The United States in Honduras, 1980–1981

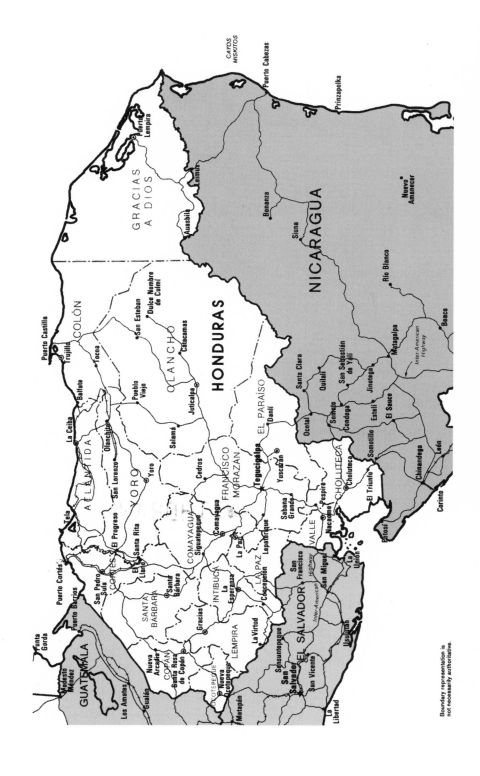

Boundary representation is
not necessarily authoritative.

The United States in Honduras, 1980–1981

An Ambassador's Memoir

by
JACK R. BINNS

McFarland & Company, Inc., Publishers
Jefferson, North Carolina, and London

Front cover: The author (right front) with U.S. General Wallace Nutting (left front) and Honduran Chief of Staff Mario Chinchilla (second from left), receiving honors at a Puerto Cortez naval base, October 1981. (Honduran Navy commander Col. Ruben Montoya is visible over Gen. Chinchilla's shoulder.)

Back cover: The author at a United Fruit Company plantation near San Pedro Sula, November 1980.

Frontispiece: Map of Honduras from U.S. Department of State, *Background Notes on Honduras.*

Diplomacy, like politics, is the art of the possible; and if we use our leverage toward an unachievable end, we will create a mess.
—George W. Ball

ISBN 0-7864-0734-4 (softcover : 50# alkaline paper)

Library of Congress cataloguing data are available

British Library cataloguing data are available

Manufactured in the United States of America

McFarland & Company, Inc., Publishers
  Box 611, Jefferson, North Carolina 28640
    www.mcfarlandpub.com

Acknowledgments

I doubt that any book of this nature—particularly by a first-time author—can be written without the encouragement, support and assistance of many people. That was certainly my experience, and I am indebted to all who contributed.

The origins of this work can be traced directly to the *Baltimore Sun*'s prizewinning series by Gary Cohn and Ginger Thompson exploring Honduran human rights abuses in the 1980s and the CIA's complicity therein. In the course of my cooperation with their investigations, Gary persuaded me that I had an important story to tell and encouraged me to tell it. Moreover, he put me in touch with the National Security Archive, without the help of which I could never have obtained the documentation needed to complete this work.

The archive's two Kates, Doyle and Martin, were extremely helpful in acquainting me with the obscure and arcane provisions of the Freedom of Information Act and my rights as a former presidential appointee. Kate Doyle set me on the right track after a shaky start. She also provided a number of documents and chronologies from the archive's holdings. Later, when I had to appeal the Department of State's initial decision to deny release of more than a hundred documents, Kate Martin was very helpful. My success with that appeal—over 90 percent of those documents were ultimately released—was due in no small part to her advice and counsel.

Once I was on the proper path, State's Freedom of Information Office, under the direction of Margaret Grafeld, was most responsive. Special thanks go to two former colleagues, Peter Lord, who expeditiously retrieved most of the requested documents, and Jack Boyle, who sped their review and release. Ken Rossman also provided assistance with my later appeal.

Thanks are also due the University of Arizona's Latin America Center for its consistent support. Associate Director Raul Saba was always responsive when I needed help. And I am particularly grateful to graduate student Megan Barrett, whose assistance in assembling and making sense of early drafts of the manuscript was absolutely critical.

I am especially indebted to several former colleagues and academic friends who generously read early versions of my manuscript and, even so, encouraged me to continue. Bill Bowdler, who bears some responsibility for my assignment to Honduras, and Bill Walker, who bears some (minor) responsibility for my actions while I was there, reviewed the complete draft for accuracy and content. Both offered extensive suggestions and many corrections, contributing greatly to the book's accuracy. George Miller did the same with a near-final version. Bob White, currently director of the Center of International Policy, reviewed parts of the manuscript, offering a number of suggestions; the center also sponsored, and invited me to participate in, a Washington symposium on the CIA's role in Honduras. Frank McNeil gave freely of his time and personal contacts when I was seeking a publisher.

My friend Nelson Polsby of the University of California's Institute of Governmental Studies was very encouraging, read the full manuscript and aided in my search for a publisher. Jacqueline Sharkey of the University of Arizona's Journalism Department, who is well acquainted with Honduras and the excesses of the 1980s, graciously read an early draft and encouraged me to persevere.

Truly, this book could not have reached print without the help of those cited above and others whom I may have failed to mention. I hasten to add that any errors of fact, omissions, misinterpretations, or misjudgments are solely my responsibility.

A final, deeply felt word of appreciation is due Martha, my spouse, sometimes severest critic and always helpmate. She struggled through the earliest drafts of the manuscript, a heroic task. She also shared my frustration with the bureaucracy at my former employer, facts that conflicted with what I remembered, computer crashes, the difficulty in finding a publisher and the struggle to cut large parts of the original manuscript.

Writing this book has been an extraordinarily gratifying experience. Having it published is an ego boost, but that is definitely secondary. The most rewarding aspect of this exercise has been the generosity, encouragement and support offered by nearly everyone with whom I have dealt. Most were strangers, yet their kindness and willingness to share information and experiences were virtually without limit. Again, thanks to you all.

Contents

Abbreviations

AID	Agency for International Development
AIFLD	American Institute for Free Labor Development
ALIPO	People's Liberal Alliance
APC	Armored Personnel Carrier
ARDEN	Democratic Revolutionary Alliance of Nicaragua
ARENA	National Republican Alliance
CAP	Central America and Panama
CARITAS	Catholic Relief Services
CBI	Caribbean Basin Initiative
CEDEN	National Evangelical Committee for Development and Emergency
CIA	Central Intelligence Agency
CINCHAF	Commander in Chief of the Honduran Armed Forces
COHEP	Honduran Private Enterprise Council
CT	Country Team
DAO	Defense Attache Office
DAS	Deputy Assistant Secretary
DCM	Deputy Chief of Mission
DEA	Drug Enforcement Agency
DIN	National Investigations Directorate
DRU	Unified Revolutionary Directorate
EFF	Extended Fund Facility
ERP	People's Revolutionary Army
ESF	Economic Support Fund
FAL	Armed Forces of the Liberation
FARN	Armed Forces of the National Resistance
FCS	Foreign Commercial Service
FDN	Nicaraguan Democratic Force
FDR	Democratic Revolutionary Front
FMLN	Farabundo Marti National Liberation Front
FMS	Foreign Military Sales

FPL	Popular Liberation Front
FSLN	Sandinista National Liberation Front
FUSEP	Public Security Force
GAO	General Accounting Office
GOH	Government of Honduras
GRN	Revolutionary Nicaraguan Government
HAF	Honduran Air Force
IADB	Inter-American Defense Board
IMF	International Monetary Fund
JAS	Joint Administrative Section
JCS	Joint Chiefs of Staff
MNR	National Revolutionary Movement
NFAC	National Foreign Assessment Center
NSC	National Security Council
OAS	Organization of American States
OPIC	Overseas Private Investment Corporation
PAO	Public Affairs Officer
PCH	Honduran Communist Party
PCV	Peace Corps Volunteer
RICO	Racketeering Influenced and Corrupt Organizations
RIG	Restricted Inter-Agency Group
RSO	Regional Security Officer
SAF	Salvadorian Air Force
SAHSA	Honduran Air Service, Inc.
SFRC	Senate Foreign Relations Committee
SI	Socialist International
UNHCR	United Nations High Commission for Refugees
URP	People's Revolutionary Union
USAF	United States Air Force
USG	United States Government
USIA	United States Information Agency
USIS	United States Information Service

Introduction

This account examines the evolution of United States policy in Honduras and Central America during the pivotal 1980–81 transition from the Carter to the Reagan administration. It lays out the story from a unique vantage point, that of the U.S. ambassador. The descriptions of events are based mainly on primary documentation, including over 1,000 pages of classified embassy and Department of State correspondence not previously available to the public.

The larger topic of our Central American policy has been dealt with extensively by others. Attention to the Honduran dimension, however, has focused almost exclusively on how those policies affected Nicaragua and the misguided effort to overthrow the Sandinista government. Yet Honduras played a central part in our regional policy under both administrations, and its importance went far beyond the "Contra" adventure.

At the time, Honduras was moving from a military dictatorship—albeit of a relatively benign nature—to democratic, constitutional rule. American policy makers saw this transition process as a unique opportunity to demonstrate that democratic government could bring social reform, socioeconomic development and, they hoped, the rule of law in a region that was woefully short of all three. Perhaps most important, the successful transition to democratic rule and movement toward a more just society in Honduras would stand in stark contrast to the Marxist model then being imposed in Nicaragua, the civil war that was raging in El Salvador and repressive elitist rule in Guatemala.

But this vision was being challenged. The principal threat came from within Honduras: its military. Having embarked on the transition process, some of its leaders began to have second thoughts about relinquishing power. Moreover, the extreme left in Honduras, inspired by the Sandinistas' revolutionary example and evangelism, did not want the transition to succeed.

There was an external threat as well. The Sandinistas had experienced the euphoria of a successful revolution. Supported by Cuba and, to a lesser extent, the Soviet Union, they sought with messianic zeal to export their

1

experience. The Sandinistas provided, directly or as a marshaling station, the material and other support that fed the Salvadoran insurgency. And with the Cubans they were training Hondurans for similar purposes. The cold war had come to Central America with a vengeance, and its arrival affected the perceptions and actions of the United States and all other players.

Geographically, Honduras occupies a strategic position in Central America. Bordering on Nicaragua, El Salvador and Guatemala, it was being buffeted by events in all three. It also separates the first two physically. Its location made Honduras a transit route for regional arms traffic, and its remote frontier areas afforded safe haven for Salvadoran and Nicaraguan insurgents. Initially, the United States sought to suppress both. Later, these factors caused it to become the operational center for the Central Intelligence Agency's (CIA) covert war on Nicaragua, as well as a base for U.S. military operations.

As the Reagan administration began to sort out its priorities and define regional policies, it experienced two major problems. First, much of its rhetoric and many of its perceptions were out of synch with reality. It also lacked effective foreign policy leadership and a comprehensive policy process. As a result, many of its policy efforts lacked discipline and cohesion. Various agencies began to pursue their own separate, often uncoordinated agendas. Although this may have had the advantage of confounding our enemies, it certainly confused our friends and, often, ourselves. The broad sweep of these early months has been engagingly described by others, most notably William LeoGrande in *Our Own Backyard* and Roy Gutman in *Banana Diplomacy*.

In some respects I became a lame-duck ambassador once Reagan was inaugurated. I was not trusted by the new administration, having been closely identified with Carter's policies. But I was not replaced for some time and kept stumbling over uncoordinated initiatives of various agencies and freelance foreign policy practitioners, such as those from the staff of Senator Jesse Helms (R-NC). Most were intent on fighting the cold war in our backyard, if necessary to the last drop of Central American blood.

The net effect was to undermine major policy goals—for example, the transition to democracy in Honduras and the encouragement of sound human rights practices—and to distort the realities of the region by viewing them through an ideological prism. The distortion destroyed the credibility of the CIA's intelligence assessment process, made a mockery of congressional oversight and led to the Iran-Contra crisis.

And there were other costs as well. The pursuit of the emerging policies and actions described herein was also responsible for the deaths of thousands, the abuse and torture of thousands more and, in my judgment, the prolongation of the so-called low intensity warfare in Nicaragua and El Salvador. One of the bitterest ironies was that Honduras's human rights record deteriorated sharply under a democratic government, in part because U.S. policy makers deliberately closed their eyes to growing abuses.

Most of that didn't happen on my watch, but the seeds were sown. That is why the recounting of these events has salience today. There are important object lessons here, and I hope the reader will draw some useful conclusions.

The purpose of this work is to bring new light to shadowed corners of U.S. policy in Central America during 1980 and 1981. But I have also sought to give the reader some sense of how a U.S. mission operated, how it related to the State Department and other agencies, and some issues an ambassador and staff dealt with on a day-to-day basis. They ranged from key questions of policy and strategies for implementation to the procedural, mundane and trivial. The latter sometimes threatened to overwhelm the substantive.

I open the narrative with a description of the process through which I became an ambassador and of the analytical underpinnings of Carter's regional policies. This defines the policy context of that which follows.

The side issues that occupied much of my time—for example, administrative support of the mission, the conduct of consular business (where we often have the greatest public impact), how we treat local (Honduran national) employees, how American employees sometimes misbehave—are largely excluded from the narrative except where they had policy implications.

I have chosen to relate the story chronologically. It is structured like a heavily annotated diary. Story lines evolve sequentially and episodically. I recount the issues and events as they occurred or otherwise came to my attention. There are also frequent insertions that summarize important events in neighboring countries or elsewhere; these are critical to understanding the context in which the actions in Honduras were playing out. Only in that way may the reader have some understanding of what it was like in the field, trying to run a large, multifaceted mission.

The conduct of foreign policy is never smooth or seamless. It is messy, full of discontinuity and occasionally chaotic. The objects of our attention are not always amenable to doing what we would like them to do, and other matters keep intruding. Sometimes these intrusions change underlying facts or assumptions; at other times they interfere with sound judgment or merely distract. Occasionally agencies seek to advance a particular agenda without regard to statute, policy, interagency agreement or common sense. At that point the ambassador must interpose—sometimes by blowing the whistle on the offender, sometimes by rapping knuckles locally. Unfortunately, I had to do a great deal of both.

The final sections of this work attempt to look briefly at some later events and the fates of some central players, and to draw some lessons from the events described.

1

Getting There Was Half the Fun

SUMMARY—Nomination as ambassador—Carter's Central American policy and challenges—Honduran transition to democracy and U.S. policy—opposition to my nomination—consultations and confirmation—events in El Salvador and Nicaragua

AN OFFER MADE AND ACCEPTED: SAN JOSE, COSTA RICA, APRIL 10, 1980. William G. Bowdler, the assistant secretary of state for Inter-American affairs, was in San Jose on official business and asked to meet privately with my wife, Martha, and me. At that meeting, he offered me the position of U.S. ambassador to Honduras, conditioned on White House approval, successful security clearance and confirmation by the U.S. Senate.

Having been assigned to our embassy in San Jose as deputy chief of mission (DCM, i.e., deputy to the ambassador, the chief of mission) the previous July after five years in our London embassy, I was relatively new to the post. Two months earlier, Ambassador Marvin Weissman had been reassigned to Bolivia. Since that time I had been in charge of the U.S. mission. I had earlier served in Guatemala and El Salvador and was familiar with the then-current challenges to U.S. interests and many of the key players.

Bowdler asked that we consider the offer and let him know our response promptly. I phoned him the following day to communicate my acceptance. He was pleased but cautioned that I should not breathe a word of this until it was announced by the White House. Too many of our colleagues had their aspirations dashed by premature disclosure of their good fortune. But leaks occur, and they began within a few weeks.

DEALING WITH CHANGE AND CIVIL STRIFE: CENTRAL AMERICA, 1979–80. The July 1979 collapse of the Anastasio Somoza regime in Nicaragua, a result of civil uprising and the Sandinista armed insurgency, struck Central America with seismic force. Before the year was out the repressive government of General Carlos Humberto Romero in El Salvador had been ousted and replaced by a reformist civilian-military junta; and in Honduras the ruling military agreed to allow elections and turn power over to civilians. Only in Guatemala, a charnel house, did the military ignore the Nicaragua lesson.

The aftershocks of Somoza's fall rocked the hemisphere, altering the structure of the cold war and, briefly, the U.S. strategic worldview. In so doing it created new stresses in our relationship with the Soviet Union and with our allies in the hemisphere and beyond. Ultimately, it gave rise to a crisis in American government known as the "Iran-Contra Affair." Clearly, the long-overdue ouster of Somoza was a historic watershed.

In early 1980 civil strife in Central America was growing, and much of the region was in turmoil. This situation was to worsen. Honduras and Costa Rica, however, were pockets of relative tranquility, although both were beginning to be buffeted by events in neighboring countries. Events and U.S. policies were to disrupt their serenity further, drawing them more deeply into the maelstrom.

The Carter administration's policy was based on the conviction that the unrest—the ouster of the Somoza dictatorship, the growing civil conflict in El Salvador, the long-running insurgency in Guatemala, new restiveness in Honduras and, to a lesser extent, Costa Rica—was the product of an inability of the unjust power structures of these nations to accommodate popular pressures for change. None, except Costa Rica, were democracies. Their traditional political, economic and social structures were, with variations and exceptions, based on an elitist triad made up of an economic oligarchy, the military and the Church. These structures were unjust and outmoded, as well as brittle.

Pressures for change were growing and came from a variety of sources. Forces for reform encompassed a growing middle class, which included businessmen and professionals who had studied abroad; an expanding trade union movement; the major academic institutions; and burgeoning numbers of the clergy, inspired by Jesuit teaching and the so-called liberation theology. Nor were the military institutions immune: the younger military in El Salvador had overthrown the Romero government; dissident ex-officers were among the more effective insurgent leaders in Guatemala; and junior officers in Honduras strongly supported the move to democratic government.

The root problems, according to this paradigm, lay in the structures themselves. Our overriding policy goal, accordingly, should be their reform and revitalization. This meant that the United States government (USG) needed to craft and carry out policies that would help, influence and, in some cases, direct the change process toward constructive ends. The United States, of course, could not and should not try to reform these structures by itself, but it could and did ally itself with those seeking change. Fortunately, there was no shortage of such allies.

If unjust, unresponsive and outmoded structures were the problem, the United States should bend its efforts toward establishment of democratic governmental forms, creation of modern economic institutions and practices, implementation of social reforms and increased social program investment, and elimination of repression and serious human rights abuses.

The Carter team sought to achieve these ends through diplomatic means. These included dialogue, good offices, mediation and suasion; leverage from increasing levels of economic and security assistance; greater utilization of "public diplomacy"; and covert action, in carefully targeted and limited situations. Covert action—the least important of this catalogue—had a place in the gamut of diplomatic tools. But its use was contingent on well-defined preconditions: clear and reasonably attainable goals; means consistent with law and national values; unlikelihood of disclosure; consistency of potential cost (financial and political) with notional gains; prior legal authorization; and a reasonable degree of deniability in the event of exposure.

The causes of the upheaval were political, social and economic, so solutions could be found only through political accommodation, social reform and economic development. Although much of the unrest was manifested as terrorism and armed violence, force was not considered a useful means of resolution. Indeed, violence was likely to accentuate differences, making reconciliation more difficult. Military force, as distinct from security assistance, was not considered a useful tool in resolving existing structural problems. Indeed, the armed forces of these countries (Costa Rica, which had no armed forces, excepted) were a major part of their structural problems. Paradoxically, it soon became clear in El Salvador that an active insurgency, supplied and supported from outside, required the military to play an important role in creating the conditions in which accommodation, reform and development could occur. This conundrum was recognized, but not resolved, before the change in administrations. It was to vex the foreign policies of both the Reagan and Bush administrations.

The role of Cuba in the overthrow of Somoza was fully recognized by the Carter administration, as was Castro's support for insurgents in El Salvador and Guatemala. The Cubans were also known to be training dissident Hondurans and Costa Ricans, as well as supporting the Sandinista government.[1] The Soviet Union was clearly abetting Cuba and in March 1980 signed a series of economic, technical and cultural agreements with Nicaragua. Yet, there was no reason to believe Central America was an important area of Soviet policy interest or activity. An opportunity to harass the United States, undoubtedly, but not an area of strategic or major interest. But the unrest in this region was not the product of international communism or the cold war.

This analytical paradigm was not universally accepted. Indeed, it was a point of almost hysterical disagreement from the right wing of the Republican Party. It is therefore noteworthy that both the Sandinista/Contra conflict and the civil war in El Salvador were ultimately resolved by diplomatic, rather than military, means. Political accommodations were eventually reached through negotiation, not warfare.

DISCORDANT ISSUES: LAND REFORM AND HUMAN RIGHTS: SAN JOSE, COSTA RICA, APRIL 16-21, 1980. A special presidential mission on Agriculture Development in Central America arrived in San Jose on April 16 from Guatemala. Headed by Dr. E. T. York, a former chancellor of Florida's state university system and noted agriculturalist, it included a number of other agriculture experts. Its purpose was to speed agricultural development and improve productivity in the region.

Although its mandate was agriculture, the mission was interested in two related issues: land reform and human rights. Both were controversial within the USG, Congress and the body politic, as well as Central America, and both impacted directly on agriculture production and productivity.

Some saw land redistribution as the sine qua non for meaningful social, economic and political reform in Central America, as had been the case in Japan, Taiwan and Bolivia. Others were concerned with the effects such programs would have on private property rights, production and productivity. And a smaller, but very vocal, group thought such programs reeked of socialism and should be opposed on ideological grounds.

In fact, land reform and redistribution were already a reality in part of Central America. In Nicaragua the Sandinistas had seized many large landholdings without providing compensation. There was relatively little redistribution, however, except to Sandinista leaders. In Honduras the military government had been distributing government-owned lands to the landless for some years, although at a decelerating pace. The real focus of contention was El Salvador.

A tiny country, with the second-highest population density in the hemisphere, virtually all its arable land was in private hands and overwhelmingly in large holdings (*latifundia*). El Salvador's new civil-military junta government regarded land redistribution as an essential step toward social justice and a popular bulwark against the Marxist-inspired insurgent movement. It had announced a redistribution program in March 1980, with Carter administration support. There was no doubt in my mind that our support for the Salvadoran program was correct and necessary. Ironically, given the source of most of the criticism of the Carter administration's policy, the Reagan administration's later support was unwavering.

The human rights issue might seem tangential to agriculture production and productivity. However, it had a direct impact on U.S. assistance policies, which, in turn, affected the agriculture sector. During its visit to Guatemala, where U.S. concerns over human rights violations had resulted in sharp cuts in our economic and security assistance, the York Mission heard a series of complaints about this aspect of U.S. policy from their Guatemalan interlocutors and the U.S. ambassador, Frank Ortiz.[2]

For their Costa Rican visit, the embassy and the Agency for International Development (AID) had arranged an intensive series of meetings for the mission over a three-day period. Members met with government officials, including President Rodrigo Carazo; leading local agriculturalists representing small, medium and large landholders; agroindustrial leaders; exporters; economists; and agronomists. We had also set up several field trips to agricultural sites.[3] Based on our observations of mission members' interaction with their Costa Rican interlocutors, we believed the mission was opposed to both our human rights policy, particularly in Guatemala, and our support of Salvadoran land reform.

Given the Carter administration's strong position on both these issues, I believed the department needed to be apprised of the York mission's apparent predisposition. Accordingly, I sent a restricted distribution[4] cable to the department, reporting our perceptions and warning of a possibly critical final report.[5] Because this information would also be of value to the other embassies scheduled to host the mission, I sent it to the other Central American posts.

The text of that document was given to York when the mission later transited Guatemala, almost certainly by Ambassador Ortiz.[6] It was to have repercussions for my nomination.

AMERICAN CONSERVATIVES ATTACK U.S. POLICY: WASHINGTON, D.C., MAY 1980. The Committee of Santa Fe, a group of ultraconservative academics and former government officials, issued a report highly critical of the Carter administration's Central American policies, asserting that "never before has the Republic been in such jeopardy from its exposed southern flank." According to its authors—several of whom would form part of the early Reagan foreign policy team—containment of this threat was not enough. What was needed was a "counterprojection of American power".[7]

MOVING FORWARD, HALTINGLY: SAN JOSE, COSTA RICA, JULY 13, 1980. Our new ambassador, Frank McNeil, arrived July 7. He was a friend from our days together in Guatemala in the early 1960s and later became an ally in the struggle to influence the Reagan administration's Central American policies. Officially, I was to remain DCM until confirmed as ambassador to Honduras. The announcement of my nomination, already overdue, was hung up at the White House. I later learned the delay was the result of a letter opposing my appointment by a member of the York mission, David Garst, who was also a strong Carter supporter. Nonetheless, Garst opposed Carter's human rights policy and support for land reform in El Salvador, and he argued against my appointment because of my advocacy of both and the cable I had sent about the York mission.

After reviewing the situation with McNeil and State, we decided that my family and I should take our scheduled home leave and enjoy a family vacation until my appointment was announced.[8] We would then go to Washington, where I would begin consultations, be confirmed by the Senate and sworn in. We left Costa Rica in high spirits.

HONDURAS: THE SETTING, SUMMER 1980. Except for a brief period in 1974 and 1975, the Honduran military had been in power since 1963, nearly 17 years. Bowing to popular and diplomatic pressure in late 1979, the military acceded to elections and a return to constitutional rule.

One of the striking attributes of the Honduran military, in addition to its moderately reformist, nonrepressive approach to government, and the corruption of many senior officers, was its cohesive, collegial leadership. Virtually all significant decisions were discussed and decided by the Superior Council of the Armed Forces, then composed of the seventy-six most senior officers. Superior Council decisions were usually by consensus, implied a kind of collective responsibility and were rarely questioned at lower levels within the institution. It was this body that had decided to hold elections and turn power over to an elected government. The transition to democracy began with the April 1980 election of a Constituent Assembly, and a new provisional government took office in late July.

Honduras differed in many critical respects from its neighbors. Although it was the poorest of the Central American states, disparities in wealth that marked the others (Costa Rica again excepted) were much less extreme. *Latifundia* was not a problem; land was available and being distributed (the largest private landholders were the United and Standard Fruit companies, and they had returned extensive acreage to the government some years earlier, increasing land available for distribution). There was no significant demographic pressure. The society was almost entirely mestizo and relatively well integrated. There was a high degree of individual freedom and few human rights violations. Trade unionism was encouraged and flourished; the Honduran labor movement was the strongest in Central America. There were few indications of incipient unrest, and the decision to hold elections had been immensely popular, as evidenced by the 80 percent–plus voter turnout in the assembly elections.

The Liberal Party had edged out its rival National Party, winning 52 percent of the vote, but two minor parties held the balance of power in the unicameral assembly. The provisional government took office July 20, with military junta president General Policarpo Paz Garcia remaining as provisional president. His cabinet included two military officers (foreign relations and defense ministers), with the remaining portfolios divided equally between the Liberal and National Parties. Roberto Suazo Cordova, the Liberal Party leader, presided over the assembly, which began work on a new constitution.

Elections for president and a unicameral legislature were later scheduled for November 1981. The government elected then would take office in January 1982, if all went according to plan.

HOME LEAVE: SOURNESS AND DISSATISFACTION: SAN FRANCISCO, CALIFORNIA, AND SPOKANE, WASHINGTON, JULY–AUGUST 1980. Arriving in the United States, we found a popular mood of disquiet and disillusion. The depth of popular dissatisfaction came as something of a surprise. The U.S. economy was stagnant, inflation and interest rates high, and there was no confidence that the Carter administration would be able to do anything about these or the other problems we faced. Internationally, the outlook was even more dismal. The United States seemed powerless to deal with Muslim fundamentalists in Iran, who continued to hold 52 American diplomats hostage; the Soviet Union's invasion of Afghanistan; Cuba and the influx of Mariel boat people; or the violence and radicalism that were sweeping Central America, historically our "backyard." And if all this weren't enough, the administration was giving the Panama Canal to the Panamanians.

Conservatives were in full throat, attacking the administration's domestic performance and foreign policy ineffectiveness. After selecting Ronald Reagan as their candidate, the Republican National Convention went on to approve a platform that stated, in part, "We deplore the Marxist takeover of Nicaragua and Marxist attempts to destabilize El Salvador and Guatemala. We will never support U.S. assistance to any Marxist government in this hemisphere. In this regard, we deplore the Carter administration's aid program for the Marxist Sandinista government in Nicaragua. We will support the efforts of the Nicaraguan people to establish a free and independent government." This statement had been written by Senator Jesse Helms and shepherded through the GOP's Foreign Policy and Defense Subcommittee by one of his aides, John Carbaugh.[9]

Actually, our experiencing the sour domestic environment while on home leave had a striking impact. The written word—which was all we had in those days before CNN—cannot adequately convey what one is able to hear and sense. Absent this experience, we could not have felt the depth of disquiet. Its consequences were to be evident in the November elections and beyond.

ALLEGED CONTRA ATTACK IN HONDURAS: TEGUCIGALPA, HONDURAS, JULY 22, 1980. The Nicaraguan ambassador to Honduras held a press conference to announce that former Nicaraguan National Guardsmen living in Honduras had attempted, unsuccessfully, to blow up his embassy in Tegucigalpa. He filed an official protest with the Ministry of Foreign Affairs, demanding that the Honduran government take action against the perpetrators. The government did not respond or take any action against those allegedly responsible.[10]

DIPLOMATIC HOSTAGES AND HIJINKS: WASHINGTON, D.C., AUGUST 1980. My nomination was finally announced July 27 and sent to the Senate for confirmation, along with a number of others. The Senate Foreign Relations Committee (SFRC) was expected to hold hearings promptly and the full Senate confirm before its Labor Day recess.

That theory failed to account for Senator Helms. A member of the SFRC, Helms strongly opposed most of the administration's policies and particularly those in Central America. Indeed, the GOP platform language he had crafted was merely an extension of fights he had earlier lost in the Democratic-controlled Senate. Helms promptly placed a "hold" on this group of ambassadorial nominations, which meant that there would be no hearings until he was ready.

I proceeded with consultations, meeting with senior officials of every agency represented in Honduras or having a serious interest in that country, as well as with State and National Security Council (NSC) officials. Martha and I attended a special seminar for ambassadorial appointees and spouses. I then spent several days in New York, meeting with leaders of American corporations and banks having interests in Honduras, acquainting myself with their operations and concerns. I also made various calls on Capitol Hill.

U.S. POLICY IN HONDURAS: WASHINGTON, D.C., LATE SUMMER 1980. Honduras was a critical test case for the Carter administration's policy of accommodating change in Central America through the encouragement of democracy, structural reform and development. The AID program at that time was the largest in the region, as was that of the Peace Corps. The World Bank and other international financial institutions were also very active. There were several large private investments pending, awaiting a promised revision of the mining code. Decisions to proceed would also be contingent on political developments. Our military assistance program at the time was small, amounting to less than $3 million that year. But that figure did not tell the whole story.

There was an unusual aspect to our security assistance effort. Major General Robert L. Schweitzer, then assigned to the office of the Deputy Chief of Staff of the Army, had visited Honduras in early 1980. A legendary combat leader and indefatigable anticommunist, Schweitzer was to become a loose cannon on the foreign policy deck during the early Reagan years. For reasons unknown to me he had a special affinity for the Honduran military.

Schweitzer had come up with the idea of increasing the Honduran army's mobility to help it exercise greater control over the frontiers with El Salvador and Nicaragua by providing helicopters for the Honduran Air Force. He arranged for the U.S. Army to lease 10 Huey helicopters to Honduras at nominal cost; all ten of these aircraft were in the country before I arrived, a nearly miraculous feat. Not surprisingly, the Hondurans considered Schweitzer their special advocate in the USG.[11]

It would be up to me, Schweitzer said, to see that the helicopters were used effectively. During my tenure they never were. The Hondurans lacked the money to maintain them or keep them in the air. But more significantly, they also seemed to lack the will to try to control their frontiers.

The overarching U.S. policy objective was the successful conclusion of elections and the transition to democracy. All other goals were supportive of, flowed from, or were contingent on that success. As early as September 1980 we had reports that some senior military officers were advocating reversal of their elections decision, and rumors of a possible coup d'etat circulated.

There were numerous secondary goals, social and economic development being a high-priority area. The flight of domestic capital, spurred by the Sandinista takeover in Nicaragua and unrest in El Salvador, posed a serious threat to this objective. These uncertainties were also deterring foreign private investment, which had a leading part to play in the development scenario. The Honduran budget deficit was growing, threatening the government's ability to continue making its counterpart contributions to development projects (development agencies routinely require recipient governments to invest a significant amount of their own funds in development projects; if the governments are unable to meet these commitments, new development investment dries up). International oil prices were also slowing the economy and threatening to bring Texaco, owner of the only refinery, and the government into serious conflict.

Governmental corruption was yet another source of U.S. disquiet. The military's power position meant that it was the largest feeder at this illicit trough, but the two major political parties were to become increasingly involved as they assumed control of government ministries; this malady infected part of the private sector as well. Addressing this pernicious problem was usually referred to euphemistically as "administrative reform."

One apparently minor issue that came up during my consultations was to assume major importance later. Both State and the CIA were curious about an Argentine military advisory presence in Honduras. We knew that some 10 to 12 officers were there, apparently working with Honduran military intelligence, but we were unable to pick up details as to their activities or goals. They were keeping a very low profile, and the Hondurans, uncharacteristically, had a tight lid on their activities. Their numbers, compared to five officers assigned to the U.S. Military Group (Milgroup), were significant. Our relations with Argentina at the time were very strained, principally over the military government's gross human rights abuses. We suspected these advisers might be helping the Hondurans set up an extralegal countersubversion operation that would resemble and emulate that of Argentina. These concerns, it turned out, were well grounded.

The Honduran armed forces were soon to embark on a program of "disappearing" suspected subversives, although fortunately on a far smaller scale than had their Argentine mentors. Moreover, we learned later that the Argentines were also working with anti-Sandinista Nicaraguans residing in Honduras. In this latter role Argentina was to become the CIA's prime contractor for mounting the clandestine Contra war against Nicaragua.[12] The wheels were to come off that operation in April 1982, when Argentina invaded the Falkland Islands, forcing the CIA to assume direct control of the Contra effort.

My consultations, particularly those on Capitol Hill, had underscored the domestic political sensitivity of human rights abuses in Central America. Although no one had expressed particular concern about Honduras, I had no doubt that Congress was becoming increasingly reluctant to authorize economic and security assistance to governments that flagrantly abused their own people. And because Congress controlled the purse strings, this was a concern policy makers had to heed, or so I thought.

In the regional context the Carter team had several worries involving Honduras: the use of its territory as a supply conduit and safe haven for Salvadoran insurgents; growing numbers of Salvadoran refugees in the frontier area; use of Honduran territory by former members of Somoza's National Guard to mount attacks against Nicaragua; the inability and unwillingness of Hondurans to make effective efforts in response to these situations; and Sandinista support and training of Honduran dissidents in Nicaragua. Each had an impact on Honduras's relations with its eastern and southern neighbors and were a constant source of preoccupation during my tenure.

The Carter administration wanted Honduras to exercise more effective control over its borders (e.g., Schweitzer's helicopters), prevent the use of its territory by insurgents, and cooperate in providing humanitarian aid for Salvadoran refugees. These steps were consistent with international law and practice.

The principal obstacle to improved Honduran relations with El Salvador was the two countries' inability to reach a peace agreement resolving a territorial dispute that had lingered since the 1969 "soccer war" between the two countries. The central issue was several pockets of disputed territory over which neither government exercised effective control.

These areas had become safe havens for Salvadoran insurgents. The Organization of American States (OAS) had maintained a small observer force in Honduras since 1969. Its mission was to keep the contending parties from renewing hostilities and monitor the pockets of disputed territory. This unit was composed of military representatives from several OAS member states, including the United States. We also provided Air Force helicopters and crews to the OAS, on a reimbursable basis, to permit the observers to access the isolated frontier and disputed areas. These aircrews were our best source of reliable information as to what was occurring in this critical, but extremely remote, area. We, along with the OAS, were working with both countries to broker a resolution to this long-standing problem. In mid-1980, negotiations on a peace treaty were nearing successful conclusion.

Honduras's relations with Nicaragua were poisoned by mutual suspicion. The former feared the Sandinistas' revolutionary evangelism, their support for Honduran dissidents and their accelerating military buildup. The Sandinistas, for their part, believed the Honduran government was abetting Nicaraguan exile attacks. Ironically, in previous years the military had allowed the Sandinistas to operate out of Honduras against Somoza with relative impunity. Indeed, some senior Honduran officers had actually sold army munitions to the Sandinistas—a prime example of corruption and greed blinding practitioners to the consequences of their actions.

As my consultations were winding up, Bowdler assigned me the task of preparing my instructions as ambassador, working closely with his deputy for Central America, James Cheek, and John Blacken, head of the Office of Central American Affairs. They were first-rate professionals and friends. This critical document laid out U.S. policy objectives, priorities and strategies for Honduras. It set out nine discrete policy goals, including ratification of a democratic constitution; elections and installation of a new government; accelerated reforms and economic development; consummation of a peace treaty with El Salvador; denial of Honduran territory to Salvadoran and anti-Sandinista insurgents; and containment of subversion with due consideration to human rights. [13]

These instructions were coordinated with other agencies (e.g., Defense, the CIA, U.S. Information Agency) and ratified by the NSC before being sent to the embassy. They constituted the Mission's marching orders and remained in force, with minor modification, throughout my time in Honduras.

EL SALVADOR BECOMES A COMBAT ZONE, OFFICIALLY: SAN SALVADOR, EL SALVADOR, AUGUST 6, 1980. The Department of Defense approved a request from our Milgroup commander in El Salvador that the country be formally designated a "hostile fire area" because of insurgent attacks on U.S. military and embassy personnel. This permitted the payment of "hostile fire pay" for all military personnel in El Salvador. Civilian personnel were already receiving "hardship allowance" for their service. [14]

MISSION ORGANIZATION AND ASSESSMENT: WASHINGTON, D.C., AUGUST 1980. The U.S. mission in Honduras consisted of nine U.S. government agencies and was scheduled to grow. In addition to the State element, they were the CIA (incorporated as part of the embassy); the Defense Attache Office (DAO—Defense Intelligence Agency); Agency for International Development (AID); U.S. Information Service (USIS);[15] U.S. Military Group

(Department of Defense); Foreign Commercial Service (FCS—Department of Commerce); Peace Corps/Honduras (PC/H); and the Inter-American Geodetic Survey (IAGS—Defense Mapping Agency). And other agencies were planning to open operations. The heads of resident agencies, together with senior members of the embassy staff, constituted the Country Team (CT), the ambassador's principal advisory and operational coordination mechanism.

The ambassador, as the personal representative of the president, is statutorily responsible for the direction and oversight of all U.S. government operations in the country to which he or she is accredited. The only exceptions to this rule are U.S. employees assigned or accredited to international organizations (e.g., the OAS observers in Honduras) or military personnel under the command of the U.S. area commander.[16] U.S. NATO forces in Germany are an example of the latter. In Latin America this exception applied only to forces based in Panama, under U.S. commander-in-chief, Southern Command. Statute and regulation, moreover, required area military commanders to obtain ambassadorial approval prior to assigning forces to, undertaking operational activities in or even visiting their countries. Differences that arise between the ambassador and mission elements or the area military commander must be referred to State for interagency resolution. This mandate was to be ignored frequently by the CIA, Defense and Southern Command following the change in administrations.

I had chosen William G. Walker, an outstanding, seasoned officer with previous experience in Central America, as my DCM. He had arrived in Tegucigalpa several weeks before me and proved an excellent choice. He later went on to be a deputy assistant secretary for Inter-American affairs and, later, our ambassador to El Salvador. In the latter capacity he was to play a major role in the negotiated settlement that ended the civil war in that country.

The embassy was organized on traditional lines, having four operational sections under the ambassador and DCM: Political, Economic, Consular and Joint Administrative (JAS), which provided logistic and administrative services for the entire mission. In theory, the other agencies reimburse State for services received, but in practice reimbursements were woefully short of actual costs.

The DCM is customarily responsible to the ambassador for the operation of the embassy and is also his alter ego for management of the entire mission. Having been DCM in Costa Rica, where Ambassador Weissman reinforced the alter ego role, I was especially conscious of the need to ensure agency heads accepted Walker in this role in fact as well as in theory. I involved him in virtually all of my sessions with CT members and insisted that he be apprised of all developments. This was to cause the CIA head—the station chief—and the AID director some heartburn.

From the Washington vantage point, there seemed to be few problems with the Economic or Consular Sections. It was acknowledged, however, that the Economic Section was understaffed. It consisted of one officer and no support personnel. The Foreign Commercial Service staff—one American officer and three Honduran employees—provided unclassified secretarial and clerical support.

Significant weaknesses existed in both the Political Section and JAS. Although the former carried out its consultative and coordination duties well enough, and did a good job reporting on events, its efforts were analytically weak. They described what happened accurately but not its significance. Nor had the section undertaken the basic "benchmark" analyses of important Honduran institutions and leaders that are essential if intelligence agencies are to evaluate the larger picture meaningfully. This section, consisting of two American officers and an American secretary, was also understaffed, especially in view of the pace and significance of events. State soon assigned two additional officers.

JAS was seriously shorthanded and had serious management problems as well. The size of the mission in Honduras had grown by nearly 50 percent in the previous four years, and the rate of increase was accelerating. Yet JAS staffing had been reduced as the overall State operating budget was cut, and other agencies were complaining about inadequate service. State management officials were not encouraging as to the possibility of additional personnel in the near term but agreed to push the other agencies to increase their contributions so that we could contract for some services. They also suggested sending an administrative team to review of the JAS operation and how it might be improved. This section proved a continuing headache and distraction until the following summer.

The CIA element was nominally part of the embassy Political Section. It also had two telecommunications support personnel (later increased to four) nominally assigned to JAS. They worked closely with State counterparts. Plans, with which I agreed, were also afoot to augment the CIA staff, and the Station grew like Topsy after my departure. These cover arrangements fooled no one in the mission, American or Honduran, as the Station was located behind a secure door in an area that was off limits to nearly all non-CIA employees. At the time, access to the rest of the Political Section was open to virtually all staff members. Moreover, CIA personnel were known to the Honduran intelligence and public security services, with which they were in regular contact.

At the time, the CIA controlled all Mission telecommunications. State messages were encrypted by the State communicators then passed to the CIA's telecommunications unit for transmission to the agency's receiving station near Washington; these messages were then sent electronically to the State Department, where they were decrypted and distributed to end users in State and other agencies.

The import of this arrangement lay in the fact that ambassadors, despite their statutory responsibility, had no way to monitor what the Station was sending to its headquarters or vice versa. Official communications from all other agencies passed through the State unit prior to transmission, and the DCM routinely reviewed the entire mission's message traffic, except for that of the CIA.

The protocol between State and CIA required the station chief to show all intelligence reports to the ambassador prior to transmission, giving him/her the opportunity to add interpretive or evaluative comments. However, CIA communications dealing with administrative or operational matters, as opposed to substantive intelligence, were exempt from this review. Although this arrangement made sense in a certain context (e.g., an ambassador has no need to know the identity of the CIA's sources or other trade craft details), it also meant there was no way for him/her to monitor what the Station was reporting or the agency is up to. Thus, the chief of mission was entirely dependent on what the station chief chose to share.

If there was good faith on both sides, this system could work. But my experiences in Honduras and elsewhere suggest that the CIA often ignores this protocol and the ambassador's statutory responsibility, as recent public cases have amply shown.[17] The agency can be as deceitful and dissembling with the chief of mission as with Congress, the media or anyone else. In sum, I do not believe agency personnel can be trusted to tell the truth, or at least all of it.

The communications arrangement also provided ambassadors with an unofficial "back channel" link with Washington officials. In such cases a message addressed to a specific person in Washington was given to the station chief, who would send it as a CIA administrative message. On receipt in Washington, the agency would hand deliver it to the addressee. There would be no official record of such communications.

AID was the largest element of the U.S. mission, except for Peace Corps. AID consisted of about 40 American and 30 Honduran employees plus an additional 40 contractors. It enjoyed an excellent reputation for design and implementation of a large, multisectorial development program. It worked with nearly 30 Honduran government and private voluntary agencies in implementing 26 social and economic development programs. In the summer of 1980 the AID project portfolio was about $80 million; this was to increase to $125 million over the next 15 months. The overall program was directed at four sectors: agriculture and rural development; population and health; urban development; and basic education. AID director John Oleson was an experienced, highly regarded and innovative program manager. I had known him for a decade and was confident we would work well together.

The U.S. Information Service (USIS) was going to have a key role to play in the attainment of our policy objectives in Honduras. Officials at its

Washington headquarters and State were very high on Public Affairs Officer (PAO, agency head) Cresencio Arcos. Although a relatively small operation—two officers and six Hondurans—the information and cultural affairs programs were well designed and apparently effective. This agency, too, was to grow in the coming months.

Hailing from Texas and fluent in Spanish, Arcos was a Russian language officer whose previous post had been Leningrad, although he earlier had Latin American assignments. He was by far the best informed of our entire staff about Honduran politics and was to become my closest and most trusted colleague next to DCM Walker. Arcos proved a superlative and energetic young officer, possessing an acute political sense and an outstanding gift for establishing relationships with people from all classes and walks of life. He was to become my principal political operative in addition to carrying out his regular responsibilities as PAO. Some years later, Arcos returned to Honduras as U.S. Ambassador.

The defense attache's office had been cut back severely several years earlier. Remaining were two Air Force officers, the air attache and assistant, accredited to all five Central American countries, three enlisted men and a Honduran secretary. Their responsibilities were regional, and they operated a two-engine Beechcraft turboprop aircraft (C-12A) that was at the disposition of the five Central American ambassadors and high-level visitors from Washington. The vast majority of their time, however, was spent in Honduras. They provided basic intelligence about the Central American air forces and aviation infrastructure. Col. William Miller, U.S. Air Force, was the defense and air attache. He was a first-rate officer, a terrific pilot and became a loyal friend.

Neither Miller nor his assistant were intelligence specialists, however, nor were they fluent in Spanish. Their ability to access the Honduran Army—the largest, most influential and most political of the armed services and hence our most important intelligence target—was quite limited. The Honduran Air Force (HAF) was their main point of contact and represented a very small but important part of the total military establishment. It was also the most professional.

The defense attache situation cried out for remedy. During my consultations, Defense agreed to assign an army officer with a Latin America regional specialization as army attache the following summer. General Schweitzer and State were both very helpful in persuading Defense to agree.

The Military Group (Milgroup) in Honduras was responsible for the administration of U.S. security assistance programs (a constant source of irritation and complaint for the Honduran military) and related advisory and training functions. This unit also served as the liaison between the U.S. mission and the Southern Command in Panama. It was commanded by Colonel Willard Goodwin, U.S. Army. He was supported by three other officers (one each, Army, Air Force and Navy), two enlisted men, two American civilians and four Hondurans. None of the officers were linguists or area specialists and often depended on one of the civilian technicians to interpret all but their most basic discussions with Honduran counterparts.

The Milgroup was one of our principal sources of information about the Honduran military, but its officers were usually kept at arm's length. Their lack of linguistic skill also limited their effectiveness. Our relations with the Honduran military were critical in our overall relationship and in the attainment of our policy objectives. Discretion and a delicate touch were essential. I was to find the Milgroup, Southern Command, Defense and representatives of the Joint Chiefs of Staff wanting in both respects. For its part, the U.S. military doubtless came to consider me most meddlesome in what it considered military affairs. I meant business about exercising my oversight role, and that was resented by some. Colonel Goodwin, however, was throughout a loyal member of the CT and—despite some serious problems— extremely helpful in keeping me apprised of what the Southern Command staff was planning and doing. That was to prove invaluable.

Colonel Goodwin also oversaw the work of the Inter-American Geodetic Survey civilian engineer. He worked with the National Geographic Institute to produce basic geodetic, mapping and cartographic surveys.

One U.S. military element in Honduras was not under my direction: the officer assigned to the OAS observer group and the USAF helicopter pilots and support personnel assigned to transport the observer mission. Nonetheless, they kept in very close touch with the defense attache, Milgroup and embassy. As indicated earlier, they were our best source of intelligence as to what was happening on the Honduras/El Salvador frontier and provided airlift when our staff wished to visit the frontier. Once the peace treaty formally ending the state of war was concluded, I found myself in a running battle with State and Defense over retaining this capability.

Peace Corps/Honduras was the second largest in Latin America, with about 200 volunteers in the field and a professional support staff of over 20 American and Honduran employees. It was run with distinction by a former Peace Corps Volunteer (PCV), Peter Lara. The volunteers did great development work at the grassroots, and their efforts were generally well coordinated with those of AID, which was not always the case. Key sectors of their activity were agriculture, natural resources, health, education, community services, rural development and adult education. It is important to note that all mission elements were specifically prohibited from using PCVs for intelligence collection: we honored that ban scrupulously.

The Drug Enforcement Agency (DEA) wished to establish an office in Tegucigalpa, Honduras at the time being covered by the DEA's regional office in Costa Rica. I was sympathetic but conscious of the embassy's administrative staffing problem. Each additional person or agency increased the workload on that section, already severely overstretched. And we had five or six additional personnel scheduled to arrive.

Overall, Washington regarded Tegucigalpa as a good—in many respects excellent—mission but one with considerable room for improvement in light of the growing attention being given Central America. Staffing, funding levels and Washington interest were all destined to increase rapidly. Consolidation of the Sandinistas' Marxist regime in Nicaragua truly had altered the stakes in the region.

HELMS ALLOWS HEARINGS: WASHINGTON, D.C., AUGUST 1980. As time slipped by, concern over the Helms hold grew. Congress was due to recess in late August and again in early October for the election campaign. In an effort to end the standoff, meetings with Helms's staff were arranged for some of the career nominees (Helms refused to lift his holds on political appointees before the elections).

I met with John Carbaugh, a highly skilled operator and raconteur. Helms, he said, had no interest in most of the career nominees. We were being held up to pressure State to do better by Frank Ortiz, who by that time had been removed from Guatemala. Ortiz had been named political adviser to Southern Command, and Helms didn't believe this post was appropriate for such a fine officer, according to Carbaugh. After further discussion, Carbaugh said Helms would be willing to lift the hold in my case if I answered a series of written questions. I readily agreed.

Three pages of questions were delivered the next day, virtually all of which were directly or implicitly critical of USG policies. Over the next couple of days I worked closely with Cheek and Blacken to prepare responses that supported our policies yet would avoid offending the senator. The resulting 20 pages of typescript was despatched to Helms's office. As promised, the holds on four of us were lifted and a committee hearing quickly scheduled. It was anticlimactic. Only one committee member, Sen. Edward Zorinsky (D-NE), bothered to show up, and his questions were all routine. We now had only to await the votes of the committee and the full Senate. Congress recessed in August without taking action, and I returned to San Jose.

UNITED STATES PUSHES FOR ELECTIONS IN EL SALVADOR: SAN SALVADOR, EL SALVADOR, AUGUST 12, 1980. U.S. ambassador Robert White, acting on instructions, urged the Salvadoran government to announce a schedule for presidential and legislative elections as soon as possible.[18] The government, however, did not respond until October 15, scheduling elections for May 1982.

OAS OFFICE SEIZED, RETURNED: TEGUCIGALPA, HONDURAS, AUGUST 15, 1980. A group claiming to support of the Salvadoran insurgents seized the OAS representative's office in Tegucigalpa; the OAS requested that the Honduran government not intervene. OAS negotiators subsequently persuaded those involved to give up peacefully in return for safe conduct out of Honduras. This marked the beginning of deteriorating security in Honduras.

COVERT AID FOR NICARAGUAN OPPOSITION: WASHINGTON, D.C., SEPTEMBER 1980. President Carter authorized $1 million for covert support of private sector opposition elements in Nicaragua. These funds were to be funneled to labor unions, media and opposition political groups in an effort to strengthen and support pluralism in an increasingly restrictive political environment.[19] Sandinista pressure on these countervailing centers escalated steadily, however. None of these funds could go to the exiled National Guard elements that constituted the principal external opposition to the Sandinistas or be used for military or paramilitary purposes.

GARST LETTER SURFACES IN HONDURAS: SAN JOSE, COSTA RICA, SEPTEMBER 2, 1980. Ambassador Jaramillo phoned from Tegucigalpa to report that the letter David Garst had written to President Carter opposing my appointment was circulating in Honduras. It characterized me as a dangerous leftist and was being handed out by Guatemalan businessmen. She thought it an effort to discredit me with the Honduran private sector—that certainly seemed to be the case—and wished to know how she should respond.[20] I sent her a copy of Garst's letter immediately—noting that the issues in dispute were U.S. policies on human rights in Guatemala and land reform in El Salvador—as well as the cable that Ortiz had apparently leaked to the York group. If my support for U.S. policy made me a dangerous leftist, so be it. That was my role, so I didn't see much to argue about.

This incident later received play in the Honduran press.[21]

CARTER OKAYS U.S. ECONOMIC ASSISTANCE FOR NICARAGUA: WASHINGTON, D.C., SEPTEMBER 12, 1980. In compliance with a congressional mandate, President Carter certified that Nicaragua was not "aiding, abetting or supporting acts of violence or terrorism in other countries," clearing the way for initial disbursement of the $75 million AID program.[22] That was clearly stretching the truth, but it was good policy. And it was small potatoes when compared to some of President Reagan's later egregious certifications. U.S. ambassador Lawrence Pezzullo and Deputy Assistant Secretary (DAS) Cheek met with Sandinista leaders prior to the first disbursement to emphasize the importance of Carter's certification and their need to refrain from supporting Salvadoran or other insurgents and acts of terrorism.[23]

SOMOZA ASSASSINATED IN PARAGUAY: ASUNCION, PARAGUAY, SEPTEMBER 14, 1980. Deposed Nicaraguan dictator Anastasio Somoza was

assassinated in a rocket-propelled grenade and machine-gun attack on his
armored limousine. The assailants, later traced back to the Sandinistas,
escaped. The news of Somoza's demise was greeted with great joy in
Nicaragua.[24]

CUBA PRESSURES SALVADORAN INSURGENTS FOR ACTION: SAN SAL-
VADOR, EL SALVADOR, SEPTEMBER 27, 1980. A CIA source within the insurgent Popular Liberation Front (FPL) reported that Cuba had threatened to
withdraw support from the insurgent movement unless a "final offensive"
against the government was mounted soon.[25] It was to be several months
before the rebel coalition acted.

ATLANTIC AREA UPRISING AGAINST SANDINISTAS: BLUEFIELDS,
NICARAGUA, SEPTEMBER 28, 1980. Anti-Sandinista demonstrations and a
general strike broke out in the Atlantic coastal city of Bluefields, a predom-
inantly Miskito Indian community. The dissidents were protesting the presence of Cuban and Soviet technicians and advisers.[26] It was the first case of
significant popular opposition to the Sandinista regime and foreshadowed
later, more serious Sandinista/Miskito confrontations and an exodus of
Miskito Indians seeking refuge in northern Honduras.

BACK TO WASHINGTON, THEN ONWARD: WASHINGTON, D.C., OCTO-
BER 4, 1980. Senate confirmation came September 26. I returned to Washington the following day. The October 1 swearing-in ceremony was somewhat
hurried but routine. After last-minute consultations I left Washington for
Tegucigalpa.

2

Learning the Ropes

SUMMARY—Organizing the mission and strategic planning—coup rumors, Paz, presidential candidates and leaders—friction with Southern Command—terrorist attacks—human rights issues—Nicaraguan exiles—refugees and strife with Nicaragua—peace treaty signed—Reagan elected, policy changes promised—meeting his transition team—growing violence in El Salvador—Sandinistas pressure opposition

ARRIVAL AT POST: TEGUCIGALPA, HONDURAS, OCTOBER 4, 1980. I was met on arrival by the Honduran chief of protocol, Orlando Carcamo, Bill Walker and, most important, my wife Martha and daughter Mimi, who had driven from San Jose. The media were also there in force. In Central America, the arrival of a new American ambassador was big news; that would take some getting used to. Carcamo conducted the party to the VIP lounge that had been set up for me to make a brief statement to the press. That duty complete, Carcamo and the press left. I then had a brief opportunity to meet the senior members of the U.S. mission and their wives, there assembled. The only familiar faces, other than my family and Walker, were my secretary, Amy Lindsey, and AID director John Olesen. Once I had made the rounds, I briefly affirmed my pleasure at having joined them, emphasized the importance of their respective efforts in advancing our national interests in Honduras and thanked them for the hospitality they had extended to my wife and daughter before I arrived. And I would see them all on Monday for my first CT meeting.

We were then off to a palatial residence we would call home.

SALVADORAN HUMAN RIGHTS ACTIVIST SLAIN: SAN SALVADOR, EL SALVADOR, OCTOBER 5, 1980. Maria Magdelena Henriquez, spokeswoman for the nongovernmental Salvadoran Human Rights Commission, was kidnapped. Her bullet-riddled body was found two days later in a shallow grave.[1]

THE CATERING ESTABLISHMENT CALLED HOME: TEGUCIGALPA, HONDURAS, EARLY OCTOBER 1980. The modern residence, purpose-built of

Honduran sandstone in the late 1960s, is set on 10 wooded hilltop acres about four miles from the U.S. Mission offices and five miles from city center. The extensive grounds were well planned and tended. A large swimming pool and bathhouse were located about 100 yards from the residence. This facility was open to all mission staff, including PCVs, and their families six days a week. It got a lot of use and was a very positive morale factor at a post where recreational activities were limited.

It was a splendid representational and catering facility and well staffed. Martha and I later calculated that we ran an average of about 100 people, mostly Hondurans, through the residence per week, hosting coffees, informal business meetings, luncheons, teas, receptions, buffet and formal dinners and other events. None of this would have been possible without the support and assistance of all elements of the mission, who suggested events, helped with guest lists and cohosted these events, and, especially, the members of the residence staff, who took great pride in their work and gave unstintingly to make these events a success.

THE CHANCERY AND FACILITIES: TEGUCIGALPA, HONDURAS, OCTOBER 5, 1980. The chancery design is similar to that of the residence had the same architect and had been built at the same time. Situated on a rise about two miles from the center of the city, the compound consisted of half a city block surrounded by a high sandstone wall. The building had three wings. One wing was two stories, the others a single floor. The executive suite accommodating the ambassador, DCM and secretaries was on the second floor. These offices had a glass wall providing a view of the city, which also represented a major security risk. The chancery housed the Political, Economic and Joint Administrative Sections, as well as several other agencies: the CIA, Defense attaches, Commerce, and later the Drug Enforcement Agency. Access to the building was controlled by a Marine Security Guard booth.

Most other Mission elements were located in an annex building directly across the street. The Consular Section and USIS occupied the ground and first floors. The remaining four floors housed AID. The Milgroup and Peace Corps were housed in converted residential properties. The former was located outside town near a military base, and the Peace Corps was near city center.

Security at all these facilities was inadequate, and a major chancery upgrade was supposed to commence shortly. Security at the annex was extremely weak, although Marine and Honduran guards controlled access during working hours. There were no practical solutions to its physical vulnerability. Although a number of improvements were to be made—most notably the installation of emergency exits from all floors—it was subjected to several terrorist attacks. A few years later it was assaulted by a mob and torched. Fortunately, all employees had been evacuated, so there were no casualties among our staff.

MEETING AND ORGANIZING THE COUNTRY TEAM: TEGUCIGALPA, HONDURAS, OCTOBER 6, 1980. The principal business of my first day was to meet with and begin organizing the CT. I also had an escorted walk through the chancery and the annex building, meeting key American and Honduran staff members. Walker had arranged for me to present credentials—the ceremony marking the host government's official recognition and confirmation of my appointment—October 10. Once that ritual was complete, I could conduct business publicly. Until then, my time would be spent exclusively within the confines of the mission.

The CT convened in the first floor conference room, its 13 members seated around two folding tables placed in the center of a sterile and cavernous room. In the future, I decided, we would meet in my office. After announcing when credentials would be presented, I asked that CT members review my instructions cable carefully and meet with me again the following day to discuss its content in detail. I wished to spend part of the next couple of weeks reviewing our policy goals, refining our strategies and making specific action assignments. At the next session I would try to address any questions, concerns or recommendations they might have; for subsequent meetings I wished to break into smaller functional groups. At the end of the process I wanted to have a joint action plan that was agreed on and accepted by all.

Next, I outlined my approach to mission management, stressing two key points:

• DCM Walker had my complete trust and confidence and should be considered my alter ego. He would be in charge when I was absent, and I wanted everyone to deal with him as if he were me. They could also expect him to be present at nearly all of my individual meetings with them.

• Although I recognized and understood their individual agency interests, I hoped to have the CT function as a cohesive, collegial unit in its pursuit of our overall policy objectives. I would count on their cooperation and support in this effort. I welcomed hearing their views on issues and encouraged dissent to the point that I would include such views in cables containing policy recommendations. Washington deserved our best judgments. Once a decision was made, however, I would expect their unwavering support.

In addition, I levied several specific tasks, explaining the rationale for each request.[2]

SANDINISTAS CLAIM BLUEFIELDS UNREST IS PART OF PLOT: MANAGUA, NICARAGUA, OCTOBER 8, 1980. A Sandinista government press conference claimed that the September 28 Bluefields general strike and Miskito Indian unrest was the product of a "counter-revolutionary" plot. Featured was a purported conspirator who told of a plan to split the Atlantic coast region off from the rest of Nicaragua.[3] Most observers considered that story specious; no other evidence was presented to support it.

JOINT MILITARY EXERCISE PROPOSAL RAISES CONCERNS: TEGUCIGALPA, HONDURAS, OCTOBER 8–9, 1980. My first significant business was Southern Command's proposal for the joint U.S./Honduran military exercise, *Halcon Vista* (Falcon View), scheduled for October. During my consultations in Washington, I had learned of our military's desire to conduct this exercise with the Honduran armed forces. State was a bit leery of the prospect but had no grounds to oppose it, especially because several years had passed without such an effort and the Honduran military supported the idea with gusto. Bowdler and others, however, had emphasized that I would need to maintain close oversight to ensure it did not adversely impact the transition process or our delicate relationship with the Sandinistas—who were certain to play the exercise as a threat to Nicaragua—or the Salvadoran situation. The last thing we wished to imply was that we were "militarizing" our Central American policy.

The exercise concept described to me earlier was for a command post exercise that would not require deployment of either Honduran or U.S. forces; it would involve only the joint exercise staff, a small control team to run the exercise and a few Southern Command support personnel. This limited activity would provide U.S. personnel an opportunity to work with and get to know some of their Honduran counterparts, to learn more about actual Honduran capabilities and to gain firsthand knowledge of terrain, road systems and so forth.

Southern Command's cable outlining the purpose and scope of the exercise revealed that the planning process was quite advanced but that there had been little consultation with either the embassy or State. The summer's command post exercise had transformed itself into one involving deployment of both U.S. and Honduran military units.

I had no problem with the central purpose of the event: to coordinate U.S. and Honduran forces in a coastal interdiction exercise and reassure the Honduran government and people of our continued support. But its scope and proposed participants were another matter entirely. U.S. forces were to include an amphibious ship with 200 Marines embarked.[4] At that time, such an action in Central America could only be considered provocative and would almost certainly trigger a negative reaction in the region and beyond. Moreover, the history of our Marine Corps in Central America—at varying times having been the instrument of direct intervention, landing and occupying parts of Honduras and all of Nicaragua—would risk a strong popular backlash. What really astounded me was Southern Command's apparent insensitivity to the political implications of its proposal. Fortunately, the exercise could not be conducted without my concurrence, and the presence of the Marines was not essential.

My first step was to consult the CT. With the exception of the Milgroup commander, who had been working with Southern Command on planning, members voiced either strong reservations or outright opposition to the exercise as proposed. Next I consulted informally with our embassies in Managua and San Salvador. Both expressed serious reservations, believing *Halcon Vista*, as conceived, was a bad idea.

I then sent a personal cable to Assistant Secretary Bowdler and General Wallace Nutting, the Southern Command commander (with copies to the Central American embassies, Defense and various military commands), in which I refused to agree to the *Halcon Vista* exercise as envisaged. I wrote:

> I have serious reservations about wisdom of including USN amphibious unit, with 200 Marines embarked, in exercise.... As addressees are no doubt aware, extreme left in El Salvador, and its allies elsewhere, including moderate left and social democrats in Europe, as well as U.S., have made repeated allegations of actual or impending direct U.S. military involvement in that country and Honduras. Similarly, FSLN [Sandinistas] in Nicaragua loses no opportunity to echo such charges, which in turn tend to feed Nicaraguan (and other) suspicions as to our real intentions toward that country.... Accordingly, I cannot concur in *Halcon Vista* exercise as planned.[5]

I went on to suggest ways in which a modified exercise, without Marines, might be structured and invited the comments of my Central American colleagues. Their support was unanimous.

I also included a section titled "Other Views," setting forth dissenting or diverging opinions. This reinforced my commitment to encourage dissent made to the CT, helping to establish my personal credibility.

This was not an auspicious way to begin my relationship with Southern Command, but I had little choice but to voice my concerns about, and opposition to, the exercise as proposed. I was most disturbed by Southern Command's lack of prior consultation with the post and its apparent unilateral expansion of the exercise scope. I was not prepared to allow the regional command to make policy in Honduras without our full consideration of the issues involved. State's response to my message was positive, reporting that the issue had been referred for interagency review.[6]

Two weeks later, still absent interagency resolution, the Joint Chiefs of Staff instructed Southern Command to proceed with negotiating a "letter of intent" with the Hondurans, laying out the exercise parameters. In the absence of an agreed interagency position as to participation of the Marines, Southern Command proposed to include its original plan in the letter of intent. The Hondurans would be asked to sign a letter that provided for the participation of the Marines, with a caveat that the scope of the exercise might be changed because of "political considerations."

I found this proposal unacceptable on two grounds and moved quickly to block it.[7] First, once the Hondurans agreed to participation by the Marines, it would be more difficult for us to block their participation in the exercise. Second, the notion of attributing any later change to "political considerations" would send precisely the wrong message to both the Hondurans and Nicaraguans. To the former it would indicate that political factors could cause us to abandon commitments, and to the latter it would suggest that they could use political pressure to force us to back out of agreements. Neither would be helpful.

The issue, however, was not resolved. The Hondurans decided they could not participate in *Halcon Vista* that year, mooting the issue. It resurfaced in 1981 and was to color our relations with Southern Command and Defense throughout my tenure.

REPORTED COUP PLANS: THE FIRST IN A SERIES: TEGUCIGALPA, HONDURAS, OCTOBER 9, 1980. The CIA station chief reported that senior military officers were increasingly displeased with President Paz (who, among other things, was accused of drunkenness and womanizing) and were planning to oust him in a legal or quasi-legal way, although it was not clear how they proposed to do that. The salons and saloons of Tegucigalpa were often abuzz with such rumors, but this report seemed to have more substance than most. Although I suspected it was overdrawn, and appended a comment to that effect before it was sent to the CIA, it was a cause for concern. Indeed, a possible coup represented a serious threat to successful transition to democratic government.

I asked Walker to call a meeting of the station chief, Political counselor, attaches and Milgroup commander to assess the situation. He recommended we also include Public Affairs Officer Arcos, since he had some of the best contacts in political circles. I agreed. This ad hoc group would soon evolve into a standing subset of the CT that would deal with political and military issues.

The consensus was that the report was probably exaggerated, although our military contingent confirmed their Honduran interlocutors' growing dissatisfaction about Paz's private affairs, and others were aware of such rumors in political circles. At this meeting we also identified several key political and military leaders as targets and assigned CT members to approach them about these rumors, which were common enough to avoid endangering the source of the CIA report. They were instructed to express our grave concern and emphasize that such action could threaten U.S. security and economic assistance. In sum, anything that would threaten the transition process would not be well received by the USG. This theme was to become a constant litany over the coming months.

Not yet having presented credentials, I had no choice but to sit on the sidelines for a couple of days. But this report underscored my need to see President Paz privately as soon as possible after the presentation. And I was also resolved to raise the issue with political leaders of all stripes, with whom appointments were already being scheduled in anticipation of the credentials ceremony.[8]

FOREIGN MINISTER ON RELATIONS WITH EL SALVADOR AND NICARAGUA: TEGUCIGALPA, HONDURAS, OCTOBER 9, 1980. Walker joined me for my initial call on Foreign Minister Cesar Elvir Sierra, an army colonel. Our purpose was to review the credentials ceremony scheduled for the following day. After outlining the procedural details, Elvir gave us a rundown on the status of the peace talks with El Salvador and other Central American issues. This was unusual for what was essentially a courtesy call and indicated to me that Elvir wished to establish an open and relatively informal relationship.

The final steps in concluding the peace treaty with El Salvador were moving faster than the public had been told, and Elvir was very optimistic that he and his Salvadoran counterpart would initial the final text in Lima on October 30. This would be followed by a formal ceremony at the OAS in Washington in mid-November, after which the pact would have to be ratified by both countries. He did not anticipate any last-minute snags and had nothing but praise for his Salvadoran counterpart, Fidel Chavez Mena, an old friend of Walker's and mine.

But he expressed concern about assembly ratification, fearing that one of the major parties might find some real or imagined political advantage in opposing the treaty. I promptly offered to support him in any way he thought might be useful, noting that I would be meeting with the leaders of both parties as soon as I had presented my credentials. He readily agreed that we should meet to discuss ways I might help.

He also reported that he was working to set up a meeting of Central American foreign ministers. Separately, he had also invited Nicaraguan foreign minister Miguel D'Escoto to visit Tegucigalpa in an effort to "clear the air" between the two countries. D'Escoto's initial response had been positive.

I was very impressed by Elvir. He had been open and friendly, was clearly very bright, and appeared to possess an agile, politically sophisticated mind. I looked forward to working with him.[9] Unfortunately, he was not a representative example of Honduran military officers.

SALVADORAN INSURGENTS UNIFY: MANAGUA, NICARAGUA, OCTOBER 10, 1980. Three Salvadoran insurgent organizations, meeting in Managua, announced the formation of a unified military command, the Faribundo Marti National Liberation Front (FMLN), to carry out their paramilitary campaign against the junta government in that country.[10]

PRESENTING CREDENTIALS: TEGUCIGALPA, HONDURAS, OCTOBER 10, 1980. Arriving at the National Palace promptly at 4 P.M., we were received with full ceremonial honors. President Paz was in a khaki uniform and seemed quite diffident, despite his position. He was about five feet, six inches tall, of slender build and distinctly Indian in appearance, which was not common among Hondurans. He had a thin moustache and a receding hairline. He did not resemble anyone's idea of a military hero, yet I knew that he had been one in the brief 1969 war with El Salvador. He had gone immediately to the front, rallied the fleeing troops, and established a defense that stabilized the situation.

During our chat Paz said that he wished to see me privately and soon, asking that I call his office the following day to set up a meeting. That was great news, given my need to see him promptly. After a few minutes, I caught a nod from Elvir, excused myself and our party retired. After laying a wreath at the National monument in front of the palace, we left.

I could now launch into what would seem an unending round of courtesy calls and visits. In addition to required calls on government ministers, legislative leaders and senior military officers, I had to follow through on the target contact lists I had requested from the CT and also work my way though the diplomatic corps. The latter was especially tedious and unproductive.

The author with the provisional president, General Policarpo Paz Garcia, at the National Palace, October 1980.

WHAT WE KNEW ABOUT THE ANTI-SANDINISTAS: TEGUCIGALPA, HONDURAS, OCTOBER 1980. The Carter administration believed that anti-Sandinista exile groups had no chance of overthrowing the Revolutionary Nicaraguan Government (GRN). That also represented the intelligence community consensus. The Sandinistas enjoyed overwhelming popular support and could not be defeated short of direct U.S. military intervention. Moreover, paramilitary operations against the GRN would be counterproductive, allowing the Sandinistas to buttress their popular support, and giving them a further rationale for repressing domestic opposition and accelerating the expansion of their army to 50,000 men.

A better approach was to try to influence their behavior through cooperation with other hemispheric democracies (e.g., Venezuela and Costa Rica), conditional economic assistance and strengthening countervailing power centers within Nicaragua. President Carter had already approved $1 million for covert financial assistance to democratic unions, political parties and media inside Nicaragua.[11] Exile groups were specifically excluded.

We were encouraging the Hondurans to restrict use of their territory by exiled Nicaraguans attacking the GRN. At that point we were unaware the Honduran military had already invited the Argentine military in primarily to organize the Nicaraguan counter revolutionaries. It also followed, as I understood my instructions, that we should avoid encouraging or appearing to support the Contra groups.

There were several thousand Nicaraguan exiles living in Honduras, many of them former National Guardsmen and their families. Tracking their activities was not a high priority. Most of the others who earlier had found refuge in Honduras had returned to Nicaragua. The exiled elite—including most senior National Guard officers—were resident in Miami or Guatemala. Those in Miami claimed to be training over 2,000 potential freedom fighters, although there was little evidence to support that. The vast majority of private sector leaders remained in Nicaragua, determined to work with, or organize a legal political opposition to, the Sandinistas.

The exile community in Honduras was fragmented. One faction included many of Somoza's former friends, close associates, and senior Guard officers; other groups explicitly distanced themselves from those tainted by the Somoza connection. Some of these groups conducted occasional raids into Nicaragua, and the frequency of these forays was increasing according to our embassy in Managua. The raids were small-scale, hit-and-run affairs—a quick attack on an isolated Sandinista guard post, the ambush of a military patrol and even cattle rustling. The raiders would then withdraw quickly to Honduras. We had information that certain Honduran military leaders were selling military arms and supplies to the exile groups, as they had done when the Sandinistas were operating out of Honduras against Somoza. We believed this represented freelance corruption rather than deliberate policy. We were wrong.

Our information about Contra activities was from three general sources: intelligence collection by the CIA and Defense attaches; routine Political Section collection from overt sources; and information gathered by two of our consular officers having friends in the exile community. They were not particularly productive. CIA sources, however, had told us that the exile community, including the Contra groups, was heavily penetrated by Sandinista informants. We still had no firm information that the Argentines were working with the Contras, although many of our military contacts had to have been aware of that link. Our principal concern at that point was that the Argentines working with the Honduran military intelligence staff might be preparing for increased repression of suspected subversives.

In retrospect it is obvious that we could easily have been, and probably were, intentionally misled by Honduran military sources.[12] Our consular staff sources picked up little of significance, and their main contact was later reported to be a Sandinista mole.

It appeared to me that members of the exile community were attempting to build closer relations with U.S. mission officials. They were, I suspected, seeking to create an impression of U.S. support for their paramilitary operations. That was definitely not a perception I wished to encourage.[13]

We needed better information. After some discussion in the CT, we decided to send a political officer and Milgroup civilian to Choluteca in southeastern Honduras, the area of most exile activity. They were also asked to see what they could discover about arms smuggling from Nicaragua into Honduras.

ASSESSMENT OF ANTI-SANDINISTA ACTIVITY ON FRONTIER: CHOLUTECA, HONDURAS, OCTOBER 10–11, 1980. Our fact-finding team returned with useful information, the full significance of which we failed to grasp. Former National Guardsmen, under the direction of a Somoza friend, Pedro Ortega, were mounting small hit-and-run attacks on Sandinista guard posts. The raiders did not penetrate far into Nicaragua and on occasion also rustled cattle. Ortega owned a local match factory and maintained contacts with other exiles in Miami, Guatemala and the southern cone. Our sources also alleged that he had Argentine advisers and received financial support from Argentina and Taiwan. We failed to pursue those leads adequately.

Cattle rustling had triggered a large counterforay into Honduras by heavily armed Sandinistas a few weeks earlier with the loss of an estimated 700 head of cattle. The cattle were reportedly hauled away by trucks of the Nicaraguan Agrarian Reform Institute. Honduran troops were then stationed on the target ranch and, two weeks later, foiled a second rustling attempt, engaging the Sandinistas in a firefight that was said to have left five of them dead. None of this seemed to alarm the local citizenry or authorities.

Even more significant in retrospect were reports that a Costa Rican trucking company was involved in shipping arms through Honduras to Salvadoran insurgents. Our fact finders came back with the name of the trucking firm, which we cabled to our embassy in San Jose, requesting any information that might be available. Nothing came of this inquiry, and we failed to follow up. That was another oversight. In January Honduran authorities would locate and close a major arms smuggling operation supporting the Salvadorans; the truck captured at that time was from this firm. Had we followed up more effectively, we might have closed that operation several months earlier.

All this information was passed to State and distributed widely within the USG, along with our assessment.[14] It failed to set off alarm bells in Washington as well. We concluded that the Contra activities were very small-scale, carried out by individuals who had been linked with Somoza (and hence discredited) and could not reasonably endanger the Sandinista government. But they were an irritant. Obviously, the Hondurans could do more to discourage this activity but probably not put an end to it.

THE PRESIDENTIAL CANDIDATES: A STUDY IN CONTRASTS: TEGUCIGALPA, HONDURAS, OCTOBER 13, 1980. My meetings with local leaders got off to a fast start on the first working day following presentation of credentials. I lunched with National Party candidate, Ricardo Zuniga, at a local watering hole much favored by the political elite, so our tête-à-tête was widely noted. Later in the afternoon the Liberal Party candidate, Roberto Suazo Cordova, came to the residence accompanied by his key aide, Carlos Flores, whose family interests included one of the largest newspapers. Suazo had requested a private meeting prior to my formal call on him as president of the Constituent Assembly, scheduled for the following day.

Zuniga was a small, cherubic man and proved an elusive and wary conversationalist. Our luncheon discussion, although cordial, was short on substance and frequently interrupted by well-wishers who greeted him and got a closer look at the new ambassador.

The National Party had lost the April 1980 assembly elections by several percentage points but hoped to reverse that outcome in the 1981 presidential and congressional elections. Historically, the party had been closely allied with the Catholic Church, but times had changed. By the 1960s its closest ties were with the military, not the clergy, and the Church had become more progressive than the Nationalists. Its major differences with the rival Liberal Party, which traditionally supported secular rule, were over social and economic policy (Nationalists were more conservative) and national sovereignty (also more nationalistic). The two parties actually disputed, and continue to dispute, the political center ground, although the Liberals at the time had a small faction that was arguably Marxist influenced.

Zuniga had been a key player in successive military governments under

Gen. Oswaldo Lopez Arellano, who ruled from 1963 to 1975. Lopez had been ousted by a military coup, following a major bribery scandal involving the U.S. banana company United Brands. Zuniga went out with Lopez. Tainted by that scandal, he had not occupied a government post since. Nonetheless, Zuniga maintained close relationships with several senior Honduran military officers but was heartily detested by others. His domination of the party and his candidacy had been unsuccessfully opposed by a number of private sector leaders who considered him corrupt and untrustworthy. But they had been no match for his guile and manipulative skills.[15]

The Zuniga meeting was disappointing, although we did agree to meet privately soon. The second meeting was much better and, in retrospect, probably marked the zenith in our relationship. Zuniga later became my leading Honduran adversary. As the political campaign unfolded, it seemed that he was headed for defeat. Thus, the USG insistence on the electoral transition process, he correctly saw, was a threat to his ambition and interests. His strategy became one of trying to persuade the military to oust the transition government and cancel the elections. From his standpoint it was better to have a measure of influence with a military regime, and retain control of the party, than to lose the election, be replaced as party leader, and be totally frozen out by a Liberal government. To accomplish these ends, Zuniga needed to discredit me and persuade the military that the USG would not react negatively to a coup.

Suazo was the antithesis of Zuniga in several respects. A large, portly man, he was a smiling glad-hander, seemingly open and candid in his dealings with others. Though he probably lacked Zuniga's raw intelligence, he was bright and not without his own measure of cunning. And he could be equally adroit and ruthless in dealing with dissent in his party: he had its left wing isolated and made virtually powerless.

Our meeting was cordial and covered a number of substantive issues: the election outlook and threats thereto, the Nicaragua and El Salvador situations, the peace treaty with El Salvador that would shortly be signed at the OAS in Washington, and the economic outlook. Regarding the peace treaty, he was ambivalent, expressing concerns about the mechanisms for resolving the territorial dispute and de facto nature of the Salvadoran government. I noted that the treaty offered both countries an opportunity that should not be missed, especially given the Central American situation. Neither country could reasonably expect to get everything it wanted from the accord, and rejection by either country would be devastating in terms of regional stability. He listened without comment but left me with the impression that he would seriously consider the points I had raised. Reporting this conversation to State, I suggested that we try to enlist the support of Costa Rican president Rodrigo Carazo, who was close to Suazo and strongly supported the treaty, to reinforce our arguments.[16]

Suazo planned to visit the United States for a medical checkup the following week and raised the possibility of his visiting Washington at that time. I welcomed this prospect and promised the embassy's full support in arranging a program. This would provide another opportunity to reinforce our support for the peace treaty and to point up the potential damage should the assembly fail to ratify.[17]

In sum, it was a useful meeting and seemed to promise a fruitful relationship. My formal call on Suazo at the assembly the following day was largely ceremonial, although he had arranged for the press to be there as our session concluded. I took the opportunity to reaffirm the USG's strong support for the transition process and free elections, which received extensive and favorable play in the media.[18] This was really the kickoff in what would become an ongoing effort to use the media to get our message of support for elections out to the public and to counter efforts to block the transition process.

ASSESSMENT: PEACE TREATY REJECTION IS REAL POSSIBILITY: TEGU-CIGALPA, HONDURAS, OCTOBER 15, 1980. We needed to get a better fix on the risk of the treaty being rejected. I therefore charged the CT with assessing this situation and devising a strategy to try to keep ratification on track. The threat seemed greater than we anticipated. However, the two minor parties that controlled the decisive votes in the event the Liberals and Nationalists split were strongly supportive, so ratification could be assured with just the votes of one major party. The Honduran military saw the strategic value of closer cooperation with El Salvador—indeed, some observers thought it was only the threat of Sandinista revolutionary zeal that had moved the two governments to reach agreement—and was solidly in favor, as were most of the media. We recommended that a full-court press be put on the leaders of both parties and every assembly member we knew. Elvir later asked that I make the same pitch to Honduran private sector leaders, which I did.

As I saw it, more was at stake than just the treaty and use of the frontier as a refuge for Salvadoran insurgents, important as they were. If the assembly should reject the treaty, the Honduran military might well block the transition. The department accepted our recommendations, and we went to work.[19]

SALVADORAN ELECTIONS PROMISED: SAN SALVADOR, EL SALVADOR, OCTOBER 15, 1980. The junta government announced that elections for a constituent assembly would be held in 1982, to be followed by presidential and legislative elections in 1983.[20]

GETTING DOWN TO BUSINESS WITH PRESIDENT PAZ: TEGUCIGALPA, HONDURAS, OCTOBER 16, 1980. My first substantive meeting with Paz was in a small reception room at the national palace. I had asked Walker to join me because I wished to demonstrate to Paz that my DCM had my full confidence. Paz was accompanied by a military aide who served as note taker for the initial part of our hour-and-a-half meeting. He left after about an hour.

Again, Paz seemed reserved and diffident, giving the impression of being uncomfortable or uncertain. After we exchanged pleasantries, he noted that he had often met with Ambassador Jaramillo at the residence, in that way avoiding the overly dramatic press speculation that usually followed his more public meetings with the U.S. ambassador, and wondered if I would be willing to continue that practice. I agreed immediately. That seemed to break the ice, and the rest of the meeting was relaxed and candid.

Paz thought the provisional government incompetent and the Constituent Assembly overly assertive. It should, he opined, stick to writing a constitution, not legislating. Party leaders, not surprisingly, were determined to legislate, as well as draft a new constitution. In response to my questions Paz discounted the precedents established by previous assemblies but said flatly that he was not prepared to confront the party leaders. Rather, he would deal pragmatically with differences that might arise. Because he had no plans for a confrontation, I assumed he was simply putting down a marker.

He also indicated distaste for the two principal political parties, expressing his unhappiness with his apparently frequent role as a mediator to resolve differences between them. Nonetheless, he said he was determined to see the transition process through.

I suggested that he might be interested in learning my instructions, which I would be pleased to share. He was and specifically affirmed the importance he attached to Honduras's relations with the United States. I emphasized the importance we placed on the successful conclusion of the transition and how critical we regarded the establishment of another democratic regime in Central America. I also described my intentions to meet as many Hondurans as possible and travel throughout the country, adding that I hoped I could count on his counsel as I sought to acquaint myself with Honduras and its people. This too seemed to please him, and he responded positively.

I then raised a couple of AID issues, one of which touched on the sensitive executive/assembly relations question. He promised to take the needed action, noting that some of the problems AID was encountering resulted from the inexperience of key ministers. He accepted with enthusiasm my suggestion that we arrange a special meeting between these ministers and AID officials to review problem areas and see what could be done to speed things up.

Finally, we touched briefly on several other issues, including the peace treaty. Paz encouraged me to work closely with Elvir, who enjoyed his full confidence.[21]

From my standpoint the meeting had been a great success. After an

With Provisional President Paz (*center*) and Foreign Minister Cesar Elvir Sierra at the National Palace, October 1980.

uncertain start Paz had been open and friendly. His affirmation of the importance he placed on the USG relationship, and his suggestion that we meet privately at my residence, indicated he wished to maintain the close link he had developed with my predecessor. That was reassuring.

Paz's commitment to a successful transition was critical to realizing our policy goals. It was apparent to me that their attainment would be tied inexorably to Paz's continuing as president. Should he be removed from office, there was no telling how far or fast the transition process might unravel.

SALVADORAN REFUGEE INFLUX GROWS: EL SALVADOR/HONDURAS FRONTIER, OCTOBER 21, 1980. The Red Cross reported that recent Salvadoran military operations in northeastern El Salvador had displaced an estimated 25,000 peasants. Most of these people sought safe haven elsewhere in El Salvador, but many moved into Honduras, increasing refugee numbers.[22]

RESULTS OF SOUNDINGS ON POSSIBLE COUP: TEGUCIGALPA, HONDURAS, OCTOBER 22, 1980. Reviewing what we had collected regarding a possible coup, we concluded that, despite efforts by some senior military officers to foment one, such action seemed unlikely at the moment. Reports of plotting (or advocacy) within the military were worrisome. These rumors, followed by endless speculation as to their significance, seemed almost a Honduran national pastime. Judging from our information, the principal promoters of a coup against Paz were Cols. Hubert Bodden, Ruben Montoya and Jose Bueso Rosa. Two of them (Bodden and Bueso) commanded major units and military districts; the third (Montoya) commanded the Navy. They were also reputed to be among the most corrupt members of the officer corps.

On occasion the names of Cols. Gustavo Alvarez and Leonidas Torres Arias also surfaced, but we were skeptical about their roles. Alvarez commanded the national police, FUSEP, and was expected to succeed Paz as armed forces commander on installation of the elected government. Torres Arias was the head of military intelligence (G-2), a confidant of Paz and thought to be Alvarez's principal military rival.

The military constituted the only real threat to the transition. Others— Zuniga, for example—might wish to block or delay the elections but could not succeed without the support and muscle of the armed forces. The principal weapon available to those who wished the transition to go forward was popular support for the electoral process. There was plenty of that. Elements favoring the transition included the political parties (Zuniga and his allies were possible exceptions, however); the private sector (less a few businessmen close to the most corrupt military elements); the media owners; the Church (although it would not take a leading role); the trade unions; and most of the intellectual community (some Marxists, however, believed frustrating elections would enhance the prospects of a popular uprising that would bring them to power).

According to a variety of sources, all coup planning (or action) had been placed in suspense, pending the outcome of the election in the United States. Evidently, our elections were going to influence, if not determine, whether the transition process would go forward as planned.

As a result, I wrote:

> On the basis of this collection effort and our assessment of the resulting information, it is my judgement that no such threat exists at the present time. All mission elements involved in this collection/assessment exercise concur in this conclusion. Nevertheless, there are grounds for continued USG concern.... Under the circumstances, it seems clear to me that we should continue our efforts to buttress the transitional government, making certain that all important sectors understand our position and expectations...several of our interlocutors have suggested that coup-minded military have merely put their plans on the back burner pending outcome of U.S. elections. According to this thesis, a victory by Gov. Reagan would encourage them to move against current government and end transition process.[23]

Little did I realize that Reagan's election would have precisely that effect and that we would be spending the better part of the coming year trying to prevent frustration of the transition.

A STRATEGIC PLAN EMERGES: TEGUCIGALPA, HONDURAS, LATE OCTOBER–EARLY NOVEMBER. Our CT had devoted several hours to reviewing our instructions and developing implementing plans. In addition, Walker had reviewed our strategy paper with the junior officers of all agencies. There appeared to be a full understanding of, and unanimous support for, both our goals and our strategies for achieving them. I was confident we had a cohesive, mission-wide policy and action plan.[24]

The CT was unanimous in believing that the United States could best support the transition process by staking out a firm, consistent position, in public and in private, in favor of elections. We would all emphasize this theme, seek opportunities to reiterate it in public and ensure that U.S. officials in Washington and all important official visitors reaffirmed it. I also asked Walker, Arcos and the head of the Political Section to work out a plan to secure maximum media exposure for our position and urged the CT to be alert to possible media opportunities and public fora that we could exploit. And in my private meetings I would emphasize that our growing economic and security assistance levels were conditioned on continued progress toward democratic, constitutional government.

On the economic side, there were growing signs of trouble. The pace of development investment was slowing, as the new government had difficulty meeting preconditions for disbursement. Tax revenues were declining, capital flight accelerating, and energy costs rising. I asked AID director Oleson and Economic officer Paul Wackerbarth to develop ideas to help ease or lessen the preconditions burden without giving away our leverage and what actions we might take to counter these other trends. Increased private investment, we believed, was essential to sustain the economic growth rate, but investors were worried about the regional environment. In the meantime we would step up our efforts with the government to overcome the procedural and bureaucratic obstacles that were slowing development programs, which I had already raised with Paz. I also asked that they and our Labor officer look at ways in which me might involve the trade unions and *campesino* organizations more directly in our development program.

, Several years earlier AID had sponsored a very successful worker housing program with unions near San Pedro Sula. It seemed to me critical that our programs be seen to be helping the less affluent sectors of Honduran society. Many were so directed, but there was little realization of that fact. Nor were the scope and diversity of our development activities fully known and appreciated by the public. We needed to get that information out, another task for our public affairs program.

Security was a vital concern to most Hondurans. We needed to ensure that they realized we would not forsake them in the face of escalating violence and subversion in the region. One important way to enhance their sense of security was by normalizing relations with El Salvador. If that country should fall to a Marxist regime, their security would be gravely threatened. They also needed reassurance that we would seek to deter any Nicaraguan notion to attack and that if attacked, we would not stand idly by. Again, media access would be critical to get these messages across. Such an approach made far more sense to me and most of the CT than a massive buildup of Honduran armaments, the course favored by the Honduran military.

Our relations with the military were critical. On the one hand, our emphasis on the elections and failure to support a major arms buildup were contrary to what many, if not most, senior officers wanted. That created a serious potential for stress and conflict. But on the other hand, the military's paranoia about the Nicaraguan threat meant that their perceived need for U.S. support was very high and apt to increase. As they saw it, security assistance from the USG—and any other sources—was vital. The flip side of that belief, which surfaced later, was their perception that Honduras was so central to our plans for containing Nicaragua that they could get away with anything: we simply would not dare to cut them off. It was precisely this kind of skewed perception that would later lead the Argentine military—after they had become the USG's "prime contractor" for the Contra effort against Nicaragua—to delude themselves into thinking the USG would stand on the sidelines when they invaded the Falkland Islands.

The Honduran military had several grievances about our security assistance, many of which were valid. Foremost was their conviction that U.S. assistance levels were woefully inadequate, given the threat posed by Nicaragua. Moreover, our growing assistance to El Salvador was to create further regional imbalance. There was only the most remote possibility that Nicaragua would attack Honduras militarily because that would almost certainly trigger an immediate U.S. military response under the Rio Treaty. The Sandinistas and their advisers, Cuban and Soviet, knew this. Nonetheless, I supported increasing our assistance level to around $10 million to assuage Honduran concerns, enhance their capability to control their frontiers and maintain our credibility. Southern Command, in contrast, constantly pushed for much higher funding. That position was to find increased favor once President Reagan took office.

Second, the Hondurans believed our assistance terms were niggardly. Virtually all our aid was provided under Foreign Military Sales (FMS) cash or credit arrangements. This meant that they were paying top dollar for what they received (training and the helicopter lease excepted). They wanted additional no-cost (grant) assistance. I was not unsympathetic, because each dollar spent for arms and equipment meant one dollar less for development and social program investment. Given the emphasis we were placing on economic and social development, and the government's difficulty in making counterpart contributions, it was self-defeating to increase FMS or credits. This same rationale applied to equipment, such as the helicopters, provided on a grant basis, although on a lesser scale. Such largess meant that the Honduran military had to assume new operational and maintenance (rather than acquisition) costs. Thus, our requests urged increased grant assistance.

Finally, the Hondurans were in constant dudgeon over our long delivery lead times on their orders and our failure to meet promised delivery dates. Senior military officers, including Paz, rarely missed an opportunity to voice this complaint. The CT felt their position was entirely justified, but the problem seemed endemic to the defense procurement system. Later a higher priority was assigned to Honduran acquisitions, easing the problem somewhat.

We also had other concerns about the Honduran military: they were not using the leased helicopters effectively, nor were they making much of an effort to prevent Salvadoran insurgents from finding refuge in Honduras. That, of course, had been the rationale for the helicopter deal. In fact, the helicopters logged very few flying hours because of operation and maintenance costs. Nor were the Hondurans doing much to discourage Nicaraguan exiles from using Honduras as a base to mount raids against Nicaragua. We were pretty much in the dark about the Argentine military advisory presence.[25]

There were additional questions that I believed we needed to focus on: the refugee situation on the frontier with El Salvador, possible Salvadoran insurgent support networks in Honduras, activities of anti–Sandinista elements in the Nicaraguan border area, purpose and activities of the Argentine military advisers in-country, status of Honduran land redistribution/reform, and how to enhance mission security and accommodate the additional personnel and agencies joining the mission. I also began to levy benchmark reporting tasks on the Political Section and other mission elements. These required further research, intelligence collection and analysis, so deadlines of several months forward were established.

From my perspective we seemed to be off to a very good start.

SAN PEDRO SULA: MOSTLY ALLIES, SOME ADVERSARIES: SAN PEDRO SULA, HONDURAS, OCTOBER 30, 1980. The CT had recommended that I make an early visit to San Pedro Sula, the second city that was also the country's commercial, industrial and agricultural center. The American Consulate there had been closed several years earlier, and our only official presence was a binational cultural center operated by USIS. We planned a program for a working visit of three days, allowing me to meet the movers and shakers—business, labor, military, media, political and so forth. Our party included Arcos, Wackerbarth, the Labor attache and the Defense attaches. The next two and a half days were a whirlwind of official calls, meetings, luncheons, dinners and receptions. Several events were particularly noteworthy.

First, my meeting with Jorge Larach, an influential but somewhat reclusive businessman whose extensive holdings included two newspapers—the conservative *La Prensa,* based in San Pedro Sula, with the largest circulation in the country, and *El Heraldo,* in Tegucigalpa. Larach had a reputation for scrupulous honesty and was a member of the National Party. However, he

With Jorge J. Larach, leading San Pedro Sula businessman and publisher of *La Prensa* **and** *El Heraldo***, in his office, October, 1980.**

detested the party leader, Zuniga, whom he regarded as a pernicious and corrupting element in Honduran society. Larach, accordingly, supported dissident elements in the party. He was also a long-standing opponent of military rule in Honduras and forthright in his support of the transition process. I found him an intelligent and perceptive observer of the domestic and regional scenes and a strong supporter of most U.S. policies in the region. We hit it off very well. Although I am sure neither of us realized it at the time, he and *La Prensa* were to become the most vocal and effective supporters of our policies.

I also called on the military district commander, Colonel Bueso Rosa, one of the leading coup plotters. I was not impressed. He was slovenly in appearance and devious in conversation. Our discussion was short on substance, dealing principally with his views on the Nicaraguan threat and the shortcomings of U.S. security assistance. He was a striking contrast to Colonel Oswaldo Lopez, the Air Force commander, who briefed me on their tactical air units located in San Pedro Sula. Lopez struck me as very professional and rational about potential threats. His forces, he asserted, could defeat anything the Nicaraguans might throw at them, though he was understandably concerned about their possible acquisition of high performance Soviet aircraft. We did not consider his assessment of the Air Force's capability mere bravado.

Leaders of the dissident, progressive faction of the Liberal Party, ALIPO, were based in San Pedro Sula and were anxious to meet with me. The CT advised that I exercise care with them, as they might try to exploit a meeting with me in their ongoing struggle with Liberal Party leader Suazo Cordova. We had finally agreed to a private dinner with the clear understanding that it should receive no publicity.

When we arrived at the designated venue, the executive offices of a local bank, we found a group of more than 20 people, *Alipistas* and trade union leaders, gathered for a large dinner. That was not what we expected. Nonetheless, it turned out to be a very amiable and informative session providing an informal opportunity to exchange views with a group of progressive businessmen and union leaders.

We were initially concerned about the presence of a photographer but our hosts assured Arcos there would be no publicity about the event. Five days later we were unpleasantly surprised to find a full page spread, including photographs, in one of the Tegucigalpa newspapers. This was not helpful but it taught me to exercise special caution when dealing with ALIPO.

CHANCERY ANNEX STRAFED BY GUNFIRE: TEGUCIGALPA, HONDURAS, OCTOBER 30, 1980. Returning to my hotel from dinner, I found a note to call Walker. He reported that the annex building housing AID, USIS and the Consular Section had been raked by semi-automatic weapons fire earlier, around 6 P.M. Although several AID employees had been in the building, none had been injured, and damage was limited to broken windows and some holes in interior walls. We had been lucky.

Walker had advised State's Operations Center, told Martha to remain at the residence and asked FUSEP to send a patrol car there to spend the night at our entry gate. He had already advised all CT of events, and I asked that he convene a special meeting the following morning to review the security situation and take any precautionary measures they thought were required. Walker clearly had things well in hand, and we agreed that there was no reason for me to interrupt my visit.

According to FUSEP, two men on a motorcycle turned into the street that ran behind the annex building, stopped, and the pillion rider fired several rounds from a Galil 9mm gun, breaking several windows. FUSEP recovered several shell casings but had no other leads. We had no idea who was responsible.[26]

AID director Oleson reported his staff members were quite concerned about their safety, but recognized there was little that could be done to protect our facilities from such hit-and-run attacks. There was less concern among the Consular and USIS personnel, but their spaces had not been hit by gunfire. Unfortunately, this was only the first of many attacks on U.S. facilities and personnel.

BOMBS AT PEACE CORPS OFFICES AND CHILEAN EMBASSY: TEGUCI-GALPA, HONDURAS, OCTOBER 31, 1980. Shortly after opening of business, Peace Corps director Lara reported that a suspicious package had been found near their offices. He had called FUSEP, and its agents discovered it was a crude bomb. FUSEP disarmed the device and took it. Almost immediately thereafter the station chief reported that a bomb had exploded at the Chilean embassy; no one was injured.

Earlier that morning, our embassy had received a phone call from a female who said, "We are not joking. We had already advised you and last night we 'advised' you again. Before the end of the year, you will hear further from us." She did not identify "us." Several media outlets had also received a flyer from a group calling itself the "Popular Revolutionary Command Lorenzo Zelaya," taking credit for the previous evening's attack. It concluded with the words "Against the signing of the treaty sponsored by yankee imperialists! Against yankee intervention in Central America! For the cessation of the repression against the Salvadoran people...Liberation or Death."[27] The security situation in Tegucigalpa was souring rapidly.

Walker and I had prearranged a phone call for that morning, and he brought me up to date on these events. Again, we decided there was no reason to cancel my visit. There was nothing I could do that had not already been done, and I wanted to continue with my program. Moreover, I did not

With trade union leader Celeo Gonzalez, San Pedro Sula, during a visit to meet leading business, political, trade union and government officials in that city, November 1980.

wish to appear to undercut Walker by dashing back to Tegucigalpa or to show that our plans could be derailed by terrorist acts.

We immediately requested a visit from the regional security officer (RSO) based in Panama, Sy Dewitt, and additional funds to increase contract guard coverage at both the annex and chancery. Dewitt came promptly, and funding was provided. We also asked State to accelerate completion of the security enhancement project, with first priority given to the annex building. Some improvements were begun, but the project was still months away from completion.[28]

In addition, we asked FUSEP to assign several officers to a permanent patrol in the chancery/annex neighborhood; this request was denied, but frequency of patrol car visits to the area was increased. FUSEP also agreed to provide a protective detail for me, supplementing our two contract bodyguards, if we came up with a car and driver. We also decided to set up fixed contract guard posts at Walker's and Oleson's residences. State quickly agreed to provide the vehicle and the needed funds. Beyond these steps, all agency heads were directed to review prescribed personal security guidelines with all their personnel and urge that they observe them. Finally, the CIA would work its assets for leads.

Later we learned that the Lorenzo Zelaya Command was a name used by the armed wing of the Peoples' Revolutionary Union (URP). The URP itself was a small group that had broken away from the Honduran Communist Party (PCH) and was committed to armed revolution. Its leaders had reportedly been trained in Cuba and Nicaragua and were receiving support from the Sandinistas.

SAN PEDRO SULA ACTIVITIES CONTINUE: SAN PEDRO SULA, HONDURAS, OCTOBER 31–NOVEMBER 1, 1980. I continued my round of meetings throughout the day, checking back with Walker several times. On Saturday morning we went to the United Fruit Company facility near San Pedro Sula, observing a broad range of activities and meeting privately with the local banana workers' union. The *"frutera,"* as United was widely known, appeared to have come a long way from its days of labor exploitation and government bribery. By all accounts it was now a good corporate citizen and employer.

Support for the transition process was uniform and enthusiastic, Colonel Bueso Rosa excepted. Essentially, I found most of my San Pedro Sula interlocutors better informed, more urbane and more fun than many of their counterparts in Tegucigalpa. I resolved to return to San Pedro Sula as often as possible.

U.S. ELECTIONS PORTEND POLICY CHANGES: TEGUCIGALPA, HONDURAS, NOVEMBER 4, 1980. Arcos and his staff had arranged a major public and media event for the U.S. elections at the USIS binational cultural center.

With workers at a United Fruit Company banana plantation near San Pedro Sula, November 1980.

I was scheduled to appear on a special telecast later, analyzing the election results. We planned to use both media opportunities to reiterate our support for Honduran elections and the successful conclusion of the transition process.

Polling data indicated that Reagan would defeat Carter. I tended to disregard much of the campaign rhetoric, believing that, if elected, Reagan would find it very difficult to adopt the kind of policies in Central America that were implied by the GOP platform and the statements of some of his ultra-conservative supporters. The realities of the situation, to my mind, simply did not leave many options. I anticipated changes in emphasis but expected key policy elements would remain in place.

While I was en route to the binational center, I learned that Carter had conceded the election. I was dumbfounded. The president had thrown in the towel before the polls had closed on the West Coast. The moment I came through the door I was surrounded by cameras, microphones and journalists from all media wanting my reaction. It was, I said, a great victory for the American people and democracy; the American people had spoken, determining who was to govern them for the coming four years. Attempting to put the best spin on events, I said that President Carter's early concession reflected acceptance of these facts. Then came my punch line: the United States remained totally supportive of the Honduran transition process, which would give the Honduran people the same opportunity to choose their leaders.

With the Honduran press on election night, November 1980.

Arcos and I then closeted ourselves, reviewed the available early returns and worked out more thoughtful and detailed responses to likely questions that would be asked in individual interviews. This allowed me to hone my comments and responses. I carefully eschewed speculation about what changes a Reagan administration might bring. My essentially anodyne comments received only limited press play the following day.

HELICOPTER FLAP: ATTEMPTING TO PASS THE BUCK: TEGUCIGALPA, HONDURAS, NOVEMBER 5, 1980. Colonel Goodwin reported that Southern Command had just asked him to advise the Honduran General Staff that the Defense Department was about to request that it be reimbursed for one of the leased helicopters that had been destroyed in a July training accident. The claim would amount to several hundred thousand dollars. The Hondurans, Goodwin maintained, were sure to be deeply angered and offended by this demand, and it would certainly damage his ability to do business. He also asserted that the claim was unfair. Neither Walker nor I had been aware of the aircraft loss, as no one in the Milgroup had bothered to apprise us of that event or this potential problem.

Goodwin explained that the accident had occurred during a training mission when a Southern Command flight instructor was in command of the helicopter. It is standard doctrine that instructor pilots are always in command and responsible for the safety of the aircraft and crew; it is their duty to ensure students do nothing that endangers either. In this particular case, a U.S. Air Force accident review board had found that the instructor pilot had placed the aircraft in hazardous position and then instructed the student pilot to carry out the unsafe maneuver, which resulted in the helicopter's total destruction. Fortunately, no one had been injured. Moreover, the review board had discovered the instructor-pilot was not qualified to act as an instructor! Accordingly, Goodwin concluded there was no valid basis for a claim against the Hondurans.

In possession of these facts and having reviewed the lease contract, I agreed entirely. I also shared Goodwin's fears that such a request would seriously harm our already unhappy relationship with the Honduran military. But I was also angry that Milgroup had failed to inform me or Walker of this potentially damaging affair. I explained why I did not wish to see a repetition. But that was a procedural problem.

The more important issue was Southern Command's effort to cover up its culpability in this affair at the expense of the Honduran government and our foreign policy goals. That was egregious. After discussing options, we sent a cable with the details to the State Department—in the STADIS channel and thus not distributed to other agencies—asking that State seek to dissuade Defense from pursuing this claim.[29] In the interim I directed Goodwin not to raise this issue with the Hondurans and to advise Southern Command of my instructions to him.

This, along with our contrarian position on *Halcon Vista*, accentuated friction with that command.

VISITING THE UNIVERSITY AND PAINTING MY CAR: TEGUCIGALPA, HONDURAS, NOVEMBER 5, 1980. As part of my courtesy call regime, I wished to visit the rector of the National Autonomous University, Dr. Juan Almendares. This proposal divided the CT. Almendares was a reputed leftist, and the university itself was widely regarded as a hotbed of communist activity. The latter, however, was an exaggeration: several schools there were in the hands of moderates, and there were non–Marxist student organizations with considerable influence. The Political counselor, the station chief and our military members were dubious or opposed, believing that I might reduce my effectiveness with conservative elements and the military. Walker and Arcos supported my initiative.

The expressed concerns were real, but I was willing to take the risk. I wished to sustain a dialogue with all elements of Honduran society, or at least try. The university was the most acceptable face of the far left, and USIS was already working with some schools there. I knew of too many embassies that limited their effectiveness by acceding to host government sensitivities regarding contacts with opposition elements, the situation in Iran under the Shah being only among the more dramatic examples. After considerable discussion, I asked Arcos to set up a meeting at Almendares's office.

When Arcos and I went to the university I deliberately left my security escort—composed of embassy contract guards and Honduran Police—at the chancery to avoid possible provocation. We went to Almendares's office and had just gotten past initial formalities when his secretary burst into the office, saying my chauffeur was outside and needed to see me urgently. Ramon reported that a group of students, having spotted and identified my car, had thrown paint all over it.

Almendares escorted us to the parking lot, where we saw the car covered with paint. A number of students were milling around in front of a nearby building. I sent the car back to the chancery and we returned to the rector's office. I called Walker to let him know what had happened, and we finished our discussion. Almendares then drove us back to the chancery. Later, my relations with Almendares became quite acrimonious. Nonetheless, the effort had been made.

This incident received some press attention the following day—"Students Bathe Car of Ambassador Binns in Paint"—no doubt thanks to the students.[30] Other fallout was mixed. Feedback from conservative contacts did not seem particularly harmful; most seemed to think I had gotten what I deserved for trying to extend a hand to the radical left. Other, more moderate elements— political and professional—expressed to me their appreciation for my effort to reach out and their chagrin at the students' behavior. The strongest reaction came from RSO Dewitt, who was highly agitated that I had gone to the university without my security detail. In fact, the decision to leave them behind was the soundest of the lot. Had they been present, there is no telling what might have happened.

HUMAN RIGHTS: THE BEGINNING OF A BIG PROBLEM: TEGUCIGALPA, HONDURAS, EARLY NOVEMBER 1980. The station chief asked that I agree to sending several FUSEP officers to an interrogation training program the CIA would shortly be conducting in the United States. Given our concerns about the deteriorating internal security situation and potential human rights abuses, he thought it would be wise to train FUSEP personnel in how to deal with suspected subversives without brutalizing them.[31] I agreed. FUSEP badly needed professional training in all fields. I was also confident that the CIA would not teach abusive techniques; indeed, abusive interrogation was an area where the Hondurans probably could have given us lessons.

The FUSEP officers attended this program, which included follow-on training in Honduras by CIA trainers. A few weeks later the station chief reported that the participants had returned and were on the job. Subsequently, he requested and received my clearance for visits of the follow-on trainers and reported on program progress. Otherwise, I gave the matter little further thought.

Years later—as a result of the *Baltimore Sun*'s investigation of human rights violations in Honduras [32]—I was to learn that these trainees had become part of the infamous Battalion 316, which was responsible for most of the Honduran human rights abuses. This unit was formed in 1982 by then General Gustavo Alvarez after he became commander of the armed forces. That action consolidated members of several groups that had been involved in disappearances, assassinations and torture into a single organization under his direct supervision. Argentine military advisers had worked with these groups and continued to work with Battalion 316. The CIA also maintained active liaison with several of the earlier groups and the consolidated unit. I doubt that CIA personnel were directly involved in human rights violations, but evidence that they were aware of these practices and ignored them is undeniable.[33] To that extent the CIA and, by extension, our government were complicit in these abuses.

SANDINISTAS BLOCK OPPOSITION POLITICAL RALLY: MANAGUA, NICARAGUA, NOVEMBER 7, 1980. The ministry of interior prohibited former Sandinista junta member Alfonso Robelo's new political party, Nicaraguan Democratic Movement, from holding a public rally. Later, the Sandinistas alleged that Robelo and the planned rally were linked to counterrevolutionary attacks along the frontier with Honduras. This incident escalated tensions between the Sandinistas and its domestic opposition. [34]

EVALUATING THE BORDER WITH NICARAGUA: TEGUCIGALPA, HONDURAS, NOVEMBER 8, 1980. In an effort to get a better feel for the frontier between Honduras and Nicaragua, I asked Air Attache Miller to fly me the length of the border. We began on the Pacific coast and followed the border to the Atlantic, a distance of some 400 to 450 air miles. Except for the coastal plain and the Danli Valley, the frontier was sparsely settled and poorly served by overland communications links. The Pan American highway running near the coast was the main all-weather link; another unpaved, improved road ran west from Danli into Nicaragua.

Much of the terrain was broken and mountainous. Vegetation ranged from semiarid near the Pacific to heavy forests in mountain areas and then broad, scrub-covered savannah as you neared the Caribbean. North of Danli signs of habitation on either side of the border were sparse, and the mountains gave way to the wide savannah. The Coco River widened and became sinuous. This part of both countries was remote and isolated; there were no apparent overland links. Then tidal wetlands and the ocean. There were several small settlements, undeserving of the label "town," on the Nicaraguan side of the river.

Heading home, we turned west, passing over the fly-specked Honduran town of Puerto Lempira. Its only claim to fame was an improved, all-weather airstrip that had been built by the United States during WWII. This desolate, isolated town was later to cope with several thousand Miskito Indian refugees from Nicaragua, as Sandinista repression of that minority increased.[35]

Based on what we had seen, we reached several conclusions. First, the only area that could possibly lend itself to a conventional military assault—in the highly unlikely event the Sandinistas should opt for such a move—was the Pacific plain. The lack of infrastructure and rugged terrain elsewhere meant that a conventional attacking force could not be supported logistically. Second, the terrain features and isolation that precluded a conventional military assault meant these areas were well suited for irregular, or guerrilla, operations. But for most of the area east of the Danli Valley, there were no significant targets. Activity in that area could serve little apparent purpose. Indeed, most of the Contra activity we were aware of seemed to originate from the coastal plain and piedmont. Third, there was no realistic way that either Honduras or Nicaragua could control their respective borders sufficiently to preclude infiltration or small-scale paramilitary operations. Neither had the capability or manpower to do the job.

We sent this assessment to Washington in the attache channel.

NICARAGUAN HELICOPTER CAPTURED IN HONDURAS: CHOLUTECA, HONDURAS, NOVEMBER 10, 1980. Honduran authorities captured a Nicaraguan military helicopter near Choluteca. It was not clear how the aircraft had been forced to land in Honduras because reports of the incident conflicted. But the Nicaraguan aircraft had dropped several small bombs and been intercepted and forced down well inside Honduras by a Honduran Air Force helicopter. In addition to the pilot, this helicopter carried the ministry of defense's information chief and a journalist from the leading Sandinista daily, *Barricada*.

Honduran authorities played down the incident, telling the Honduran media that the pilot was "not very well trained in recognition of the border" and had entered Honduran airspace "by mistake." Nonetheless, the pilot and passengers were taken to Tegucigalpa for interrogation before being returned to Nicaragua. The helicopter was returned several days later.

Choluteca, however, was calm. Local officials told embassy officers who visited the area the following day that Sandinista troops were still crossing the border frequently and that it was not uncommon to hear exchanges of gunfire at night. These officers noted no signs of stepped-up military alert or activity.[36]

POLICY SPEECH RESONATES: TEGUCIGALPA, HONDURAS, NOVEMBER 11, 1980. The first opportunity for a major public statement of U.S. policy came in the form of an invitation to speak at the American Association's Veteran's Day luncheon. In addition to building relationships with the resident American community, we could ensure fairly extensive media coverage by briefing key journalists and distributing translations of my remarks to the media.

Drawing on a raft of official U.S. policy statements and unclassified analyses, Walker, Arcos and I crafted an overarching review of the regional situation and explication of U.S. policy objectives. The central point would be our strong support for the Honduran transition process. Other key points follow:

• The United States believed that change is natural and inevitable. Peace and democracy in Central America would depend on socio-economic and political reforms that increase the well-being and rights of individuals. A brief description of the state of play in each of the Central American countries, drawn from unclassified briefings and statements, followed.

• The United States would support reform initiatives but would not seek to impose its own views or models. Nor would it use military force where only domestic groups were in contention. But if Central American countries were subjected to external attack and wished to make use of the Rio Treaty, I was certain the United States would honor its commitments.

• External influences, particularly Cuba, were seeking to exploit the change process and unrest in the region to impose new, undemocratic structures. This unrest was the result of domestic pressures for change, not the external factors. We would help countries of the region resist such outside intervention.

• Regarding Honduras, successive governments had carried out important reforms, avoided repression and human rights violations and opened the way for a peaceful return to democratic government. Consequently, Honduras had avoided the violence and disorder experienced by its neighbors. It could count on continued U.S. support. Our policy in Honduras had four major elements: firm, unequivocal support for the transition process and elections; continued economic assistance in support of development and reform programs; increased security assistance to strengthen Honduras's ability to defend itself and control its frontier areas; and encouragement of Honduras's vigorous and constructive role in the region and beyond, exemplified by the peace treaty with El Salvador.

• The problems facing the region could not be resolved by governments alone. The private sector, including foreign investors, had a major role to play in their resolution. Support for peaceful change and for the emergence of equitable democratic societies was a goal all should support. Failure to do so could only help the enemies of freedom and human dignity.[37]

We expected reasonably heavy coverage in local media, and our expectations were exceeded. The daily newspapers gave them extensive treatment; two published the entire text and provided analytical comment. Both TV channels had clips with Spanish voice-over on the parts about Honduras, and most radio stations read excerpts to their audiences. All emphasized the importance of the democratic transition.

Totally unexpected was the speech's resonance outside Honduras. Excerpts were played by major media outlets in all the Central American countries, reportedly causing some unhappiness in official Guatemalan and Nicaraguan circles. It also received extensive treatment in the U.S. Spanish-language newspaper, *Diario las Americas,* and in major capitals throughout the hemisphere. Newspapers in both Santiago, Chile, and Bogotá, Colombia, reprinted the entire text.[38] This was especially surprising because the speech contained nothing that had not been said before, much of it many times, and by more important people than I. It was definitely old wine in a new bottle.

Overall reaction in Honduras was highly positive. But there were dissenting voices. Some military officers, the Zuniga faction of the National Party and the extreme left thought my remarks about Honduras went beyond diplomatic norms, infringing on Honduran sovereignty. The Zuniga crew also made sure Senator Helms and other right-wing contacts in the United States were aware of what I had said about the possible direction of the Reagan policies.[39] That aside, public diplomacy had paid off in a big way. There is always a risk of giving offense in any public articulation of policy. From our standpoint the gains far outweighed any negative side effects.

To Washington: Treaty, Transition and Consultation: Washington, D.C., November 12–21, 1980. The El Salvador/Honduras peace treaty saga was nearing its end. The pact had been initialed by both governments and the formal signing ceremony set for November 18 at the OAS in Washington. It would enter into force once the two governments exchanged ratified instruments, an act accomplished in Tegucigalpa the following month. The signing ceremony provided me with an opportunity to travel to Washington for consultations, as well as to participate in the ceremony. I was anxious to learn how the election had affected the Inter-American bureau and to get a feel for the new administration's likely policy directions. Bob White, our ambassador in El Salvador, also went to Washington for the ceremony.

Uncertainty was the watchword at State. No one had a clue about what the future might hold in terms of our Central American policy, but everyone was reading the tea leaves assiduously. The signs were not heartening. In the interim they all kept doing what they had been doing, our policies remaining unchanged.

At the time, the new secretary of state had not been designated. A transition team for the department was in place, and I learned from a friend in the secretary's office that its dealings with department officials were marked by an unusually high degree of partisan friction. The Inter-American bureau transition unit was headed by Pedro A. Sanjuan, a right-wing Cuban American ideologue. Of even greater concern, however, were reports that he was working very closely with Senator Helms's lead staff aide, John Carbaugh. Both were foreign policy lightweights. Fortunately, neither was to occupy a position of responsibility within the new administration. But their views helped shape the transition team report on Latin America.

My interview with Sanjuan was the most memorable event of these consultations. When he was offered an opportunity to meet with White and me separately, his response was less than enthusiastic. Indeed, he declined to meet with White, an anathema to the right wingers. He also deferred scheduling a session with me to the point that I had to delay my return to Tegucigalpa. The interview was an anticlimax. Sanjuan asked for an overview of the situation in Honduras and our policy. When I concluded, he had no significant questions. We engaged in polite chatter for a few minutes and I departed. His lack of interest could not have been more obvious. That didn't bode well.

His later report to the head of the transition team accused ambassadors of engaging in social change experimentation in their countries of accreditation, citing White as having helped "to develop and implement a new theory of social change," that is, the land and banking reforms.[40] This assertion was nonsense. Although it was true that White (and the Carter administration) supported those reforms, both were originated in El Salvador by Salvadorans. In fact, both had been the subject of political debate and legislative initiative a decade earlier. Not surprisingly, both had been vigorously and successfully opposed by that country's oligarchy. Sanjuan's position clearly seemed driven as much by ignorance as by ideology. The transition memo went on to praise our former ambassador in Guatemala, Frank Ortiz, whom, Sanjuan asserted, "was severely penalized for performing with distinction in the role of a bona fide ambassador." More nonsense, as Ortiz had been removed for his ineffective support of our policies.

In retrospect, the most amusing and ironic part of Sanjuan's exposition was his largely inaccurate critique of the Carter administration's Latin American policy process. Today it reads eerily like a description of what actually occurred under Reagan.

> The role of the Bureau, as the vehicle for theories propounded by individuals not representing the carefully considered policy of a President, is most disturbing. The advocacy of policy and doctrines the implementation of which in the U.S. would cause violation of our own constitutional guarantees cannot be permitted to affect U.S. relations with other countries without a proper review at the top levels of the national security apparatus, including the President himself. It matters not that such advocacy comes from ambassadors in the field or NSC staffers acting outside the NSC system or other government officials who have no mandate other than the existence of an informal relationship with the President. All initiatives that radically affect those traditional constraints placed upon the implementation of U.S. foreign policy for the purpose of preserving the essential elements of national security, must be presented to, debated and decided by the President and his top national security advisors.[41]

The imperative contained in Sanjuan's last sentence—the need to observe an orderly policy process—was sound. But while the process in the Carter years may have left much to be desired, it was far more coordinated and effective in the Latin American region than that which was to follow.

SANDINISTAS CRACK DOWN ON PRIVATE SECTOR: MANAGUA, NICARAGUA, NOVEMBER 17, 1980. Cracking down on opposition leaders, the Interior Ministry arrested seven leading businessmen. The vice president of the Superior Council of Private Enterprise, Jorge Salazar, was later killed by government forces. The government alleged that Salazar was shot while transporting arms for the counterrevolution; witnesses say he was unarmed and assassinated because of his effective opposition to the government. These events triggered the withdrawal of the private sector and opposition political parties from the Council of State.[42] Tensions between the Sandinistas and opposition elements had reached a new high.

ANTI-SANDINISTA LEADER PAYS A CALL: TEGUCIGALPA, HONDURAS, NOVEMBER 18, 1980. Walker fielded a phone call from a Nicaraguan claiming to be a leader in one of the anti-Sandinista groups, the "Democratic Revolutionary Alliance of Nicaragua" (ARDEN). He requested an appointment to see me. Informed that I was away, he asked to see Walker. Knowing our mission policy of avoiding any encouragement to such groups, Walker suggested that he meet instead with our Political counselor. The meeting produced more puffery than substance.

In addition to claiming there were about 2,000 anti–Sandinistas actually operating inside Nicaragua (a nonsense), this individual asserted that his group had the support of: most private sector leaders in Nicaragua (highly improbable); some 200 ex–National Guard officers "who were not tainted" by Somoza connections (a oxymoron); and six Sandinista *comandantes* (incredible). He had sought this meeting because he believed the new Reagan administration would no doubt be "assuming a more active role in support of the anti–Sandinistas," and he wished to be among the first to establish regular contact with the embassy.[43]

He was thanked for stopping in but given no encouragement. We reported this initiative, our wariness at becoming openly associated with this or similar groups and our highly skeptical assessment of his various claims. We had learned nothing that caused us to change our earlier assessment.

HELICOPTER FLAP: DEFENSE BACKS DOWN AND TEMPERS FLARE: TEGUCIGALPA, HONDURAS, LATE NOVEMBER 1980. Following my November 25 return, Central American Affairs director Blacken called to advise that State had convinced Defense to abandon its claim against Honduras. He wanted to alert me, however, that a number of people at the Pentagon, and presumably Southern Command, were very upset over our cable and State's intervention.

I passed this information on to Goodwin, who was pleased. If he was concerned about the reactions of some of his Pentagon and Southern Command colleagues, he didn't show it.

I got an earful of Pentagon anger shortly, however, in the form of a phone call from General Schweitzer. He was irate. Our cable, he asserted, was out of place, having aired our military's "dirty linen" (investigative reports of aircraft accidents are never made public, he claimed). In so doing, he said, I had jeopardized the embassy's and his ability to help Honduras in the future.

My response was that if these were the consequences of our actions it was indeed unfortunate but that I had seen little option, given the damage the spurious claim would have caused. No one had bothered to raise the issue with me before telling the Milgroup commander to approach the Hondurans, which, I pointed out, might be construed by some as an effort to subvert the ambassador's authority under Public Law 93-475. And it would certainly have impacted our larger policy objectives. Such actions simply could not be taken without consulting the ambassador. As to airing dirty linen, I hardly thought a classified, restricted distribution cable could be equated with going public. In the future, I suggested, we could avoid such misunderstandings by ensuring the embassy is consulted before any actions were decided on or instructions given. Schweitzer took this suggestion without comment. It was a message I was to reiterate in my dealings with both Defense and Southern Command, to little apparent avail.

Although we prevailed in this dispute, it would be months before Defense finally completed all the paper work to relieve the Hondurans of responsibility for the loss.

3

The Circus Begins:
Challenges and Diversions

SUMMARY—More coup plotting—policy vacuum in Washington—grow-ing security threat—ratification of peace treaty and U.S. role in 1969 conflict—OAS observer mission saved—insurgent arms seized—"good offices" in Salvadoran conflict fail—congressional visitors—Americans murdered in El Salvador by military and rightists—promised policy changes and unofficial visitors undermine Honduran transition—Sal-vadoran insurgent "final offensive"—pressure on Nicaraguan opposition increased as U.S. aid suspended

COUP RUMORS RESURFACE, ACTION RECOMMENDED: TEGUCIGALPA, HONDURAS, NOVEMBER 26, 1980. There had been a resurgence of coup rumors, the subject of several embassy reports, during my absence. Their gist was that the military was becoming increasingly dissatisfied with Paz, with the assembly, and with the "inefficiency" of the transition government. None of this was news. Meanwhile, there was rising concern about the sagging economy among the private sector and others. The result was a growing sense of popular unease and uncertainty that fueled speculation about a coup.

At a meeting with chief of staff General Mario Chinchilla I decided to confront the issue directly, asking his opinion of the reports, including one that alleged the Armed Forces Superior Council had recently voted, by a majority of a single vote, to retain Paz in office. Chinchilla acknowledged widespread disquiet about the effectiveness of the transition government and the assertiveness of the assembly but stated flatly that reports of military plot-ting against President Paz were baseless. As to the alleged Superior Council meeting, the council had indeed met over the weekend to discuss retirements, but neither Paz nor the government had been the subject of any part of that session. He added rather dryly that whoever was circulating the story about the alleged vote on Paz's continuation was unfamiliar with Superior Council proceedings. Except in very rare circumstances, its decisions were by con-sensus; open votes were exceedingly rare.

Chinchilla's response seemed to have been open and candid, a judgment that was shared by Colonels Goodwin and Miller, who had accompanied me. Later, we confirmed Chinchilla's account of the Superior Council meeting from other sources.

Our inquiries also revealed a variety of curious sources of this spate of rumors. One had been an assessment by the Honduran Communist Party (PCH), which had considerable resonance in left-wing circles. Tracing another report, we found the source was President Paz himself! And both the Liberal and National Parties also seemed to be busily spreading reports of a conspiracy against Paz. In the latter case we theorized that the Liberals were attempting to preempt the suspected plotters by surfacing reports of their intentions. In other cases the rumors were probably designed to create uncertainty. We seemed to have entered a hall of mirrors. The prevailing view in the CT was that if all this smoke did not indicate the existence of a fire, someone might decide to light a fire to justify the smoke. In other words, these rumors might become self-fulfilling.

The final El Salvador/Honduras peace treaty ceremony, scheduled for Tegucigalpa December 10–11, seemed to offer an unparalleled opportunity to reaffirm in dramatic fashion U.S. support for the transition. Senior officials, including several chiefs of state and foreign ministers, would be in attendance, and the United States would presumably send a high-level delegation. Why not use this event to make this point unequivocally?

I cabled Bowdler, assessing the recent round of coup rumors and their possible significance, together with recommendations for a U.S. response. I urged that Secretary Muskie or another senior official head the U.S. delegation and that it include a senior member of the Reagan transition team. While here, this group could reiterate publicly and privately our support for elections.[1]

It was not to be. Indeed, given the hostility between the Carter and Reagan camps, that part of the recommendation was unrealistic. In the end Bowdler headed our delegation but was distracted by critical events in El Salvador. The closest State could come to a Reagan representative was a former (Republican appointee) ambassador to Honduras, Phillip V. Sanchez, who had no formal role in the transition.

SALVADORAN OPPOSITION LEADERS SLAIN: SAN SALVADOR, EL SALVADOR, NOVEMBER 27, 1980. Six leaders of the Democratic Revolutionary Front (FDR), the political wing of the insurgent movement, were abducted by a band of armed men and later found dead, with signs of severe torture. Among the victims was Enrique Alvarez Cordova, scion of one of El Salvador's leading families, a former cabinet minister and president of the FDR. He was certainly no Marxist.

Ambassador White reacted quickly, communicating the seriousness with which the United States viewed this development to junta members, senior military officers and the foreign minister.[2] Subsequent information confirmed that these brutal killings were carried out by government security forces under the command of Salvadoran military officers.[3]

REAGAN TRANSITION TEAM PROMISES INCREASED MILITARY ASSISTANCE: WASHINGTON, D.C., NOVEMBER 28, 1980. Leading members of the Reagan transition team—including Jeane Kirkpatrick, Roger Fontaine, James Theberge and Constantine Menges—told representatives of the Salvadoran private sector that the Reagan administration would increase U.S. military assistance to that country once Reagan was in office.[4] Most Salvadoran private sector leaders opposed the junta and its reform policies. That commitment, given to this group at this juncture, could hardly have been more irresponsible or counterproductive, undermining our efforts to stem the military's gross human rights violations. A few days later the CIA station in El Salvador reported that the military had concluded that the "election of Ronald Reagan to the U.S. presidency will mean that the US will no longer take a hard line against repression against the left in El Salvador."[5]

PERSONAL ATTACKS BEGIN: TEGUCIGALPA, HONDURAS, LATE NOVEMBER 1980. *El Heraldo* published a letter accusing me of intervention and other sins. This was the first of what was to become a series of such attacks.[6] *El Heraldo* had ties with the Zuniga faction, and Arcos suspected that Zuniga was the source. I trusted his judgment in these matters, especially because the use of media cutouts was part of the Zuniga modus operandi.

It was a warning signal. Our impression was that Zuniga was not gaining ground on Suazo Cordova. If he thought he was likely to lose the elections, he would seek to block them.

PEACE TREATY RATIFIED UNANIMOUSLY: TEGUCIGALPA, HONDURAS, NOVEMBER 28, 1980. The Constituent Assembly, in a rare unanimous action, ratified the peace treaty with El Salvador, thus clearing the way for the December 9 exchange of instruments.[7] The Liberals had gotten the message from all sides and done the right thing.

REAGAN TRANSITION AND HELMS REACH INTO HONDURAS: TEGUCIGALPA, HONDURAS, DECEMBER 1, 1980. I had received a phone call from Richard McCormack, a member of Senator Helms's staff, who implied that he had some connection with the Reagan transition team and requested an appointment. He said he was visiting Honduras privately and wanted an opportunity to meet with me before returning to Washington. I agreed to see him and quickly called State to verify his credentials. Although unaware of

McCormack's travels, they confirmed he was a Helms aide. He was not among those identified as members of the State Department transition team but was well plugged into several of those who were.

McCormack was pleasant and relatively open in our discussion, quite unlike Sanjuan. He had come to Honduras at the invitation of a "friend," who turned out to be Ricardo Zuniga. McCormack was en route to Nicaragua and would return to Tegucigalpa on his way back to Washington. He had already met "unofficially" with a number of leaders, including President Paz and Colonels Torres Arias and Alvarez. Most of his interlocutors, however, were Zuniga supporters. He met no one from the National Party's dissident faction, the opposing Liberal Party or the two minor parties.

From our discussion it was evident that McCormack had swallowed the Zuniga line completely. The National Party, he repeated, was the only one the United States could trust. The dominant Suazo Cordova faction of the Liberal Party was sympathetic to the Sandinistas in Nicaragua, he asserted, and the dissident ALIPO faction was even worse. Moreover, the embassy was seen as favoring the Liberals, who were rigging voter registration in their favor.

I disputed the Liberal/Sandinista canard and sought to bring greater balance to his appreciation of the local scene. I urged that on return he meet with the opposition and private sector leaders who were not in the Zuniga camp. He professed a willingness to do so but declined my offer to set up any meetings.[8] When he returned, he again failed to meet with those outside the Zuniga group and the military. This was to be the pattern followed by all Helms's aides when they visited Honduras.

McCormack also asked if he could meet with the Milgroup commander, and I set up an appointment. Colonel Goodwin subsequently reported that McCormack had asked about the helicopter issue and sounded him out about Nicaragua and El Salvador. Regarding the latter, Goodwin said he had been very guarded, claiming to know nothing about "politics."

McCormack left me with a sense of acute unease. First, I felt that he was a naif as far as Central America and Honduras were concerned and clearly under Zuniga's sway, evidently taking everything he heard as gospel. I smelled trouble. We learned later that Zuniga had emphasized the alleged "communist infiltration" of the Liberal Party and provided McCormack with "documentary evidence" that the "Honduran Communist Party provided the Liberals with $3 million dollars."[9] That was nonsense.

His visit had as yet received no publicity. I felt Zuniga was certain to use it to suggest the Reagan administration supported him and might not be unsympathetic to postponement of the elections. I reported these qualms in a NODIS cable, noting: "Given Zuniga's reputation and the continuing coup talk, I suspect that the invitation for this [McCormack's] visit was designed to construct the beginning of a facade of future US approval for a coup. Or at the very least it was designed to make that a more viable option."[10] Ambassador White in El Salvador, meanwhile, was having a similar experience with a visitor falsely claiming ties to the Reagan team.

A few days after McCormack's return visit *La Prensa* picked up on his presence, characterizing him as "foreign affairs advisor of President-elect Ronald Reagan." This item also reported that he had "totally passed over the Ambassador and his advisors, which has everyone asking what Reagan's advisor was doing here," meeting with Zuniga and senior military officers. According to a friendly journalist, the characterization of McCormack came from Zuniga. We responded with a letter to the editor over my signature. It read in part:

> I wish to inform you that Mr. McCormack does not form part of President-elect Reagan's transition group, although he is a member of Senator Jesse Helms' staff.... Mr. McCormack came to Honduras on a private visit that was not related to his position in the Senate. Mr. McCormack met not only with yours truly, but also with other representatives of this Embassy. Because of the recent controversy surrounding the alleged activities of individuals who have presented themselves as representatives of President-elect Reagan, you would do both Mr. McCormack and me a favor by publishing the above points at the earliest opportunity.[11]

I asked State to pass the text of our statement, which was duly printed, to McCormack.

AMERICAN CHURCHWOMEN SLAIN IN EL SALVADOR: SAN SALVADOR, EL SALVADOR, DECEMBER 2, 1980. Three American nuns and one layworker, having just arrived in El Salvador, were abducted, raped and murdered by five Salvadoran National Guardsmen. Their bodies were buried in shallow graves near San Salvador and discovered the following day.[12] This atrocity, coming on the heels of the murder of the six FDR leaders, blew the lid off U.S./Salvadoran relations and deeply affected popular opinion in the United States. Its repercussions were to last for years.

Ambassador White was appalled and outraged. The United States immediately suspended all military and economic assistance and dispatched a special presidential commission to investigate. The commission was headed by Assistant Secretary Bowdler and one of his predecessors, William D. Rogers. Their mandate was to determine the facts surrounding these brutal murders and determine what the junta government was prepared to do to turn the deteriorating human rights situation around. There was no doubt that Salvadoran security forces were responsible. The only question was how high up the chain of command responsibility reached. That question was never answered satisfactorily.

The Reagan transition team kept a very low profile on this issue, but congressional Republicans demanded immediate resumption of security assistance because suspension "presumes (Salvadoran) government guilt" and was needed to prevent a communist take over.[13] Initially, the United States made further aid contingent on (1) progress in the investigation of the murders, (2) junta government efforts to reduce violence, (3) initiation of a dialogue between the junta and the democratic opposition (many of whose leaders had been killed by the military a few days earlier), and (4) a commitment from the junta to continue the agrarian and banking reforms. The United States resumed economic and nonlethal military assistance on December 17 and lifted the ban on other military aid on December 31 in the face of the deteriorating military situation and congressional pressure.[14]

ANOTHER MEETING WITH ZUNIGA: TEGUCIGALPA, HONDURAS, DECEMBER 8, 1980. I had scheduled a meeting with Zuniga before McCormack's visit, wishing to sound him out on a range of issues—coup rumors, the Constituent Assembly, and growing economic problems (e.g., budget deficit, possible new taxes). In our discussion he was pleasant and measured on all the issues, although clearly disingenuous about the coup reports and his party's willingness to cooperate in the Assembly. He also expressed concern about the "extreme left," which he carefully avoided associating with the Liberal Party. The leftists, he claimed, were seeking confrontation with the government, as evidenced by student disorders and strikes by unions affiliated with the Honduran Communist Party. Fortunately, he spared me the other tales he had spun McCormack.[15] This meeting did nothing to allay my concerns over his manipulation of McCormack and other matters.

SECURITY ASSESSMENT UPDATE: TEGUCIGALPA, HONDURAS, DECEMBER 8, 1980. The CT had been watching the security situation very closely, searching for indicators of popular unrest or events that might foreshadow the nascent stages of an insurgency—kidnappings, bank and payroll holdups, urban terrorist actions. We were deeply concerned about the inadequate physical security of our facilities. Shortly after my arrival, a State survey team had recommended major renovation and security upgrade of the chancery building and annex. Progress on the needed improvements was slow, much to my dissatisfaction and that of RSO Dewitt. The JAS, responsible for our overall security posture, was just not moving with any sense of urgency, despite continued prodding by Walker and Dewitt. Nor was State timely in providing engineering drawings and hardware—secure doors, bulletproof glass, television monitors—so construction work had not started.

Intelligence indicated that the PCH had formed a paramilitary action group, Cuba and Nicaragua were training dissident Hondurans, and the Salvadoran insurgents were operating clandestine supply/support networks in Honduras with support from the PCH.

We were, moreover, beginning to see troubling signs. FUSEP was reporting an apparent increase in holdups and armed robberies outside Tegucigalpa, in the San Pedro Sula area and north coast. Our Economic Section and Foreign Commercial Service officers confirmed this trend based on what they were hearing from their Honduran business contacts.

Accordingly, we prepared an updated appraisal, noting recent indices of a deteriorating security environment, including the insistence of Cuban officials that the PCH and other leftist groups prepare for guerrilla warfare; the August 1980 amnesty that freed hundreds of common criminals and violent elements; the link up between these criminal elements and radical leftist groups to stage bank, payroll and other robberies in part to fund terrorist operations;[16] the "slop over effect" of guerrilla groups in all three neighboring countries; and increased Cuban funding and training of subversive-terrorist groups.[17]

PEACE TREATY CONSUMMATED: TEGUCIGALPA, HONDURAS, DECEMBER 9–11, 1980. The state of war between El Salvador and Honduras concluded with the formal exchange of instruments in Tegucigalpa. The border was reopened, allowing traffic on the Pan American highway after more than a decade. Diplomatic and commercial relations were also restored.[18] This event brought Salvadoran president Napoleon Duarte to Honduras—a good and respected friend from my time in El Salvador—and high-level diplomatic delegations from 20 hemispheric nations.

The U.S. delegation was headed by Bowdler, who flew in briefly from El Salvador, where he and Bill Rogers were investigating the murder of the four American churchwomen. Our delegation also included my predecessor, Mari-Luci Jaramillo, and Ambassador White arrived with Bowdler on our attache aircraft. Both White and I had been "in at the beginning," along with Bowdler, who had been our ambassador in El Salvador. At the onset White was serving as political counselor in Tegucigalpa; I occupied the same position in San Salvador. Now, 11 years later, we were "in at the conclusion," this time having switched countries and risen to be the respective chiefs of mission. But the most extraordinary aspect of this conflict has never before been made public.

The commander of the U.S. Military Group in El Salvador, and his Army section commander, were directly engaged in planning the Salvadoran mobilization and attack on Honduras. Their actions were in direct violation of U.S. policy, the specific instructions of Ambassador Bowdler and standing directives for Milgroup operations and activities. Moreover, in the months leading up to the actual attack, these two officers repeatedly misled and lied to the CT regarding activities of the Salvadoran armed forces. At the time, the United States was actively seeking to prevent conflict between the two countries, and their duplicity and deception was directly responsible for an intelligence failure of the first order.

Top: With Assistant Scretary of State for Inter-American Affairs William G. Bowdler, shown arriving in an embassy aircraft for ceremonies concluding the El Salvador/Honduras peace treaty, which officially ended the 1969 "soccer war"; Ambassador to El Salvador Robert E. White is shown in center background, December 1980. *Bottom:* Col. Gustavo Alvarez Martinez (*left*), Commander of Honduran National Police (FUSEP) and later Commander in Chief of the Honduran Armed Forces, and Deputy Assistant Secretary of State Frederick L. Chapin during the El Salvador–Honduras peace ceremonies, December 1980. Chapin replaced Ambassador White in El Salvador on an interim basis in February 1981.

With predecessor ambassadors Mari-Luci Jaramillo (then Deputy Assistant Secretary of State for Inter-American Affairs) and Phillip V. Sanchez (1973–1976) at the embassy, December 1980.

Bowdler only learned of their complicity after the fact when, through an unusual chain of circumstances, he received a document, partially in the Milgroup commander's handwriting, that revealed their unequivocal involvement. Both were removed immediately and shortly thereafter retired from the U.S. Army.

It was nearly a year later that we learned, from the chief of staff of the Salvadoran armed forces, the full extent of these officers' activities and how they had affected Salvadoran perceptions of U.S. attitudes. Because of the direct engagement of these two officers in planning the Salvadoran military's mobilization, offensive strategy and even tactical moves, the Salvadorans had reasoned that our repeated diplomatic representations opposing military action were simply cover for public consumption. How could it be otherwise, when our two most senior officers were deeply involved in planning the attack?[19] But for their actions, it is entirely possible that the Salvadorans would have been dissuaded from their folly and the conflict, with its many consequences, avoided.

There is no simple explanation for the behavior of these officers. They placed their loyalty to the host country armed forces ahead of that to their own government, seriously damaging our national interests. Part of the problem may arise from the fact host governments fund some of the Milgroup's operational costs,[20] sometimes giving rise to a mistaken perception that the organization works exclusively for the host country, not our government.

Indeed, I have heard officers attached to Milgroups assert this. But although they do assist the host military, they do so strictly as agents and employees of the United States. They are not some kind of official mercenaries at the disposition of the local armed forces. Indeed, the notion that they owe primary allegiance to their hosts is so clearly wrongheaded that it cannot be credible to a reasonable person.

HONDURAN BANKER KIDNAPPED: TEGUCIGALPA, HONDURAS, DECEMBER 18, 1980. The station chief came to me with a shocker. Paul Vinelli, president of Banco Atlantida and my frequent tennis partner, had just been kidnapped. His armored Mercedes limousine, en route from home to his office, had been stopped on a busy street about six blocks from the chancery by two other cars. Vinelli was dragged from the vehicle by several armed men, thrown into one of the cars and driven off. He had no bodyguard, and his driver had not been harmed. FUSEP was interrogating the driver and several witnesses. At that point no ransom had been demanded.

I immediately summoned Walker and the JAS chief and called State's Operations Center. A cabled report followed. I instructed the JAS chief to alert the Marine security detachment and bring additional Marine guards into the chancery, advise the civilian guard force and ensure their men were alert, and tighten entry procedures at all our facilities. Walker was to advise the heads of all other agencies and have them ensure their personnel followed our personal security guidelines. He would also set up a CT meeting as soon as possible and arrange a situation reporting schedule. I also asked the station chief to send one of his officers to FUSEP and keep someone there as long as necessary. In addition, I tasked him with canvassing his covert sources to see if they could shed any light on what had happened.

Our involvement in this case was to be at the margin. Vinelli had renounced his American citizenship and become a naturalized Honduran several years before. Thus, legally he had no claim to U.S. protection services, nor was the Honduran government under any obligation to keep the embassy informed. But Vinelli's children were U.S. citizens, and they were able to bring enough pressure to bear on Honduran authorities to ensure we were kept informed. We later learned that the bank and family had retained someone to assist in their dealings with the kidnappers and government. The ransom demand followed shortly, triggering extended negotiations between the bank and family on one side and the kidnappers on the other.

FUSEP, meanwhile, made no progress in locating Vinelli or identifying those responsible. Ultimately, he was released, shaken but otherwise unharmed physically. He immediately left for Miami and did not return to Honduras for several months.

We later learned that he had been kidnapped by the Popular Liberation Front (FPL), a Salvadoran insurgent group formed in the early 1970s by dissident members of that country's traditional Communist Party.[21] This kidnapping, then, clearly demonstrated that at least one Salvadoran insurgent group had a covert support apparatus in Honduras, and it was pretty effective. Further evidence would surface later.

This incident caused us to reevaluate the security environment. The threat was growing, our personnel and facilities were increasingly at risk, and we had pretty well exhausted what we could do with existing assets to improve things. As a result, we requested additional assets, including assignment of a full-time security officer, additional funds to beef up contract guard posts at Walker's and Oleson's residences, temporary assignment of someone to train FUSEP protective services personnel, and expedited action on improving the physical security of our facilities.[22]

PEZZULLO'S CONCERN OVER RECENT DEVELOPMENTS GROWS: MANAGUA, NICARAGUA:, DECEMBER 11, 1980. Ambassador Pezzullo advised State that the assassination of private sector leader Salazar, the Salvadoran insurrection and the election of Ronald Reagan had heightened tension between the Sandinistas and their domestic opposition. He went on to warn that "the fragile situation here can turn on us if the utmost care is not taken." He was granted permission to go to Washington for consultations.[23]

SURVEYING THE SALVADORAN FRONTIER: SOUTHERN HONDURAS, DECEMBER 13, 1980. The AID disaster relief officer, Peace Corps director Lara and I boarded a USAF helicopter assigned to support the OAS observer mission to visit the frontier with El Salvador. Only by visiting this area and refugee camps could I gain adequate knowledge of the situation and gain some idea of how it might be improved. We also planned to overfly at least one of the disputed areas, or pockets, that served as safe haven for Salvadoran guerrillas. That leg of the journey would be accomplished at a high altitude because OAS choppers had drawn ground fire on several previous occasions. Our flight was no exception, so we didn't tarry in the area.

Both sides of the border were very rugged, semiarid, isolated and generally inhospitable. Most of the countryside was covered with scrub growth, although stands of pine trees were occasionally visible. Where there was water, near settlements or in sheltered valleys, vegetation was lusher.

We visited four towns, only two of which were then providing refuge for significant numbers of displaced Salvadorans. The first was Colomoncagua, a tidy, well-kept town of 3,000 to 4,000 people, plus an estimated 3,000 refugees. It had two refugee camps. The one we visited was a 15-minute walk from the town and located on a partially wooded hillside. It was well laid out, with several rows of canvas tents that served as shelter for the nearly 2,000 residents. There was water nearby, and several kitchens had been set up under plastic tarpaulins. Sanitary facilities were also in place. In sum, it seemed to be a well designed and administered operation, although quite primitive.

With a Honduran Army detachment commander (*center*) at Colomoncagua and OAS observer Major Edwin Merwin, USAF, in a refugee camp for Salvadorans, December 1980.

Most of the refugees were women and children, although we did see a few elderly men. Those with whom we spoke did not seem unfriendly, and one woman offered us tortillas she was cooking. There were no young or able-bodied men in either camp; our guide speculated that the male partners of these families were either active in the insurgency or working in San Salvador or the Pacific lowlands. Little guerrilla activity was reported in the area. But men, presumably Salvadoran insurgents, were seen around the camps frequently at night or the early morning hours.

In contrast to Colomoncagua, La Virtud, the other refugee site, appeared to have come on hard times. It was larger—population about 6,000 in the principal village, with another 26,000 living in 12 other villages making up the municipality. Many of the buildings hadn't seen paint in years. The military barracks near the square was particularly seedy.

Refugees there were not in organized camps but dispersed throughout the area. Some 14,000 refugees were officially registered. We spoke with a number of people in the community—the town clerk and military, local merchants and a French nurse working with Physicians Without Frontiers. All reported a relatively high level of guerrilla activity on the Salvadoran side; it was often possible to hear exchanges of gunfire. The Honduran military unit was not very active, mostly staying in the barracks at night. All agreed there was considerable movement, by males, back and forth across the border. Most of our interlocutors also believed the number of refugees was substantially lower than the official figure; their highest estimate was 10,000. In addition, we sensed concern or tension that had not been present elsewhere.

The refugees were dispersed because the relief organizations lacked the resources to establish and operate camps to accommodate the entire refugee population. The Salvadorans were registered centrally, then assigned to small encampments in outlying villages. Medical services were provided by a central government clinic or volunteers such as the Physicians Without Frontiers group. Foodstuffs and supplies were doled out from a central warehouse, with allotments based on the registered population of refugees in each outlying area. This decentralized administration made accountability difficult. Nor did there appear to be mechanisms for verifying head counts or assuring that food given out reached the intended recipients.

Visiting a food distribution warehouse, we saw a dozen people with pack animals gathered at the door as relief workers meted out large bags of flour, beans, dried milk and other commodities. They seemed to be working from a list of refugee numbers at specified sites and allotting food on that basis. The bags were loaded onto the pack animals, and off they went. Most of those receiving these foodstuffs were males, which seemed curious based on our observations at the Colomoncagua camps. The man in charge refused to answer our questions regarding the process we had witnessed or the procedures and controls. Our questions had to be referred to his superior in Santa Rosa de Copan.

We reported our observations, conclusions and action recommendations to State.[24] In my judgment, there was no reasonable possibility of the Hondurans controlling the border effectively. The terrain, isolation and absence of communications meant the task of stopping arms traffic or preventing Salvadoran insurgents from finding safe haven was far beyond the Army's capability. Existing troop numbers, meager firepower (against increasingly well-armed insurgents), limited mobility, low skill levels and poor communications meant that Honduran forces were inadequate for the task. With additional personnel, material and training, however, they could do a better job, making it more costly for the insurgents to operate. We could help with this, assuming they could be persuaded to address the problem seriously.

As to the refugee situation, we reported a number of apparent problems. Their numbers in the La Virtud area seemed greatly overstated, perhaps by as much as 40 percent. This was significant because foodstuffs and other supplies were allocated on a per capita basis. Taken with the apparent absence of controls and accountability, it seemed likely that significant quantities of food were being diverted to the insurgents. This situation cried out for remedial action, and I wanted the CT engaged in working out some possible solutions. To that end I circulated a memorandum outlining key issues and possible strategies for dealing with them, asking that they be prepared to help develop a plan to address and monitor the identified problems.[25] It seemed to me that the critical step would be consolidation of refugees in camp sites located away from the immediate border. An accurate census of refugees, periodically verified, was also needed, as was improved accountability and control of food and other supplies.

I had been through a refugee camp establishment process earlier in the year while chargé d'affaires in Costa Rica, and had a pretty good idea of what could be done. There, we had expected over 10,000 Cuban refugees, Mariel boat people, and we had planned and laid out actual camp sites. In the end the refugees had not come, but that experience proved very useful.

CONTRAS BOMB RADIO STATION, KILL THREE: SAN JOSE, COSTA RICA, DECEMBER 13, 1980. In what was apparently its first significant operation, the September 15 Legion, one of the Nicaraguan counterrevolutionary groups advised by the Argentines, bombed a leftist radio station. This attack failed to destroy the station, but it did kill three Costa Rican employees.[26] The Costa Rican government was understandably outraged.

ECONOMIC ASSISTANCE FOR EL SALVADOR RESUMED: WASHINGTON, D.C., DECEMBER 17, 1980. A $20 million Economic Support Fund (ESF) grant for El Salvador that had been suspended following the slaying of the four American churchwomen was reopened. Ambassador White was also instructed to advise President Duarte that the full range of economic assistance was being resumed. At the same time, the Inter-American Development Bank announced approval of a $45 million credit for agricultural equipment in support of the land reform program. These actions were justified on the basis of the Salvadoran government's "commitment to a thorough, professional and expeditious investigation" of the murders of the churchwomen.[27] The investigation would meet none of these criteria.

HONDURAN PROPOSES U.S. "GOOD OFFICES" IN SALVADORAN CONFLICT: TEGUCIGALPA, HONDURAS, DECEMBER 24, 1980. Jorge Arturo Reina, a leading member of the Liberal Party's dissident ALIPO faction, called on me with an "urgent matter." He had met with Assistant Secretary Bowdler and Deputy Assistant Secretary Cheek in Washington the previous week to propose a negotiated settlement to the emerging civil war in El Salvador. Many of the opposition leaders, he claimed, were interested in a "political solution" rather than continued warfare and violence, but only the United States could bring the two sides together.

Reina told Bowdler that he had met with Salvadoran opposition leaders in Mexico and believed they would negotiate. He urged that we take the lead in working out a peaceful settlement and, as a first step, meet with leaders of the Democratic Revolutionary Front (FDR). Bowdler responded to the effect that we would welcome such an outcome—indeed, we had repeatedly urged both sides to try to work out their differences at the conference table rather than on the field of combat—but we could not "negotiate" for the Salvadoran government.

If, however, there seemed to be a basis for bringing the two sides together, we would certainly support it. Bowdler outlined five discussion themes that might serve as a basis for an exchange of views with leaders of the FDR. He emphasized, however, that any such discussions would not be "negotiations." The themes were cease-fire arrangements, reorganization of the junta, reorganization of the military and elimination of repressive units, continuation of reform programs and free elections.

Reina believed he had been authorized to broach these discussion points with the Salvadorans and had gone directly to Managua for that purpose. He met with Guillermo Ungo, leader of the FDR, and several others, including Hector Oqueli, a former Christian Democrat, and Cayetano Carpio, one of the principal guerrilla leaders.[28] Reina claimed he had stressed the need to: find a negotiated end to the conflict before it worsened; U.S. willingness to support such an approach—with the understanding that we could not negotiate on behalf of the Salvadoran government—and that talks must center on the suggested themes.

Reina said they were interested but needed to discuss the proposal with other leaders, political and paramilitary. Although he wasn't specific, Reina implied that he had also discussed this proposal with several Sandinista leaders. I reported this information to Bowdler.[29]

Reina apparently left FDR leaders somewhat confused. Oqueli approached our embassy in Managua to confirm U.S. interest and clarify other points. The FDR's understanding of the proposed themes was also at variance with Bowdler's proposal.

For example, they believed one topic would be the elimination of Salvadoran "security forces" (i.e., the National Guard, Treasury Police and other non-Army groups associated with death squads and human rights violations) and reorganization of the armed forces. These questions were sent to State and later repeated to us.[30]

State's response confirmed the Bowdler/Reina meeting and said that we "had no special messages for the FDR." Nonetheless, the Managua embassy was instructed to tell Oqueli that we encouraged a dialogue between the Salvadoran government and the FDR.[31]

Reina was a somewhat mercurial, democratic leftist. He knew, and was in touch with, much of the Latin American democratic left, particularly those affiliated with the social democratic Socialist International. His efforts to defuse the Salvadoran conflict were, I thought, sincerely motivated if somewhat quixotic.

MAJOR INSURGENT ATTACK IN EL SALVADOR: CHALATENANGO, EL SALVADOR, DECEMBER 26–27, 1980. An estimated 1,000 rebels launched a series of coordinated attacks on police posts in Chalatenango province, which abuts Honduras. Many posts were overrun, but army counterattacks ultimately dislodged the guerrillas. Large numbers of them reportedly escaped into Honduras. This appeared to have been the largest guerrilla offensive operation to that date.[32] At the same time, insurgent leader Fermin Cienfuegos told U.S. reporters that the rebels planned to launch a "final offensive" prior to the January 20 inauguration of President Reagan.[33]

NEGOTIATIONS WITH VINELLI'S KIDNAPPERS UNDERWAY: TEGUCIGALPA, HONDURAS, DECEMBER 30, 1980. Representatives of Vinelli's family came by to provide a status report. They had established contact with the kidnappers and confirmed they were from the Salvadoran Popular Liberation Front (FPL). Negotiations were in progress. The Honduran government was aware of the negotiations, and security forces had promised to take no action without first consulting the family. I reported these developments to State.[34]

FDR CONSIDERS GOOD OFFICES PROPOSAL: TEGUCIGALPA, HONDURAS, DECEMBER 30, 1980. Reina phoned to report he had spoken with Ungo, and the Salvadorans were still considering the good offices proposal. Reina remained optimistic and hoped to have a final response shortly after the New Year. I reported the state of play.[35]

POSSIBLE CLOSURE OF OAS OBSERVER MISSION: TEGUCIGALPA, HONDURAS, DECEMBER 31, 1980. With the conclusion of the El Salvador/Honduras peace treaty, State asked if the OAS observer mission should be continued. The USAF helicopter support agreement was due to expire, and the OAS wished to eliminate the expense.

The OAS observers provided our best intelligence about the border and refugee camps, as well as affording the best means for moving embassy personnel into that area. Accordingly, I told State that we strongly supported its continuation. Our San Salvador embassy, for similar reasons, agreed.

I found Foreign Minister Elvir fully supportive of continuation. The Hondurans doubted Salvadoran intentions in the disputed areas and wanted the balanced information only the OAS could provide. He also offered to raise the issue with his Salvadoran counterpart, Fidel Chavez Mena, to ensure Salvadoran support.[36] Shortly thereafter, I learned from State that the Salvadoran government had acceded to closure of the mission. I quickly passed this on to Elvir, who was surprised and contacted Chavez Mena. It turned out that the Salvadoran military had agreed to termination, considering it a military matter. Chavez Mena was able to turn that decision around; his government officially supported a six-month extension.

AMERICAN ADVISERS SLAIN BY SALVADORAN RIGHTISTS: SAN SAL-
VADOR, EL SALVADOR, JANUARY 4, 1981. Michael Hammer and Mark Pearlman, two American employees of the American Institute for Free Labor
Development (AIFLD) who were official advisers to the Salvadoran land
reform program, were killed by three gunmen while eating at the Sheraton
Hotel. Murdered with them was the Salvadoran chief of the agrarian reform
program.[37]

I was shocked and deeply grieved. Hammer was a good and respected
friend of mine for many years, and his tireless efforts on behalf of others I
greatly admired. We had worked together closely in El Salvador in the late
1960s, helping to develop the trade union movement and establish agricultural cooperatives. It was later learned that these killings had been ordered
on the spur of the moment by two Salvadoran landowners who had seen the
group in the hotel dining room. The identities of the assassins were known
and their responsibility established beyond any doubt. They were ultimately
arrested and charged with the crime but later released on an alleged legal tech-
nicality.

INTELLIGENCE DATA TRIGGERS NICARAGUAN AID CUTOFF: WASH-
INGTON, D.C., JANUARY 6–7, 1981. A special CIA report, drawing in part on
recent aerial photography, confirmed continued Sandinista material support
for the Salvadoran insurgency, thus providing "conclusive proof that the
Nicaraguan government was providing significant amounts of aid to the insurgency in El Salvador." Ambassador Pezzullo was instructed to advise the
Nicaraguans that we had conclusive evidence they had been providing arms
and other assistance to the insurgents in violation of their repeated assurances
to the contrary. This triggered the antiterrorist clause in our assistance agreements, cutting off all further aid; that action was formalized January 16, 1981.[38]

RECOMMENDATIONS ON REFUGEE PROBLEM: TEGUCIGALPA, HON-
DURAS, JANUARY 6, 1981. Our deliberations produced a series of action recommendations and strategies for their implementation. These recommendations were designed to alleviate human suffering, husband scarce resources,
facilitate Honduran efforts to control the frontier area and make it more
difficult for the Salvadoran insurgents to find safe haven in Honduras. Several of the proposed courses of action had been taken in Costa Rica the previous year, and all were realistic and feasible.

The key to success was U.S. assumption of leadership and influence to
move the other players—the Honduran government, the UN High Commission for Refugees (UNHCR), and the voluntary agencies working with the
UNHCR. Without a strong commitment from us, little was likely to happen.
In the case of the Mariel boat refugees, we had exercised that leadership.

We urged immediate interagency agreement to work for establishment

of several central refugee camps somewhat removed from the immediate frontier area, with part of the initial costs assumed by the United States. These
costs would be deducted from our future payments to the UNHCR. This
offset arrangement had been adopted in the Costa Rica case. To accomplish
our ends, we needed to do the following:

• Persuade the Hondurans, UNHCR and voluntary agencies that the
dispersal of refugees was uneconomic, caused unnecessary human suffering
and hampered Honduran efforts to control its frontier.
• Offer to provide site survey, layout and construction supervision services for the proposed camps, using AID disaster relief and Southern Command personnel. This had been done expeditiously in Costa Rica.
• Provide UNHCR, on a reimbursable basis, tents and other required
equipment needed to establish the camps from AID disaster relief stores, as
was done in Costa Rica, and provide military air transport for UNHCR-
owned stores still located in that country.
• Advise the Hondurans, UNHCR and others that the United States
would find it very difficult to justify the continued provision of foodstuffs and
other relief supplies without agreement on establishing central camps and
improving controls over supplies.[39]

State's Refugee Affairs and the AID's Disaster Relief offices were reluctant in the extreme to adopt an active role in Honduras. The Inter-American Bureau was sympathetic, but in the waning days of the Carter administration there was no political will to undertake this initiative. Southern
Command was prepared to assist if authorized. There was no interagency
effort, although parts of our recommendations were adopted, willy-nilly, later.
We continued our efforts, but results were slow in coming.

OAS OBSERVER MISSION SAVED: TEGUCIGALPA, HONDURAS, JANU-
ARY 7–8, 1981. State responded to our recommendations by proposing closure of the OAS mission and substituting "Salvadoran and Honduran forces
themselves with appropriate [helicopter] bilateral support from the US."[40]
This notion, in my judgment, was fatuous. The idea of providing U.S. helicopter support directly to Salvadoran and Honduran forces operating in the
region, which risked drawing us directly into the conflict and giving the Salvadoran insurgents an extraordinary propaganda target, was particularly mindless.
I quickly transmitted a reclama, with copies to San Salvador and Southern Command, taking the arguments in the State cable apart point by point
and concluding:

In sum, I continue to believe the OAS presence directly serves our interests and that withdrawal would be seriously damaging in terms of inhibitions on major actors, reliable intelligence, ability to move US personnel into and out of area and possibly domestic US political environment. No other option offers as many potential benefits. I therefore strongly urge that USG agree to extension of helicopter support contract for an additional six months. At the end of that time, we can reevaluate need for OAS observers in light of existing circumstances.[41]

Ambassador White and Southern Command quickly endorsed my arguments, and State backed down. The helicopter contract was extended and the observer presence assured through June.

FDR/DRU MEETS WITH REINA: MANAGUA, NICARAGUA, JANUARY 8, 1981. Reina met with the combined FDR/paramilitary leadership to outline his proposal and Bowdler's five thematic points. Several of the principals, including Ungo, demanded "direct negotiations" with the United States and were adamantly opposed to sitting down with Duarte or the Christian Democrats. They asked, alternatively, if we would accept their negotiating with the Salvadoran military rather than the junta government. A larger faction, however, seemed completely opposed to any talks.

No decisions were made at this meeting, but Reina left with the impression that the proposal was still under consideration. The proposal, and suggested discussion points, were being circulated in each of the member organizations making up the coalition to see if a consensus would emerge.

I cabled Reina's report to State.[42]

A VEXING QUESTION: NUMBERS OF SALVADORAN REFUGEES: TEGUCIGALPA, HONDURAS, JANUARY 8, 1981. We had been trying for weeks to get a fix on the total number of Salvadoran refugees in Honduras. It was a bit like pulling teeth to get these data from the various refugee relief organizations, but we finally succeeded. We also received the Honduran Immigration and UN High Commission for Refugees (UNHCR) numbers. In theory Immigration had to certify each entrant. The figures varied widely: Immigration, 8,000; UNHCR, 12,000; Catholic Relief Services, 20,000; and CEDEN, an evangelistic group, 23,000. CARE did not have an updated figure.[43]

These wide variations seemed to substantiate our belief that the numbers used by the relief organizations were greatly exaggerated. Obviously, inflated figures could be used to provide cover for the diversion of foodstuff and supplies to Salvadoran insurgents and also to Hondurans living in the border area. We soon confirmed the latter transfers; hard evidence that significant quantities were reaching the guerrillas was harder to come by.

TOUGH INSTRUCTIONS FOR MOSCOW AND HAVANA; MILITARY AID FOR EL SALVADOR: WASHINGTON, D.C., JANUARY 9, 1981. Secretary

Edmund Muskie instructed our embassy in Moscow and the U.S. Interests Section in Havana to warn their hosts that "their intervention in El Salvador is contrary to the interests of all the peoples of that country and threatens peace and security of the region." At the same time, an interagency dispute over the resumption of military assistance to El Salvador was resolved with approval of a $5 million package that included military transport, communications equipment and the cost-free lease of six helicopters.[44] This assistance was considered "non-lethal."

MEETING WITH INTELLIGENCE CHIEF TORRES ARIAS AND THE PRESS: TEGUCIGALPA, HONDURAS, JANUARY 9, 1981. Colonel Leonidas Torres Arias was something of a mystery man to the embassy. He was always in evidence at official functions, believed to have great influence with President Paz, apparently intelligent and ambitious, and outwardly amiable, yet very self-contained. Over the years no one in the American mission had been able to establish a friendly, informal relationship with him. Apart from official functions, he seemed to avoid Americans. Consequently, when I made my first formal call on him at the National Palace, both the station chief and Defense attache wished to come along. Why not?

Torres Arias proved to be as elusive and equivocal as reputed. He was charming, articulate and impossible to pin down: intelligent, without doubt; devious, equally without doubt. Physically attractive, possessing a winning smile and favoring civilian clothes, he wore a large gold Rolex on his left wrist, heavy gold chains about his neck and right wrist, and Gucci shoes. Not your typical Latin American officer. Nothing of substance came of the meeting.

Emerging from the palace, we were nearly overwhelmed by reporters, which made the station chief notably uncomfortable. They seemed to read great significance into our meeting with Torres Arias (they had obviously been tipped off) and were dying to know what monumental plans we had been hatching. The truth was, none, and I said so. But that didn't slow the freewheeling questions that echoed current rumors and disinformation: 30 U.S. military advisers were in-country, training Honduran military (incorrect at the time, and so denied); U.S. plans for direct military engagement in El Salvador (nonsense, and so belittled); Cuba's important role in Central America (confirmed); and stationing a U.S. aircraft carrier near Costa Rica (nonsense and denied).

In response to a Cuba question, I stated that there was extensive evidence that Cuba was "training Central Americans in an effort to change the governmental, social and economic systems of CA." This, together with responses to questions on El Salvador, received extensive coverage in Honduras and beyond. Some of it was mind-boggling in its inventiveness. For example, *El Heraldo* quoted me as saying, "Cuba Prepares Armed Invasion of

Central America." That story, however, was picked up by wire services and received unwarranted play, hitting the front page of Miami's *Diario las Americas*.[45]

LETTER OF RESIGNATION: TEGUCIGALPA, HONDURAS, JANUARY 10, 1981. State earlier cabled all serving ambassadors, reminding them that "in keeping with established custom", they should submit their resignations to President Reagan, effective at his pleasure. I complied.[46] Normally, career Foreign Service officers could expect to remain at their posts two to four years. But times were far from normal in Central America.

I thought there was a high probability I would be replaced early, especially in light of my experience with the Reagan transition team. Once the new leadership team was aboard in the bureau, however, I planned to point out that a change in ambassadors prior to the November 1981 elections would be perceived as signaling a major change in our Honduran policy. It would certainly help those seeking to block elections and could well trigger a coup that would preclude realization of our central policy objective.

SALVADORAN INSURGENTS LAUNCH "FINAL OFFENSIVE": SAN SALVADOR AND SANTA ANA, EL SALVADOR, JANUARY 10–12, 1981. The newly unified insurgent groups, the Faribundo Marti National Liberation Movement (FMLN) launched a major attack on military installations in San Salvador, Santa Ana and smaller cities. This was by far the largest military operation mounted by the rebels and enjoyed some initial success: the Salvadoran military were very much on the defensive. FMLN and FDR issued a declaration saying the attacks were the beginning of the promised "final offensive" to wrest power from the junta and calling for a national general strike. The strike call was an attempt to emulate the tactics used in Nicaragua to bring down Somoza.[47] A 70-man military unit in Santa Ana mutinied and joined the rebels but didn't alter the outcome.

The general strike did not occur: on Monday, January 12, the first workday after the onset of the fighting, an estimated 90 percent of all workers in San Salvador were at their jobs. Within a few days the military drove the insurgents out of the cities and back to their rural base areas. There were heavy casualties on both sides and among the civilian populace caught in the crossfire. Major cities also were severely damaged.

REINA REPORTS FDR/DRU KEEP OPTIONS OPEN: TEGUCIGALPA, HONDURAS, JANUARY 12, 1981. Reina phoned to report that he had received a "declaration" from an FDR leader that left the door open for negotiations. He did not, however, provide the text or other details that supported his conclusion. I confessed some perplexity. Since the FMLN was conducting its "final offensive," didn't it expect a military victory, as Carpio had predicted earlier? If that were the case, why would they be open to a negotiated settlement? I also reiterated that the United States was not going to negotiate with FDR, although we were willing to talk about the subjects on the suggested agenda. Finally, I emphasized that he was not representing the United States in his talks. He acknowledged these points and assured me that he had made them clear to FDR.

I reported Reina's assessment to Washington.[48] I couldn't see how the rebels could enter into talks about a negotiated settlement in good faith while engaged in a major offensive against the government. Their purported interest in this initiative, it seemed to me, was just a smoke screen or tactical ploy.

Reina phoned again the next day in an excited state. Ungo had just phoned him from Mexico City and wished to come to Tegucigalpa "immediately" to meet with me. The FDR had agreed to the proposed thematic discussion points, and he wished to come today. Taken aback, I told Reina that I would get back to him after checking with State.

I suspected that Ungo's proposed visit may have represented an effort to gain access to an American official so that the FDR could later claim the United States had given it de facto recognition as a belligerent. That would allow the rebels to score useful propaganda points. At the time, I was not aware that the final offensive had been broken, but Ungo and others probably knew. That, together with general strike fiasco and concerns about the posture of the incoming Reagan administration, may have moved some of the FMLN and FDR leaders to seek talks. There was also a chance that Ungo wished to come to Honduras to meet with a congressional delegation due in Tegucigalpa the next day. Whatever its purpose, a meeting with Ungo did not seem like a good idea.

I phoned Bowdler immediately for guidance.[49] He agreed with my assessment and instructed me not to meet with Ungo. I then phoned Reina, asking that he so advise Ungo. I hoped that would end the entire episode. It did not.

MILITARY ASSISTANCE TO EL SALVADOR REINSTATED: WASHINGTON, D.C., JANUARY 13, 1981. Responding to the "final offensive," President Carter decided to resume shipping lethal military assistance, suspended since 1977, with the allocation of $5 million from a contingency fund. Congressional approval was not required,[50] but this action was supported by the leadership of both chambers and a head-count majority in the House.

This decision represented a major shift in our policy and was a very clear signal that the United States would not sit on its hands in the face of a major leftist effort to seize control of El Salvador. The incoming Reagan administration shared that view in spades.

CONGRESSIONAL DELEGATION IN HONDURAS: TEGUCIGALPA, HONDURAS, JANUARY 13–19, 1981. Over the two previous months, the embassy had been working with John McAward of the Unitarian Universalist Service Committee on a Central American tour for three congressional representatives and their staffs: Gerry Studds (D-MA); Robert Edgar (D-PA) and Barbara Mikulski (D-MD). The group was to visit Costa Rica, Nicaragua, Honduras and El Salvador.

Congressional delegations usually travel on official business, with the local embassy handling their entire program, making all appointments and other arrangements. Costs, in these cases, are paid by Congress. But this trip was different. It was "unofficial" and would be almost entirely a Unitarian show. They were footing the bills and calling most of the shots. This arrangement was in large part the product of suspicion and hostility toward the Carter administration's Central American policy on the part of many American liberals. They simply did not trust an embassy to give them a fair, balanced picture of what was happening and why. In that sense, they were much like their ideological opponents on the far right.

We had agreed to give the representatives and their staffs a classified briefing on the Honduran situation (McAward and the others would be excluded, because they lacked the requisite security clearances) and arrange meetings for them with President Paz, assembly president Suazo Cordova and a few other officials. I also agreed to host a large cocktail-buffet reception in their honor the second evening and a working luncheon the following day.

I wished to ensure balance by bringing the representatives together with a wide range of Hondurans: members of the Honduran legislature and representatives of all legal political parties, business leaders and trade unionists, military officers and clerics, media leaders and professionals. We expected McAward's program would be tilted well to the left of center and were not disappointed.

Our travelers arrived from Managua, where they had spent several days, in midafternoon. I met them at the airport and the representatives and staff came to the embassy for the briefing. They were slightly euphoric from their experiences in Nicaragua. They had been deeply and favorably impressed by the Sandinistas, proudly showing off a large photograph of the three of them, grinning and flanked by two Sandinista *comandantes*, all holding a large Sandinista flag. Blessed, I thought, are the naive, for they are eternally credulous—except when dealing with their own embassy.

The briefing went reasonably well. The three principals asked good questions and readily acceded to our request that they stress the importance of the transition process and elections in their meetings with Honduran officials and media. They met that commitment in all the meetings we arranged. I also asked if they would share with us their impressions at the conclusion of their program; they agreed to do so.

The official part of their visit began January 14 with a call on President Paz. It went very well, as did the other visits, although our visitors found that the Hondurans did not share their sanguine view of the Sandinista regime in Nicaragua. They seemed somewhat taken aback.

The reception that evening initially seemed to go swimmingly. Embassy officers were on hand to act as interpreters when the representatives or staffers were speaking with Hondurans who did not speak English, and guests seemed to be flowing easily between groups. Suazo Cordova, Zuniga and key military leaders were on hand, getting plenty of attention. Although circumstances did not afford much opportunity for in-depth discussion, our visitors were at least exposed to a wide swathe of the Honduran political scene.

Following the official meetings and luncheon the next day, the delegation began McAward's program. Edgar and Mikulski headed for the El Salvador/Honduras frontier in separate parties. A third party, consisting of two staff aides, went elsewhere on the frontier. Studds, however, took a chartered flight to San Salvador (our embassy there had earlier recommended that the delegation not visit El Salvador because of the military situation and attendant risk).

Three days later they reappeared on our radar screen and were ready to brief us on their findings. A session was quickly arranged, this time with Unitarian staff participation.

Their travel and other arrangements had been handled by various private refugee relief organizations, several of which we suspected were very sympathetic to the Salvadoran insurgents. Edgar and Mikulski had been impressed by the rugged terrain and relative isolation of the frontier area and were highly complimentary of the work being done by the relief organizations. Mikulski, referring to our earlier briefing, said she had detected "no hint of misuse" of relief supplies but went on to note that "Hondurans in the border area are receiving their share of relief supply benefits." The distribution of these supplies to Hondurans, of course, was a clear misuse. The greatest unmet needs, they said, were adequate health care and housing. Both reported no evidence of problems with the Honduran military and Mikulski observed that relations between the Salvadoran refugees and Hondurans seemed very good.

However, both repeated stories from refugees about alleged atrocities committed by the Salvadoran military and claimed to have proof that these stories were true. Their "proof" was a tape recording of statements by various refugees, selected by the relief agencies, recounting various killings, rapes, bayoneting of pregnant women, beatings and other atrocities. They played it for us, and we were not impressed. Three things seemed curious about the taped stories: similarities in descriptions of discrete events, particularly the use of the same phrasing by different people describing widely separated occurrences; the use of vocabulary that was uncommon in the speech of Salvadoran *campesinos*; and inaccurate translations of actual remarks (also on the tape) by the Unitarian interpreters. It was our impression that the testimony

With then–Representative Barbara Mikulski and Constituent Assembly deputy and *campesino* union leader Julien Mendez at the embassy, January 1981.

had been rehearsed and that the speakers had been guided in what they should say.

I thanked them for sharing their impressions, which were helpful and in many respects reinforced our views. But I also expressed reservations about some of their findings and particularly the atrocity stories. I acknowledged there was no doubt that the Salvadoran military was committing many, and often gross, human rights violations—as were the rebels—but did not find the stories on the tape particularly credible. Nor did they constitute "proof" of such violations. I then explained the reasons for my dubiety, which were seconded by Arcos, Walker (who had also lived in El Salvador for three years and was familiar with common speech patterns, vocabulary and so forth) and other staff members. Our comments precipitated a sharp discussion and did not endear us to our visitors.

We reported the substance of this meeting, the summary of the "findings" they planned to issue at a Miami press conference, and messages the representatives wished sent to President Carter and President-elect Reagan. The latter were especially critical of Carter's Central America policies. They opposed, inter alia, resumption of military aid to El Salvador announced January 14. They also opposed the earlier suspension of economic aid for Nicaragua.[51]

This cable brought a quick telephone response from State. The administration's decision to resume military aid to El Salvador, I was advised, had been supported by congressional leaders and most major newspapers. Accordingly, I was asked to suggest to Studds that they might wish to withhold any statement until they returned to Washington. I located Studds and passed on the message. He took umbrage, accusing me and State of trying to muzzle them. He stated flatly that they would go ahead with their press conference and condemn the decision to resume military assistance. This, too, I reported back to State.

Their Miami press conference was not reported by the Honduran media, but their later similar statements at a press conference in Washington were. At that event they announced the introduction of legislation prohibiting military aid to El Salvador. They also made a number of charges that received local coverage: the Salvadoran "conflict has every possibility of becoming another Vietnam"; State had advised them not to visit El Salvador because of the security situation and had "tried to manipulate the delegation [while] in CA"; State later sought to dissuade them from making their findings public on advice of the embassy in Honduras, "which believed that the information we gathered from Salvadoran refugees was not valid"; and State had lied to them regarding the investigation of the murder of the four American missionary women by Salvadoran security forces.[52]

As a result of these assertions, I initiated correspondence with Studds and the others that was to last several months and, in the end, seemed to allay concerns on both sides. Later, however, we were to have further problems with one of Studds's aides who visited Honduras.

The bill suspending military aid did not prosper. Later, however, Congress imposed—correctly, in my view, given the continuing human rights violations and death squad activity—a variety of conditions and limitations on our assistance to El Salvador.

PAZ AND HONDURAN VIEWS ON THE SALVADORAN SITUATION: TEGUCIGALPA, HONDURAS, JANUARY 16, 1981. I was instructed to contact Paz and senior military leaders to determine their reactions and expectations as to the Salvadoran guerrillas' final offensive. Specific points of interest included whether they had been in touch with Salvadoran officials, and what steps they could take to tighten security on the border and interdict arms traffic.[53]

I was meeting with Paz at my residence when this cable was received and covered most of the points. When I returned to the chancery I asked Walker to advise the Political Section and Colonels Miller and Goodwin to get in touch with their contacts. We would meet later in the day to go over what they had turned up. As a result of the Codel program, I had spoken to several senior military commanders about El Salvador in the past several days, so I had a pretty good feel for their views. I also asked Walker to track down a draft cable with our recommendations for improving the Honduran military's ability to police its borders that was circulating for final clearance and get it out. It could hardly have been more timely.

My meeting with Paz had been extended, frank and relaxed. He was very concerned about the security situation on the Salvadoran border and believed the uncontrolled presence of the refugees precluded effective control of the frontier. Yet the establishment of refugee camps would be very costly, and his government did not have the resources to undertake that task. His discussion was laced with broad hints that we should be forthcoming financially to help with this problem. Then engaged in attempting to advance just that position—without success—I couldn't give him much encouragement.

Paz finally got to the point, saying: "We will do whatever you want us to do on both the refugee and security issues." This was an extraordinary opportunity. He had put the ball in our court, clearly implying that we foot the bill. I had no idea if we would meet the challenge.

I responded by outlining our position that the refugee problem was one for the UN High Commission for Refugees (UNHCR), in which Paz had earlier told me he had no confidence, and other agencies to deal with. Then, exceeding my brief, I told him that I was actually trying to convince State that we had to become directly involved in helping Honduras deal with this problem. But I had no luck and was not very optimistic. As to frontier security, I said we had been working on a proposal to improve Honduran capabilities and had a number of suggestions. When I suggested that we meet with Chief of Staff Chinchilla and other officers to review these proposals— which they would be free to reject, modify or accept—he not only agreed but said he would chair the meeting.

Paz expressed his satisfaction with the U.S. decision to resume military assistance to El Salvador, reiterating that he would help the Salvadorans in any way we suggested. Again, unstated, was the implication that we would have to pay for whatever we recommended. He did not mention any contacts the Honduran military may have had with their Salvadoran counterparts or anything they were doing to help but opined that the Salvadoran army would turn back the insurgent offensive.

In reporting this meeting I again urged that we help Honduras deal with the refugees and move quickly in so doing.[54] That was hopelessly unrealistic. There was no way the Carter administration would grasp that nettle, and Reagan transition officials were studiously ignoring State and the embassy. While I was drafting this cable, Walker was putting the finishing touches on our recommendations to enhance the Honduran military's control of the country's frontiers. That cable was dispatched to Washington shortly after mine.[55]

After comparing notes with members of the Political/Military group, we put together a response that covered the points not addressed in the earlier messages. We characterized the Honduran attitude as one of concern but not alarm; they seemed to believe the Salvadoran army was capable of controlling the situation, as long as it did not run out of ammunition and maintained an airlift capacity. They were pleased with our decision to resume military assistance, although they probably thought we were tardy in coming to it.

We had also learned that two Salvadoran officers had been in Tegucigalpa earlier in the week. The purpose of their visit was to apprise the Hondurans of their operational plans for the border area. This was well beyond the fairly routine informal contacts between units of the two armies in the border area. Finally, we had discovered that Honduran chief of staff Chinchilla was miffed that his new Salvadoran counterpart had yet to communicate with him and suggested that our embassy might wish to recommend that the Salvadoran initiate contact. There was nothing like a bit of personal pique to sour cooperation.[56]

NICARAGUAN AID FORMALLY SUSPENDED: WASHINGTON, D.C., JANUARY 16, 1981. The United States formally suspended economic assistance to Nicaragua. When Ambassador Pezzullo notified the Sandinistas, they promised to close the Salvadoran rebel radio, *Radio Liberacion*, and halt the arms traffic.[57] Nevertheless, arms continued to flow, but by increasingly sophisticated means. The radio station later moved to rebel-controlled territory in El Salvador.

PRESS QUERY ABOUT U.S. TALKS WITH THE FDR: TEGUCIGALPA, HONDURAS, JANUARY 16, 1981. Alan Riding of the *New York Times* phoned Walker to verify a story that was running in the Mexican press: State had approached FDR about holding talks with rebel leaders in Tegucigalpa; the FDR had accepted and sent a representative, whom I refused to meet. Riding also reported that FDR leaders had told him they still wished to open the discussions in Tegucigalpa.

Walker stated flatly that no discussions or negotiations were taking place in Honduras, nor were any planned. He was aware that I had met with Reina and that Reina claimed to be in touch with the FDR. Beyond that, he could only confirm that I had received telephonic instructions following the onset of the insurgents' final offensive, as he had been present. He suggested Riding call Bowdler or Cheek regarding their content. He also knew that I had not met with Ungo or anyone representing the FDR.[58]

The FDR/DRU was clearly the source of this report and had decided to demonstrate that they were willing to negotiate about the future of El Salvador, while the United States was being unreasonable.

PAZ ON IMF PROBLEM: AT LOGGERHEADS: TEGUCIGALPA, HONDURAS, JANUARY 16, 1981. We had been urging Paz and his economic ministers to rein in central government expenditures and increase revenues in order to renew the International Monetary Fund (IMF) extended fund facility. This was essential for Honduras to make required counterpart contributions to various ongoing development programs. This agreement, we stressed, was essential for further development lending from AID and other donors, such as the World Bank and the Inter-American Development Bank.

Paz, on repeated occasions, had assured me that he would trim outlays and introduce a tax increase package in the assembly. But State had recently reported that the IMF had broken off negotiations because the Hondurans had decided against introducing a proposal. This was an unpleasant surprise.

I raised this report with Paz during our meeting, and he confirmed it. Unalterable opposition from the private sector, together with the assembly's reluctance to enact new taxes in the election run-up, caused the cabinet to abandon the idea. Consequently, the IMF decided there was no point in continuing negotiations. When I asked Paz how he proposed to deal with this, he simply shrugged his shoulders and said it was a problem for his minister of finance to resolve. It was an uncharacteristically cavalier response.[59]

This was very bad news. Without the extended fund facility and foreign exchange from development lending, Honduran foreign exchange holdings would be quickly depleted and the economic decline would accelerate. And if the government continued to print money to finance the budget deficit, inflation was likely to surge. We had to redouble our missionary efforts with the private sector, political parties and government economic ministers to get these negotiations back on track.

DEBATE OVER SALVADORAN REFUGEES CONTINUES: TEGUCIGALPA, HONDURAS, JANUARY 16, 1981. State's Office of Refugee Affairs had been steadfast in opposing greater U.S. involvement in the refugee problem, reiterating that the UN High Commission for Refugees (UNHCR) was the appropriate organization to deal with refugee relief and that the United States did not wish to incur additional refugee-related costs. Their response to our January 6 cable recommending several actions therefore came as no surprise. But it included a number of new arguments, for the most part fatuous, for rejecting our recommendations: e.g., establishment of well run camps would draw additional refugees from El Salvador; there was no "evidence" that setting up camps would reduce leakage of supplies to insurgents; an improved standard of living in refugee camps would create resentment among Hondurans.[60]

This was the kind of pettifogging that drove me wild. I fired back a cable rebutting point by point their arguments and emphasizing that the refugee problem was a central element in the larger security issue on the frontier, which was threatening some of our principal foreign policy interests. To view it solely in humanitarian terms was misguided, and failure to address it adequately would only make the realization of other critical goals—survival of the Salvadoran government, prevention of a Marxist takeover, avoidance of an insurgency in Honduras—more difficult. Accordingly, the mindless repetition of pat answers and specious theories was not enough. We needed action.[61]

It was not the time to be trying to launch new initiatives, but this cable did cause Refugee Affairs to send a special survey team to Honduras to have a firsthand look at the situation.

FOREIGN MINISTER REPORTS APPROACH BY FDR: TEGUCIGALPA, HONDURAS, JANUARY 17, 1981. Foreign Minister Elvir, who had just returned from the UN General Assembly, summoned me to discuss information received from his ambassador in Managua. When I arrived, I found him visibly upset. His ambassador had been approached in Managua by FDR leaders who asserted that the final offensive was going to succeed and that they wished to open a dialogue with the Honduran government before reaching power. They claimed their organization was committed to respecting the recently signed peace treaty but had other issues to discuss. This approach deepened Elvir's concerns about developments in El Salvador and their implications for Honduras. He professed to see similarities between this situation and that which prevailed in Nicaragua in 1979, shortly before Somoza fell. He wanted to know how we saw these events.

Realizing that he had been out of touch and had apparently not yet seen Paz or any military colleagues, I said that we believed the Salvadoran military were now in control. The insurgents had suffered very heavy losses and failed to hold any of their initial territorial gains. Although the threat had not ended and the violence would continue, the Salvadoran government was not in serious danger. The resumption of U.S. military assistance should also help stabilize the situation. I also noted that I had discussed these matters with President Paz and Chief of Staff Chinchilla.

As to the FDR's approach, I opined that it was pulling out all stops in its efforts to obtain de facto recognition governments to bolster its legitimacy. Honduran government contact with this group, no matter how innocent, would be distorted to serve its purposes. Speaking personally (I had no instructions), I recommended that his government refrain from further contact and, if approached, voice its displeasure with the lies and false reports the FDR and its allies were disseminating about alleged Honduran involvement in El Salvador.

Elvir agreed with the latter point but also noted that countries supportive of the FDR might try to raise the Salvadoran situation at the General Assembly. We should prepare for that contingency, he stressed.

Changing the subject, he expressed his disappointment with his government's decision, taken while he was away, to drop the tax proposal. An agreement with the IMF was essential, and he planned to continue arguing this case within the cabinet and elsewhere. I agreed completely and promised to emphasize the importance of the IMF facility and increased tax revenue in my conversations with the political and private sectors, as well as with union and government leaders. He welcomed my commitment.

By the time I left, Elvir had calmed down, apparently reassured by my assessment of events in El Salvador and the FDR's strategy.[62] However, I failed to tell him that I had earlier been approached with a proposal to meet with the FDR. That was an error. When the story broke shortly thereafter, it no doubt left him and others feeling—correctly—that I had not been candid with them.

HONDURANS MAKE MAJOR ARMS SEIZURE: TEGUCIGALPA, HONDURAS, JANUARY 19, 1981. The station chief bounced into my office Monday morning, happier than I had seen him in some time. He was bearing great news. FUSEP had discovered and seized a major arms cache near Comayagua, some 60 miles northwest of Tegucigalpa, two days previously. A local officer had become suspicious of truck traffic at a local warehouse and decided to investigate while the building was unoccupied. Initially, he found a small quantity of arms in a Costa Rican semi trailer with the top of its refrigerated compartment and the interior cooling pipes removed. The truck was being used to smuggle arms, hidden in the pipe spaces, into Honduras, for purposes at that point unknown. This officer quickly notified his headquarters, which sent reinforcements and technicians to the site.

A thorough search of the building revealed a hidden cellar containing several tons of rifles, automatic weapons, ammunition and other munitions, along with an assortment of identity documents, passports and so forth. In all, it was three and a half tons of arms.[63] FUSEP had uncovered a major arms smuggling operation. Moreover, shortly after the FUSEP reinforcements had arrived, an apparent member of the smuggling ring had driven up in a pickup truck. He was carrying a Salvadoran passport that proved false and had been taken into custody. Inspection of his vehicle revealed that it too had secret compartments in the doors, body and flat bed; it was evidently used to carry arms from the cache to end users.[64]

When the police went to arrest the Honduran owner of the warehouse, a shoot-out ensued in which several people were killed and two wounded. All were suspected of being Salvadoran insurgents or support staff. The building owner escaped.

We subsequently established that this operation was based in Costa Rica, funneled arms to the Salvadoran insurgents, and that the arms themselves were originally provided by Cuba for the Sandinistas but had not been delivered before Somoza fell. They had been stored in Costa Rica since then, under Cuban control. Some serial numbers on these weapons were traced to U.S. stocks that had been abandoned in Vietnam.

This was an extremely important development. It provided irrefutable confirmation of our intelligence, proving the Cubans and Sandinistas were involved (trucks had to transit Nicaragua) and that at least some of the insurgents' arms were still passing through Honduras. FUSEP cooperated fully with us in exploiting this seizure, allowing CIA personnel to inspect the materiel, gather manufacturing data and serial numbers and take a complete set of photographs. And we provided them with the information our analysis revealed. We also used this information in a worldwide effort to persuade other governments of Cuban and Nicaraguan involvement, to counter Nicaraguan denials and to justify our continued military assistance to El Salvador.

The Salvadoran from the pickup would not talk, and his identity could not be established. At about this time, the extreme left in region began a major publicity campaign alleging the Hondurans had captured Facundo Guardado, a major insurgent leader, and demanded his release. Initially, FUSEP denied any knowledge of Guardado's whereabouts but soon realized that the pickup driver was Guardado. Their immediate reaction was to offer to exchange him for the kidnapped banker, Paul Vinelli.[65] We sought to discourage that idea. Ultimately, Guardado was released. We weren't very happy with that outcome, either, but Honduran authorities claimed they had no legal basis to hold him.

When the Honduran military announced this seizure several days after the fact, spokesmen denied knowing who was responsible or for whom the weapons were destined. Their reasons for taking this position were never clear to us, but they may have seen it to be in their interest to encourage speculation that the arms were for a Honduran insurgency. In any event, this difference between Honduran and U.S. public postures was soon to cause trouble.

Guardado was not only a major insurgent leader. He reportedly had masterminded the Vinelli kidnapping as well. In 1989, during another rebel "final offensive," he commanded FMLN units in San Salvador, nearly capturing the OAS secretary general, who was staying in the Sheraton Hotel at the time. Subsequently, Guardado strongly opposed the peace accords ending the civil strife in El Salvador. He was among the hardest of the hard core.[66]

EL SALVADOR MILGROUP ORDERED TO RECOMMEND MAJOR INCREASE IN AID: SAN SALVADOR, EL SALVADOR, JANUARY 19, 1981. The Milgroup commander advised Ambassador White that he had been directed to recommend a major increase in U.S. assistance levels to that country, including the addition of 55 more U.S. advisers and "huge amounts of lethal military equipment."[67] White, who had been pushing to tie increased assistance to improved human rights performance and a thorough investigation of the murders of the four American churchwomen, was furious. The Pentagon and Southern Command were jumping the gun in anticipation of President Reagan's inauguration, and acting without coordination with State or other agencies. That pattern would continue.

REAGAN INAUGURATED, BOWDLER BOUNCED: WASHINGTON, D.C., JANUARY 20, 1981. Ronald Reagan was inaugurated as the fortieth president of the United States. A few days earlier Assistant Secretary Bowdler had been told by Undersecretary David Newsom, State's senior career official managing the transition, that he had to clear his office no later than noon, January 20. When Bowdler inquired about an onward assignment, Newsom was evasive. Absent an assignment, Bowdler's career was effectively over. Unbeknownst to Newsom, however, Bowdler had earlier submitted his retirement papers, having inferred from the transition team that he would have no future under President Reagan, despite over 30 years of loyal service to Republican and Democratic administrations alike.[68]

The abrupt removal of senior officials was not without precedent, but the termination of a Foreign Service officer's career for having loyally served a previous president was reasonably rare. According to Roy Gutman, the Reagan transition team initially demanded the immediate dismissal of all Carter appointees, political and career.[69] Newsom convinced Secretary-designate Alexander Haig that this would create chaos in the conduct of our foreign policy and seriously damage the career service. Haig appealed this decision to transition team head Richard Allen, the national security advisor-designate. As a result, it was agreed that Newsom would provide Allen with a list of career appointees (there was no question about noncareer officials, they were out), and Allen would identify only those that were unacceptable. Bowdler was targeted by the ultraconservatives, with Senator Helms's aide John Carbaugh, an ex-officio member of the transition team, leading the charge. The new administration's treatment of Bowdler sent shock waves through the Foreign Service, which viewed it as an ominous start.

The Foreign Service was created to ensure that our nation had a corps of skilled, highly trained men and women to assist in formulating our foreign policy, conducting our diplomacy and providing the secretary of state and president with the best possible information and advice on our international relations. Frequently this advice and analysis is unwelcome to our political leaders. But if Foreign Service officers tailor their advice to what their political masters wish to hear, they would not be doing their jobs. Once a policy or proposed action is determined by lawful authority, however, members of the Service must carry out their instructions unerringly and loyally, regardless of personal views. If an officer cannot, in good conscience, do so, he or she should resign or request reassignment.

The notion of punishing those who meet their constitutional responsibility by loyally and faithfully carrying out a president's policies strikes at the heart of the Foreign Service. If career officers are to be punished for loyal service to an outgoing administration, how can loyalty to the incoming administration be assured when it might well lead to future dismissal?

Bowdler's abrupt departure left the bureau largely adrift at a critical juncture. The new administration was exceedingly slow getting out of the blocks, while Central American leaders, as a result of campaign rhetoric, were expecting new directions or reaffirmations, and soon. And events in the region were moving apace.

Principal Deputy Assistant Secretary John Bushnell took over management of the bureau on an interim basis until a successor to Bowdler could be appointed and confirmed. That process was to take several months. Bushnell, however, was not trusted, and was to have only limited influence on policy.[70] The upshot was to be a period of uncertainty and drift.

Bureaucracy, like nature, abhors a vacuum. There was no shortage of volunteers rushing to fill the policy void in Central America. The NSC process, at that point, was virtually nonexistent and was to remain so until Richard Allen's replacement in January 1982. Absent an effective coordinating process and discipline, agencies and individuals began to speak about Central America in many tongues and to undertake unilateral initiatives with mindless abandon. Little consideration was given to how their actions might mesh or conflict with other policy activities or to possible secondary and tertiary effects. The instructions given the Milgroup commander in El Salvador, described above, exemplified this.[71]

4

New Administration Brings Confusion, Interagency Conflict

SUMMARY—Policy vacuum continues despite promised changes—security assistance woes—political maneuvering—Southern Command visit and new stress points—CIA begins unilateral covert action planning—response to growing disinformation—problems with IMF—Colonel Alvarez foreshadows government repression—building support for U.S. policies—dispute with Texaco—security threat grows—ambassador to El Salvador replaced as assistance increased—diplomatic initiative against Nicaragua as Contra attacks grow

FRONTIER AND POLICE TRAINING ON AGENDA: TEGUCIGALPA, HONDURAS, JANUARY 21, 1981. The only news we had from State was that Bowdler was out and John Bushnell was acting as assistant secretary until a replacement was named.

Nonetheless, we were moving ahead. Milgroup officers and I met with Paz and the General Staff to review our recommendations for improving frontier security. As we outlined our recommendations, it was clear that they were falling well short of what the Hondurans had expected and wanted. They wanted more hardware—heavy weapons, munitions, aircraft and troop-lift capability. But we were in no position to even hint at increased security assistance levels, let alone satisfy their appetite. From the desultory discussion that followed our presentation, it was clear that they weren't buying what we had tried to sell.

Having heard us out, Paz raised the issue of U.S. training for police forces. Aware of our existing bar on such training programs, which he characterized as shortsighted, Paz noted that he understood the Reagan administration planned to amend the law to permit their resumption.[1] If this were the case, he wished to ensure Honduras was among the first in line to receive training.

Having no idea as to the new administration's intentions in this regard,

I said I would apprise Washington of his concerns and desire to participate in these programs if and when they were reauthorized. I did so, endorsing his request.[2]

In the light of FUSEP's later record of gross human rights violations, I still don't have a clear sense of why Paz raised this issue. True, criminal activity was on the upswing, and some of it was seemingly the work of aspiring insurgents. It was also likely that the Superior Council of the Armed Forces was considering ways to deal with this growing problem. Based on later discussions, it is certain that FUSEP commander Alvarez was arguing strongly for the extralegal "Argentine approach" for dealing with suspected subversives. That approach was subsequently adopted. Was Paz trying to give me a heads-up or simply trying to prod the new administration to reverse the ban on police training programs?

PRESS ON "NEGOTIATIONS" WITH FDR: TEGUCIGALPA, HONDURAS, JANUARY 21, 1981. Arcos received a call from *La Prensa,* inquiring about a report that I was an intermediary for aborted negotiations between the United States and Salvadoran rebels. This was the first local interest in the issue. Arcos had persuaded the caller to hold the story until he could talk to me. The thrust of this report was that we had missed an opportunity to reach a peaceful solution to the Salvadoran conflict. Although we could not be sure, the FDR appeared to be the source, although Reina was a possibility. The reporter was friendly, and Arcos thought he would play it the way we wished if we gave him an exclusive background briefing.

I needed guidance before proceeding and phoned State for help. Absent Bowdler, no one was familiar with all the foreplay or had any bright ideas on how to deal with this situation. My impression was that no one wanted to touch it. I took that as carte blanche to deal with it as best we could.

Arcos recommended that I give the reporter a "not for attribution" interview, laying out our version of the Reina initiative. I accepted his recommendation. Unwittingly, I began to build on my relationship with *La Prensa* owner Jorge Larach. It was to become "a beautiful friendship," cementing our relations with that newspaper. In all our dealings with *La Prensa,* I found a level of rectitude that was, in my experience, almost unparalleled. Full credit goes to Larach's integrity and oversight of the paper and to Arcos's superb ability to judge people and build productive relationships.

I met with the reporter and Arcos that afternoon. After receiving a commitment that I would be referred to only as "an Embassy source" and Reina would be described as a "Honduran intermediary," we began. I related the evolution of this initiative, emphasizing that it had come from the Honduran intermediary, not the United States or FDR; there was never any question of our "negotiating" with the rebels; the "five points" were merely suggested discussion topics, not negotiating points; and the insurgent coalition had undermined its own credibility by launching its final offensive while ostensibly considering discussions to explore a political solution. I also suggested that the timing of FDR's delayed effort to initiate these talks—after the failure of the general strike and final offensive—indicated its members were seeking de facto U.S. recognition. Moreover, I suspected that their decision to go public was dictated by the failure of the final offensive and fear that the new administration would take a much tougher line.

The article of the following day carried our spin flawlessly.[3] It couldn't have been better if Arcos had written it. And it snowballed. It was repeated locally, and then the FDR made a renewed effort to exploit our "failure to seize the opportunity for a negotiated solution" in a story given to the *Miami Herald*.[4] That paper then called Arcos for comment, and we had our version of the story replayed two days later. We thought we had countered this FDR propaganda initiative quite effectively.

All of this only reinforced my belief that the FDR had not been seriously interested in a negotiated settlement; rather, its leaders sought de facto U.S. recognition in order to claim status as belligerents under international law. Once the final offensive collapsed, they sought to portray their acceptance of the Reina initiative as an act of statesmanship designed to avoid further bloodshed. From start to finish it was a cynical effort to gain a propaganda advantage.

REBEL RADIO IN MANAGUA CLOSES: MANAGUA, NICARAGUA, JANUARY 21, 1981. The insurgent radio station *Radio Liberacion* ceased broadcasting from Managua, apparently as a result of the Sandinistas' earlier commitment to Ambassador Pezzullo.[5] It later began broadcasting from El Salvador.

DISINFORMATION ON HONDURAN TROOP DEPLOYMENTS: TEGUCIGALPA, HONDURAS, JANUARY 21, 1981. The FDR and Coordinator for Solidarity with the Salvadoran People asserted that the Honduran military had deployed 3,000 troops along the border with El Salvador and were engaging in joint operations with the Salvadorans. These spurious charges had been voiced publicly by the Studds/Mikulski/Edgar congressional delegation, and then played back in the Honduran media. Wire services also carried statements of guerrilla leader Cayetano Carpio, making this same allegation. They clearly represented a disinformation effort.

Our Milgroup's Army Section commander had visited the southern border January 19–20, stopping at the three military district garrisons responsible for frontier security: Santa Rosa de Copan, Marcala and Cucuyagua, none of which are located on or near the frontier. Each garrison consisted of a single battalion of about 800 men. One company from each battalion was actually deployed in towns near the border. This was unchanged from their deployments prior to the signing of the peace accord. The total number of Honduran troops facing the border was no more than 2,400, with fewer than 400 men actually deployed at posts on the frontier. Nor did this officer see any signs of a military buildup.

The Marcala garrison, he learned, had conducted a training exercise over several weeks that involved a single company (100-plus men) and, for a few days, five air force helicopters. That exercise, however, had been conducted well away from the border area and was reported by the OAS observers and our attache.

The 3,000 troops allegedly operating on the border represented roughly one fourth of the Honduran army. Even if all their trucks and support equipment were operational, an unprecedented situation, the Hondurans would have trouble moving that number of men, let alone providing sustained logistical support. These facts demonstrated the allegations were untrue, and we so reported to State.[6] The correction of disinformation about Honduran military activities, however, was not our responsibility.

SUSPENDED NICARAGUAN AID PROGRAM CANCELED: WASHINGTON, D.C., JANUARY 23, 1981. The new administration ordered a formal review of the AID program for Nicaragua, which had been suspended January 16. Some $15 million remained undisbursed, along with $50 million authorized for fiscal year 1981.[7] Pezzullo argued that by holding these funds in suspense we would have a carrot to influence Sandinista behavior; cancel the program completely, and we would lose that leverage. The administration, however, canceled the program, and the funds were reprogrammed to other countries.[8]

DEALING WITH DISINFORMATION ABOUT THE UNITED STATES: TEGUCIGALPA, HONDURAS, JANUARY 26, 1981. Several CT members had voiced concern about a growing number of spurious and terribly distorted stories in the media designed to cast the United States in a bad light. Some of these accounts were speculative, apparently extrapolated from Reagan campaign rhetoric, statements by transition team members or others purporting to speak for them, but most seemed to be deliberately fabricated.

We had earlier noted an increasingly sophisticated disinformation campaign to discredit the Salvadoran government and military, although their known actions were appalling enough without additional burnishing. But the United States was now a target as well. Many, if not most, of these stories dealt with alleged activities in the border area and originated with the Coordinator for Solidarity with the Salvadoran People. Several Catholic priests in the Santa Rosa de Copan area were involved with that front group, and we suspected some refugee relief workers also cooperated with it. The Church hierarchy was trying to deal with the priests, but the refugee voluntary agencies were another matter.

Arcos had routinely called or written editors when an especially egregious piece appeared, correcting the report and urging that they check with him before publishing stories about supposed U.S. actions or intentions. That had not produced much result. In his usual direct style Arcos now suggested that we compile a listing of the principal published "myths" about what we were doing in Honduras and Central America, develop a statement of fact for each myth and hold a press conference. In any event he believed I was overdue to meet formally with the press, and a conference would provide a controlled environment to counter this disinformation. After consideration by the CT, I agreed. We also decided that we would respond, promptly and in writing, to stories that seemed to constitute disinformation about the United States. Arcos would be the point person in that effort.

We identified seven myths—outright falsehoods and half-truths—that were receiving continued media play: the United States and Honduras were converting the Honduran army into the principal military force in Central America; we had rejected an opportunity to negotiate a peaceful solution to the Salvadoran problem; 36 American military advisers had entered Honduras between January 8 and 15 to train the Honduran army for an incursion into El Salvador; several U.S. ships carrying arms had arrived recently in Honduras and the arms had been trucked to San Pedro Sula, and during the January 14–22 period "various US Hercules aircraft had taken off from Toncontin [Tegucigalpa airport] for unknown places"; the United States was planning a direct armed intervention in El Salvador; a U.S. aircraft carrier with 3,000 Marines embarked was anchored off the Salvadoran coast, waiting to attack; and we were sending Green Berets, vast quantities of arms and other assistance to the Salvadoran military.[9]

For each myth we prepared factual responses drawn from previously published or unclassified material. Although difficult to prove the negative (e.g., that the United States had no intention of intervening directly in the Salvadoran conflict), we could lay out the facts. We also prepared responses to anticipated questions from the media. I felt confident that I could handle anything thrown at me during the press conference.

CONCERNS ABOUT NICARAGUAN EXILES: TEGUCIGALPA, HONDURAS, JANUARY 28, 1981. My disquiet about our staff's dealings with the Nicaraguan exile community was growing, as was my curiosity about what the new administration might have in mind *vis-à-vis* Nicaragua. The fact that the Sandinistas had used entrapment to discredit their enemies, together with our certainty that the exile community in Honduras included Sandinista agents, had earlier caused me to instruct the staff that they should refrain from seeking out Nicaraguan exiles and use the utmost discretion in any unsolicited meetings. With U.S.-Nicaraguan relations deteriorating rapidly, I thought the Sandinistas might try to create an incident to use against us. Thus, I cabled State, requesting guidance on dealing with such contacts.[10]

After a week or so without response, I called Deputy Assistant Secretary Cheek, soon to be replaced and banished to Nepal as DCM, another victim of loyal service to the Carter administration. He said that no one wished to deal with the issue I had posed, so I was on my own. This vacuum needed to be filled. I asked Walker to prepare a statement of mission policy, outlining our concerns and reiterating the need to avoid Nicaraguan exiles and to be extremely discreet in any official, social or other meetings. This time I wanted it circulated to every officer in the mission. They were to sign it, indicating their understanding of the guidance, and return it to Walker. Moreover, they were instructed to report any and all such encounters to him. This turned out to be a useful step.

ENGAGING AMERICAN BUSINESSMEN: TEGUCIGALPA, HONDURAS, JANUARY 28, 1981. One of my priorities was to increase and broaden our interaction with the managers of American businesses in Honduras. Although the embassy—particularly Economic officer Wackerbarth and Commercial attache Bob Higgins—had excellent relations with this community and met frequently with the local managers, it seemed to me important that we strengthen these relationships with higher-level attention. There were several reasons for this.

These businessmen all had extensive contacts with their Honduran counterparts and government officials and could provide us with additional information about, and perspectives on, local developments. And sometimes they picked up important information before we did. I also felt that by keeping them fully apprised of our policy goals and why they were important, they would be more supportive of our efforts. And we could use all the support we could get. Finally, they often came to us for assistance when their companies had problems with the Honduran government but usually only after the issue had reached a critical juncture. If we maintained regular contact and could win their trust, we would probably learn of emerging problems earlier and perhaps be able to aid their resolution before they developed into crises.

I had already included several American businessmen in all my larger social functions, was visiting most of their operations and had spoken to them individually about setting up a regular monthly meeting with key mission staff members. Almost without exception they thought this an excellent idea. To deal with the problem of geographic dispersal, we agreed to hold occasional meetings in the San Pedro Sula area. This would ease the travel problem for managers located in the north.

Our first meeting was an informal luncheon at my residence. I outlined our overall policy goals and asked various mission officials to provide brief overviews of their respective activities and concerns. Our guests were encouraged to ask questions or comment on what they heard and in turn were questioned by us about various aspects of the business, banking and economic environment. The feedback was very positive, and there was unanimous agreement that these meetings should continue on a regular basis.

DISINFORMATION PRESS CONFERENCE AND REACTION: TEGUCIGALPA, HONDURAS, JANUARY 28–29, 1981. We had an excellent turnout. We then handed out a five-page statement describing each myth and laying out the factual response and began the conference. In my initial remarks I outlined our concerns regarding what we believed to be a major disinformation campaign and suggested that when reporters heard of alleged U.S. intentions or actions, that they first seek confirmation, clarification or comment from Arcos. And I committed the embassy to respond to such questions as quickly and candidly as possible.

Their initial questions focused on the myths, but once that ground was covered, they moved on to other topics. Our homework was paying off; most of the questions addressed issues we had identified and prepared for. Their questions also gave me several opportunities to reaffirm our continued support for Honduran elections and the transition process. This was especially important in view of the new administration and Ricardo Zuniga's continued machinations.

But my response to one critical question was to further damage my relations with the Honduran military. Responding to questions about the covert arms smuggling operation uncovered at Comayagua, I said that these munitions had been shipped from Costa Rica, were from Cuban stocks and had been destined for the Salvadoran insurgents. This information had been made public in Washington, but I had overlooked the fact that Honduran authorities were continuing to deny any knowledge of origin or end use. So I had unthinkingly placed myself on record as contradicting them. That was not smart. In retrospect, it is difficult to understand how neither I nor others picked up on this point as we worked on responses. On the other hand, it is equally difficult to believe that I would not have used this information in any event, as it was a critical part of the picture we wished to paint. But at least I would have created this new problem with the military wittingly.

We soon learned that some in the military were outraged. Indeed, they would later accuse me of violating confidentiality and their trust by having made these statements. This incident became another item in their growing list of grievances against me, the foremost of which was my outspoken support for elections and opposition to a military coup.

The impact of the press conference exceeded our expectations. The evening television shows ran clips of some of my comments, and various radio newscasts ran excerpts of my statements and responses to questions. The heaviest coverage, however, was in the morning newspapers—headline stories in all, with extensive stories describing the myths and detailing our responses thereto.[11] *La Prensa* and *Tiempo* both published the complete text of our statement, as well as other, more interpretive stories. Associated Press also highlighted our denial that the United States was seeking to make the Honduran military its cat's paw.

By any standard the conference had been a public diplomacy success. Having directed the public's attention to the disinformation campaign, we laid out clear factual responses. That achievement, in my judgment, far outweighed any negative consequences for my relations with the Honduran military. We did not, however, have much success in getting the reporters or editors to call Arcos to verify their stories about United States policy before going to press. Nor did we stop the flow of disinformation. But by raising the issue with the public, we hoped to encourage a healthy skepticism about such stories. We had also set a precedent by responding factually to disinformation efforts, a practice we continued.

VISIT BY GENERAL NUTTING APPROVED: TEGUCIGALPA, HONDURAS, JANUARY 28, 1981. Southern Command had phoned Colonel Goodwin to request authorization for General Wallace Nutting, the area commander, to visit Honduras February 11–13. That seemed to me a good idea because it would provide me a chance to meet Nutting, brief him on the situation in Honduras and our policy goals, and allow him to meet Honduran military leaders. I was required, however, to clear all such visit requests with State and promptly sent a cable relaying the request and recommending approval.[12] It was granted, and we began working on a program for the visit.

HONDURAN COMMISSION RECOMMENDATIONS ON REFUGEES: TEGUCIGALPA, HONDURAS, JANUARY 28, 1981. A special commission on the Salvadoran refugee situation, appointed earlier by Foreign Minister Elvir, published its recommendations. It advocated granting formal status to the refugees and resettling them in camps located away from the frontier.[13] We were pleased with both recommendations, but implementation would prove exceedingly slow and would be left to the elected government.

AMBASSADOR WHITE REMOVED FROM EL SALVADOR: SAN SALVADOR, EL SALVADOR, FEBRUARY 1, 1981. In one of its first diplomatic moves, the new administration dismissed Ambassador White.[14] He was to be replaced by an interim charge d'affaires sent from Washington, Frederick L. Chapin, until a new ambassador could be confirmed. White, offered no further suitable assignment, retired, another victim of loyal service. Which of the remaining Carter holdovers—Pezzullo, McNeil or me—would be next?

UNITED STATES LAUNCHES MAJOR DIPLOMATIC INITIATIVE AGAINST NICARAGUA: WASHINGTON, D.C., FEBRUARY 2–4, 1981. Secretary of State Alexander Haig approved a major worldwide diplomatic initiative against

Nicaragua, Cuba and the Soviet Union for their support of the Salvadoran insurgency. We laid out information on arms smuggling and the U.S. position that "no U.S. government can sit idly by while the Soviet bloc arms terrorists seeking to overthrow a legitimate friendly government in Central America" in démarches made in major world capitals. We also released previously classified intelligence and captured documents describing Soviet and Cuban agreement to support the insurgency. Lawrence Eagleburger, assistant secretary for European affairs, and representatives of five other agencies were sent to European capitals on this mission. Later, State published a supporting white paper, "Communist Interference in El Salvador."

The latter, released with great fanfare, was found to contain a number of factual errors, speculative assertions and exaggerations that undermined its credibility. Its author, career officer Jon Glassman, subsequently explained that in the rush to publish "we completely screwed it up."[15]

This initiative met with only limited success and was not helped by the botched white paper.

TEXACO REFINERY DISPUTE COMES TO FORE: TEGUCIGALPA, HONDURAS, FEBRUARY 2, 1981. Trouble between the Honduran government and Texaco, which owned and operated the only oil refinery, had been brewing for months. It was essentially a commercial dispute between the government and a company enjoying a monopoly position. As petroleum prices had risen in the world market, the government saw an increasing part of its critical foreign exchange going for oil imports, to the detriment of other sectors of the economy. The government also controlled gasoline prices and for political reasons did not wish to pass the full market cost on to consumers. As a result Texaco's profit margins were being squeezed.

The two parties were deadlocked, and neither welcomed our involvement. Texaco had a long tradition of eschewing U.S. assistance in disputes with foreign governments, and local representatives wanted no help from the embassy.[16] The Hondurans, for their part, feared our involvement would bring pressure to meet Texaco's demands. We were happy to watch from the sidelines.

The situation changed dramatically early in the year, however, when Mexico and Venezuela announced a special concessionary "oil facility" for Central America. Under this scheme these two countries provided petroleum at below-market prices to ease the strain on their foreign exchange positions. It was a form of economic assistance, but it also had major implications for Texaco.

First, Texaco, which had previously supplied the crude used by its refinery, was to be deprived of the profit from those sales. Second, according to the company, the refinery was not designed to handle the crude supplied by Mexico and Venezuela, so it could not refine this product without a major investment in new equipment. Further complicating matters was Texaco's experience with an earlier government: according to Texaco, that government had reneged on a firm commitment to raise retail prices. The company did not wish to get burned again and adopted a very tough negotiating approach.

Texaco advised the Honduran government that the refinery agreement would have to be amended to allow the company to make up the loss of profit from crude oil sales. In addition, the government would have to finance the additional refinery investment. Predictably, the Hondurans were outraged by what they considered attempted extortion. In a singularly ill-advised move, the government had gone public almost immediately, converting what had been a straightforward commercial dispute into a major political issue.

Hard-line nationalists in the media, legislature and military saw the confrontation as a reason to expropriate the refinery, and they were beating that drum with vigor. Although Texaco was willing to sell the refinery, it rightfully insisted on full, immediate and effective settlement of its resulting claim if nationalized. If those criteria were not met, it would seek full reimbursement from the Overseas Private Investment Corporation (OPIC), a U.S. government organization that provides insurance coverage against such risks. The dispute would then become a government-to-government issue. That could trigger suspension of economic assistance and other cooperation until the claim was resolved.[17] Few things, in my judgment, could be more damaging to our policy interests in Honduras. Washington concurred..

In meetings with Paz, Elvir and others I had taken the position that this dispute should be resolved without our involvement. Once the expropriation issue surfaced, however, I was compelled to point out the potential consequences of such action. We recognized that a decision to nationalize a privately held asset was a sovereign act, which Honduras had every right to make. We also took the position that in the expropriation of an American-owned asset, the owners were entitled to be compensated promptly. Absent such settlement, OPIC would be obliged to pay the claim and we might suspend economic assistance and other cooperation until the government paid OPIC.[18]

Paz and Elvir assured me that they did not wish to nationalize or otherwise assume responsibility for the refinery. Others in the government, however, were advocating expropriation, with Zuniga's National Party at or near the forefront. And several newspapers were fanning the fires of public outrage over Texaco's tactics.

We were following this matter closely and keeping State fully apprised. We were also very circumspect in discussing the issue with only the two principals. But the media wouldn't rest. Following a long-scheduled meeting with the "economic cabinet"—the ministers of economy, finance, natural resources and the chair of the planning council—to review our development programs, AID director Oleson, Economic officer Wackerbarth and I were almost overwhelmed by reporters waiting outside the National Palace. Convinced we were there to pressure the government on the Texaco dispute, which had turned nasty over the previous weekend, they were not persuaded by my denials or those of the minister of economy. I reiterated that it was a commercial dispute that didn't involve the embassy.[19] That didn't dampen their speculative fires.

This dispute continued to simmer for the duration of my time in Honduras without resolution. We managed to avoid becoming engaged. Small victories can be important too.

IMF PLAYS HARDBALL: TEGUCIGALPA, HONDURAS, FEBRUARY 2, 1981. I was astounded to learn from the International Monetary Fund's (IMF) local representative that the fund had broken off negotiations with the Honduran government on the extended fund facility (EFF). Tiring of the dilatory Honduran negotiating style, he told them that their proposed austerity plan was inadequate. However, they could have "90 days to see if it had the desired effect" in reducing the public sector deficit but would not have the benefit of the EFF during that period.

I feared that this development would undo much of our work of the previous month. We had been urging the government to come to terms with the IMF as a first step in getting its financial house in order and reestablishing business confidence. I had beaten this drum with President Paz, cabinet ministers, key private sector leaders in Tegucigalpa and San Pedro Sula (asking that they pressure the government) and senior military officers. AID director Oleson and Economic officer Wackerbarth had been drumming the same beat to their contacts. As we saw it, the fund's action would make the Hondurans less likely to accede to its conditions and also undermine our credibility.[20]

I cabled State for guidance; we were instructed to continue our efforts.

SECRETARY HAIG MEETS WITH FOREIGN MINISTER ELVIR: WASHINGTON, D.C., FEBRUARY 3, 1981. Secretary of State Haig and Acting Assistant Secretary Bushnell met briefly with Foreign Minister Elvir and the Honduran ambassador at OAS headquarters. Haig assured Elvir of our continued support for Honduras, adding that there would be "certain changes in U.S. policy toward Central America." Haig also stressed the Cuban role in the current unrest in the region, stating that Honduras was "itself threatened by this intervention and was high on the Cuban list" of targets. He went on to say that President Reagan considered Cuban intervention "totally unacceptable and is prepared to take whatever steps are necessary to terminate it." He apparently did not elaborate.

Elvir assured Haig that his government shared our concerns and was "ready to cooperate in any action program the U.S. might undertake to deal with this problem."[21] Based on the record of that conversation, Elvir was left with no real idea of what we might want but was no doubt reassured by Haig's tough talk. He certainly passed the details of the conversation on to Paz and senior Honduran military officers. Zuniga almost certainly learned the gist from one of them or his son, who was serving in the Honduran embassy at that time. The vague "changes in U.S. policy" formulation could easily be interpreted as signaling a weakening in our support for the transition to constitutional rule, if one so chose. That concerned me. Similarly, the talk about "taking whatever steps are needed" regarding Cuba was no doubt read by the Hondurans as encouraging the Honduran-Argentine effort to develop the anti-Sandinista operation.

State's cable reporting this meeting kept me in the policy loop but provided no basis to respond to Paz's earlier request.

A HEADS-UP FROM A FRIEND: TEGUCIGALPA, HONDURAS, EARLY FEBRUARY 1981. I received a phone call from Raymond G.H. Seitz, the department's deputy executive secretary, alerting me that my name was on the transition team's "hit list" of ambassadors to be replaced. Though expected, the news was disheartening. I resolved to soldier on, providing the best policy advice I could, even when it might be unwelcome, and carrying out instructions scrupulously. The central problem at that time, of course, was the absence of new guidance or instructions to carry out.

A few weeks later Seitz again phoned to report that Haig had decided to ignore the transition team recommendations. Nonetheless, we agreed that I was closely enough identified with the Carter administration to be a prime candidate for early replacement.

BUILDING PUBLIC SUPPORT FOR OUR ASSISTANCE PROGRAM: TEGUCIGALPA, HONDURAS, EARLY FEBRUARY 1981. Information about our economic and social development activities, and their importance for Honduras, was not getting out to the public. In many of my meetings with Hondurans who were not part of the government, I had been struck by their rather shocking ignorance about our programs and aims. In other cases factual ignorance was coupled with a high degree of cynicism—these programs really didn't reach those in need or were mainly sources of income for corrupt politicians, military or officials. Efforts to publicize our programs—special ceremonies each time we signed a new loan or project agreement, issuing press releases and making speeches—weren't having much impact. We usually received minimal coverage and no follow-on. Consequently, we spent a lot of time trying to figure out ways to resolve this problem.

We ultimately came up with two sound ideas: making a special presentation on our development program activities to Honduran private sector leaders; and taking a group of working journalists to visit a number of actual project sites, followed by an in-depth review of the full range of our development program activities. If successful, the journalists' program scheme would give us a cadre of informed newsmen and -women that we could approach in the future. And for all we knew, it might trigger someone's interest in doing an in-depth, results-oriented story. In addition, over the duration of the trip we should be able to build some useful relationships with the working press.

The Private Enterprise Council (COHEP) quickly accepted our proposal, and an early March meeting was set. In the meantime Oleson and Arcos squeezed their respective budgets to find funds to rent buses and cover other expenses for the journalists' tour, which was to last five days. They worked out an itinerary and developed program and background information packets for the participants. Our target date for this tour was the second week in March.

Arcos then had to sell newspaper editors, television program directors and others on the idea that it would be worthwhile to assign good journalists to our project, in effect losing them for five days. It was not always an easy sell, but he did it.

FUSEP LEADER ON REPRESSION AND ARMS TRAFFIC: TEGUCIGALPA, HONDURAS, FEBRUARY 6, 1981. My meeting with Col. Gustavo Alvarez, FUSEP commander and designee to become commander of the armed forces, proved to be extraordinarily frank and insightful. Accompanied by the station chief, I was seeing Alvarez to discuss and assess FUSEP's follow-up on the Comayagua arms-trafficking network.

Once we had covered that business, I asked Alvarez for his views on the apparent increase in domestic subversion and how it could best be handled. His response was candid in the extreme. Western democracies, he stated, are soft, perhaps too soft for their own good, in dealing with communist subversion. The Argentines, on the other hand, had met this threat effectively, identifying and "taking care of" the subversives. That was an effective way to deal with subversion. Continuing, he asserted that Argentina's laws allowed suspected subversives to be held for up to five years before filing charges or bringing them to court. That, he thought, was quite admirable.

Honduras, he continued, needed to modify its outdated criminal code, which, for example, did not cover kidnapping. The judiciary, too, required reform to make the courts more efficient and less corrupt. Absent such changes, he stated flatly that he would opt for the extralegal methods to deal with subversion.

At one point I interrupted his monologue to suggest that extralegal action by a government against subversives and terrorists robs the government of its legitimacy, subverts the legal system and blurs the moral distinctions between the government and the outlaws it is trying to control. That process, as we had witnessed in Nicaragua under Somoza and were now seeing in El Salvador and Guatemala, feeds the opposition and is self-defeating. Might it not be better, I asked, to work within the legal and judicial framework, amending laws and perhaps suspending certain rights and procedures for the duration of a crisis? The British, for example, had done that in Northern Ireland. In this way the government's legitimacy and rule of law are preserved.

Alvarez did not respond directly but asked if I would try to persuade the civilian political leaders (for whom his contempt was evident) of the need to reform the criminal code and the judicial system to deal with subversion. I agreed to do so, having already urged assembly leaders to expedite revision of the criminal code in response to a request from Foreign Minister Elvir. But I stressed that I could not involve myself in the details of defining criminal acts, prescribing penalties or other matters.

In reporting this conversation to State, I noted that Alvarez supported and understood the need for social and economic development programs and change. He was not a "caveman" in that sense. But when it came to subversion, "he would opt for tough, vigorous and extralegal action".[22] At that time we had no evidence FUSEP or the military were engaged in extralegal action in any systematic way, although indices of domestic subversion were mounting. All too soon, however, officially sanctioned abuses appeared. When they did, I cited Alvarez's prophetic comments in my recommendations that we take prompt action to dissuade the Hondurans from pursuing these policies.

Looking back, I suspect Alvarez wished to send a message to the new administration. He was fully aware that several leading figures in our new foreign policy establishment—most notably UN ambassador Jeane Kirkpatrick and Secretary Haig's special emissary, General Vernon Walters—had expressed admiration for the Argentine government and its handling of suspected communists. That being the case, Alvarez was probably telling us that the Honduran military were prepared to follow Argentina's example. Although demurral on our part might have caused them to reconsider, it seems unlikely that we could have changed the course of events absent strong and forthright action. But our failure to respond to Alvarez's remarks was almost certainly interpreted as a green light.

Regarding arms smuggling, Alvarez said that interrogations indicated the arms had been landed in Nicaragua, then taken to Costa Rica for transshipment to give the Sandinistas deniability. The detainees had identified the lead operative in Costa Rica only by his pseudonym and claimed that the captured truck had made only two trips when discovered. Alvarez believed that other vehicles were involved and that the network had been operating about six months.

He also referred to reports that one of Costa Rican president Carazo's sons was directly involved in this clandestine traffic. This came as no surprise. When I had been in Costa Rica, we had information that this son had received big money from the Cubans for facilitating their operations in support of the Sandinista insurgency. Costa Rica had served as the Sandinistas' principal logistics support base.

When we returned to the embassy, I quickly reported this information.[23]

GENERAL NUTTING'S VISIT: TEGUCIGALPA, HONDURAS, FEBRUARY 11–
13, 1981. General and Mrs. Wallace Nutting, accompanied by several members of the Southern Command staff, were welcomed by chief of staff Gen. Mario Chinchilla and other senior officers. Martha and I, and the mission's military officers and spouses, were also at the airport to greet them. Following the arrival ceremony, Martha and Mrs. Nutting were driven to the residence, where the Nuttings stayed. I took the general and others to the chancery for a CT briefing, which was followed by a working lunch at the residence to review our military assistance program. During that session I stressed the need to be extremely circumspect in discussing increased assistance levels with the Hondurans because they tended to interpret the slightest reference to a given figure or piece of equipment as a commitment. I had earlier played this refrain for Nutting as we drove to the chancery. I also noted that the Hondurans had a voracious appetite for military hardware, which our Milgroup constantly sought to dampen.

From his questions during the political portions of the briefing session, I had the impression that Nutting was having trouble grasping the importance of the central element of our Honduran policy—the transition process and elections. Nor did he appear to see its importance in the regional context. It also seemed evident that Nutting and his aides considered our security assistance recommendations—a modest increase in military sales credits and sharply increased training fund grants—insufficiently proactive. And they didn't appear to recognize the pernicious conflict between military assistance levels and development investment. Fortunately, the Defense Department didn't control security assistance allocations.

Following lunch we proceeded to General Staff headquarters where Nutting met President Paz in his capacity as armed forces commander. The service commanders, including Alvarez, all of whose headquarters Nutting would visit later, and senior staff officers, including Torres Arias, were also present. The Hondurans gave us an elaborate briefing, addressing their threat perception and military needs. The briefers spoke in Spanish, so our visitors needed interpreters to keep up. They saw several potential threats. Foremost were two from Nicaragua: Sandinista-sponsored subversion and a possible frontal military attack by the rapidly expanding Sandinista military machine. El Salvador, too, figured in the threat equation, despite the peace treaty. The expansion of its forces and armaments, aided by the United States, along with the Nicaraguan buildup, changed the regional military balance. Although relations with El Salvador were improving, they might deteriorate again, and Honduras had to be ready to defend itself. That required redressing the imbalance. Finally, Guatemalan forces were larger and better armed, creating another potential threat, although bilateral relations were good, if not close.

I found the presentation alarmist in the extreme and was thankful that neither Costa Rica nor Belize had armies. Nutting's aides had been nodding in assent throughout. To respond to these threats, the Hondurans recommended an extensive buildup of their forces. The briefers quickly ran through a long list of equipment and armaments Honduras needed to defend itself—tanks, artillery, aircraft and other goodies. Our Milgroup later came up with a rough cost estimate in excess of $100 million. That compared with our 1981 military assistance funding of $10 million and our total AID program of about $50 million. Even Nutting and his staff were taken aback. Nutting's response indicated sympathy, while carefully avoiding any statement that might have been construed as a commitment of future U.S. assistance. He also found an opportunity to reaffirm the importance of a successful transition. He had gotten the message.

That evening, the Honduran military hosted a gala reception and dinner for the Nuttings and staff at the Air Force officer's club. The Milgroup and attache staff, as well as several other senior mission officials and their wives, were invited. Nutting and I were seated at a table with the senior Honduran officers. It was a bit awkward in that only Chinchilla and Air Force commander Walter Lopez spoke English, and Nutting didn't speak Spanish. But we were getting along.

Over coffee and cigars Nutting commented that the new Panama Canal treaty would probably force the closure of the School of the Americas, a U.S.-operated military training facility for Latin American officers. Consequently, Southern Command expected to need a new school site. Would the Hondurans be interested, he asked? This question came as a complete surprise. Apparently an offhand remark, it had major policy implications. Nutting, although we had plenty of private time together, hadn't raised this subject with me nor indicated any interest in Honduras as a possible site.

Lopez translated Nutting's comment and question for the others. I could almost see the wheels spinning in the Hondurans' heads as they calculated how they might turn this situation to their advantage. Initial comments were positive. Alvarez, however, remained silent. After aimless speculation about the school's possible economic impact and other considerations, Alvarez spoke. He suggested that Honduras might allow the school to be set up in the Olancho area or near Trujillo. Both were extremely remote, undeveloped areas near the eastern frontier with Nicaragua. The other Hondurans nodded sagely, impressed by Alvarez's strategic grasp, since they were worried about possible Nicaraguan incursions into those areas. The presence of a U.S. military facility would provide an additional insurance policy against the exceedingly remote possibility of a Nicaraguan attack. Nutting didn't have a clue as to the significance of Alvarez's response nor the isolation of the areas in question but said he would keep their interest in mind if it became necessary to move the school.

I raised this matter with Nutting the next morning at breakfast, noting that I would have appreciated some warning that he was going to raise this issue with the Hondurans, since I was responsible for our bilateral relations. I also explained the significance of Alvarez's rejoinder and some of its potential consequences. I then urged that his command give us advance notice, and a chance to comment on, any plans it might develop that involved Honduras—including *Halcon Vista*, which was back on the calendar for later in the year. He agreed to do so but seemed displeased with my implied criticism.

Nutting went off on a round of visits to service headquarters and military units, including a quick flying trip to the Honduran Air Force operating base in San Pedro Sula. Colonel Goodwin and other Milgroup officers accompanied the Nutting party on these calls. I had other business: an economic policy review meeting; a review of the mission's operating budget accounts, which were at a critical point, and spending plans; and swearing in a new group of Peace Corps volunteers. I had asked Goodwin to be alert for any untoward comments or commitments; he reported that there had been none.

That evening I hosted a return reception for about 200 people—military, political leaders, government officials and businessmen—in honor of the Nuttings. It seemed to go well.

At noon the next day, after a brief departure ceremony, Nutting and his party headed back to Panama. His commitment to consult with the embassy on plans involving Honduras, repeated on later occasions, was honored largely in the breach. And I continued to make an issue of it at every opportunity.

INTERNATIONAL NEWS REPEATS HONDURAN TROOP BUILDUP CANARD: TEGUCIGALPA, HONDURAS, FEBRUARY 12, 1981. The French wire service, AFP, reported the spurious allegations that Honduras had deployed large numbers of troops along the border with El Salvador and was engaging in military operations in that area. Further, this account alleged that the troop buildup was the result of "American advisors who entered Honduras in January." AFP specifically attributed this story to the Coordinator of Solidarity with the Salvadoran People.[24]

This was a clear case of deliberate disinformation accepted as reality. It would not be the last time I wrote an unclassified cable refuting such allegations point by point. I sent it to Paris and our other European embassies, as well as State, the Central American posts and military addressees.[25]

HONDURAN PRIEST ARRESTED, RELEASED: TEGUCIGALPA, HONDURAS, FEBRUARY 13, 1981. Father Fausto Milla, a Honduran priest from the Copan diocese, was arrested as he returned from Mexico. He was carrying $36,000 in cash when detained and was charged with introducing "subversive materials" into the country and foreign currency violations. The money was confiscated.

Presenting General Wallace H. Nutting, commander in chief, U.S. Southern Command, to Constituent Assembly president (and Liberal Party leader) Roberto Suazo Cordova; Martha Binns and Suazo Cordova aide Carlos Flores are shown in background February 1981.

Milla was a chief propagandist for the Coordinator for Solidarity with the Salvadoran Peoples. In Mexico, according to our sources, he had been working with Salvadoran insurgent groups to develop disinformation alleging Honduran army atrocities on refugees.[26] We also knew that Milla had earlier been involved publicizing the spurious May 1980 "Rio Sumpul massacre," in which the Salvadoran army was alleged to have killed several hundred Salvadoran refugees trying to enter Honduras. He was one of the most active of the Copan priests supporting the Salvadoran insurgents. And there was little doubt that the money he had been carrying was destined for the insurgent support network.

He was released February 17.

ANOTHER MEETING WITH ZUNIGA, AND MORE: TEGUCIGALPA, HONDURAS, FEBRUARY 16, 1981. I lunched again with Zuniga at a local restaurant, knowing that he was trying to undermine my position with both the Honduran military and the Reagan administration. And he knew that I knew, which was part of a delicate minuet. I didn't like the rogue, but I respected his skills, cunning and sheer gall.

On this occasion he seemed exceedingly self-confident, even smug, and in good humor. We chatted with friends and acquaintances who stopped by our table. Most observers would have guessed we were having a grand time.

The substance of our conversation was minimal, focusing on elections preparations and his complaints about them. The Liberals, he said (repeatedly), were cooking the electoral registration rolls in their favor, removing or refusing to register National Party members. This was a perversion of simple justice and a violation of electoral law. Unless the chicanery ceased, the Nationalists would propose an indefinite delay in the elections, thus blocking the transition.

I didn't wish to get into an argument, but neither did I wish to be considered a pushover or a fool. So I pointed out that the Liberals were making similar claims about his party in areas where they were in control. And officials handling the registration rolls—under supervision by representatives of all parties—had told us they believed these problems could be resolved by review of the rolls, once they were closed, several months prior to the actual elections. Accordingly, current irregularities did not appear sufficient reason to delay elections. And in any event, I added, the United States remained firmly committed to elections and the transition process: we would vigorously oppose any effort to delay or frustrate them.

Zuniga knew I was bluffing about our resolve on the elections. The new administration had not yet reaffirmed our support for the transition process nor my instructions, and he knew it. On the other hand, my instructions were still valid, and I was sticking to them. He also knew many of his Washington friends bought into his allegations about the Liberal Party and irregularities in the voter rolls and were working to sell these views to the new administration.

At about the same time, Arcos was getting an interesting earful from Suazo Cordova and his aide, Carlos Flores. Zuniga, they claimed, was still burning with resentment over the loss of the assembly elections the previous April. He blamed former ambassador Jaramillo for that, believing that her influence was what had persuaded the military to hold open, honest elections. That had deprived him of victory. Similarly, he considered me an obstacle to realization of his ambitions by virtue of my outspoken support for the electoral process. Consequently, Zuniga had launched a campaign—locally and in the United States—to discredit me by citing my contacts with trade unionists and the Liberal Party's ALIPO faction as evidence that I was a "dangerous social democrat." They also claimed that Zuniga was fomenting labor and student unrest in order to provoke a preemptive military coup and foreclose the promised elections.

Customarily, when we are told of the alleged sins of one party by its major opposition, we take the information with several grains of salt. In this case, however, their accusations were entirely consistent with what we knew from other sources—prominent businessmen, dissident National Party members, and others. They all squared with actual events. Further substantiation would soon be at hand.

When Arcos related this I realized that reporting it would make me appear self-serving. Yet it was important, and Washington needed to know how leading figures assessed the local political environment. I therefore asked Arcos to work with Walker to produce a report they felt comfortable with; I would have no role in its preparation or editing. The upshot was an outstanding assessment of Zuniga's apparent plans, goals and likely actions.[27] Although it was well received in the Inter-American bureau, it was almost certainly discounted elsewhere in government as a self-serving effort.

ANOTHER ATTACK: ALLEGED MEETING WITH SALVADORAN MARXISTS: TEGUCIGALPA, HONDURAS, FEBRUARY 18, 1981. A local radio newscaster having close ties to Zuniga broadcast that I had met with "leaders of El Salvador's Marxist insurgency" the previous day, that I had a "preference for the Latin American left" and that I was acting contrary to U.S. policy in the region. These fabrications were designed to undermine, and we were certain they were planted by Zuniga. He seemed to be stepping up his campaign against me.

Arcos urged that I authorize a press release denying the allegations in the strongest terms. Walker agreed. After weighing the pros and cons, I gave Arcos the go ahead. The statement he prepared characterized the allegations as "false, absurd, tendentious and slanderous," adding that they were designed to undermine relations between the United States and Honduras. I approved it, and out it went.

The press gave our statement prominent treatment, with *Tiempo* going all out. It carried a headline story, an item in its political column that ridiculed the radio report, and a cartoon lampooning it.[28] We believed we had won that round, at least in Honduras.

I later learned that the original story, like others that followed, was sent to Senator Helms's aide, Richard McCormack. He then spread the clippings around Washington, as evidence of my leftist sympathies and disloyalty to the administration.[29]

I also learned similar allegations had earlier been circulated in the United States by "Hemisphere Hotline," a private newsletter published by Virginia Prewett that circulated among the far right. That item was accompanied by a particularly nasty fiction that "Amb. Binns is also reported to be maneuvering and applying pressures to get conservatives out of the Honduran cabinet and get liberals into those jobs before he can be recalled to Washington and replaced."[30] Anyone at all familiar with the transition arrangements dividing cabinet positions evenly between the two parties would know it was ludicrous. This slander too was planted by Zuniga or his allies.

IMF ISSUE: PRIVATE SECTOR WEIGHS IN, MOVES PAZ: TEGUCIGALPA, HONDURAS, FEBRUARY 17–18, 1981. Pressure on the government to come to terms on the extended fund facility (EFF) was increasing. The head of the San Pedro Sula Chamber of Commerce phoned to report that he had been summoned to a meeting of the economic cabinet later in the day. Speaking for the chamber, he would urge the government to increase tax revenues and take the other steps needed to meet the Fund's conditions. This was an important development, and several influential Tegucigalpa businessmen and bankers had already informed the government that they were prepared to accept increased taxes to secure the EFF.

More surprising was the attitude of National Party leader Ricardo Zuniga. After vigorously criticizing the government for having allowed the economic situation to deteriorate to its current point—which was somewhat ironic, as both the Finance Ministry and Central Bank were controlled members of his party—he agreed in principle to support a tax measure that would meet the IMF's requirements.[31] I had yet not had a chance to speak with Suazo Cordova, but expected that he would agree if the National Party was on board. Since he expected to lead the next government, it was in his interest to alleviate the economic situation before it became a full-blown crisis.

I met with President Paz the next day at my residence. Briefing me on the economic cabinet meeting, he said that his private sector advisers were as one on the need to increase revenue to meet the IMF's conditions. To forge a consensus behind the tax package, his advisers had gone from the cabinet session to a meeting with the Honduran Private Enterprise Council (COHEP). We agreed that COHEP support was essential.

Once the private sector was on board, Paz could deal with the assembly. If the civilian political leaders balked, he was prepared to impose it by decree. It was essential, he asserted, that the government move quickly to resolve this problem.[32] This was a big shift from his passive attitude a few weeks earlier, but there was still some way to go before the EFF agreement would be in place.

SECURITY SURVEY TEAM VISIT: TEGUCIGALPA, HONDURAS, FEBRUARY 21–28, 1981. Our deteriorating security environment caused State to dispatch a seven-member Security Enhancement Team to survey our facilities and devise solutions to our many security problems. Unlike earlier groups, this one included structural engineers, an architect and other professionals from State's Office of Foreign Buildings who could come up with design proposals on the spot, as well as security officers.

The team was in town for ten days and worked hard. They were able to improve the several projects we had underway or planned and developed new approaches to several physical security problems. Their plan to make the AID annex building safer was imaginative and innovative, although costly. They also surveyed all residential properties, suggesting a series of relatively low-cost steps that would enhance the security of all our employees and their families. The team also endorsed our view that the location of the Marine house was a potential danger in an emergency. They were soon moved to a house very near the chancery.

This team also addressed longer-term issues, endorsing our recommendation that State acquire the other half of the block on which the chancery was located. It was a large parcel containing a small, unoccupied restaurant building. That vacant property represented one of the chancery's most serious vulnerabilities.[33] Shortly before this team's arrival, we had discovered what appeared to be an attempt to tunnel under the chancery wall from behind the abandoned restaurant. We staked out this site for several days, but no one had shown up to continue the excavation. The hole was filled in and we established a regular perimeter patrol to preclude recurrence. State quickly authorized us to lease the property, with an option to buy. Later the sale was concluded and the chancery expanded.

The CT was very pleased with this group's work, and their visit had a positive impact on post morale.

HONDURANS OFFER TO EXCHANGE ARMS TRAFFICKERS FOR VINELLI: TEGUCIGALPA, HONDURAS, FEBRUARY 21, 1981. The Vinelli family advised us that the government had offered to exchange the 12 Salvadorans and Costa Ricans arms smugglers captured in Comayagua for Vinelli's freedom. The family, near settlement with the Salvadoran kidnappers, thought this would complicate negotiations. They declined the offer.

We knew the Hondurans were probably going to release the traffickers because Honduras's outdated penal code required that they be granted bail. Once freed, they would be out of the country in a flash. But to exchange them for a hostage, we thought, would be a serious error. It would only encourage future kidnapping whenever anyone involved with insurgent supply networks or other subversion was captured.

Because of that concern, I asked State for permission to approach senior officials to see if they could find some way to hold these prisoners and ultimately try them. State did not respond.[34]

SANDINISTAS ACCUSE INDIAN LEADERS OF PLOTTING: MANAGUA, NICARAGUA, FEBRUARY 23, 1981. The Nicaraguan government charged that Miskito Indians, under the leadership of Steadman Fagoth, were engaged in a plot to split the Atlantic coast area away from the rest of Nicaragua. Fagoth and other Indian leaders were arrested.[35] This increased pressure on the Miskitos soon led to their mass exodus into remote regions of northeastern Honduras, creating another refugee problem.

OAS PROPOSAL FOR GOOD OFFICES ON EL SALVADOR: TEGUCIGALPA, HONDURAS, FEBRUARY 24, 1981. The Organization of American States

(OAS) proposed a consultative meeting on El Salvador to explore a possible negotiated settlement in that country. We had no instructions to discuss the issue with the Hondurans, so we went about our regular business. Then we received a cable from Fred Chapin, our charge d'affaires in San Salvador, urging in the strongest terms that the United States oppose the OAS effort. After reading Chapin's arguments, I had serious doubts about them. Briefly summarized, he argued:

• The Marxist paramilitary groups in the FDR/DRU would probably be unwilling to negotiate and, in any event, would be unacceptable partners in a transition government (probably true).
• Ungo's National Revolutionary Movement (MNR), an affiliate of the Socialist International, had never demonstrated significant popular support and included another faction composed of those who were not in exile or opposed to the junta. Consequently, the Ungo group lacked legitimacy and should be ignored (I disagreed—the Socialist International recognized Ungo's faction, giving it international standing), especially since it would not negotiate with the junta as then constituted (probably true).
• The Salvadoran military opposed negotiations with the rebels (questionable), as did the Christian Democratic Party, which controlled three of the five seats on the junta (not entirely correct, as Duarte had earlier told me that he was willing to talk with Ungo and others, although Chavez Mena later said that if he advocated talks with the rebels, he would be killed by a right-wing death squad).
• The OAS was an ineffectual institution, and we should go to great lengths to block its involvement in El Salvador (largely true, but the OAS often played a useful role).
• Therefore, the United States should oppose the OAS initiative and instead encourage only negotiations between the junta and opposition groups that remained in the country (e.g., labor organizations, the private sector, the MNR dissident faction) over an electoral process that would be open to all (this argument ignored the U.S. domestic and international political dimensions of the conflict, and we were losing in those arenas).[36]

Chapin was missing a critical point: we needed to influence congressional and international perceptions, as well as strengthen the junta and move the country toward democracy. I discussed this cable with Walker, who knew El Salvador and many of its players as well or better than I did. He agreed. Before we had our arguments fully developed, Ambassador Frank McNeil in Costa Rica responded to Chapin's cable, taking issue with his views on a possible OAS role and noting that Costa Rica was supporting this initiative.[37]

I decided to weigh in, sending a cable arguing in favor of engaging the rebel coalition in talks with the junta because it would be useful in strengthening our international position and credibility.[38] It was sent to our embassies in the major European and Latin American capitals, as well as to State.

Chapin, however, won the argument. We refused to support any efforts to negotiate an end to the bloodbath in El Salvador for nearly another decade. Ironically, when the United States finally came around to supporting a negotiated solution, Bill Walker was our ambassador in El Salvador and played a key role in its attainment. A further irony: in the late 1980s, when the Salvadoran peace talks began to get serious, it was the UN that managed the negotiations, and the United States would have been happy with OAS directing the show.

DISINFORMATION: ALLEGED MASSACRE OF SALVADORANS: EL SALVADOR/HONDURAS FRONTIER, LATE FEBRUARY 1981. On February 23, 1981, the *Miami Herald* alleged that over 300 Salvadorans were killed when caught by a joint Salvadoran/Honduran military operation as they crossed the Sumpul River, which marks the border.[39] This got our attention.

Our initial soundings produced no evidence of unusual Honduran troop movements in the area. The *Herald* account, however, bore a strong resemblance to an attache report of the previous week involving an incident near Colomoncagua wherein Honduran troops turned back a group of some 300 Salvadorans, barring their entry into Honduras. The critical differences were that there were no Salvadoran troops in the area, no shots were fired and no one was injured. This incident had been witnessed by a French physician.[40] I decided to send a political officer to the frontier for further information.

He brought back little that was new. He had spoken to the French physician who witnessed the (improper) stopping of Salvadorans seeking refuge in Honduras and confirmed there had been no Salvadoran forces in the area nor any shots fired. By his account, several hundred Salvadorans, mostly women and children, but including a few men, arrived at the river. A Honduran patrol approached as they started to cross, ordering them to remain in El Salvador. They turned back. As the Hondurans were armed, a threat of force may have been implied, but there were no threats.

We reported these findings and our judgment was that the *Herald* story was typical disinformation.

PROPOSED ASSIGNMENT OF U.S. TROOPS TO HONDURAS: TEGUCIGALPA, HONDURAS, FEBRUARY 24, 1981. Colonel Goodwin came to my office on urgent business. He had just spoken to a Southern Command officer who advised him that the command had sent the Joint Chiefs of Staff (JCS) a very hush-hush proposal to deploy covertly up to 100 U.S. troops along the border with El Salvador. He had no other details.

By the time Goodwin, Walker and my secretary, Amy, were able to pull me down from the ceiling, I had decided to lodge an extremely strong dissent and protest. Clearly, Nutting and his command were continuing to ignore my repeated requests to review and comment on their plans involving Honduras. I considered this incident especially egregious, not only because of the serious policy implications of the proposed action but also because Nutting had been in Honduras less than two weeks before, assuring me he would consult. If he considered the informal call to Goodwin fulfillment of his commitment, he and I needed to work on definitions and semantics.

I sent a NODIS cable addressed to Acting Assistant Secretary Bushnell, vigorously opposing such action. I could not send an information copy of this cable to Southern Command because State regulations prohibited lateral transmission of NODIS messages. My arguments were these:

• The Honduran government would probably refuse to permit assignment of U.S. troops.

• If it could be persuaded to agree, it would be at very high cost; would trigger a strong anti-U.S. backlash, alienating many Hondurans who were then supportive of USG policies; would provide the incipient Honduran insurgents with a new cause; and would make our bilateral relationship more difficult.

• Moreover, this step would prove the left's allegations that the United States was preparing to intervene militarily in the Salvadoran conflict and was seeking to use Honduras as our tool. This would undermine our credibility, as well as give Nicaragua, Cuba and the USSR new propaganda weapons.

In my judgment this proposal was singularly harebrained. It also seemed evident to me that such action would trigger a political firestorm domestically. But advice on domestic politics from ambassadors is never welcomed, so I held my tongue. Concluding, I wrote:

> From where I sit, we would be hard pressed to find another proposal which at this time would be more self-defeating than the assignment of a large number of U.S. military to Honduras.... What we need is a coordinated, low-key approach to the frontier problem which: involves increased U.S. civilian presence (through visits) in frontier areas; provides modest levels of carefully targeted additional assistance to the Honduran military; and encourages the Honduran military to better utilize its existing equipment and manpower. Such a response would be measured and cost-effective, and would not trigger serious counter-reactions. I also believe—as you are aware—that by helping the GOH [Government of Honduras] manage the Salvadoran refugee problem we would greatly facilitate GOH efforts to control the security situation in the frontier area, as well as meet very real humanitarian needs.[41]

Atypically, response to this cable was swift, although not exactly what I had expected. The next morning I received a phone call from Bushnell, who was easily as angry as I had been the previous day but for other reasons. My cable, he said, caused a storm in State. The Southern Command proposal had been very closely held, known to only three people in State prior to my cable, which had blown it open (NB. Only 20 copies of my NODIS cable had been printed, and their distribution was controlled by Haig's secretariat). When I argued that this was a serious issue on which I was entitled—no, obligated—to comment and pointed out that NODIS is the most limited distribution I was able to use, he had no answer. Bushnell calmed down a bit in the course of our discussion, but it was clear that he had been reamed by the secretary's office, and was still smarting. That my cable made a contribution to the swift demise of this proposal is questionable. The idea was so absurd and politically risky, it no doubt fell of its own weight. But if I did help, hurrah.

The notion of a covert operation of extended duration on the frontier with El Salvador, involving 100 or so U.S. Special Forces troops, was an oxymoron. That area, isolated though it was, was crawling with Salvadoran insurgents, refugees, refugee workers from several countries, Honduran clergy who supported the insurgents, Honduran military and civilians, and, most significantly, journalists from several countries. The chances of keeping such an operation secret were nil.

WHITE URGES CONGRESS TO OPPOSE MILITARY ASSISTANCE FOR EL SALVADOR: WASHINGTON, D.C., FEBRUARY 25, 1981. Testifying before a congressional committee, former ambassador Robert White strongly opposed resumption of military assistance to El Salvador, stating that "the chief killer of Salvadorans is the government security forces" and that resumption of this aid would undermine "a fledgling government headed by civilians who are desperately trying to bring a recalcitrant military under control."[42]

SOCIALIST INTERNATIONAL MEETING IN PANAMA: PANAMA CITY, PANAMA, FEBRUARY 26, 1981. The Socialist International (SI) convened a special regional meeting of Latin American social democratic parties to discuss the Central America situation, ways to find a negotiated solution to what was becoming a civil war in El Salvador and avoid a larger conflict in the region.[43] Although not an SI affiliate, the Sandinista National Liberation Front (FSLN) attended.

As a result SI secretary General Bernt Carlsson, a Swede, was authorized to approach the United States, offering good offices to try to negotiate a solution to the Salvadoran conflict. I had seen a lot of Carlsson when assigned in London and had great respect for his intelligence and integrity. We did not always agree, but we had become good friends.

Carlsson met with Acting Assistant Secretary Bushnell on March 3 to formally offer the SI's good offices. Bushnell told Carlsson that it would not be useful for the United States to become involved.[44]

PROPOSED COVERT OPERATIONS IN CENTRAL AMERICA: WASHINGTON, D.C., FEBRUARY 27, 1981. The CIA proposed an extensive set of covert actions in Central America designed to counter Cuban subversion and meet the challenges of local conflicts. These proposals were subject to interagency review, prior to presidential approval. The embassy was not consulted about, nor privy to, these proposals or deliberations, although the Station may have been.

State Department Counselor Bud McFarlane this date sent a memo to Secretary Haig regarding this initiative, emphasizing that "the key point to be made now is that while we must move promptly, we must assure that our political, economic, diplomatic, propaganda, military and covert actions are well coordinated."[45]

That was excellent advice although, in light of McFarlane's later performance at the NSC, rather ironic. Such coordination proved largely unattainable. The pursuit of separate agendas, primacy of ideological considerations, lack of interagency and interpersonal trust and the absence of effective oversight and coordination mechanisms sowed the seeds that later grew into the Iran-Contra scandal.

HINTON NAMED AMBASSADOR TO EL SALVADOR: WASHINGTON, D.C., FEBRUARY 28, 1981. The White House announced the nomination of Deane Hinton, a career officer with extensive Latin American experience, as ambassador to El Salvador, replacing White.[46]

ADMINISTRATION REQUESTS EMERGENCY AID FOR EL SALVADOR: WASHINGTON, D.C., MARCH 2, 1981. The White House requested Congress approve $100 million in emergency economic assistance and $15 million in military aid for El Salvador. Public statements and Senate testimony indicated that this assistance would not be linked to human rights performance by the Salvadoran government.[47]

KIDNAPPED BANKER FREED: TEGUCIGALPA, HONDURAS, MARCH 3, 1981. I received an evening call from Walker reporting that Paul Vinelli had been released. Vinelli had lost considerable weight, 30 to 40 pounds, but otherwise seemed in good condition. He and his wife had left immediately for the United States. That was great news.

5

Improving Environment Sours Quickly

SUMMARY—More security assistance complaints and coup rumors—arms interdiction plans and problems—congressional visitor—fabricated press attack and rebuttal—Milgroup misjudgments create new problems—irrational Honduran military plans and bizarre Paz effort to meet Reagan stress relationship—more terrorism and a hijacking—diversion of refugee supplies—military stalemate in El Salvador—Sandinistas protest Contra activities

ASSESSMENTS AND ANALYSES ARE FLOWING: TEGUCIGALPA, HONDURAS, EARLY MARCH 1981. The mission was beginning to hit its stride. The previous month had seen the completion and dispatch of several important policy assessments—especially our recommendations for the Honduran armed forces and the World Bank and International Monetary Fund (IMF) programs—and others were in their final stages. Arcos's review of the Honduran Church and its role was ready to go;[1] the study of corruption in the government, which Walker and I had taken over from the Political Section, was in final review stages;[2] and the working group on the arms infiltration problem was due to complete its analysis and recommendations shortly.[3]

Finally, Walker's historical assessment of Zuniga and his record in various governments was progressing.[4] Beyond that, I thought our day-to-day reporting was becoming crisper, better focused and increasingly analytical.

I thought Oleson's shop was doing first-rate work. USIS, under Arcos's strong leadership, was doing a terrific job. Recognizing the Milgroup's lack of linguistic skills, the often prickly nature of its relations with the Hondurans and the pressures it was under from Southern Command, I was satisfied with its work.

The same went for the rest of the mission, with the exceptions of Joint Administrative and the Consular Sections.

119

NICARAGUAN JUNTA REORGANIZED: MANAGUA, NICARAGUA, MARCH 4, 1981. The Sandinistas reorganized the governing junta, converting it from a five- to a three-person body, in the process eliminating the two junta members that were not members of the Sandinista National Liberation Front (FSLN). It was now an exclusively Sandinista body, with Daniel Ortega as the junta coordinator.[5]

MEETING WITH HONDURAN BUSINESS GROUP: TEGUCIGALPA, HONDURAS, MARCH 4, 1981. Our economic team met with the Honduran Private Enterprise Council (COHEP) to discuss the economic outlook and brief business leaders on our AID program. There was a broad coincidence of views between the COHEP and the mission on the Honduran economy. I stressed the pivotal nature of domestic investment, if Honduras were to continue to grow. Flight of private capital was, at the time, one of the most critical negative economic factors. The council members were responsible for much of it, so I laid in on them. Their concerns were largely political (e.g., growing instability in the region, as well as the uncertainties surrounding the transition to democracy), so I again affirmed USG support for Honduran security and the transition process. And I emphasized that we would oppose any action to delay or block the elections.

AID director Oleson described the scope and direction of our assistance efforts, and our hosts seemed impressed. Many, however, voiced concern that our assistance dollars were being siphoned off by corrupt officials, creating additional debt and leaving nothing. Oleson explained how development agreements worked, how they were monitored and funds disbursed in tranches as the government met performance criteria, and how actual expenditures and records were audited by AID. This impressed them, although some were still dubious that we were preventing the "leakage" of development funds. They undoubtedly knew more about corruption than we did, especially because some of them may have been involved in questionable practices.

This was the first time COHEP had received a formal briefing of U.S. policy goals and development programs. This session was also extremely important for us in the way of feedback. It was, at least in part, a precursor of our later Economic Support Fund (ESF) grant proposal designed to encourage increased domestic investment and deter private capital outflows. It was approved after my departure.

The most interesting aspect of this session was, however, political. Support for the transition was nearly unanimous, but most had qualms about the uncertainties that lay ahead. Two members expressed serious reservations and seemed to favor delaying elections—one was close to Zuniga, and the other was a front man for several military investments. But it was the Council president, Fernando Lardizabal, who dropped the bomb. Noting that he was speaking for himself, he suggested that a military coup might not be such a bad idea. An outspoken opponent of military rule and corruption, openly contemptuous of Zuniga, and very conservative, he was much respected. His comment stunned most of his colleagues who, after regaining their composure, made it clear that they did not agree.

Explaining his view, Lardizabal asserted that Paz was becoming increasingly non compos, the two principal presidential candidates were incompetent rogues leading corrupt parties, and with the military they at least knew what they were getting. It was hard to disagree with these assertions, but there were few present who shared the leap in logic that this required a coup, with all the consequences that would follow.

Everyone was awaiting my response. I thanked Lardizabal for his candor and emphasized that I would respond in the same vein because I did not wish anyone present to be in any doubt as to our position. First, the nature of the Honduran government was a matter only the Hondurans could decide. However, my instructions were clear: the United States fully supported the transition process and the earlier decision to return to a democratic regime. We had not wavered on that point.

The private sector, military, political parties and virtually every other institution in the country had decided that a return to constitutional rule via elections was the best course. As a result, a Constituent Assembly had been elected to write a new constitution. This had lifted and excited the expectations of the Honduran people by promising an elected president and Congress. Should that decision now be reversed, frustrating these expectations, I feared they would reap a whirlwind of popular discontent. I also noted that frustration of the transition would make it more difficult for the United States to continue its assistance programs.[6]

From the nodding of heads and subsequent comments of other COHEP members, it was evident that the overwhelming majority agreed. In the next few days a number of the dozen participants contacted me in person or by phone to express their shock and sharp disagreement with Lardizabal. Without exception, these businessmen urged me to keep the pressure on. But they also reported a resurgence of coup rumors.

This meeting drew attention from the media. We had, however, coordinated what we would say to the press, in effect speaking with a single voice. Lardizabal and I met jointly with the press immediately after the meeting. It had been, we said, a very useful exchange of impressions about the current situation, prospects for the future and our AID program.[7]

COUP AND OTHER DISQUIETING REPORTS: TEGUCIGALPA, HONDURAS, MARCH 5, 1981. My concern about renewed coup rumors was growing, especially in the light of the feedback I had received from businessmen. I was also troubled by wide speculation that the Reagan administration was opposed to Suazo Cordova because of alleged Sandinista sympathies and would accept a coup in order to block his election. There was no doubt within the CT that Zuniga was the source of these canards, aided by his U.S. allies (or dupes). Military officers opposing the transition, of course, were happy to encourage these rumors any way they could. Stepping up our collection effort, we confirmed that rumor mills were again operating at high speed, despite very strong support for elections.

Most of the coup rumors centered on the military's alleged dissatisfaction with Paz. I had also sensed a change in him, a kind of distancing, but nothing I could put my finger on. He had asked me on several occasions if I had a reply to his earlier question about what the United States wanted him to do on the frontier, but I had nothing to report. He was aware of Haig's meeting with Elvir, but that had not provided an answer. His uncertainty about our intentions, coupled with swirling speculation about possible changes in our policy, deteriorating relations with—and the enormous arms buildup of—the Sandinista regime and the military stalemate in El Salvador must have weighed heavily on him.

He had not visited my residence for some time and seemed tentative and less candid than previously. There were reports that he had again fallen off the wagon. Initially, I supposed that his behavior change stemmed from his increased drinking and stress from renewal of coup rumors, of which he had to be aware. In fact, the situation was much worse than I realized, as I was soon to discover.

ARMS INFILTRATION ASSESSMENT AND RECOMMENDATIONS: TEGU-CIGALPA, HONDURAS, EARLY MARCH 1981. I had earlier set up a working group to look at the arms infiltration issue and devise strategies to help deal with it. Members were Walker, the station chief, Political Section chief, the Defense attaché and the Milgroup commander and his Army Section chief. We examined the three principal infiltration routes: air, land and sea. The traffic originated in Nicaragua, Costa Rica (from Cuban-held stocks) and, possibly, Panama. The importance of the air and sea routes was growing. Honduras lacked the capability to interdict those routes, although its cooperation would be important for anything the United States might try to do. Overland routes were another story. The Hondurans could play a critical role in disrupting or closing down this traffic with the right assistance and support.

Interdicting overland traffic looked like a manageable challenge. The earlier seizure near Comayagua indicated that the contraband weapons were being hidden in heavy trucks that moved most of the cargo in Central America. The arms were then consolidated at a depot and later divided into quantities that could be hidden in door panels of cars or small trucks for delivery to the insurgents along the frontier.

The most effective place to direct our efforts was at the larger shipments as they entered the country, which we called the "wholesale" side of the traffic, rather than trying to stop the many smaller shipments that were actually delivered to the rebels, which we labeled the "retail" side.

Virtually all overland cargo moving into Honduras from the south moved on the Pan American highway. It was the only road connection of consequence. And traffic flow on secondary and tertiary roads was so light that any vehicles could be thoroughly searched without seriously disrupting commerce. Attempting to interdict the flow of arms from Honduras into El Salvador— the thrust of Southern Command's earlier troop deployment recommendation—would be far more difficult, less effective and more apt to lead to direct armed confrontation with the insurgents.

There were many unimproved roads leading to the Salvadoran frontier, and literally hundreds of trails and paths crossing the border in this topographically rugged area. The manpower and other resource demands to exercise even a modicum of control would be far greater than needed to suppress the wholesale traffic. Moreover, success, in terms of quantities seized, would be far less significant.

Our principal recommendation was the formation of an interagency survey team that included the CIA, DEA and Customs and that would work with the mission and FUSEP to develop a comprehensive plan to control the wholesale traffic.[8] As FUSEP had primary responsibility for stopping contraband, and our military were generally prohibited from working with police agencies, we saw Southern Command's role as secondary. But they could work with the Honduran military to disrupt the retail traffic along the Salvadoran frontier and train the army as a backup to FUSEP.

Several Southern Command staff officers came to Tegucigalpa to review the problem with the mission. We found a relatively high degree of agreement as to the nature of the problem and the strategy to address it. Washington, however, was another matter. Both the notion of an interagency approach and the logic of our wholesale/retail argument were resisted.

The initial response to our analysis and recommendations, for example, dealt solely with a military survey team from Southern Command, ignoring FUSEP's primary responsibility for controlling smuggling and frontier commerce. Emphasis on that approach precluded concentrating our efforts on entry points from Nicaragua, the wholesale end of the traffic. The Salvadoran frontier, Washington opined, offered "better opportunities for military operations."[9]

Ultimately, we hosted separate survey teams from the CIA and Southern Command, each developing its own discrete interdiction plan. We tried to coordinate their activities and recommendations with some success, but there was never much action during my tenure. Indeed, the CIA soon became enraptured by its covert Contra operation, while our military focused on building up operating bases and joint exercises. Consequently, an opportunity was lost. The absence of a coordinated approach reflected individual agency agendas and the absence of an effective interagency coordinating mechanism. The NSC under Richard Allen was simply not up to the task, and the Inter-American bureau was awaiting Enders's confirmation.

NICARAGUAN EXILE GROUP MOVES TO HONDURAS: GUATEMALA CITY, GUATEMALA, EARLY MARCH 1981. The Argentine intelligence service assisted a Nicaraguan counterrevolutionary force in Guatemala to move to Honduras, where a training camp was established. Later, a group of 60 Nicaraguan exiles, mostly ex–National Guardsmen, was sent to Argentina for training in intelligence, sabotage, psychological and tactical operations.[10] We were unaware of these developments.

SUGGESTED REGIONAL MILITARY ASSISTANCE FOR EL SALVADOR: WASHINGTON, D.C., MARCH 6, 1981. The NSC and the Inter-Agency group for Latin America were seized with the deteriorating situation in El Salvador. Their efforts to find ways to turn things around led to a notion that Honduras and Guatemala might be able to provide the Salvadoran military with direct military assistance—"materiel, training and advisors."[11] I couldn't speak for our embassy in Guatemala, but to me this idea illustrated starkly the new administration's lack of understanding of the regional situation generally and that of Honduras specifically.

The Honduran military had been using every meeting with U.S. officials, as Washington well knew and we had been reporting for months, to express: their deep concerns over what they saw as a strategic threat arising from the regional arms imbalance; their need for more materiel and munitions; their inability to adequately fund routine operations; and their grim budgetary outlook. It seemed apparent that no one in Washington was paying attention to the Hondurans or reading our reporting. Even more absurd was the notion that Honduras's ill-trained military could provide Salvadoran forces, with nearly two years of often intensive combat experience, with useful training or advisory services.

Because we had been asked for our views, I convened key staff to prepare a response. Our cable concluded that there was little chance Honduras could provide useful assistance, unless we increased our materiel transfers to Honduras, which might then allow them to transfer obsolete arms and equipment to the Salvadorans. Financing modern equipment for Honduran forces so that obsolete materiel could be given to El Salvador was neither rational nor cost effective.[12] Fortunately, we heard no more of this scheme.

REGIONAL MILITARY ASSISTANCE FUNDING REQUEST: WASHINGTON, D.C., MARCH 8, 1981. Acting Deputy Assistant Secretary Bushnell appeared before the House Foreign Affairs Committee to present our regional security assistance request for Fiscal Year 1982. The requested total for the hemisphere was $81.5 million in Foreign Military Sales (FMS) credit, of which $35 million was earmarked for Central America and $7.2 million for training grants. The Honduran shares were $10 million and $750 thousand, respectively.[13] We so advised the Hondurans; they were gravely disappointed.

REAGAN APPROVES COVERT ACTION IN CENTRAL AMERICA: WASHINGTON, D.C., MARCH 9, 1981. President Reagan signed his first Presidential Finding, authorizing covert action in Central America. It built upon that signed earlier by President Carter, which authorized covert financial assistance to opposition groups—unions, political organizations, media—inside Nicaragua. The stated purpose of the Reagan finding was "to provide all forms of training, equipment and related assistance to cooperating governments throughout Central America in order to counter foreign-sponsored subversion and terrorism."[14]

Although I received no formal notification of this development, the station chief did advise me that a finding had been approved to allow the CIA to send a team to Honduras for the purpose of developing an arms interdiction program with FUSEP. He also assured me that I would be involved in the development of this plan and be kept fully informed of resulting activities.

The CIA interpreted this finding broadly. Congressional oversight committees were told that its purpose was exclusively to interdict clandestine arms traffic. According to a later report in the *Miami Herald,* the CIA had immediately advised Nicaraguan exile groups that the president authorized covert operations in Central America, implying that they would be beneficiaries. The finding, however, referred only to "cooperating governments," which clearly excluded exile groups.[15]

JOURNALISTS VISIT DEVELOPMENT PROJECTS: HONDURAS, MARCH 9–12, 1981. Our program to have Honduran journalists visit AID and Peace Corps development projects was underway. The deputy AID director, Leo Ruelas, led the tour as the three four-wheel drive vehicles pulled out of Tegucigalpa with eight journalists and a TV camera crew. An assistant Peace Corps director and a member of the USIS press section also went along. At each site the party was met by the responsible AID and/or Peace Corps technicians, along with their Honduran counterparts. They visited a variety of project sites between Tegucigalpa and Tela. The tour ended the evening of March 11 at a beach-side resort. This was a small reward for the participants for the discomfort they had endured over their three-day adventure on Honduran byways.

Arcos and I flew to Tela in the late afternoon to meet the party. They were all tired and retired shortly after dinner. The next morning we gave them a complete briefing of our development program activities, of which they had seen just a small part. At its conclusion, several of the reporters had asked Arcos if I would grant them interviews. Seeing another opportunity to drive home the election message and dampen enthusiasm for a coup, I agreed.

They asked pointed and provocative questions, focusing on allegations floated by the Zuniga crowd that the administration favored his candidacy because of the Liberals' leftist tendencies. I opted for candor, which, although undiplomatic, seemed to be in order, given the circumstances. Following these interviews, Arcos and I flew home; the travelers spent the rest of the morning on the beach, then drove back to Tegucigalpa.

We debriefed Ruelas and the other guides in Tegucigalpa the following morning. All agreed that it had been a useful exercise and disabused the journalists of some of their more cynical views about our assistance programs. Nearly all of them had been impressed that our projects were actually reaching the grassroots and meeting real needs. Bread had been cast upon the media waters.

DIVERSION OF REFUGEE SUPPLIES CONFIRMED: SAN SALVADOR, EL SALVADOR, MARCH 13, 1981. A former Salvadoran insurgent who had taken advantage of an amnesty program reported that the insurgents were receiving foodstuffs and other supplies from refugees located in the La Virtud area. That was where we had observed foodstuffs being distributed with virtually no control or accountability. This was the first confirmation of what we were certain had been happening to part of those supplies.

I cabled State, San Salvador and the U.S. Mission in Geneva, where the UN High Commission for Refugees (UNHCR) was headquartered, urging that this information be shared and used to force the UNHCR and relief agencies to tighten up on their handling of these supplies.[16] This recommendation seemed to have been ignored, possibly because the CIA did not wish to risk exposing the source.

PRESS PLUGS TRANSITION, REPORTS MY INDISCRETIONS: TEGUCIGALPA, HONDURAS, MARCH 14, 1981. Reading the Saturday morning newspapers over breakfast, I saw that coverage of my interview in Tela was featured in both *La Prensa* and *La Tribuna*. There was very little about our assistance program, however. Both papers covered the principal themes I had sought to emphasize: our continued support of the transition process and confidence that elections would occur on schedule; Cuba, supported by the USSR, was encouraging and supporting insurgencies in the region; and the United States was trying to strengthen the Honduran armed forces to help ensure they had the capability to defend their country, not to become our surrogate in the region. But the journalists' interpretations of my remarks, plus my less-than-thoughtful responses to several questions, produced some pretty sensational news.

Most troubling was *La Prensa*'s version of my response to a specific question about rumors that the Reagan administration favored Zuniga as next president. I had flatly denied the United States had a favored candidate and emphasized that we would recognize and support whoever was chosen by the Honduran people. Seeking to reinforce that point, I had thoughtlessly added that if Cantinflas, the great Mexican comedian, were elected, we would recognize and work with him. That undiplomatic comment was highlighted in a way that made it appear I had referred to Zuniga as a clown, which was not the case. *La Tribuna* reported more accurately, but both misinterpreted a comment I had made about U.S. military advisers. I had referred to the approximately 50 advisers then in El Salvador, but both reporters understood me as having said there were 50 U.S. military advisers in Honduras.[17] That was wildly off the mark. Our Milgroup then had only five officers, and rarely were there more than a half dozen temporary duty trainers in-country. We sent a letter to both papers, correcting that misapprehension, which they both printed.[18] But there was nothing I could do about the Zuniga faux pas.

Walker was troubled and virtually certain the *La Prensa* article would blow back on us. He was still working on his in-depth analysis of Zuniga's historical role and knew more about the man than anyone on our staff. Zuniga, he noted, was already feverishly trying to undermine me, and that story would cause him to redouble his efforts: I should prepare for some very heavy attacks. Later Arcos echoed these sentiments. They were right.

My Cantinflas statement was out of line, drawing attention away from the substance of the message I sought to convey and creating problems we didn't need. The lesson here was unequivocal: no more press conferences or open-ended interviews without adequate preparation. We had to work out artful responses to anticipated awkward questions.

CONSENSUS EMERGES ON TAX PLAN: TEGUCIGALPA, HONDURAS, MID–MARCH 1981. The soaring budget deficit had become a major problem, threatening the IMF standby agreement and development program funding. However, we had been lobbying the government, businessmen and politicos on the urgent need to cut spending, increase revenues and reach agreement with the IMF. After several months of deadlock, the three parties finally agreed on a modest tax increase. It was less than the government sought, more than business wanted and all that the assembly would enact. It would not close the deficit gap, but something was better than nothing.[19] Our efforts had helped tip the balance.

GROWING DISQUIET OVER SECURITY ASSISTANCE: TEGUCIGALPA, HONDURAS, MID–MARCH 1981. Colonel Goodwin reported that he and his staff were coming under increasing pressure and criticism from the Honduran military over what they perceived as our nonresponsiveness on security assistance. They wanted increased assistance from us, and they wanted it now. Their complaints and aspirations were not new—we had all been over them many times—and we had made little headway in improving delivery and response times. But we were not prepared to increase funding to a level they regarded adequate.

Goodwin and the Army Section chief had been called in by General Chinchilla for a special roasting. Their threat litany was unchanged. They were alarmed about the arms buildup in Nicaragua—at that time rumored to include Soviet tanks, as well as increased military manpower—and the growing arms imbalance with El Salvador. On the heels of that meeting came an intelligence report outlining the Superior Council's concerns and a plan to force U.S. action, dictated by their perception that the embassy was preventing Washington from hearing their message. They would send a group of senior officers to Washington in order to gain our attention.

I reported these developments, reiterating the causes of their concern, and the failure of General Nutting's visit to dampen their frustration. If anything, his visit had only whetted their appetites. When nothing happened, it strengthened their conviction that the embassy was the key obstacle. In addition to their principal assistance grievance, they had three specific complaints on which they harped continually: extension of the helicopter lease, formal relief of financial liability for the lost helicopter and an unmet request for a temporary duty intelligence adviser. The first two had been dragging on since shortly after my arrival, and the intelligence adviser request was several months old. They consistently drew invidious comparisons between our swift responses to Salvadoran needs and our "business as usual" attitude when it came to their requirements.

I did not favor a further increase in our security assistance, just upped to $10 million, or the proposed trip to Washington, but I thought their disquiet over the three specific cases was valid. "What is really needed," I wrote in my cable to State, "is expeditious action on those irritants that have been digging into their emotional skin for a long time: the helicopter lease, financial responsibility relief and intelligence advisor issues. While we understand the reasons for the various delays, the host military do not, and the upshot is that despite our best efforts, we are—at least in these terms—our own worst enemy.... Action requested: I urge the Department to do everything possible to expedite favorable decisions on the two helicopter issues and the assignment of a temporary duty intelligence advisor."[20]

The next day President Paz unloaded on me with the same complaints. We had met, at his request, to discuss the tax and IMF negotiations issues. At the conclusion of that discussion, he raised the issue of overall security assistance level in El Salvador, compared to that of Honduras, covering familiar ground. I acknowledged the growing gap between the two countries and noted that we would soon increase Honduran FMS funding to $10 million, which was news to him. I also observed that Honduras did not face a comparable threat. We intended to continue cooperating with Honduras to ensure that a threat such as the one in El Salvador did not eventuate. Finally, I reported that the new administration had requested authority to extend concessionary FMS credit terms to the Central American countries in fiscal year 1982. That would mean that nearly half of the credit for Honduras would be under these new terms. I cautioned, however, that there was no assurance Congress would agree.

Paz then observed that our assistance often had a serious near-term impact on the Honduran military operating budget that might not be fully appreciated. The helicopter lease arrangement, for example, had been unanticipated and required significant unplanned outlays—fuel, spare parts, maintenance—that caused the armed forces to delay other planned expenditures. He would like to see a return to the days when we released excess equipment to friendly governments at "token" cost, thereby minimizing the longer-term impact on the military budget. As to the status of the helicopter lease extension, he recalled that General Nutting had promised to follow up, but he had heard nothing more. I confirmed that Nutting was trying to expedite action, and we were hopeful that the matter would soon be resolved. Paz was skeptical.

My attempts to allay his concerns were neither persuasive nor successful. Although he was pleased with the increased FMS level and the possibility of concessionary FMS, he did not seem to consider them an adequate response.[21]

Despite Paz's obvious impatience, I failed to realize the extent of Honduran anxiety/paranoia over the perceived Nicaraguan threat, the imbalance with El Salvador and uncertainties about our policies. With Zuniga's help, Paz would shortly embark on a singularly bizarre adventure.

My plea for action from Washington didn't produce much, but it did get Southern Command's attention. Their efforts to help, however, backfired as a result of the conjunction of zeal, misinformation, poor judgment in our Milgroup and Murphy's Law. These circumstances would bring my already poor relations with the Honduran military to a crisis point.

BOMB INJURES MARINES IN COSTA RICA: SAN JOSE, COSTA RICA, MARCH 17, 1981. An embassy vehicle carrying three Marine security guards was severely damaged by a remotely controlled bomb; all three Marines were wounded, one seriously. The following day the Honduran embassy in San Jose was damaged by another bomb. Those claiming responsibility said they had taken these acts "in reprisal for U.S. and Honduran support" of the Salvadoran government. The Costa Rican government promptly deported 25 Salvadoran and Nicaraguan asylees suspected of involvement.[22]

ALLEGED SLAUGHTER OF SALVADORANS NEAR BORDER: CHALATENANGO, EL SALVADOR, MARCH 17–18, 1981. Salvadoran helicopters allegedly attacked an estimated 4,500 fleeing Salvadoran refugees, mostly women and children, as they tried to cross the Lempa River and enter Honduras, according to reports in the U.S. press. These reports indicated there were 20 "confirmed dead and 189 missing."[23] This incident became known as the "Rio Lempa Massacre."

HAIG REMARKS STIR PROTEST, "CLARIFICATION": WASHINGTON, D.C., MARCH 18, 1981. Secretary Haig, testifying before the Senate Foreign Relations Committee, suggested that the four American churchwomen slain in December may have been killed when they tried to run a roadblock.[24] This triggered a storm of protest. Subsequently, UN ambassador Jeane Kirkpatrick alleged that these women had been "political activists," adding further fuel to the fire. Two days later State issued a "clarification" of Haig's remarks, to the effect that what he had suggested was that the women may have inadvertently run a roadblock, precipitating an "exchange" of gunfire in which they died. He had not wished to suggest the women had engaged in a gun battle.[25]

ANOTHER CONGRESSIONAL DELEGATION: TEGUCIGALPA, HONDURAS, MARCH 18–20, 1981. Representative Clarence Long (D-MD), accompanied by Central American Affairs director John Blacken, arrived in Honduras for a quick review of our AID operations. Long was interested in "appropriate technology," that is, unsophisticated technologies that could be understood and applied by peasants, who are often illiterate, to improve their lives. Following a CT briefing that dealt primarily with the transition process and AID program, Long and his aide met with Oleson, Walker and me, treating us to an extended dissertation on AID's failure to adequately utilize appropriate technologies.

Next, we were off to see President Paz. I asked Long to emphasize to Paz how important it was, in terms of continued U.S. economic assistance, for the elections to proceed as planned. Long did a masterful job of massaging Paz and then repeated the performance with the local media.[26] His visit provided another opportunity to get our message out.

I hosted a small reception for Long and his party that evening. The following day he visited the Assembly, where he met with Suazo Cordova and the leaders of all parties. Once again he emphasized the importance of holding elections as planned. This time, however, there was no press coverage.[27]

ZUNIGA ATTACKS: MEETS SWIFT REBUTTAL FROM ALL SIDES, TEGUCIGALPA, HONDURAS, MARCH 20–23, 1981. Walker and Arcos had been right. Zuniga attacked amain, but in so doing he overreached. The fabricated allegations he launched this time were so absurd as to lack all credibility—in Honduras. The headlines and article were, however, clipped and sent to Washington for circulation within the Reagan administration.[28]

El Heraldo led with the front-page headline "Binns Will Be Separated for Intervention in Honduran Politics," with a photo of me; the page-two story headline read: "Binns Will Be Fired for His Intervention in Honduran Politics." However, the substance of the fantasy spun by one of Zuniga's favorite flacks was easily refutable. It began: "The Reagan administration has been better informed about Honduran politics than its ambassador, who does not agree with the general policies of the new government … and for that reason it has decided to retire him from the Foreign Service." It then moved into a series of fatuous allegations (the facts follow in parentheses) including:

• Since late 1980 I had pressured President Paz and political party leaders to hold elections in August 1981. (Fact: I had, indeed, urged all of them to hold elections pursuant to the transition agreement they had worked out, but never, at any time, did I suggest a general or specific election date.)

• On January 27 I met with eight well-known dissidents from various parties and independents, cited by name, at the house of a third party. Subsequently, I held three further meetings with this group. (Fact: I had, at various times, met separately with only two or three of those named, but most, including the owner of the house in which the first meeting allegedly occurred, were completely unknown to me.)

• The purpose of this meeting was to establish a Social Democratic Party, the members of which would seek "to penetrate and take over the traditional parties [*sic*]." (Fact: I had never advocated formation of a new party, of any stripe, in Honduras or anywhere else.)

• On January 28 I had lunched with a group of business leaders at the Chico Club, pressing them to support August 1981 elections. (Fact: I had lunched with American businessmen at my residence on that date and had reviewed U.S. policy objectives, including the transition to an elected government, but did not mention any date or dates for the election.)

• I had visited San Pedro Sula and met with business and union leaders for the purpose of gaining their support for the new Social Democratic Party. (Fact: never, in any of my meetings in San Pedro or elsewhere, did I advocate formation of such a party.)

• I had intervened, in writing, with the Honduran Supreme Court to obtain the resolution of a case pending before the court on terms favorable to the American plaintiffs. (Fact: I was unaware of the cited case and had never discussed or written court members concerning this or any pending case.)

• I was supporting Jorge Arturo Reina, identified as the intermediary for the aborted talks with the Salvadoran rebels, as a future Liberal Party candidate for president. (Fact: I had never advocated Reina, or anyone else, as a candidate for anything.)

The article concluded that "these acts of open political intervention by Binns, from every point of view contrary to the actual policies of the Reagan administration, have caused it to retire him quickly."[29]

The principal purpose of this slander was less to discredit me in Honduras—although it certainly had that end in mind—than to demonstrate my alleged opposition and disloyalty to the Reagan administration. This article, with a poorly prepared English translation, was sent to McCormack and other Zuniga contacts in Washington, who saw that it reached senior levels at State and, presumably, elsewhere.[30] Refutations of the allegations, drew headlines and extensive space in Honduras but were not circulated in Washington.

Walker, Arcos and I huddled immediately to plot our actions. Arcos would call the editors of all newspapers and other media outlets to assure them the story was false and that we would be issuing a strong rebuttal later that day. We decided that it should take the form of a letter to the editor of *El Heraldo* from me, which we would then send to all other media outlets. I would draft point-by-point rebuttal statements, Walker would review them, and they would be incorporated in the letter Arcos was drafting. We would all review the final draft before delivering it, by hand, to the media.

We cabled the complete text of the article to State. Walker also had our political officers call their contacts who were mentioned in the article, asking that they correct the record. Their response was overwhelmingly positive. Our initial cable was soon followed by others with the text of our rebuttal and subsequent fallout.[31]

My letter characterized the original article as a "complete distortion and apparent effort to discredit me personally, the diplomatic mission over which I preside and the U.S. government" and provided a detailed refutation of the five most egregious allegations. We had decided to limit the points rebutted for space considerations. It concluded: "A number of the points in the article I willingly acknowledge. I have made trips to San Pedro Sula, I have held discussions on politics, economics, and other subjects with a wide range of Honduran citizens, and I have attempted to become as cognizant as possible of the problems and aspirations of the Honduran government and people before whom I am charged to represent my government. As long as I remain in Honduras, I plan to continue to travel, to meet as many people as possible and to exchange opinions and experiences with them. I trust this will not be misinterpreted by *El Heraldo,* nor by its readership as further evidence of 'interventionism.'"[32]

The letter dominated the local news March 21, with all papers, including *El Heraldo,* printing the complete text, along with letters and statements from several of the alleged participants in the imaginary meetings. All denied its substance.[33] The most curious coverage, however, was that of the original source, *El Heraldo.* It devoted several articles and two full pages to the issue, with every article rebutting the original account. It even printed an interview of a member of the Liberal Party who explicitly tied the "Embassy intervention" thesis to Zuniga, and his repeated assertions that the embassy favored the Liberals.[34] It was extraordinary and puzzling to see a newspaper devote so much space to debunking one of its own stories.

The extreme left also leapt into the fray, attacking me from the opposite side. The *U.R.P.,* an irregular tabloid calling itself the "Propaganda Organ of the People's Revolutionary Union," published a long, polemical diatribe. It took me and the Reagan administration to task for our "imperialistic" actions in Honduras. It also alleged that the administration was seeking to overthrow the Nicaraguan government and "subjugate" the peoples of Central America. I was said to be the chosen agent of the Reagan administration in this nefarious enterprise.[35] Later, the editor of *U.R.P.,* Tomas Nativi Galvez, would become the second or third Honduran arrested and "disappeared" by Honduran security forces, as they stepped up repression of suspected subversives.[36]

The story reverberated for several days. *La Prensa* summed it all up in a spirited March 23 editorial defense of both U.S. policy goals in Honduras—which it said coincided with the desires of the Honduran people—and my actions. It also contained a thinly veiled allusion to Zuniga and his crowd, as being responsible for this "fairy tale."[37] And to demonstrate evenhandedness, the editorialist also picked up on the *U.R.P.* allegations as a counterpoint and excoriated the Marxist left as well. I thought it was an excellent piece of work.

Arcos later learned why *El Heraldo* had refuted its own story with such vengeance. *La Prensa* owner Jorge Larach also owned *El Heraldo* but normally exercised little editorial oversight. When the story first appeared, he severely reprimanded the *El Heraldo* editor for printing this patently bogus report.[38] To atone, the editor printed everything he could find that cast doubt on the original report.

This was just another installment in my running battle to counter false allegations from the Zuniga group and also the extreme left. *El Heraldo,* however, was never again a major player in that game.

CONTRA TRAINING IN UNITED STATES DRAWS OFFICIAL PROTEST: WASHINGTON, D.C., MARCH 21, 1981. The Nicaraguan government, responding to press reports that former members of the National Guard were being trained near Miami for paramilitary operations in Nicaragua, lodged an official protest with the United States.[39] Subsequent FBI investigation of this training, conducted by Cuban exile groups, failed to find grounds for prosecution.

U.S. MILITARY MISJUDGMENTS CASCADE: TEGUCIGALPA, HONDURAS, MARCH 23, 1981. Southern Command, responding to our cables concerning the Honduran military's deepening dissatisfaction with our security assistance program, phoned Colonel Goodwin with "unofficial" information about pending decisions that would affect Honduras. He was advised that Defense had agreed to extend the helicopter lease three years; the prospects for increased funding for the coming fiscal year were very good, with a possibility we would grant concessionary sales terms; and, if Honduras could provide a listing of all undelivered materiel and items wanted in the coming year, in priority order, Southern Command would try to expedite delivery. Goodwin recognized that, except for the helicopter lease extension, there was not much substance to this information, although it might excite Honduran expectations.

Judging it a routine matter, Goodwin opted to wait until our regular CT meeting the next day to advise Walker and me. Had he taken no action until he had advised us, it is unlikely that we would have had the problem that eventuated. But he acted, and that was the first misjudgment in what was to become a cascade of errors.

Because the Hondurans needed to prepare the priority listing of materiel on order and desired under the coming year's FMS, Goodwin asked the American civilian technician who managed security assistance procurement, monitored deliveries and tracked the Hondurans' use of materiel provided to pass the information on to his Honduran counterpart on the General Staff. This technician was Milgroup's only fluent Spanish speaker, married to a Honduran woman and, it turned out, almost totally lacking in judgment. Given the delicate nature of our relationship with the Honduran military, we needed to consider whether it was advisable to pass all or part of this nebulous information on. We also needed to think about how and to whom it should be passed so as to avoid raising expectations. By asking a low-level technician having little understanding of the sensitivities involved to carry out this task, Goodwin erred. The technician charged forward with gusto, much to our later chagrin.

After hearing our technician's report, the Honduran contact asked if the technician would brief the Superior Council of the Armed Forces, the highest body in the military structure, the following day. Our man evidently thought that was a neat idea and agreed to do so without consulting or advising Goodwin. He did, however, send Goodwin a memorandum describing these events after the fact. Another judgmental error. Next, he compounded that error with a display of independent initiative. Again without informing Goodwin or his other superiors, he phoned Southern Command for additional details, striking a mother lode of dubious data, which he later shared with the Superior Council.

Suddenly, seemingly routine information had become misinformation and was shared with the highest level in the Honduran armed forces without the knowledge of senior U.S. officials. The misjudgments had reached a critical mass.

Following our regular CT meeting, Goodwin advised me of the Southern Command phone call and the action he had taken. I immediately realized that we needed to think through what, if anything, we wanted to do with this information. I asked Goodwin to keep his technician from passing this information along, if possible. If it had already been passed, we both assumed it was unlikely to provoke a major problem. The technician was meeting with the Superior Council as we spoke. We turned to other matters. Circumstances intruded, and it would be several days before I became aware of the full magnitude of the problems that had been created.[40]

PRESIDENT PAZ TRIES TO GO TO WASHINGTON: WASHINGTON, D.C., MARCH 23–25, 1981. The Honduran Ambassador, Col. Federico Pujol, phoned State's Honduran desk officer with an unusual request. Could State arrange for President Paz to have a medical examination at Walter Reed Hospital during a visit to Washington that was to begin March 25? In the course of this conversation, Pujol said that the principal purpose of Paz's visit was to meet with President Reagan and Secretary Haig and that these meetings had already been arranged outside official channels.[41]

That news was, to put it mildly, a shocker. Foreign chiefs of state do not just turn up in Washington unannounced and uninvited for "unofficial" meetings with the president and secretary of state. Even private visits by chiefs of state and heads of government require extensive, time-consuming preparations and are carefully orchestrated by the White House and State. Nor are there intermediaries who can arrange for private visitors to have such high-level meetings without observing established procedures.

This information set off alarm bells in the bureau and, later, Haig's office. After frenzied calls to the White House and further discussions with Pujol, it turned out that Paz had no appointments. Zuniga and the Honduran embassy had asked Richard McCormack of Senator Helms's staff to set these meetings up, and they apparently assumed he had done so. When State contacted McCormack, he acknowledged that he was trying to orchestrate the visit but as yet had no confirmed appointments.

Indeed, it was not until the following day, March 24, that McCormack delivered a memorandum to State Department counselor Bud McFarlane, setting out a case for "short circuiting Ambassador Binns, and establishing direct links between Washington policy makers and senior Honduran officials."[42] Such action was necessary, McCormack's memo continued, because "cooperation with Honduras is very important in containing the Nicaraguan and El Salvadoran [sic] problems." While disclaiming any "first hand information," he also wrote that "Binns is more sympathetic to the left than is to their liking...and is not trusted by the President of the country." McCormack supported this contention by enclosing a clipping of the fabricated Zuniga-sponsored article from the March 20 *El Heraldo*. The memo also went on to describe how Paz "went on a week long bender—and his Defense Council was not certain he would be physically able to represent the country in his semi-intoxicated state" and was only "given the green light to visit Washington" that morning.

In his conversations with State officials, McCormack repeatedly alleged that Paz believed I "had leaked confidential information to the press" and was allowing the diversion of AID money "to leftist causes." Consequently, Paz had "determined that I could not be trusted."[43]

We subsequently learned that the projected visit originated with Zuniga. His daughter, Elizabeth, and her brother, Major Ricardo Zuniga, the assistant army attache in the Washington embassy, had made the initial approach to McCormack, an eager participant. McCormack later told State officials that he thought Paz's overriding purpose for coming to the United States was "to sound out the new administration about the possibilities of a coup that would perpetuate Paz in office," a plan McCormack claimed he tried to discourage.[44] Although Senator Helms's office, through McCormack, was sponsoring this venture, it is unclear to what extent the senator was aware of his aide's activity. The Honduran embassy was only made privy to this initiative after planning was underway.[45]

State frantically sought to block this quixotic trip. But it ignored its most effective tool, the embassy. Pujol was urged to inform Paz that no appointments had been arranged and would not be; moreover, an abortive trip to Washington would probably be politically embarrassing for him in Honduras. McCormack was asked to carry the same message. These messages were apparently delivered but produced no feedback.

Unsure of the situation, State officers tried to reach Paz by phone March 25 to dissuade him from coming. Yet they still had not advised the embassy of these developments. Instead of Paz, they reached Colonel Torres Arias, who indicated the president was indisposed and could not travel for another week at the earliest. Torres Arias also indicated that Paz had never left Honduras.[46] In fact, Paz had departed Tegucigalpa for Washington via a Honduran Air Force plane the morning of March 25, but that flight turned back before reaching the United States.[47]

There are several aspects of this adventure that deserve further examination. First, State did not advise me or the embassy of these events, which began March 23, until four days later. That was absolutely inexcusable. Although Paz may have lost confidence in me, the embassy and I could have worked key local contacts to prevent the trip far more effectively than State could from Washington. Second, Paz was evidently under growing stress, and it was affecting his behavior and judgment. Third, and most important from the standpoint of U.S. interests, it appeared that Paz had fallen under the influence of Zuniga to an alarming degree, a cause for serious concern.

Just why this scheme arose remains a puzzler. In retrospect, I believe that

Zuniga's claimed influence with the new administration, together with McCormack's earlier visits, had gotten Paz's attention. Paz—troubled by the deteriorating situation in the region, his waning power, a drinking problem, our nonresponsiveness to his questions and pleas, and the perception that the embassy was blocking his ambitions—was easily convinced that Zuniga was well plugged in with the Reagan administration through McCormack. Paz took the bait, and Zuniga set the hook.

Having gained Paz's confidence, Zuniga was able to play on the latter's desire to remain in power to advance his own goal of delaying elections. Theirs was an unfortunate coincidence of interests. Because Zuniga considered me one of the principal obstacles to blocking the elections, he lost no time in spreading lies about my sympathies and actions and in fabricating spurious news stories to support those allegations. As State officials later noted in a masterpiece of understatement, "We believe that Ricardo Zuniga and the Nationals (and there may be others) appear to have decidedly poisoned the well among top government of Honduras officials concerning you and the Embassy."[48]

PEZZULLO COUNSELS AGAINST PARAMILITARY OPERATIONS: WASHINGTON, D.C., MARCH 24, 1981. Ambassador Pezzullo, recalled to Washington for consultations, met with CIA director William Casey for an assessment of the Sandinista movement and government. In that meeting Pezzullo made two main points: the Nicaraguan government responded to diplomatic pressure, as evidenced by its cutoff of the arms flow from Nicaragua to the Salvadoran insurgents and closure of the rebel radio station; and popular support for the Sandinistas was very strong, so a covert military operation was likely to fail.[49] Pezzullo's views were shared by nearly everyone who had knowledge of Nicaragua. Indeed, most knowledgeable observers felt a U.S.-backed insurgency would only serve to strengthen the Sandinistas in the near term, being counterproductive. Casey was not persuaded, however, and moved forcefully to change his agency's assessments, corrupting the intelligence process.

Assistant Secretary Thomas Enders subsequently sought to use the threat of covert military action as a lever to force the Sandinistas to accept a diplomatic arrangement, but that initiative failed. For his temerity, the administration's war party forced him from office. That was the effective end of U.S. diplomatic efforts for nearly a decade. Bud McFarlane later admitted that while NSC adviser he had not believed the Contra operation could succeed and therefore should have been ended. He never offered that counsel to the president, however, because "if I had done that, Bill Casey, Jeane Kirkpatrick and Cap Weinberger would have said I was some kind of commie."[50]

GOING BACK TO SAN JOSE: TEGUCIGALPA, HONDURAS, AND SAN JOSE, COSTA RICA, MARCH 25–27, 1981. Several weeks previously, Colonel Miller invited Martha and me to fly to Panama on the Mission aircraft, which required routine maintenance, departing the morning of March 25 and returning the morning of March 27.[51] We had no particular interest in going to Panama but welcomed an opportunity to get away for a few days. We had a standing invitation from Frank McNeil to visit San Jose, so I asked Miller to drop us off and pick us up there en route and obtained permission to leave the country.

So, we spent a couple of days in San Jose, blissfully unaware of the unfolding Paz trip scenario or that the day before we left the Milgroup technician had briefed the Superior Council of the Armed Forces in a way that left its members with visions of dancing sugarplums. As we were about to leave McNeil's residence for the airport, the embassy communications center called to say they had received an immediate EXDIS cable for me. They would send it to the airport. We had to delay our takeoff a few minutes until the messenger arrived.

Once we were airborne I opened the envelope and read the message. It was titled "The Almost Visit of General Paz," and began "On March 23 at 3PM, the Honduran Ambassador called the desk officer...."[52] By the time I had finished, I was stunned, too shocked to be angry. This incident had arisen four days before, when I was still in Tegucigalpa, and I had not been advised. That was, based on my experience, virtually without precedent.

After a few minutes' reflection, I walked to the cockpit and asked Colonel Miller to radio the embassy to have Walker meet me at the airport on our arrival. I knew he would have seen the cable.

CONSTITUENT ASSEMBLY BUILDING BOMBED: TEGUCIGALPA, HONDURAS, MARCH 26, 1981. A small bomb exploded at the Constituent Assembly building, injuring three people, one seriously.[54] The Popular Revolutionary Command Lorenzo Zelaya, *Cinconeros,* the paramilitary action wing of the People's Revolutionary Union (*URP*), claimed responsibility.

STARTING DAMAGE-CONTROL OPERATIONS: TEGUCIGALPA, HONDURAS, MARCH 27, 1981. By the time we landed the shock had worn off. I was furious with the desk officer and the bureau. But I had used the time to come up with several recommendations as to how we should respond. Walker met me and was as furious as I with the cable. And he had other problems on his mind.

As we drove to the embassy he gave me my first news of the Milgroup technician's briefing of the Superior Council. It's a good thing I was not given to shooting messengers bearing bad news. At that moment I was probably angrier than I had ever been or would be again. But within a couple of minutes we began to laugh. How in the world were we going to clean up these two extraordinary messes?

Anticipating my desires, Walker had a working group waiting in my office: the station chief, Political Section chief, Colonel Goodwin (looking extremely chagrined) and Arcos. Colonel Miller joined us after securing the aircraft. Our first task was to assess the aborted Paz visit. I reviewed my preliminary thoughts, asked for their views and, after some discussion, made a series of intelligence collection assignments to try to get a better fix on what had happened, and why. We would regroup on Monday.

When that meeting broke up, Goodwin and Walker stayed to assess the scope of the Superior Council briefing fiasco and what needed to be done to limit damage and fix accountability. It was even grimmer than the preceding session. The more I heard, the worse it seemed. It was at this juncture that I first learned of the technician's independent initiative with Southern Command to gain more information and the general content of what he had relayed to the Superior Council.

He had evidently told the Hondurans that the United States was prepared to provide all the equipment they could use and afford (whatever that meant), provided they came up with good justifications. He also apparently told them that current year funding would be increased by up to $12 million and that we would even consider a request for F-5 aircraft (at the time, we opposed transferring such high-performance aircraft to Central America). Moreover, he advised them that we were prepared to grant concessional terms for Foreign Military Sales credits, at an interest rate of 3 percent, vice commercial rates. And, in a final burst of glory, he had indicated that we would help the police (FUSEP) obtain equipment and training. That, of course, was generally prohibited by law.[53]

No wonder Goodwin looked hangdog. His guy had just given away the pass in terms encouraging exaggerated Honduran expectations.

How this could have happened without Goodwin's knowledge boggled my mind and to some extent still does. Yet he denied all awareness of the technician's actions beyond his original instructions. Our subsequent inquiries produced no contrary information.

I had not determined how to handle this matter. As a first step I reviewed with Goodwin what seemed to me to be the basic misjudgments that led to this debacle, with critical comments (i.e., I chewed him out royally). I also asked that he bring the technician in Monday for a fact-finding session. In the meantime I would think about what we needed to do. Goodwin left shaken and anguished. I was not sympathetic.

After Goodwin left, Walker and I defined some parameters. If it became clear that the technician had actually acted on specific instructions from Goodwin, I would have the latter removed promptly. That action would create a new source of discord with both Defense and Southern Command, but I could see no realistic alternative. It would also no doubt make waves with the Honduran military. The best that could be said of Goodwin's role was that he displayed an appalling lack of judgment (an offense with which I had a more than passing acquaintance).

If the technician had acted largely on his own, as appeared to be the case, I had more options. But the dilemma was, in some respects, more acute. The gravity of the offense, both Walker and I agreed, justified his removal. But I could not ignore the fact that it would reverberate strongly in Honduran military circles (his Honduran wife assured that), further debasing my currency in that market. And he might decide not to leave Honduras, becoming kind of a running sore in our relations with the Honduran military. It would also leave the Milgroup with a vacancy that would last for months at a critical juncture.

It had been a hell of a day. Walker and I had a drink and another sardonic laugh before heading homeward for the weekend.

HONDURAN AIRLINER HIJACKED TO NICARAGUA, THEN PANAMA: TEGUCIGALPA, HONDURAS, AND MANAGUA, NICARAGUA, MARCH 28–30, 1981. Walker called me at home to report that a Honduran Air Service (SAHSA) Boeing 737 en route from Tegucigalpa to New Orleans had been hijacked and was seeking permission to land in Managua. Following established procedures, he had already notified State's Operations Center; Wackerbarth was trying to get through to Honduran civil air authorities to determine if American citizens were on board; the station chief was trying to get further information through liaison and Colonel Miller was working his contacts in the Honduran Air Force. I asked Walker to set up a meeting later in the day.

By the time we met the airliner was on the ground in Managua, surrounded by security forces. Thirty-four passengers were soon released to the Honduran embassy, and the rest were reportedly safe. Approximately 50 people remained on the aircraft; eight to ten were thought to be American citizens. The URP's *Cinconeros* again claimed responsibility. The hijackers demanded the release of 15 Salvadorans they claimed were being held by Honduran authorities, eight of whom had been arrested in connection with the January arms-smuggling bust. Insurgent leader Facundo Guardado was among them.

The hijackers also had several other demands and asserted that the Honduran military had targeted 12 Honduran leftists and progressives for assassination. They promised to "hold the government responsible" for the safety of the alleged target group, which included political leaders, retired military, university leaders, former government officials, journalists and teachers. Among those listed were dissident Liberals Jorge Arturo and Carlos Roberto Reina; another was Tomas Nativi, leader of the URP. Several months later Nativi would be arrested and "disappeared" by Honduran security forces. The others were not harmed.

The Nicaraguans were consulting with the Honduran government. The hijackers, however, demanded that Honduran negotiators be sent to Managua by 2 P.M. March 29. The Hondurans suspected Sandinista collusion with the hijackers and were not inclined to negotiate. Let the Sandinistas deal with the problem, since they probably had something to do with its origins.[55]

We passed this information to the Operations Center. With the aircraft in Managua, the embassy there was the principal point of contact. Our role was secondary, keeping in touch with Honduran authorities and passing them any information or advice we received from Washington. We continued to monitor events around the clock.

The Honduran refusal to negotiate initially seemed to be working. The hijacker's deadline passed without incident, although no more passengers had been released. Several hours later, however, the hijackers asked that the aircraft be refueled. The Nicaraguans obliged, and the plane and passengers departed for Panama about 5:30 P.M. The Honduran government thereupon asked Panama to receive the aircraft. Soon after its arrival, the Panamanians persuaded the hijackers to release the remaining passengers, crew and aircraft in return for a promise to seek the release of the Salvadoran prisoners and to allow them and the hijackers to seek asylum in Cuba.

I was instructed to make various diplomatic representations, or démarches, to the Hondurans. First, urge that they not release the Salvadoran prisoners. Later, I asked that they urge the Panamanian government to prosecute the hijackers. To these ends I met with Foreign Minister Elvir and G-2 chief Colonel Torres Arias and spoke to President Paz by phone. I also delivered a personal message to Paz from Secretary Haig. It was all to no avail. The Honduran prisoners were released after the passengers and aircrew were returned to Tegucigalpa. But that had been inevitable because of Honduran penal code defects. And, having asked the Panamanians to do them a favor by receiving the aircraft and returning the passengers and crew, the Hondurans were not inclined to pressure them about prosecuting the hijackers.

This was not a desirable outcome. Successful hijackings tend to encourage repetition. Moreover, it turned out that at least some of the hijackers remained in Panama, rather than going to Cuba. As a result, the United States sought to organize a joint démarche by all ambassadors from signatory countries of various antihijacking agreements, urging that Honduras ask the Panamanian government to prosecute the hijackers. There was little enthusiasm for this idea, either in the respective capitals or among my colleagues in Tegucigalpa. Finally, four other governments—Britain, Germany, Italy and Japan—agreed to a joint approach. We made our representations, with predictable results. The Hondurans took no further action.[56]

Looking back, I suspect that this incident and the assembly bombing were key factors in convincing the Honduran military that they had to resort to harsh, extralegal repression of suspected subversives.

FIXING ACCOUNTABILITY WITH MILGROUP: TEGUCIGALPA, HON-
DURAS, MARCH 30, 1981. Walker and I met with Colonel Goodwin and his
technician. Although this meeting was principally fact finding, I also wished
to make it educational by examining the root causes of our military assistance problems with the Hondurans and the specific lapses in judgment that
had led to the current snafu. I wanted both Goodwin and the technician to
understand my concerns and position. Goodwin was familiar with the message, but I sensed that the technician did not grasp my explanation of the
problems he had created. But he was left in no doubt as to the gravity with
which I viewed his actions.

The technician's account of events was consistent with Goodwin's and
the memorandum he had sent Goodwin. He had no explanation for his failure to advise Goodwin of the invitation to meet with the Superior Council
or his initiative to gain additional information from Southern Command.
Nor did he believe it unusual for him to brief the Superior Council, since he
invariably went along as an interpreter whenever senior Milgroup officers
briefed that group. But he acknowledged that he had not previously had a
solo performance. He didn't grasp the distinction between an interpreter and
a spokesperson.

The details of what he had told the Superior Council were even worse
than I had inferred, but he claimed they accurately reflected what Southern
Command had told him. He had told Superior Council that:

• The United States "was in a position to help them acquire all of the
equipment they could use and afford if they would present a package and justify it," and "the time is especially propitious for seeking additional equipment because of the great interest the USG is focusing on Honduras";
• Speaking "unofficially," "the possibility existed that they could augment this year's FMS by 10 or 12 million dollars if they would present a package" and that "they should be thinking of F-5 aircraft... because it would not
be considered out of line for Honduras to request such airplanes";
• "The USG was searching for the best way to help FUSEP (police
forces) obtain equipment and training, realizing that the police was [sic] the
first line of defense in the event of urban disturbances";
• "They should think of requesting an increase in this year's Foreign
Military Sales (FMS) credit immediately"; and
• We were considering an interest rate of "three percent" on the next
year's FMS credit.[57]

In aggregate, this represented a major shift in U.S. policy and was apparently based on Southern Command recommendations to Defense. But security assistance policy decisions and allocations are made in an interagency forum,
not by Southern Command or Defense, and State controlled the purse strings.

What the Hondurans made of the briefing I cannot say, but I suspected the worst. Much of what had been implicitly promised didn't come to pass, even with the largess of the Reagan years; other implied promises took years to fulfill. The Hondurans never received anything like what they wanted in materiel, although they were to receive increased FMS, as well as important "in kind" grants. The F-5 aircraft remained an illusion until 1987. The fiscal year 1981 program had already been bumped up, and there was no further growth. It was too early to tell what Congress would do to our FY 1982 funding request, so that was anyone's guess. It may be that our military later found an under-the-table means to help FUSEP, I don't know. Honduras did receive a concessional FMS interest rate, but it was higher than the indicated 3 percent. This was a case study in how to mismanage a security assistance relationship. But we had to live with the consequences.

The official reprimand minuet began. I wrote to the technician, advising him of my intention to reprimand him and giving him 15 days in which to offer information in extenuation or mitigation. He responded April 3, failing to provide anything new or persuasive; indeed, his letter only reaffirmed my intent. On April 6 I issued the reprimand. That action, unfortunately, could not undo the damage.

INCREASED AID FOR EL SALVADOR: WASHINGTON, D.C., MARCH 31, 1981. The administration announced a 100 percent increase in current year economic assistance for El Salvador, making the new total $126.5 million, vice $63 million.[58] It was not conditioned on improved human rights or other performance criteria.

MEETING WITH AMERICAN BUSINESSMEN: TEGUCIGALPA, HONDURAS, MARCH 31, 1981. Our monthly meeting with the American business community was particularly important because of recent events. Their principal concerns were recurring coup rumors and the deteriorating security situation, as evidenced by the assembly bombing, SAHSA hijacking and events on the borders. The recent tax agreement between the local private sector and government was also of interest. Wackerbarth also reported they were very curious about Zuniga's press attack on me and our denials. Finally, garbled rumors about Paz's aborted trip to Washington were floating and had reached their ears. Given the candor we strived for in these meetings, I could see no reason why I shouldn't give them a brief recap of these latter points, although the Paz trip was a very delicate topic.

Our discussion was very useful. Their perceptions of the security situation were—not surprisingly—very negative, especially in its effect on the economy. And their reports of the reactions of their Honduran counterparts were even more bearish, confirming what we had been reporting. All had taken measures to increase their personal security. Because of their concerns, we arranged for RSO Dewitt to brief them on personal security measures when he was next in town.

They were ambivalent on the tax issue. Most felt the tax package would not raise sufficient revenue and was only a stopgap; a further boost would be needed. They thought the Honduran private sector had erred in not biting the bullet on the first go. Others, however, felt the only solution lay in rather sharp cuts in government spending.

Addressing the political matters, I explained our program that had taken journalists to visit a number of AID projects and how my impolitic remarks had been played by the press. Although this may have affected the nature of Zuniga's subsequent attack, I explained, it was not its cause. His actions were rooted in far more profound differences—whether the embassy and USG should openly (or covertly) support the Zuniga candidacy and whether elections should be delayed to avoid Zuniga's possible loss of the presidency and control of the National Party. As long as we avoided helping either party and opposed postponement of elections, we would incur Zuniga's wrath. Although there were elements in our Republican Party that supported Zuniga, their influence on the administration, as far as I could determine, was limited. Our official position remained that of being evenhanded and supporting elections as scheduled. Consequently, they could expect to see further such attacks.

As to Paz's trip, there was little I could say. Paz had a strong desire to go to Washington, and the embassy had recommended an official visit through regular channels. Competing demands on President Reagan's time, however, meant that such a visit was unlikely in the near term. Aware of this, Paz had sought to use informal channels to arrange a visit. That initiative had involved Zuniga and had not been successful. We were busy trying to work out a solution that would meet Paz's needs, but I could not be more specific.

They seemed grateful for this information, and we were certainly happy to have their views of the security and economic situations.

6

Damage Control, Honduran Schemes and Covert Plans

Summary—Dealing with Paz and supporting elections—extraordinary Honduran military plans—misuse of AID resources—appetite for arms grows—CIA deceit and Honduran duplicity—policy uncertainty and uncoordinated actions—General Walters's visit—new friction with Southern Command—human rights abuses—efforts to ease regional tensions—Washington consultations—Salvadoran conflict unabated—clashes on Nicaraguan border escalate

CONFLICTING VIEWS: ARMS INTERDICTION AND SECURITY ASSISTANCE: TEGUCIGALPA, HONDURAS, APRIL 1, 1981. Our differences with Washington over a strategy to control the illicit arms flow continued. The joint State/Defense recommendations focused on the "retail" side of the traffic rather than interdicting it at the Nicaraguan border, the "wholesale" side. Southern Command was to be the main actor, and General Nutting was pushing to send an initial survey team before we had even agreed on a scope of work. Our military's ability to work with the Honduran police, who had primary responsibility for controlling this traffic, was strictly circumscribed by law. That meant their effectiveness would be limited. Moreover, our recommendations for a coordinated interagency approach were being ignored.[1]

Meanwhile, Honduran anxiety was reaching near-hysterical levels. Their demands for security assistance were growing almost daily, and they were constantly stressing the need to make their requirements known to the "highest level" of our government. That was a clear reference to Paz's desire to meet with President Reagan.

To force action we reiterated our arms interdiction position and called for decisions, began working with Southern Command on a scope of work for their survey team and recommended a small increase in security assistance.[2] These steps, I hoped, would reaffirm our commitment and ease the growing disquiet.

145

AID TO NICARAGUA OFFICIALLY TERMINATED: WASHINGTON, D.C., APRIL 1, 1981. State formally terminated U.S. assistance for Nicaragua, suspended since January. Curiously, the notice acknowledged that Nicaragua's response to U.S. pressure "has been positive" and that we had "no hard evidence of arms movements through Nicaragua during the past few weeks, and propaganda and some other support activities have been curtailed."

Sandinista leader Daniel Ortega, in Managua, called our move an act of "true aggression against Nicaragua." Ambassador Pezzullo cited this decision as the turning point in our relations with Nicaragua by which "we dealt ourselves out of the game for no reason...because of small-mindedness on our side."[3]

MORE DAMAGE CONTROL: DEALING WITH THE PAZ VISIT ISSUE: TEGUCIGALPA, HONDURAS, APRIL 2, 1981. Our damage control group met several times to review Paz's aborted trip to Washington, how it came about and its significance. At this point, we had received only one report from State.[4] It contained few details, but referred to the possibility that Secretary Haig might send Ambassador-at-Large Vernon Walters (a retired lieutenant general and former deputy director of the CIA under President Nixon) down as a special emissary. Letters from Central American Affairs director John Blacken and Deputy Director Rich Brown—much richer in detail—were en route via diplomatic courier and did not reach me until several days after our analysis and recommendations were transmitted.[5]

Our local collection effort had been very productive, and most of what we had developed was confirmed by the information we later received from Washington. I drafted an analysis of how and why the trip had eventuated, what it meant for our relations and what we might do to restore some equilibrium in my relationship with Paz. Included were a series of recommendations addressing Paz's perceived needs and ways to undo some of the damage. It was circulated to the working group before being sent to State.[6]

My thesis was that the root causes were frustrated Honduran perceptions and expectations: Paz and the military saw us as insensitive to their security needs, and they had expected the new administration to alter U.S. regional policy quickly and dramatically. Zuniga, in particular, played on these expectations, claiming close ties with the Reagan crowd and using people like McCormack to reinforce that perception. In Zuniga's view I was the problem. He told them that I had failed to convey their concerns to Washington and opposed their requests for sharply increased military assistance. The Honduran embassy in Washington, we learned later, was reporting similar impressions, based on the contacts Ambassador Pujol and Zuniga's son had with the far right and senior U.S. military officers. I suspect that the gist, if not the detailed content, of some of our more sensitive cables concerning military assistance had been leaked to the Honduran embassy. As a result of these efforts, he had gained an alarming degree of influence with Paz and his associates. His goal: a preemptive coup or elections rigged in his favor.

According to our sources, Zuniga had also targeted Milgroup commander Goodwin and the station chief for removal from Honduras. That struck me as odd, since Arcos was by far our most effective operator in the Honduran milieu and was not included on Zuniga's hit list.

To safeguard our political and security interests, and to try to restore relationships, I emphasized that we must speak with a single voice. Otherwise, we would appear disorganized and lack credibility. That, of course, was precisely the case at that time, and it didn't change much.

In addition, I recommended the following steps:

• Either inviting Paz to Washington for an official visit or sending a special high-level emissary. The former was more desirable and would go some way in restoring my credibility as President Reagan's representative, but I knew it was highly unlikely.

• In either case we needed to emphasize our understanding of Honduran security concerns, continued support for the transition process, willingness to increase security and economic assistance in a measured fashion, and commitment to defend Honduras under the Rio Treaty should it be attacked.

• To lend substance to this message we had to make additional, but fairly modest, assistance commitments. For example: finalizing the agreement to relieve the Hondurans of financial liability for the damaged helicopter; offering a program to assist with arms interdiction, as already recommended;[7] increasing security assistance modestly; and approving additional economic assistance, preferably Economic Support Funds (ESF).

The final point was the most important, as ESF was a grant that could be directed at selected targets. The cable concluded with a request for feedback.

The response was unusually prompt and largely reflected our recommendations. Later, when General Walters met with Paz, his talking points included more of our recommendations. Our official commitment to the transition would never waver, despite the cacophony of voices with which we continued to speak, some lukewarm endorsements by senior officials and the efforts of Zuniga and his friends.

The analysis contained in our cable was surprisingly accurate. It described what had motivated Paz; how our interests conflicted with those of Zuniga, Paz and some other senior officers; how Zuniga was attempting to deal with that conflict; and how some senior military officers might seek to preempt elections with a coup. Ultimately the success of our policy would turn on how the military institution as a whole viewed the transition process.

There was, however, one critically important factor that had driven Paz that we were unaware of: he wished to meet with President Reagan and Secretary Haig in order to broach a Honduran plan to attack Nicaragua and oust the Sandinistas. Otherwise, our assessment erred only in underestimating the elected successor government's likelihood of remaining in power.

PRESS DETAILS NICARAGUAN EXILE CLAIMS AND GOALS: NEW YORK, APRIL 2, 1981. The *New York Times* reported the plans of Nicaraguan exile groups in Honduras to invade and "liberate" Nicaragua. The story quoted exile leaders as claiming the "support of some sectors of the Honduran Army and hoping for a 'green light' from Washington" for their plan. Three groups—the September 15 Legion, the National Liberation Army and the Nicaraguan Revolutionary Armed Force—were identified as forming this paramilitary coalition.[8]

ENDERS NOMINATED AS ASSISTANT SECRETARY: WASHINGTON, D.C., EARLY APRIL 1981. President Reagan nominated Thomas O. Enders, a distinguished career officer, to become assistant secretary for Inter-American affairs. Enders was Haig's choice but encountered considerable opposition from the far right. Senator Jesse Helms blocked his confirmation hearings for several months.

Although Bushnell remained acting assistant secretary, Enders moved into the bureau front office and was soon running it on a de facto basis. Although he was able to revitalize the bureau, the delay in his confirmation prevented State from gaining a firm grip on the interagency policy process. The administration would continue to speak in many voices and engage in uncoordinated actions.

MISUSE OF AID FUNDS: TEGUCIGALPA, HONDURAS, APRIL 3, 1981. Over the preceding months, AID director Oleson had reported several instances of misuse of AID funds or AID-provided equipment. They involved agencies under the direction of both the National and Liberal Parties. Most involved the diversion of resources—vehicles, salaried employees and travel funds—for electoral purposes rather than project implementation. We also had AID inspectors investigating what appeared to be an attempt to rig bids in an agency controlled by the Liberals. In addition, Zuniga's daughter Elizabeth, serving as the number two in the government's industrial development agency, had attempted to force AID-funded employees to kick back part of their salaries to the National Party.

Oleson believed the time had come to raise the issue officially. Indeed, if the bid-rigging allegations proved true, it was hard to see how we could keep it from becoming public. I shared Oleson's concerns, and recognized the need to deter further misuse of our resources as the election campaign approached. But I was very chary about making an official issue of it, given my standing with Paz and our overall relationship, the details of which Oleson was only partially aware.

After reviewing options, Oleson agreed that I would send an EXDIS cable laying out a proposed course of action and seeking the concurrence of State and AID/Washington. It proposed that Oleson and I approach Paz, explaining the issue in general terms, emphasizing that both parties were involved, and that, with his permission, we wished to meet separately and privately with the two parties' leaders. Assuming he agreed, we would repeat this to the party leaders, tell them that we had raised the issue with the president, and warn them that if such practices did not cease, we would formally request the government take corrective action. If that failed, our future ability to extend economic assistance to Honduras could be jeopardized.

We also planned to proceed with an "institutional evaluation" of one of the agencies controlled by the National Party, which could surface officially some of the irregularities we had detected. That action, we believed, would deter further irregularities in other agencies, regardless of party affiliation.[9]

MEXICO AND VENEZUELA CALL FOR SALVADORAN NEGOTIATIONS: MEXICO CITY, MEXICO, APRIL 9, 1981. The presidents of Mexico and Venezuela, Jose Lopez Portillo and Luis Herrera Campins, issued a joint communiqué calling for a negotiated solution to the strife in El Salvador and urging the Salvadoran government to open talks with its opponents.[10] Like its several precursors, this initiative went nowhere. It did, however, strain relations between the United States and these two countries.

CLARIFICATION OF PROPOSED MILITARY ASSISTANCE LEVEL: TEGUCIGALPA, HONDURAS, APRIL 9, 1981. The local press picked up a wire service report of the fiscal year 1982 military assistance funding request presented to Congress March 7. And it got the funding levels wrong. Accordingly, I asked Arcos to prepare a press release that described the correct figures, explained what the congressional presentation meant, and stressed that Congress might reduce or increase the requested levels. It would emphasize what had been requested for Honduras: $10 million in Foreign Military Sales credit and $750 thousand in training grant funds. This was essentially what we had recommended, well below the levels recommended by Southern Command and far less than the Hondurans wanted. We had, however, advised the Hondurans of the FY 1982 request.

This clarification, I feared, could irritate the Honduran military further. Their expectations had already been fired by the misinformed and mindless briefing of the Milgroup technician, and a public statement by the embassy would rub salt in their wounds of disappointment, heightening their displeasure. Yet I didn't want the misinformation to stand. So I also asked Colonel Goodwin to hotfoot it over to the Honduran military headquarters and tell them we were going to issue a press release clarifying the issue. He reported that their unhappiness was palpable. They tended to regard all information concerning military funding, U.S. or Honduran, as highly sensitive, despite the fact that our data were matters of public record.

The media printed our press release.[11]

ARMS INTERDICTION: GENERAL STAFF ACCEPTS OUR PROPOSAL: TEGUCIGALPA, HONDURAS, APRIL 10, 1981. We finally persuaded Washington to give priority to stopping the "wholesale" traffic from Nicaragua and agreed on a scope of work for Southern Command's survey team. Our interagency approach, however, remained an orphan. Nonetheless, we set up a meeting with the General Staff to outline our proposal. To help control the illicit flow of arms we were prepared to bring a military survey team to Honduras promptly to work with the Honduran military in developing a plan to help close off this traffic. I stressed that this team would not be able to work with FUSEP. However, we hoped we would soon have a proposal for a non-military survey group that could work with police units.

There would be no cost to Honduras for this team or any follow-on training and related activity; costs would be funded on a grant basis. At the conclusion of the survey we would offer recommendations, which they could decide to adopt or not. We were prepared to collaborate in implementing agreed-upon recommendations, although I could not commit the United States to providing further funding to this end. I stressed the final point.

General Chinchilla agreed to the proposal. The earliest the Hondurans could receive the team was May 4.

We then agreed on the following survey targets:

• Identify potential overland infiltration and exfiltration routes and potential choke points with emphasis on the Salvadoran frontier.

• Recommend improvements in Honduran intelligence collection capabilities.

• Evaluate Honduran communications capability and determine additional equipment needs.

• Recommend ways to improve existing vehicle inspection stations at border choke points.

• Train crews to man checkpoints and recommend technical means to detect contraband cargo.

• Evaluate earlier border surveillance training and recommend additional training and materiel.

• Recommend possible technical and psychological deterrents and incentives (e.g., a rewards system) to reduce arms traffic.

• Develop training proposals for a military "quick reaction" group that could be called to respond to reports of arms infiltration or border crossings.

• Study the feasibility of training mobile military checkpoint teams for deployment on secondary roads near the Salvadoran frontier and elsewhere.[12]

The Hondurans seemed enthusiastic, although actual progress in getting the program underway was to prove slow. The scope of work also proved to be overly ambitious for the Southern Command group. Several of these goals—particularly those involving inspection stations at choke points and on secondary roads and related training—were left to the CIA team that later worked with FUSEP.

SECRETARY HAIG'S LETTER TO PRESIDENT PAZ: TEGUCIGALPA, HONDURAS, APRIL 11–15, 1981. Holy Week, a national holiday period in Honduras, began April 11. Virtually the entire country closed down until after Easter. Although we could not close the mission, very little business could be conducted. In keeping with local practice, Walker and I had decided to operate with a skeleton staff, allowing most Honduran employees to join their families and keeping only a few American officers and secretaries on duty each day. Walker would remain in Tegucigalpa through Wednesday, while Martha, Mimi and I went to Tela with Honduran friends. We would return Wednesday, and Walker and his family would take their holiday.

Walker phoned Saturday afternoon, reporting receipt of an EXDIS cable containing the text of a letter for President Paz from Secretary Haig. It directed me to seek an early appointment to deliver the letter and discuss its content. With most government officials, including the president, off the radar screen, and Walker's judgment that the cable did not require urgent action, I asked that he try to set up a Thursday meeting with Paz. If that was not possible, he should set something up for the following week. In the interim he should have the cable text typed and translated and advise State that Holy Week was delaying our action.

ZUNIGA ASSESSMENT TRANSMITTED: TEGUCIGALPA, HONDURAS, APRIL 13, 1981. Walker sent the assessment of Ricardo Zuniga to Washington in my absence. He had been responsible for its preparation and its coordination with the Political Section, Arcos, and others. Apart from saying that I wanted him to be evenhanded, it was his project. I recused myself and did not review it.

It described many of Zuniga's nefarious dealings, especially during the 1963–71 period when he effectively ran the government for dictator Gen. Lopez Arellano. It touched on Zuniga's corruption, double dealing, violence and use of entrapment, as well as his interactions with my predecessors and other embassy officials, usually involving Zuniga's trying to compromise or discredit them. He had, for example, entrapped one of my predecessors by arranging for someone to sell him stolen colonial period artifacts then accusing him of trying to smuggle these items out of the country.

This report also focused on his personal enrichment during his early years of power and influence. One of his favorite ploys was to extort money from foreign firms wishing to do business in Honduras. His modus operandi as minister of government in 1967 was to demand 10 percent of any foreign company's deal. Later, in 1971, he masterminded efforts to extort money from the two large U.S. banana companies. Zuniga and his associates arranged strikes and labor unrest, raised taxes and imposed retroactive tax levies, and even threatened possible nationalization of the companies. Ultimately, these actions led to the 1975 "Banana-gate" scandal that toppled the Lopez Arellano regime and damaged the United Brands' corporate image. In 1972 Zuniga led an extortion effort against an American construction firm that had a contract to build the Tela-La Ceiba highway. The company was forced to kick back $50 thousand to have specious legal actions against it dropped. In that case the firm showed the actual payoff check to an embassy official.

The report also detailed how Zuniga had "borrowed" money from the government, set up enrichment schemes for himself and others, and sought to destroy or neutralize those he could not control. It also detailed how Zuniga had used threats, lies, planted press stories and entrapment to discredit his enemies—including U.S. ambassadors and embassy officials—and minimize their influence. A favorite ploy to "prove" his influence was to claim that he had arranged the removal of ambassadors and other officers with whom he had differences when they were routinely transferred.

Finally, Walker's assessment examined Zuniga's self-proclaimed anticommunist credentials, which were his main selling point among ideological warriors in or near the Reagan administration. After describing some of Zuniga's activities, Walker concluded that although Zuniga had sometimes engaged in effective anticommunist activity, he had also on occasion made common cause with communist-dominated unions and student organizations and actively encouraged anti-American sentiment when it served his interests.[13]

It was an excellent effort. Had anyone paid attention to it, the information could have been used to counter some of the pro-Zuniga sentiment in Washington. Instead, it seemed to have been largely ignored. I have always hoped that one of Zuniga's friends in the administration told him of this cable, because I am certain it would have driven him up the wall.

HONDURAN MILITARY OFFICERS TO VISIT WASHINGTON: TEGUCIGALPA, HONDURAS, APRIL 13, 1981. Several weeks earlier the station chief had asked me to approve an invitation his agency wished to extend to Colonel Alvarez to make an orientation visit to the agency's headquarters. At the time, it seemed like a benign request, so I agreed. In fact, it marked the beginning of U.S. involvement in the effort to overthrow the Sandinista regime and of deliberate efforts to prevent me from knowing what the CIA was planning.

The agency's invitation was quickly expanded to include Alvarez's deputy, Col. Juan Lopez Grijalva, who commanded the police intelligence unit, the National Investigations Directorate. Then, during an April 10 meeting on another subject, Alvarez told me that he would be joined by the Air Force and Navy commanders, Cols. Walter Lopez and Ruben Montoya. Could I arrange for this group to meet with Secretary Haig, or his designee, and General Schweitzer? This request was especially awkward in light of Paz's failed visit. But I had no option to forwarding it. Although a meeting with Secretary Haig was out of the question, it would be useful for these officers to meet with State officials, if only to ensure they had that perspective. In forwarding Alvarez's request, I suggested that Enders receive them. I hoped that he would allay some of the misunderstandings and bad feelings generated by Paz's ill-fated initiative.[14]

To ensure Schweitzer received them, I sent him a personal message, providing background on recent developments and suggesting responses to their anticipated concerns.[15] It seemed like a good idea at the time; with hindsight, it was a bad call. Schweitzer only encouraged their paranoia and bizarre plans.

I assumed—correctly, it turned out—that Lopez and Montoya were joining this delegation in order to lend weight to the Honduran military's "urgent" plea for increased security assistance, as outlined in an earlier briefing of our Milgroup. I wasn't happy at the prospect of Alvarez and these senior officers wandering around in the chaotic environment existing in Washington during the early days of the Reagan administration. But I was aware of only part of their agenda. Shortly after Alvarez left for Washington, escorted by our station chief, we learned that he would also broach a scheme for launching a military attack on Nicaragua in order to oust the Sandinista government. This was utter madness.

In the event, Lopez and Montoya dropped out at the last minute, probably because of their exclusion from the CIA visit. Alvarez and Grijalva went alone and met with Casey, Schweitzer and others, as well as Enders.

The report of the Enders meeting indicated that they did not meet with Schweitzer.[16] Gutman, however, cites Alvarez as confirming that he met with Schweitzer on this trip.[17] It may be that State was unaware of that meeting or that Alvarez delayed his return a day in order to see Schweitzer after having met with Enders. Whatever the explanation, this trip was pivotal in terms of our engagement in the ill-conceived effort to use the Contras to oust the Sandinista regime.

NEW YORK TIMES ASSESSES HONDURAN TRANSITION: NEW YORK, APRIL 15, 1981. The *New York Times* featured an Alan Riding report examining the political situation in Honduras. It highlighted the uncertainty about the transition to democracy, Zuniga's efforts to exploit expectations about Reagan administration policy and the growing security threat.[18] It was a first-rate account of events and how they were being influenced by the administration's failure to come down forthrightly in favor of elections.

Riding had spent over a week in Tegucigalpa and met with a wide range of political and government leaders, including Zuniga and Suazo Cordova. He also met several times with Arcos, who suggested people he ought to see and helped arrange appointments for him, and with Walker, a friend of long standing. I also gave him a brief interview on a "not for attribution" basis, describing how we saw events.

From our standpoint, Riding's story could not have been more useful. Among my adversaries in Washington, however, it no doubt was seen in a different light.

SALVADORAN OLIGARCHS ARRESTED FOR MURDER OF AMERICANS: MIAMI, FLORIDA, AND SAN SALVADOR, EL SALVADOR, APRIL 15–17, 1981. Two major Salvadoran landowners, Ricardo Sol Mesa and Hans Crist, were arrested and charged with complicity in the January 1981 murders of American agrarian reform advisers Hammer and Pearlman. Crist was arrested in Miami and immediately extradited; Sol Mesa was arrested in San Salvador.[19]

According to one of the actual gunmen, Sol Mesa and Crist saw the Americans in the Sheraton Hotel dining room and ordered their own bodyguards to kill them as they ate dinner.[20]

MEETING WITH PRESIDENT PAZ: TEGUCIGALPA, HONDURAS, APRIL 16, 1981. On my return to Tegucigalpa I reviewed the text of Secretary Haig's letter and my instructions. Walker had been able to locate Paz and set up an appointment. The letter and translation were ready for delivery. State had accepted most of our suggested strategy. Paz would not be going to Washington, however. Instead, General Vernon Walters would come to Honduras as Haig's personal representative.

The letter had one important weakness, however. The affirmation of support for elections was weak, almost offhand. It did include a strong statement of understanding for Honduran concerns, promised increased U.S. assistance and encouraged Honduran cooperation with the IMF. It also asked Paz to work with me on the Walters visit and concluded with a statement of Haig's "full confidence" in the embassy. That was all helpful.[21]

Paz appeared in good condition, and the meeting seemed to go well. Although clearly disappointed that he would not be going to Washington in the near future and that no specific assistance was promised, Paz evinced great interest in meeting Walters, whose background I briefly outlined. Unfortunately, he was already committed for the entire May 4 week and could not change his schedule; could Walters come the week following? I had to inquire and suggested that he give me the name of someone I could work with in developing a mutually acceptable date and program. Colonel Torres Arias was designated.

I reported the meeting, initiating considerable back-and-forth attempting to find a suitable date. We finally agreed on May 13–15. Torres Arias and I then began work on the program. Despite Haig's casual endorsement of Honduran elections, I saw Walters's visit as a unique opportunity to reaffirm our support for the process. It was, and Walters did a terrific job.

This effort did not dampen Paz's efforts to get to Washington by bypassing the embassy, however.

DISINFORMATION: HONDURAN GROUP ALLEGES MASSACRE IN EL SALVADOR: TEGUCIGALPA, HONDURAS, APRIL 18, 1981. The Coordinator for Solidarity with the Salvadoran People issued a press release alleging that the Salvadoran Air Force (SAF) had recently bombed and killed 1,200 refugees in El Salvador.[22] This report contended that the refugees—mostly women and children—were trying to escape a strafing and bombing attack as they made their way to safe haven in Honduras. Seeking refuge from aircraft fire, they had entered a large cave. The SAF then repeatedly bombed the cave entrance, causing its collapse and entombing those inside. All were alleged to have perished. The story was picked up and disseminated internationally by the wire services.[23] It was a total fabrication.

The Salvadorans immediately denied this report. We investigated and after nearly two weeks work found nothing remotely substantiating the alleged events. All sources, including refugees themselves, denied knowledge of the movement of 1,200 people, and we could find no one who claimed knowledge of a sizable cave in the area, let alone one large enough to hold 1,200 people.

NICARAGUAN REFUGEE INFLOW RAISES CONCERNS: PUERTO LEMPIRA, HONDURAS, APRIL 21, 1981. Honduran authorities reported a relatively slow but steady influx of Miskito Indians from Nicaragua into the Puerto Lempira area. Some 200, fleeing growing Sandinista repression, had already entered, and their numbers were growing.[24]

This was an extremely remote, isolated and sparsely settled area. There was no significant overland access, and virtually all supplies came in by air or small coastal boat. The Hondurans were allowing these refugees to stay but were hard pressed to provide much support. They had contacted the various refugee relief organizations, urging that they provide the needed assistance. It was slow in coming. Living conditions for the Miskito refugees were extremely primitive, even when compared to those in the camps along the Salvadoran frontier. Once the rainy season began, much of the area would be under water for several months. Even the higher spots would resemble bogs. This meant there was a very high probability of serious disease outbreaks unless something could be done to improve their situation.

We reported this development and urged State to bring it to the attention of the UN High Commission for Refugees and support the Honduran request for assistance.

MEETING WITH SUAZO CORDOVA: TEGUCIGALPA, HONDURAS, APRIL 23, 1981. At his request I met with Liberal Party leader Suazo Cordova and his aide at the residence.[25] Suazo was concerned—understandably—about Zuniga's maneuvering, Paz's behavior and the possibility of a coup. I couldn't offer much reassurance. However, I did tell him that Secretary Haig was sending a special emissary to meet with Paz and to reaffirm our commitment to elections. I did not identify the envoy, and stressed that the dates for the visit were still open.

I also assured him that I would do my best to ensure that this emissary met with him and other political leaders (Zuniga) during the visit. I asked, without much hope that my request would be honored, that he hold this information very closely. I assumed, correctly it turned out, that Torres Arias or someone else had already told Zuniga of the planned Walters visit.

WALTERS VISIT PREPARATIONS AND PROGRAM: TEGUCIGALPA, HONDURAS, LATE APRIL–EARLY MAY 1981. The delay in finding a date for the Walters visit gave President Paz an opportunity to renew his request to visit Washington in lieu of waiting for Walters. He was not pleased with my customary response.

Program coordination with Torres Arias went smoothly, with only one unexpected issue. On several occasions he noted that Paz wished to meet alone with Walters, evidently a reflection of Paz's lack of confidence in me. Each time, I responded to the effect that U.S. diplomatic practice was for our ambassador to be present at all meetings; indeed, should Paz go to Washington and meet with President Reagan, I would go along. But it was a warning flag.

As part of our preparations, we cabled State with our suggestions for Walters's agenda and talking points, which conformed with our earlier recommendations: the military situation and security assistance, the transition and elections, corruption and related problems, and the economic outlook and U.S. assistance. Curiously, State's response suggested that Walters raise the matter of media attacks on me and the embassy, particularly the one that alleged I had tried to start a new, left-wing political party. I argued against including this topic. The government had not been responsible and could not control the media. And no amount of cajoling was likely to dissuade Zuniga from having another go at me. It was dropped.

In my cable reporting the first planning session I noted that Paz was eager to release details of the visit to the media in order to demonstrate his country's close relationship with the new administration. I urged that we go along, requesting that State provide draft press guidance that we could propose to the Hondurans. I was unwilling to undertake this, as there were too many traps that could arise from the visit (e.g., speculation about U.S. or Honduran intervention in El Salvador or Nicaragua, rekindled coup rumors, Sandinista accusations of a conspiracy against them). In any event, that request and follow-ups brought no response. I could only tell Torres Arias that I agreed we should have a joint statement and had requested guidance from Washington. This was a missed opportunity to demonstrate our willingness to collaborate; instead, a leak in Washington preempted a formal announcement, breeding further resentment.[26]

CHARGÉ CHAPIN MAKES TOUGH DÉMARCHE: SAN SALVADOR, EL SALVADOR, APRIL 26, 1981. Chargé d'Affaires Fred Chapin and his deputy met with Salvadoran defense minister Garcia and National Guard commander Vides Casanova to communicate growing government and public impatience with the failure to prosecute those responsible for the murders of the American churchwomen and agrarian reform advisers. They also urged an end to the other gross human rights violations committed by various elements of the military. Failure to expedite action in the American cases, Chapin emphasized, would jeopardize continued U.S. assistance.[27]

This démarche was long overdue, yet it produced little. Our military and economic assistance flows, however, increased, and we made no effort to attach conditions to this aid. Given our behavior, and the several voices with which the administration was speaking, it was not surprising the Salvadoran military chose to ignore Chapin's tough talk.

HONDURAN PLANS TO ATTACK NICARAGUA AND ABORTED PAZ VISIT: TEGUCIGALPA, HONDURAS, APRIL 27, 1981. The day before, we had received a report that the Honduran military were planning a direct military assault on Nicaragua, using their own forces and the Contra groups then operating out of Honduras. According to our source, President Paz's unrelenting efforts to get to the United States were driven by his desire to broach this plan with the new administration and seek U.S. support; it was also what motivated his quixotic March effort to meet with President Reagan and Secretary Haig. This source also reported Paz was still trying to arrange such a trip extraofficially, despite Haig's letter, the proposed Walters visit and my cautionary comments.

The attack plan was utter madness. The Honduran military had no capability to mount a sustained attack on anyone. And the Contra movement at the time was a travesty, a ragtag amalgam of several poorly trained and armed groups capable of little more than hit-and-run attacks along the border. This scheme, according to Honduran officers, had the support "in principle" of El Salvador and Guatemala, as well as indications of support from Brazil and the Southern Cone. The plan had no chance of success, and none of the purported supporters had the capability to assist a Honduran operation. Such an action would only plunge the region more deeply into armed conflict, possibly precipitating a direct confrontation between the United States and the Soviet Union under circumstances in which we were likely to have little international support.[28]

Irrationality of the plan aside, we judged the report credible. The views attributed to military commanders were entirely consistent with those we had repeatedly heard them express. Finally, it provided a rationale for Paz's behavior, which we had been struggling to explain. If his country was planning to go to war with Nicaragua, he wanted to be damn certain he could count on our support before launching an attack. I had to take this report seriously. Because of its extreme sensitivity, I shared it only with Walker.

After reflecting overnight and discussing it with Walker, I decided that the time had come for some blunt talk with Paz. I was also concerned that Colonel Alvarez, then in Washington accompanied by our station chief, would broach this wild-eyed scheme. The mind-sets of some of those claiming to speak for the administration with whom he might come into contact, the administration's apparent lack of internal coordination,[29] and the Hondurans' ability to see a commitment in the blandest of responses seemed to me to create a high probability of catastrophic misunderstanding. We needed to act quickly: it could not wait two weeks for General Walters.

I sent a NODIS cable outlining my assessment of the report, my concerns and the need for prompt action on the possibility of an attack on Nicaragua and Paz's continued insistence on visiting Washington.[30] Bearing in mind the need to protect the source, it would be necessary to approach the issue indirectly. Therefore, I proposed that I be instructed to raise the visit issue with Paz again. I would reiterate that his request for an official visit was still pending; the Walters visit responded to his sense of urgency, but would reduce the priority of his visit request; and further efforts to arrange a visit outside embassy channels simply would not prosper. If following General Walters's visit he still felt it necessary that he go to Washington, State would support his request and do what it could to expedite it.

At that point I proposed to shift to the anti-Sandinista movement. I would tell him that I had also been instructed to voice growing U.S. concern over a variety of reports that his government was considering providing direct support to the Contras. Although we understood and, to a large extent, shared Honduran concerns, we felt that increased Contra operations would be counterproductive in Nicaragua and destabilizing in Honduras. Any support for such operations would quickly be known, trigger increased Cuban presence in Nicaragua, increase Sandinista-sponsored subversion in Honduras and greatly complicate our efforts to bring international pressure to bear on Nicaragua. Hence, we expected that Honduras would make good-faith efforts to deter use of its territory by the anti-Sandinistas.

Finally, although we thought a Nicaraguan attack was highly unlikely, we were prepared to honor our Rio Treaty commitments should it eventuate. The implied message was that if we opposed support of the Contra operation, it followed that we would certainly oppose a direct Honduran attack.

I went on to recommend that State—preferably Enders—make a similar presentation to Colonel Alvarez and that I also be authorized to make similar démarches to the foreign minister and Colonel Torres Arias. It was essential, I argued, that we get this message across in fairly forceful terms.

I soon received authorization to approach Paz with a watered-down version of my proposal. Something was certainly better than nothing. Moreover, my cable influenced the substance of Enders's and Bushnell's meetings with Cols. Alvarez and Lopez Grijalva. Acting Assistant Secretary Bushnell told them that "care must be taken that provocative actions against Nicaragua do not give the Sandinistas a reason to establish a totalitarian state, and even offensive actions before the interested countries work out a general approach...will help, not hurt, the GRN [Revolutionary Government of Nicaragua]." He also told Alvarez that any Honduran action on the border with Nicaragua "would be counterproductive, and we would discourage it."[31]

That didn't phase Alvarez. In a later meeting with Enders he urged the United States to decide quickly how it was going to handle Nicaragua. "Immediate action is necessary," he said, for "as long as the Sandinistas control Nicaragua there will be no peace." He went on to assert that the

> GOH [Government of Honduras] had consulted with Argentina and Chile about the problem. These countries, with Paraguay and Uruguay, are now ready to make common cause with Honduras in actively opposing the GRN. They have offered to meet with their Andean counterparts to enlist support for acting to expel communism from the region.... A move against Nicaragua would receive support from El Salvador and Guatemala. Even Costa Rica might endorse it, as they are beginning to understand the communist threat.[32]

This was a clear reference to the plan to attack Nicaragua that Paz wished to lay before the United States and that Alvarez had raised with Casey and Schweitzer in greater detail. In response, Enders "emphasized that calm and peace were crucial to the area. A confrontation between Honduras and Nicaragua would be unhelpful, given the current violence in El Salvador. He asked that the GOH restrain Nicaraguan exiles in Honduras and not allow any incident to take place that would provide the GRN a pretext to unite its people in facing foreign intervention, thereby removing the spotlight from the internal problems that weaken the GRN."[33]

Enders and Bushnell had made the recommended points unequivocally. The problem was that the administration had no single vision of what it wished to do, and others didn't want to deter actions against the Sandinistas. Several years later I learned that the visit of Colonel Alvarez represented the beginning of the CIA's meaningful involvement in the Contra operation.

Alvarez met separately with CIA director Bill Casey and General Schweitzer, then at the NSC.[34] Our station chief was present at the CIA meetings, including that with Casey. I don't know if he attended the meeting with Schweitzer.

According to Roy Gutman, in both meetings Alvarez laid out a plan that involved clandestine U.S. support for the Contras, who would be led by former National Guard officers. Once these forces were activated and operating in Nicaragua, the plan was to provoke the Nicaraguans into attacking Honduras, at which point U.S. forces would intervene and defeat the Sandinistas. Alvarez's vision included a key role for the Honduran armed forces, which would be re-equipped and upgraded by the United States. Casey and his deputy for Latin America, Nestor Sanchez, were noncommittal, according to Gutman.[35] But Casey did tell Alvarez that he would analyze the proposal closely and consult with President Reagan. Alvarez's experience with Schweitzer was quite different. Having listened to the Hondurans' presentation, Schweitzer was enthusiastic, and Gutman quotes him as telling Alvarez "We'll do it."[36] Alvarez, who had heard three different responses to his proposal, returned to Honduras convinced that he had our backing.

The plan described by Gutman, based largely on interviews with Alvarez, varied significantly from that reported by our source, as it did not envisage a direct Honduran attack on Nicaragua. I believe our version was the more accurate, as we later acquired a military document justifying that strategy. Whichever was correct, the Honduran military soon went on a major arms-buying spree financed by the Treasury.

HONDURAN SECURITY FORCES DETAIN SALVADORAN GROUP: TEGUCIGALPA, HONDURAS, LATE APRIL 1981. The press had reported the detention of two Salvadoran families, a total of 14 people, on April 22. Reports of arrests of this nature were uncommon but by no means unheard of. This case drew the embassy's attention for several reasons: the number of people arrested, which reportedly included several children; it had been witnessed by a Dutch citizen who worked for the United Nations; and Honduran authorities denied all knowledge of these people.[37]

We assumed the members of these two families, Barrillas and Navarro, would ultimately turn up, but I asked our human rights officer to be sure to report the incident. I also asked the CT to see what light their contacts might be able to shed on this incident. We needed to know if FUSEP or military elements were responsible and, if so, what had become of the detainees. With that, I turned my attention to other matters.

AMBASSADOR PEZZULLO VOICES CONCERN OVER POSSIBLE HOSTILITIES: TEGUCIGALPA, HONDURAS, APRIL 29, 1981. We received an information copy of a Managua cable indicating that the Sandinistas planned to mobilize their forces in the face of a perceived Honduran military threat.

Ambassador Pezzullo was concerned over increasingly frequent and serious clashes between the Contras and Sandinista forces and the comments of senior Sandinistas. Both indicated bilateral tensions were nearing a critical point. If something was not done to defuse the situation, he thought a direct conflict might result.

According to the Sandinistas, the Honduran army had greatly strengthened its units along the border with Nicaragua, and the Honduran Air Force (HAF) was on alert in anticipation of a preemptive attack. Consequently, the Sandinistas were planning a mobilization. To avoid direct confrontation, Pezzullo recommended that I be instructed to approach President Paz, urging that he accept a pending Sandinista invitation for high-level meetings.

I was fairly certain that the Sandinistas' fears about the threat were exaggerated, although they were consistent with what we knew of the Hondurans' longer-term intentions. Pezzullo, however, had not been apprised of that information. There seemed no denying that tensions were rising and that an effort to ease them was needed. Pezzullo's suggestion that I urge Paz to accept the Nicaraguan invitation made sense: it might well calm both sides down. And if I could meet with Paz on that topic, Washington might also seize the opportunity to have me communicate the other message urging Honduran restraint that I requested permission to deliver.

But before I supported Pezzullo's proposal, I wanted to know whether the Honduran military were in fact mobilizing or otherwise preparing for action against Nicaragua. I asked the Defense attaches and Milgroup officers to look into what was going on and report back as quickly as possible. They did, and their information was reassuring. The Honduran army had not reinforced either of the two battalions responsible for the Nicaraguan frontier area, although they had moved two companies, less that 250 troops, from rear areas to border posts. That looked to us like a defensive move rather than mobilization preparations. As for the HAF, there were no signs of an alert or other offensive preparations, and at least a third of its aircraft were grounded with serious maintenance problems. Nicaraguan concerns were clearly exaggerated. Nonetheless, I wanted firsthand information about what was going on along the frontier and dispatched a joint embassy, Defense attache and Military Group team to the Choluteca area.

I reported our initial information and endorsed Pezzullo's recommendation. I also added two additional points: that State make a parallel approach to the Honduran ambassador in Washington and that I be authorized to urge Paz to restrain the Contras.[38]

The Choluteca group confirmed there had been no reinforcement of the units responsible for the Nicaraguan border nor any signs of mobilization. Moreover, Honduran troops were under orders not to return fire from Nicaragua, although Contras reportedly fired into Nicaragua at night in efforts to provoke firefights between the two forces. Our team also learned later that the local Honduran commander met with his Nicaraguan counterpart April 30, with the result that Sandinista forces had drawn back one kilometer.

We reported this, along with our assessment that tensions seemed to be easing.[39]

HALCON VISTA PROPOSAL RESURFACES: TEGUCIGALPA, HONDURAS, APRIL 30, 1981. Like the proverbial bad penny, the joint U.S./Honduran military exercise *Halcon Vista*, canceled in 1980, was back on our agenda. Southern Command was pushing to begin planning with the Hondurans, and the initial concept again called for the participation of U.S. Navy ships carrying Marine Corps landing forces. If anything, the then-existing tensions in the region and Honduras were even higher and more dangerous than they had been the previous year. And now we had the Honduran military secretly pushing a harebrained plan to attack Nicaragua. This, coupled with Southern Command's more aggressive posture, accentuated my disquiet. However, there was no chance of getting a cancellation or postponement. Faced with an inevitable exercise, our only viable strategy would be to try to control its scope and nature, preventing anything that might be unnecessarily provocative, such as the Marine presence. That would prove a major challenge.

I remained ignorant of the administration's intentions toward Nicaragua, but it seemed clear that it was eager to engage in thinly veiled military threats. *Halcon Vista* fit nicely into that category. The Hondurans, of course, were at least equally eager to have the joint exercise, their views being far more extreme than ours.

My first move was to cable State, flagging the problem of embarked Marines and urging that the views of our other Central American embassies be canvassed before beginning discussions with the Hondurans. I was quite sure they would support my position.[40]

ASSEMBLY PASSES EMERGENCY ECONOMIC PLAN: TEGUCIGALPA, HONDURAS, APRIL 30, 1981. The Constituent Assembly overwhelmingly approved the government's emergency economic plan designed to raise additional revenue and bring Honduras into compliance with its Extended Fund Facility arrangement with the IMF. As a result, Honduras would be eligible to borrow up to $60 million from the fund to augment its foreign exchange account and strengthen the Lempira.[41]

SOUTHERN COMMAND ARMS INTERDICTION SURVEY: PRESS GUIDANCE, TEGUCIGALPA, HONDURAS, EARLY MAY 1981. With the Hondurans preparing to receive the arms interdiction survey team, we needed to deal with the public affairs issue. There was no way we could keep the presence of the survey team from becoming public knowledge, and we needed to agree on what we would say when that happened. Given speculation about U.S.

intentions and the likelihood that the Coordinator for Solidarity with the Salvadoran People would have a disinformation field day when our military were spotted in the border area, we needed a credible explanation for their presence. After careful discussion and review, we came up with press guidance, which we sent to State and Southern Command for approval.[42]

There was the usual word smithing and back-and-forth about what we should say, but ultimately we worked out satisfactory language. We would soon need it.

THE DECEIT BEGINS: STATION CHIEF RETURNS FROM WASHINGTON, TEGUCIGALPA, HONDURAS, MAY 4, 1981. I had eagerly awaited the station chief's return from Washington, where he had remained a few days after Alvarez's departure. I wanted to know what Alvarez had said about Honduran plans for Nicaragua and the Contras and, especially, how our officials had responded. According to the station chief, Alvarez had not broached either subject; rather, his main pitch had been for additional police and military assistance. I pressed on this point, but the station chief stuck with his story. Alvarez, he claimed, had reviewed the alarmist Honduran threat assessment we all had heard many times but had said nothing about a Honduran attack or aiding the Contras. Casey, he said, had raised the arms-traffic issue, and Alvarez had responded by welcoming anything we could do to help. Later, the station chief and Alvarez had met with working-level officials to discuss ways to interdict this traffic. This account struck me as quite curious, especially in light of the reports of Enders's and Bushnell's meetings with Alvarez.

The station chief had several meetings on the arms-traffic issue following Alvarez's departure. The agency agreed to send a team to assess the situation and make program recommendations, assuming, of course, that I agreed. I did, since I had been pressing for nonmilitary action. The station chief, however, claimed not to know whether this team would be interagency in its composition. When it arrived a few days later, it was not.

The station chief also reported that he had taken some flak from his supervisors for the Station's and embassy's reporting on human rights issues. "Tell your Ambassador to back off all that liberal stuff," he was advised. I thanked him for that feedback but pointed out that as far as I was concerned, we had a legal mandate to report on human rights and would continue to do so.

I had little reason to doubt what the station chief told me, although it called into question the reliability of the source of our earlier information. As far as I was then aware, the station chief had always played square with me, and I assumed he still was.

In fact, he deliberately lied about the content of the Casey/Alvarez meeting. About that there can be no doubt. And he was almost certainly doing so on direct orders from his superiors. This probably marked the beginning of the agency's effort to cut me out of the picture by engaging in active deceit and duplicity. I cannot, however, be sure that this strategy had not been underway for some time. For example, the activities of the Argentine military advisers had been a target for agency collection since before I had arrived, yet I had seen no intelligence on this subject. Were the agency's employees too busy with other targets, incompetent, or actually getting data they failed to share with me? If the latter, it was a clear violation of statute and agreements between State and the CIA.

This deception surrounding the Contras also served to further undermine my position with President Paz and the military. Alvarez no doubt lost little time telling Paz and his colleagues that the United States would support their plan to back and beef up the Sandinistas, and, probably, that we were prepared to strengthen their army so that it could prevail over the Sandinistas. This cut the ground from under my position and cast serious doubt on my credibility on all subjects, including the transition. That was intolerable. Had I been aware of it, I might well have resigned on the spot.

And how did Alvarez square what he had heard from Enders and Bushnell with what he took away from the meetings with Casey and Schweitzer? I suspect it was the same rationalization used by the Salvadorans in 1969, as they prepared to attack Honduras. They chose, not unreasonably, to read the Milgroup's collaboration in their mobilization and attack planning process as reflecting the "real" U.S. position. We really had no objection to their aggression but couldn't say that openly. The embassy's warnings, in that case, were perceived as "cover," future deniability, if you will. The Argentine government made a similar miscalculation the following year when they decided to attack the Falkland Islands.

HONDURAS/NICARAGUA RELATIONS: CAUTIONS AND ASSURANCES: TEGUCIGALPA, HONDURAS, EARLY MAY 1981. I met with President Paz on May 4 to convey our concerns about possible Honduran actions against Nicaragua. In the interim I received State's report of Enders's and Bushnell's meetings with Alvarez, so I drew on their comments to strengthen the original instructions. I ran through my talking points, which had ignored Pezzullo's suggestion about meeting with the Sandinistas, commending Honduran restraint in the face of Nicaraguan provocation, our shared concerns and support for Honduras, the Walters visit, and the Sandinistas' growing internal problems before getting to the principal point: that they continue to exercise restraint and avoid any incident, including those by anti-Sandinista groups operating out of Honduras. In sum, we asked that they take no action against provocations or threats from Nicaragua and make a greater effort to control the exile groups.

Paz responded by assuring me his government would continue to exercise restraint. Specifically, he reiterated that Honduran military units on the frontier had standing orders not to return fire from Nicaragua. He also acknowledged that Contra units in Honduras often fired on Sandinista guard posts or units, hoping to provoke a confrontation. He said nothing and gave no indication that they would do anything about the Contras, however. Nonetheless, even limited assurances were useful, although I was skeptical as to their value. They were soon tested.

Winding up, I took the opportunity to alert him to the growing interest of American media in anti-Sandinista activities and the Honduran role therein. We knew the *Washington Post* was about to come out with a story that synthesized statements of Contra leaders, Alvarez's recent trip, and Walters's forthcoming visit to advance a theory of an emerging conspiracy to oust the Sandinistas. Moreover, a CBS television crew was then in Tegucigalpa filming an anti-Sandinista training camp. Reports of this nature, I noted, could be damaging to both our interests. He agreed, then again inquired about his visit to Washington. My response was unchanged.[43]

ASSURANCES TESTED: NICARAGUAN ATTACK ON HONDURAS: HONDURAS/NICARAGUA FRONTIER, MAY 5, 1981. The Honduran military reported that a Sandinista Army force of some 300 men had entered Honduras 50 kilometers due east of Danli, cutting a road linking two Honduran villages, Cifuentes and La Trojes. This force withdrew into Nicaragua after about an hour.

Details as to what might have provoked this attack were vague, but a Milgroup source reported there had been a six-hour firefight in the area prior to the Nicaraguan attack, suggesting that the incident had been provoked by Contras thought to be operating nearby. We also suspected the reported size of the Nicaraguan incursion was exaggerated, given the area's rugged terrain, isolation and sparse population.

The Honduran reaction was relatively rapid, measured and defensive. Because the police, rather than the military, were best acquainted with this area, a crack FUSEP unit was ordered to the area to direct two platoons of troops from the nearest military unit. Four Huey helicopters left the Tegucigalpa air base midafternoon, less than an hour after the initial report, transporting the FUSEP unit. The choppers later ferried in the army troops and were back at their base before nightfall.[44]

Within a few days most of the deployed forces were back at their respective bases.

A QUICK VISIT TO MANAGUA: MANAGUA, NICARAGUA, MAY 7, 1981. Larry Pezzullo called me several days earlier to suggest that we get together for a *tour d'horizon* and invited me to make a day trip to Managua. The invitation could hardly have been more timely, and I accepted immediately. I would go over in the morning and come back the same afternoon in the

Attache aircraft. As the Air attaches were accredited to Nicaragua and visited there occasionally, the presence of their aircraft would not attract particular attention. Pezzullo would advise the Nicaraguans of the visit and arrange for my customs and immigration clearance to be handled outside regular channels.[45]

For my part I didn't wish to stir up the Honduran military—goodness knows how they would have interpreted this visit—or give Zuniga another opportunity for a potshot, so we kept a lid on it. At post, only Walker, the station chief, the Air attaches and my secretary, Amy, knew that this orientation flight would land in Managua. I also cleared the visit with John Blacken in Central American affairs, who agreed that because I would not be out of the country overnight, no formal request to leave the post was required.

I found Pezzullo, who was one of the most resourceful and energetic of my colleagues, very downbeat about the future of U.S. relations with Nicaragua and the outlook for Central America generally. The Reagan administration, he thought, had no sense of how to deal with the Sandinistas, and it had already thrown away several opportunities. Moreover, its apparent penchant for military approaches—whether in El Salvador, Nicaragua or Honduras—did not bode well.

He was very concerned about Nicaragua/Honduras relations, fearing a mindless action (e.g., an act by the Contras) could trigger a rash Sandinista response. He pressed me hard as to Honduran intentions. I couldn't allay his concerns. I described how sentiment in the military was shifting toward possible preemptive action against Nicaragua but stressed that the Hondurans did not have the capability to mount a meaningful offensive. If they should attack—highly unlikely without assurances of our support—it would be a replay of the 1969 El Salvador/Honduras conflict: a small salient on a single front, followed by exhaustion. In such a case, however, I suspected the Sandinistas would be able to throw the Hondurans back in fairly short order, perhaps turning an attack into a rout.

I did not share with Pezzullo what we knew about the wild-eyed Honduran scheme to oust the Sandinista regime. My reasons were several. First, the extreme sensitivity of the information. If Washington wanted Pezzullo to know, it was their responsibility to advise him, not mine. Second, the plan was so harebrained that it was not credible, at least to me, and I had no doubt that it would be rejected by our government. I saw no reason to get Pezzullo exercised about something that seemed so absurd. In retrospect, I probably erred; on the other hand, it's hard to see how my advising him would have changed later events.

As for the Contras, we both believed that some in the Honduran military were helping them, along with the Argentines. But from what we could tell, they had no meaningful military capability. They could harass the Sandinistas, yes, but that was about it. If the tide of public sentiment should change inside Nicaragua, however, it might be a different ball game.

I told Pezzullo what I had learned of Alvarez's meetings in Washington, our pleas for restraint and Paz's assurances. He was not reassured and certainly would have been alarmed if I had told him what had actually transpired. But I didn't know. The key problem, in Pezzullo's view, was the administration's unwillingness to grasp the nettle and tell the Hondurans firmly that we opposed any military action against Nicaragua. Our equivocation on that point, he thought, could cause them to take some action that could not be undone.

Our only differences involved the Contras; he thought they represented a serious threat. Their cross-border raids, regardless of their military insignificance, were sorely trying the Sandinistas and could lead to a blowup, he argued. I agreed that they were an irritant but did not believe they represented a real threat.

Given this bleak outlook, we spent some time discussing ways to ease tension. About all we could come up with—apart from the high-level bilateral meetings—was some kind of regional approach, (e.g., a meeting of heads of state to air grievances and allay security concerns). The Central American foreign ministers were at the time discussing just that option, but agreement appeared unlikely. How such a meeting could be convened and kept on a constructive track escaped us. Later, Pezzullo elaborated on this notion, suggesting the United States seek to engage a number of other Latin American countries in sponsoring such a meeting. And he was active in trying to push the Sandinistas in this direction.

Neither of us had solid information about where the Reagan administration wished to go. And at the time it didn't know either. There were too many ideas in play, most of them ill-advised. It is difficult to conduct foreign policy without well-defined goals and impossible to be effective without adequate coordination. We didn't meet either test.

Midafternoon I headed home.

WALTERS VISIT STORY BREAKS: RELATIONS WITH NICARAGUA: TEGUCIGALPA, HONDURAS, MAY 8, 1981. I was scheduled to see Colonel Torres Arias to finalize the details of General Walters's program. Neither the government nor the embassy had yet announced the visit; indeed, just how we would do that was on my agenda for Torres Arias. We were preempted. The *Washington Post* featured a story alleging that Honduras was preparing for war with Nicaragua, which it linked to the Walters visit, blindsiding our hosts. Even worse, the thrust of the article was that Honduras, with U.S. support, was increasing its armed forces and weaponry in order to attack Nicaragua and block the transition process.[46]

This triggered a media feeding frenzy. Hyperactive imaginations were stoked by the conjunction of the Walters visit, incidents on the Nicaraguan border, speculation about postponing elections, the administration's loose rhetoric and the *Washington Post*'s theory. It smelled like big news. Arcos's phone was ringing off the hook, and he was stonewalling. But when I was seen entering the National Palace, the media sharks gathered to await my exit.

Torres Arias expressed displeasure at the leak of the Walters visit and thrust of the story, but we quickly got down to work on the program. Walters's first appointment May 13 would be with Foreign Minister Elvir, who would accompany us to meet the president at the National Palace. This would be a courtesy meeting. It would be followed by a threat assessment briefing at the General Staff. The critical session with the president and his closest military advisers was set for the following day at General Staff headquarters. Around these official sessions we set up meetings with Zuniga, Suazo Cordova, the private sector and others. I would also host a reception the first evening. Finally, Walters would meet with the press the morning of May 15, before departing.

Torres Arias then launched a discourse on Nicaragua and "Honduran moderation in the face of Nicaraguan provocations." Honduras, he insisted, had no intention of going to war with Nicaragua, as evidenced by its failure to reinforce frontier forces or to begin mobilization. "You would have to be crazy to advocate such a thing," he said, adding that "we may be backward, but we are neither fools nor lunatics." I indicated my total agreement with the former statement but withheld my reservations about the latter. He also threw in a caveat: nonetheless, Honduras had the right and responsibility to defend itself if attacked.

Continuing in an apparently candid fashion, Torres Arias touched on several other aspects of the relationship, most of which Paz had touched on a few days earlier. But he added a new wrinkle. Honduran leaders were deeply resentful of Nicaraguan assertions that they wished to block elections and overthrow Paz, had received massive amounts of military supplies from the United States, were acting as a cat's paw and were helping anti-Sandinista groups. He also asserted that the government was not helping the anti-Sandinistas in any way.

He was lying through his teeth. In sum, most everything he said was a con, but I couldn't say that. I responded by running through the usual "appreciate your restraint" recitation, and moved on to the *Washington Post* piece. The author, Chris Dickey, had spent some time in Honduras and had met with several Contra leaders, as well as government officials and dissidents of various stripe. Indeed, in retrospect, Dickey's was an excellent example of solid, in-depth reporting, although at the time we considered it quite exaggerated. I told Torres Arias that it was difficult to dispute many of Dickey's facts. We believed that he reported the statements and attitudes of the Contra leaders accurately, for example. Torres Arias agreed, noting that the Contras had often approached him and his colleagues, claiming that they had the support of Guatemala, the southern cone and the CIA, but everyone "knows they exaggerate greatly."

Continuing, I noted that we were both aware that the Contras' actions fed Sandinista paranoia. Honduran claims of innocence, accordingly, would be much stronger if they were accompanied by evidence that they were trying to control the anti-Sandinista groups. Even though they had not been able to stop the Sandinistas, they had made a good-faith attempt to do so. They should try the same with the Contras.

Torres Arias didn't respond. I wondered if he thought I believed him; if so, he must have considered me a nitwit. I reported this discussion, noting that Honduran concerns seemed to be increasing sharply.[47]

We also spent a few minutes discussing what to say to the press as I departed. Torres Arias escorted me out, and we both said we had met to plan the Walters visit, which had been in the works for some time. It had nothing to do with the recent tension between Honduras and Nicaragua. Helpfully, Torres Arias flatly denied that Honduras had any intention of attacking Nicaragua. He then headed back to his office.

I noted that the Honduras/Nicaragua situation seemed to be quite delicate but that we were in no position to tell two sovereign states how to behave. However, from our discussions with leaders of both countries, it seemed that they wished to resolve their problems amicably. Consequently, we were confident that a peaceful solution would be found. As to Dickey's story, I said the following: "I believe the newspaper added up a series of facts and constructed a thesis that is definitely irrational and incorrect. It is a thesis that is very mistaken and one which I do not agree with."[48] Asked if the United States continued to support the transition process and elections, I said there had been no change in our policy and we continued to do so.

Coverage was overwhelming, with some version of my comments making front-page headlines in all major newspapers. *El Heraldo* and *La Tribuna* played the support for elections on the first page, and *La Prensa, Tiempo* and *El Cronista* chose to go with pacific resolution of the problems with Nicaragua.[49] All carried reasonably accurate accounts of my comments, no small accomplishment. It was a good press day, and I had made the most of another opportunity to get the support-for-elections message out.

WASHINGTON CONSULTATIONS SCHEDULED: TEGUCIGALPA, HONDURAS, MAY 11, 1981. I had requested my annual consultations in Washington; ambassadors are normally allowed one consultation a year (my November trip to Washington was related to the peace treaty ceremony and did not count as a consultation visit). I had been at post almost seven months and was feeling increasingly uncertain about where the administration was headed. The request was quickly granted and the dates set for May 25–June 5.[50]

This trip would also give me an opportunity to discover whether and how soon I was to be replaced and to make my case for remaining on the job at least until after the November 29 elections. I was firmly convinced that a change in ambassadors before that time would be regarded as signaling a shift in U.S. policy on elections, thereby possibly triggering a coup.

ZUNIGA MEETING: WALTERS VISIT AND ELECTION COMPLAINTS: TEGUCIGALPA, HONDURAS, MAY 12, 1981. When I phoned Zuniga to arrange a meeting regarding the Walters visit, he asked to meet at the residence. When he arrived, we reviewed the agenda for his session with Walters, which didn't take long. That done, he launched into an extended critique of voter registration and election preparations, alleging various fraudulent actions by the Liberal Party. He then asked that I raise these matters with Suazo Cordova. If they were not stopped, he stated, the National Party would withdraw from the elections. That was a tough threat.

I responded by noting that I had recently spoken to the leaders of the two smaller parties regarding election preparations. They both confirmed that irregularities were occurring and thought that both major parties were involved. However, the numbers of such instances were relatively small, and each believed that procedures then in place provided an adequate means to challenge suspicious cases. Continuing, I suggested that the electoral registry, jointly controlled by all the parties, had sufficient authority and adequate mechanisms to correct abuses such as he had described. That being the case, he ought to take his allegations to that body. Nonetheless, I promised to raise this issue with Suazo Cordova, as he requested. As to his threat, I reaffirmed my expectation that everyone would agree that the best way to assure political stability was to have a democratically elected government carrying out the popular will. Delaying elections, whatever the pretext, would only play into the hands of those who sought to impose authoritarian or Marxist models on Honduras. From our continuing soundings at all levels of Honduran society, we had found very few people who wished either of those alternatives.[51]

I also suggested that Zuniga raise these subjects with General Walters, who would be interested in hearing his views. I expected that Walters would reaffirm the U.S. position in strong terms, and he did.

REFINERY DISPUTE: MEETING WITH TEXACO OFFICIALS, TEGUCI-GALPA, HONDURAS, MAY 12, 1981. Several Texaco officials were in town in an effort to resolve the continuing standoff with the Honduran government over the refinery and briefed us on the state of negotiations.[52] This was a significant departure from Texaco's customary practice, and we attributed it to our efforts to reach out to the American business community.

According to Texaco, the government had backed away from expropriation. This retreat was the triumph of realism over emotion. As the Hondurans looked more closely at that option, they realized they lacked the technical capacity to operate the plant and the money to pay for its acquisition. They also expressed their appreciation for our role in emphasizing the U.S. position that nationalization would require prompt, adequate and effective compensation.

The principal outstanding issue was how to handle the Mexican and Venezuelan crude provided under the oil facility. Although they were deadlocked, several options were being explored: Texaco was willing to provide refining services for a fixed fee, with Honduras remaining the owner of both the crude and refined product. A swap arrangement to allow continued processing of Saudi crude was another option, as was a possible blending of crudes, with some price adjustments. Also still at issue was a tax question then before the courts. As yet, Texaco saw no role for us. We agreed.[53]

MISUSE OF AID RESOURCES: PART 2: TEGUCIGALPA, HONDURAS, MAY 12, 1981. We received authorization to address the misuse of AID resources. When I met with Paz on May 4 he had no objection to what we proposed. Indeed, he expressed his disgust with the "irresponsibility" of the two parties, which I thought a bit rich.[54]

What with the campaign activities of both Zuniga and Suazo Cordova, and other matters demanding my time, it was more than a week before I was able to set up the next appointment. Zuniga, whose party seemed to be the worst offender, was first, but only by circumstance. In broaching the subject I cited as examples the national cadaster and nutritional planning projects, where vehicles and per diem payments were being misused. I told him that we had already discussed these problems with the officials responsible and with President Paz; I was now raising the issue with him because I was certain he would not want members of his party involved in activities that might prejudice our continued assistance in these areas.

His response was defensive, asserting that the Liberals were doing the same thing, only more so. The Liberal-controlled Agriculture Ministry, he claimed, was an especially egregious example. I told him we were aware of problems with the Liberal Party, and I would be raising this issue with Suazo Cordova as well. Although I would look into his charges about Agriculture, I did not think it appropriate for me to discuss these matters with anyone other than the responsible ministers, the president and the respective party leaders. Accordingly, I would not discuss our problems with National Party ministries with the Liberals, and vice versa. That calmed him down, and after further discussion of the specifics, he assured me that he would direct all of his people in government that they were to ensure AID resources were used strictly in accord with the respective project agreements.[55]

His allegations concerning the Agriculture ministry, it turned out, were incorrect as far as AID was concerned. Hardly any of its vehicles had been provided by AID, and there was no evidence of misuse of the few vehicles we had supplied. We could not, of course, interfere in the ministry's use of its non-AID resources.

I subsequently made the same pitch to Suazo Cordova, who promptly assured me that he would look into each of the cases I cited and make certain the abuses ceased. He also promised to advise all Liberal ministers and program directors to make sure they did not violate AID project agreements and asked that I inform him promptly of any future violations.

These approaches had the desired effect. Although cases of misuse did not disappear, their incidence fell.

GENERAL WALTERS COMES TO TOWN: TEGUCIGALPA, HONDURAS, MAY 13, 1981. Walters arrived midmorning from Guatemala, accompanied by an aide, Lieutenant Commander Lee Martini. Walters was a large, ebullient man with a craggy countenance. He towered over me and most Hondurans, and his impressive girth made him hard to miss. We went directly to the residence. Once they had settled in their rooms and unpacked, we went over the program. The first meeting with Paz would be ceremonial. The next day's meeting would be the business session at the General Staff, and Paz would be accompanied by several senior military officers. Walters and I would be the only representatives from our side.

I explained to Walters that Paz wanted a private meeting with him but that I had pointed out U.S. diplomatic practice was for the ambassador to be present at all meetings with the chief of state. In this case, given reports that I was soon to be replaced and that the Honduran military distrusted me, I thought it especially important for me to be present to demonstrate I had the administration's confidence. Walters nodded and indicated that he understood but said he would wait to see how the actual meeting played out. In other words, I couldn't count on him to insist that I be there.

I also asked if he would be willing to meet informally with the CT to exchange views and perspectives in an unofficial setting. He agreed to do it at the residence the next afternoon, following his final meeting with Hondurans. I advised Walker and he alerted members of the meeting.

After lunch the three of us and Arcos drove to the Foreign Ministry. This session was more substantive than expected. Elvir had just returned from a meeting on the border with Sandinista officials designed to ease tensions. He wished to share his impressions. The Nicaraguan side had included both Daniel and Humberto Ortega, Foreign Minister D'Escoto and intelligence chief Cerna; President Paz led the Honduran group, which included Chief of Staff Chinchilla, Defense Minister Flores and Torres Arias, as well as Elvir. The meeting had lasted five hours.

Elvir said the Sandinistas acknowledged they were building a large army but had stressed that this was in response to U.S. threats and not to be used against their neighbors. They claimed, as expected, to have stopped arms shipments to and logistical support for the Salvadoran rebels. Finally, they expressed considerable concern about Nicaraguan exile groups in Honduras.

With special emissary General Vernon Walters (center) and Honduran Chief of Staff General Mario Chinchilla, May 1981.

For their part, the Hondurans denied incursions into Nicaragua or helping the exile groups. They also registered their profound unhappiness over the plight of two Honduran agricultural workers whom the Sandinistas had recently arrested and accused of spying. According to Elvir, these exchanges were cordial, all the Sandinistas' vitriol being reserved for the United States. They agreed to hold further talks among the foreign, defense, and economy ministers.

Elvir then escorted us to the National Palace. After we took seats in a large sitting room, Paz formally welcomed Walters, who responded by saying Secretary Haig had sent him to listen to what he, Paz, and others had to say about the current situation in Central America and how best to deal with it. That, he understood, would be the agenda for the next day's meeting.[56] Walters then launched into several humorous stories, all appropriate for the context of his visit, and soon had our hosts relaxed and laughing. His ability to interact with people, charming and dominating them, was almost magic.

Exiting the National Palace we were besieged by the press. Walters towered over the journalists who were deluging him with questions. He smiled and said nothing until the din subsided. At that point he told them—in colloquial Spanish—that he had just arrived, would be meeting with and listening to a broad range of Hondurans and would meet with the media prior to his departure on May 15. Until that time, he would have nothing to say.[57] They would have an opportunity to ask their questions then.

Our next stop was General Staff headquarters for a threat assessment briefing. We were met by General Chinchilla, the service chiefs and several staff officers. After an exchange of pleasantries, the Hondurans launched their standard threat briefing, followed by a summary description of their security assistance needs, which were continuing to grow.

Walters responded by saying there had been changes in the United States, and we were now determined to redress the worldwide military balance. Some $35 billion this year would go to strengthen our allies throughout the world. The United States, however, had assistance priorities. We would give sympathetic consideration to the Honduran request, and he personally would review their detailed listing, but we could make no promises until we reviewed the "whole question" in a global context. He twice repeated assurances that the United States would honor its commitments under the Rio Treaty if Honduras were attacked. At the same time he cautioned that an attack on Nicaragua would be counterproductive.

That done, we headed back to the residence to get ready for the evening reception. We had an excellent turnout—Walters was big news—and nearly everyone wanted to meet him. We had invited a full spectrum of the Honduran polity, including the leaders of the two minor parties who would not be meeting separately with Walters, businessmen, trade unionists and military officers.

MANAGEMENT PROBLEMS: SOLUTIONS AT HAND OR IN SIGHT: TEGUCIGALPA, HONDURAS, MAY 13, 1981. We had turned up serious problems in the management of the Consular Section. Our efforts to change the Consul's behavior were unsuccessful and, after consulting with State's consular affairs bureau, resulted in the exercise of close oversight by DCM Walker. That was an unnecessary burden. The arrival of our new Consul, Sarah Horsey, was welcome. She was highly touted, very professional, well briefed on our problems and seemed to know what was needed. We were both mightily relieved to welcome her aboard, Walker especially so.

Horsey spoke fluent Spanish, knew sound consular management and practices and seemed to possess a wry sense of humor—a great asset in her job. I thought she would be a fine addition to the CT, as well as our consular operations. Most of the problems we had been experiencing—arbitrary case decisions, adverse public reactions and low employee morale—were soon behind us.

A few week later, George Clift, our new head of the Joint Administrative Section (JAS)—about whom I had strong reservations—arrived and demonstrated that he too was a first-rate professional. These two changes would put most of our management problems behind us.

DAY TWO: WALTERS MEETS WITH MILITARY AND POLITICAL LEADERS: TEGUCIGALPA, HONDURAS, MAY 14, 1981. Following breakfast we were off to meet with Paz and his key advisors. Paz opened with a brief recap of the meeting with the Sandinistas the previous day, followed by a variation of the standard threat assessment. He added an internal subversion dimension to what we had heard the day before. Shifting gears, he next affirmed the armed forces' commitment to holding free and honest elections November 29, the date that had recently been fixed. That goal, however, had become increasingly problematic because of growing hostility between the major parties over the voter registration and national identity document issues. As a result, the Nationalists were threatening to abstain. The way Paz described the situation, I sensed a wavering of his commitment to elections, as did Walters.[59] Concluding, Paz affirmed his desire to come to the United States for political talks as soon as possible.

Walters's response was artful. He repeated essentially what he had told the general staff and service commanders previously—no commitments of additional assistance—at the same time leaving the impression that we would be responsive. He came down hard on the importance of completing the electoral process, noting that he would make the same point to Zuniga and Suazo Cordova. Failure to meet this commitment, he stated, would have far-reaching consequences in the region. As to Paz's desire to visit Washington, Walters noted that both the president and Secretary Haig had very full schedules in the coming months, but such a visit might be possible later. We would, he said, keep in touch with him on this subject.

Much to my surprise, Walters then told Paz that governmental corruption was damaging Honduras's reputation internationally. Paz took this coolly, agreeing and placing the blame on the two major parties and some of the military. He himself had taken nothing, he claimed. But he did not suggest constructive action to reduce the problem.[60] I found his willingness to finger his military colleagues surprising.

After more than an hour the discussion wound down. Walters and I stood, and he expressed our appreciation for their candor and hospitality. We shook hands all around and moved into the reception area outside Paz's office. Just as we reached the door leading to the courtyard, Torres Arias called to Walters and said that Paz wished to see him. Walters glanced at me, turned and headed back. As I turned to accompany him, Torres Arias blocked my path. To go with Walters, I would have had to force my way past Torres Arias. Recognizing a Hobson's choice, I sat down, picked up a magazine and seethed. Torres Arias continued to guard the door to Paz's office.[61]

Walters exited after about 20 minutes, inscrutable. Once we were in the car, I asked what Paz had said. According to Walters, he had raised two topics. The first was Honduran concerns over the perceived threat from Nicaragua (Walters did not indicate anything had been said about their reported plan to attack that country). The second was that the military distrusted me. Walters claimed he had told Paz I had Secretary Haig's confidence and that he should rely on me. I was dubious. Walters gave no indication that the elections issue had been discussed, nor did he offer further details of their tête-à-tête.

It was back to the residence to meet with business leaders, editors of the major newspapers, Zuniga and Suazo Cordova. In every case Walters emphasized the importance of the elections. Both the Zuniga and Suazo Cordova sessions focused on narrow partisan issues rather than the larger picture, but they were left in no doubt as to our continued support for the electoral process. When our last guest left, Walters and I discussed the substance of these meetings briefly. He had not been impressed by either. As we had time before the CT meeting, we opted for a rest.

Walker was the first to arrive, wishing to discuss some business before the others came. Shortly before 5:00 P.M. they began gathering on the patio, where tables had been placed together. Walters and Martini joined the group, and after introductions and chitchat, we sat around the tables, ready to start.

I opened the discussion by asking Walters's impressions of the situation and outlook in the region. After his customary introductory anecdotes, he gave an overview of our relations with Guatemala and the administration's efforts to ease tensions. This included a brief commentary on his meetings there with President Romeo Lucas Garcia and others. From his remarks, it was fairly clear that human rights concerns were no longer on the U.S./Guatemala relations agenda.

Moving on to El Salvador, he characterized the conflict there as a well-defined battle between democracy and communism, with the insurgents acting as surrogates for Cuba and the Soviet Union. Consequently, we needed to give our full, unqualified support to the Salvadoran government and military. He then made a statement that, to me and all the others assembled, was not only blatantly false but reflective of a breath-takingly dogmatic mindset. Reports of human rights violations and alleged atrocities on the part of the Salvadoran military, he asserted, were untrue: such reports were entirely the product of communist disinformation. Glancing quickly at my colleagues, I could see that they were astounded.

His assertion was absurd. Embassy and CIA reporting over the years had described, often in great detail, incidents where the Salvadoran Army and security forces had severely abused and murdered their own people. Sometimes these atrocities were carried out by regular forces, other times by clandestine units or "death squads" that were definitely linked to the military. There were also private, right-wing death squads, but most of the carnage lay at the military's doorstep. This had been going on since well before the onset of the current conflict and was amply documented.

Both Walker and I had served in El Salvador. We were familiar, in considerable detail, with the Salvadoran military's violent and vicious ways. And every member of the CT—most especially the station chief—had seen dozens, if not hundreds, of embassy and agency reports detailing Salvadoran human rights violations, some as recent as that very week.

Neither Walker nor I could allow these comments to pass unchallenged. I began by telling Walters that during my four years in El Salvador I became familiar with the practices of the security forces and found official U.S. reports of the military's human rights violations credible. Following that comment and knowing that Walters was Catholic, I asked what he thought about the December killing of the four American churchwomen by members of the National Guard. It gave him no pause. These women, he said, supported the insurgency, were well meaning but naive, and probably tried to run a government roadblock when they had been killed.[62] Good grief! Didn't he recall that Haig had tried that canard and been forced to retract?

Walker, becoming increasingly exercised, jumped in, describing his experiences and stating firmly that Walters did not know what he was talking about. He had spent three years in El Salvador watching the military abuse their own people and knew they were responsible for gross and frequent human rights violations. Walters had noted that he knew several senior Salvadoran officers personally and found them to be "honorable and professional soldiers." Walker asked Walters how long he had spent in El Salvador to be able to make such a judgment; the answer was two days. But from his meetings with them in Washington, Walters knew they were victims of communist disinformation.

Walters was not used to being challenged in this way and clearly didn't like it. His face reddened and his voice rose as he responded, asking whether we agreed that the insurgents and their allies were using disinformation to blacken the Salvadoran military's reputation. We did. The rebels had an active disinformation campaign underway, and we were spending a lot of time and energy trying to counter it. But that didn't mean the military's hands were clean. The intelligence and other reports we were referring to often came from Salvadoran military officers themselves.

We went back and forth in this vein for several minutes, voices and tempers rising. I could see that the CT members were very uncomfortable, as was Martini. The station chief's eyes had gotten as large as saucers at Walters's first blanket denials, but he quickly put on a poker face. Arcos and Colonel Miller were probably the coolest, observing closely and betraying no emotion. Colonel Goodwin appeared stricken by what was going on, and AID director Oleson had physically shrunk back into his chair, as although trying to distance himself from the argument. All were aghast.

Then Walters delivered his clincher: "I do not believe the Salvadoran military engage in human rights abuses, because to do so would be self-defeating, and they are not stupid." That was followed by silence. No one said a word. No response was possible. That comment was so vacuous that it defied challenge. Such behavior, of course, was self-defeating, but the Salvadoran military were engaging in it with abandon. The point was precisely that they were behaving in a profoundly stupid manner. And for us to support them without trying to change their behavior seemed criminally negligent, as well as stupid. But we held our tongues. It was evident that Walters would not be swayed by fact or reason. It called to mind George Orwell's observation about Stalin's defenders: beyond a certain point, refusal to accept such facts amounted to intellectual crime or a form of insanity.

Our little get-together had come to an abrupt and crashing end. I thanked Walters for having met with us and stood. Walters shook hands with each of the officers and headed for his room, followed by Martini. I escorted the others to the door. Walker was still steaming, Arcos was chuckling in sardonic disbelief and the others just wanted out of there. We would, I suggested, discuss this further the next day.[63]

When I joined Martha in our quarters, she remarked that it must have been some party judging from the loud voices and shouting she had heard. I assured her that it had and that I would fill her in on the details after Walters was gone. My concern was composing myself enough to face dinner with Walters, Martini and my family. By the time we sat down together, tempers had cooled and Walters was back in a storytelling mode. But after dessert and coffee, we retreated to our respective rooms.

WALTERS PRESS CONFERENCE AND DEPARTURE: TEGUCIGALPA, HONDURAS, MAY 15, 1981. Walters was smiling, confident and articulate as he opened his airport press conference with a brief statement. He had come to Honduras to meet with, and listen to, the views of Honduran leaders about the political, economic and military situation in the region; having done so, he felt quite optimistic about the future of Honduras, which he characterized as "an oasis of tranquility in the midst of the storm raking Central America."[64] With that, the floor was open.

He responded to the first, long-winded question based on the assertion that the United States was arming Honduras so that it could become the "gendarme of the region" with a terse, "That's not true." Several follow-on questions made the same point in different words and drew the same response. He then elaborated, saying that "President Reagan does not wish to use Honduras as a base against Nicaragua, but we do wish to help friendly republics defend themselves against those who don't want democracy." That shifted the focus to Honduran elections. Walters praised Honduras as "a true example for Central America," explicitly endorsing the elections scheduled for November 29. And in responding to other questions, he found several other opportunities to reiterate our support. His statements were strong, direct and unequivocal.

He also addressed several militarization questions by observing that military force rarely resolved political problems, and should be avoided. It was his hope and prayer, he said, "that [the Central American] peoples can find peace, stability and prosperity without going to such extremes." He then stressed that the Reagan administration was adamant in its opposition to Soviet involvement or intervention in the region.

Walters handled the other topics skillfully until asked if "the U.S. will offer increased military assistance to our country?" His reply was not a direct response. Instead, he stated, "I believe we have already announced special sales of $10 million for this year," which was true.[65] It would be misunderstood.

Once his plane was airborne, I headed for the embassy with a sense of relief. Walker and I spent some time discussing the substance of his visit and meetings—very positive for those we knew about and troubling for the one we didn't know about. We also agreed that the previous evening's confrontation had been extraordinary. It seemed abundantly clear that Walters was blinded by ideological zeal, which caused him to take a mindless position on the Salvadoran military. It was the product of deliberate self-delusion. He didn't wish to believe intelligence reports of Salvadoran human rights abuses, so they either didn't exist or were false. It was especially bizarre for someone who had once been a senior CIA official.

CONTRAS AND SANDINISTAS CLASH NEAR JALAPA: JALAPA, NICARAGUA, MAY 16, 1981. In what was one of the largest engagements to that time, an anti-Sandinista column operating out of Honduras ran into a well-armed Sandinista Army unit near the border town of Jalapa. This area is a few kilometers southeast of Danli, Honduras, not far from the site of the earlier Nicaraguan incursion into Honduras. Reportedly, 17 Contras and one Sandinista were killed in the clash. *Radio Sandino* later claimed that the Contra unit had been "committing murders, holdups, rapes and robberies and burning state-owned farms for several months."[66] Tensions were again escalating.

WALTERS FALLOUT: THE MEDIA, OUR RESPONSE AND ASSESSMENT: TEGUCIGALPA, HONDURAS, MAY 16–18, 1981. Coverage of Walters's press conference was extensive and mostly accurate. The headlines, however, focused on military assistance, not his endorsement of elections—by far the most significant of his statements—or other topics. The elections endorsement was pretty well buried. Moreover, all misinterpreted what he had said about military assistance, reporting that he had announced a $10 million increase in funding.[67] In fact, all he had done was confirm the previously announced funding: that Honduras would receive a $10 million credit in the coming fiscal year.

There wasn't much we could do to change the spin the media had placed on Walters's remarks, but I wanted to set the record straight on military assistance. Arcos quickly put together a letter, which we sent to all the papers the following Monday, pointing out that Walters had not announced an increase in military assistance. All responded by printing the text of our letter, with *La Prensa* also reprinting the complete text of our April 9 press release, which had described the Honduras program levels in detail.[68]

The Walters visit, apart from the informal meeting with the CT, was a great success, achieving all of our desired goals. The Honduran military had an opportunity to register their concerns about developments in the region and present their requests for sharply increased security and economic assistance to Secretary Haig's personal emissary. And Paz had been able to reiterate his desire to visit Washington without me as a filter. For his part Walters had reassured them of our continuing interest and support, especially as regarded consulting closely and standing by our Rio Treaty commitments should they be attacked. Finally, he had counseled against any rash actions that might be self-defeating in terms of relations with Nicaragua. I was hopeful this would relieve some stress.

Most important, Walters had reaffirmed our continued support for the transition, elections and restoration of constitutional rule. He had made these points in the official meetings and in his sessions with the private sector, media and leaders of the major parties. He had also warned of the dangers of governmental corruption in both the official and private sessions. Feedback was uniformly favorable.[69]

Perhaps inevitably, there would be a down side, but it would take weeks to surface. It would be our slowness in responding to Walters's commitments. He had explicitly promised to look into the possibility of transferring patrol boats to Honduras, à la Schweitzer's helicopter lease arrangement, and increasing the exchange of intelligence about developments in Nicaragua. Despite the embassy's repeated reminders (and caustic Honduran comments), nothing came of either initiative during my time in Honduras.

SECURITY FORCES BELIEVED RESPONSIBLE FOR DISAPPEARANCES: TEGUCIGALPA, HONDURAS, MID–MAY 1981. Our efforts to confirm responsibility for the disappearances of the 14 Salvadorans detained April 22 and discover what had happened to them had only limited success. Our information tended to substantiate what was widely believed: that the National Intelligence Directorate, then part of FUSEP, had been responsible. But we lacked confirmation.

Our sources believed that these detentions had been officially authorized and carried out by that organization. Moreover, it was difficult to believe that a nonofficial organization would have the capacity to detain and hide a group that large: one or two people, à la Vinelli, sure, but not a group of 14, including children. Honduran authorities, however, continued to deny any knowledge of this group. Nevertheless, we felt reasonably certain one or another element of the security forces had been responsible and so reported to State. If our convictions were correct, this case represented a very troubling escalation on the human rights front. Absent confirmation of official responsibility, however, we had no basis to make a specific démarche.

I again asked that CT members be alert to any further information.

SALVADORAN REFUGEE UPDATE: COLOMONCAGUA AND LA VIRTUD, HONDURAS, MAY 17–21, 1981. We had not had a firsthand report on the Salvadoran refugee camps for some time, so we dispatched two officers, one from the embassy and the other from AID, to take a new look. On their return a cable summarizing their observations and interviews with relief workers, refugees, military and local residents was sent to State.[70] Their information indicated about 12,000 refugees were in the La Virtud area, with another 4,000 in Colomoncagua. There may have been a couple of thousand elsewhere, at most. These numbers were substantially lower than "official" UNHCR figures, which put the total number of Salvadoran refugees in the border area at 27,000.

Our officers judged the relief effort to be as well organized and efficient as could be expected under the circumstances. Overland travel was difficult, and the onset of the rainy season was certain to cause serious transportation and health problems. They found the Honduran military relaxed, citing few problems. This was somewhat at variance with what we had been hearing from other sources. Our officers also reported a problem with recently arrived refugees in Colomoncagua. The Salvadorans, for reasons that were unclear, were refusing to allow themselves to be documented as asylees. The patience of Honduran authorities was wearing thin: if they continued to refuse to register, they would be forced back to El Salvador.

The decentralized food distribution system noted previously, with its potential for leakage, remained unchanged. Moreover, our officers confirmed that large numbers of Hondurans continued to benefit from relief supplies and services. In large part this was because so many of the Salvadoran refugees were billeted with or near Honduran families. How could you keep the host families from sharing the foodstuffs given to the refugees? They also learned that Hondurans accounted for about 60 percent of those receiving medical treatment. It was good that they now had access to such care, but it was being underwritten by refugee relief funds. That was a misallocation of refugee resources.

There was no quick or easy fix for these problems. But they again underscored the desirability of getting the refugees into well-organized camps away from the immediate frontier. That, I remained convinced, was the only way to exercise adequate control of the resources earmarked for refugee relief. Needless to say, this step would also reduce the likelihood of supplies being diverted to the insurgents.

ARMS INTERDICTION SURVEYS: TEGUCIGALPA, HONDURAS, MAY 18–
20, 1981. Our arms interdiction survey teams from the CIA (using cover of
another agency) and Southern Command had been in-country and working
separately for about a week. They were beginning to formulate their recommendations, and it was imperative that we speak with a single voice when
presenting our conclusions to the Hondurans.

We had several sessions with these teams to ensure they were not dupli-
cating each other's efforts or taking radically different approaches to the common problem. We set up a joint review of their findings and recommendations so we would have a cohesive plan to present to the Hondurans. In view
of our strained relations with Southern Command, and to reduce the likelihood of the recommendations being subjected to an extended round of second guessing, argument and revision, I invited General Nutting and/or senior
members of his staff to participate in this review. Southern Command was
unable to send anyone to this meeting, but we cabled the joint recommendations to Panama for the Command's approval, which was forthcoming.[71]

We brought the leaders of these two teams together with our political-
military committee. There were no significant conflicts in their recommendations, although we did do some fine-tuning. I was, however, surprised by
the tentative nature of the Southern Command recommendations. Their team
had been in-country longer and was three times the size of the CIA group,
yet most of its recommendations were for additional surveys to provide "in-
depth" assessments and for training Honduran forces. They were not operational. Actually, that pleased me.

HONDURANS ACCEPT ARMS INTERDICTION PROPOSALS: TEGUCI-
GALPA, HONDURAS, MAY 21, 1981. We met with President Paz and the General Staff to present our recommendations. The recommendations for FUSEP
emphasized five themes: training, communications, incentives for outstanding performance (e.g., rewards, extra vacation, bonuses), establishment of
regional inspection stations at transport choke points, and improved capability to conduct counterintelligence operations. The recommended training
and advisory services would be provided at no cost. The CIA was also exploring the possible provision of in-kind assistance to implement some of the recommendations.

Southern Command, in addition to follow-on survey teams, proposed a
series of basic tactical and intelligence courses—a second phase of interme-
diate training that would include counterinsurgency, combat engineering and
other more specialized courses. These activities were to be supplemented by
actions to improve communications and the intelligence system, establish a
public relations program, and acquire detailed maps and aerial photographs
for operational use. Once those steps were completed, Southern Command
would begin an advanced training program.[72] All of the later training and

associated costs would be charged against Honduran assistance program allocations, although we had promised to increase grant aid to cover these costs.

After a relatively short discussion, President Paz and the General Staff accepted our proposals and agreed to begin implementation. I suspected that implementation of the Southern Command recommendations would accomplish little beyond making work for our trainers. Those of the CIA, on the other hand, seemed practical and focused. And the police, not the military, had responsibility for customs inspections, criminal investigations, traffic control and other functions directly related to illicit arms traffic.

Moreover, the preliminary phases of the recommended military training cycle would require up to nine months to complete. Only when that stage was complete would the more advanced training begin. The Honduran military was basically a conscript force (with more than half the draftees being illiterate), having an 18-month period of service. By the time the troops would complete their basic training and the full proposed training package, their terms of service would be near completion.

When I left Honduras five months later, little had been accomplished. The CIA's attention had been diverted by the Contra operation, and Southern Command had sent survey teams, which caused problems, and was doing some training. By that point, moreover, sea and air traffic had replaced the overland as the principal means of arms supplies for the Salvadoran insurgents.

PLANNING FOR A COUNCIL OF THE AMERICAS MISSION: TEGUCIGALPA, HONDURAS, MAY 21, 1981. Paul Vinelli had returned to Honduras some weeks earlier and sought our assistance arranging for a special visit of the Council of the Americas. His bank was a member of the council, an organization composed of businesses, mostly American, with interests in Latin America. It counted among its members several Fortune 500 companies, as well as large Latin firms. It was based in New York and influential.

The purpose of this mission was to bring a number of American businessmen and potential investors to the country to meet with their Honduran counterparts and government officials. He believed it would be helpful for the council to see and endorse the transition and might result in new investment opportunities. All of the Honduran business organizations, Vinelli said, had agreed to support this initiative, as did we. We also thought his initiative could complement what we were trying to accomplish with our AID program activities.

The council responded favorably to Vinelli's initiative, and the visit was scheduled for late July.[73]

CENTRAL AMERICAN CHIEFS OF STATE MEETING: TEGUCIGALPA, HONDURAS, MAY 21, 1981. Efforts to have a meeting of Central American chiefs of state as a means to ease tensions were beginning to pay off, with the strongest support coming from Mexico, Venezuela and Panama. The Central American governments were less enthusiastic. Recently, however, Honduras and El Salvador had joined Costa Rica in backing the notion, seeing it as a possible means to edge Nicaragua away from Cuba and the Soviet Union. They weren't optimistic but thought it would be worth a try. As this scheme began to gain momentum, however, Guatemala remained an obstacle.

The Guatemalans objected to involvement of non-Central American countries. Their position, if sustained, would ensure that Mexico and the other countries retaining marginal influence with the Sandinistas would be on the sidelines. Guatemala also objected to the proposed meeting site, Panama, insisting that it be held in one of the Central American capitals. But even if these objections were accommodated, the Guatemalans refused to commit to participating. We were skeptical that it would accomplish much but were inclined to be encouraging.

That was the state of play when Foreign Minister Elvir briefed me on recent developments. He was now proposing a preliminary meeting of the Central American foreign ministers in late June, which would set the agenda for the later chiefs of state meeting. All except Guatemala had agreed on this point, as well as on holding both meetings in Central American capitals. He had offered Tegucigalpa as the venue for the preliminary session, but Guatemala was still demurring. Salvadoran foreign minister Chavez Mena had been deputized by the other three ministers to persuade the Guatemalans to participate.

The four foreign ministers were working on an agenda focusing principally on economic issues. It would, he said, include unspecified "economic incentives" for Nicaragua to draw the Sandinista government more fully into regional affairs, helping to moderate its behavior. Nicaragua's growing economic difficulties, he thought, would impel it to cooperate.[74]

I was not optimistic but agreed that it was certainly worth a try. In reporting Elvir's comments I urged that State accept a suggestion made by Ambassador McNeil that we encourage Guatemala to participate.

SEEKING TO EASE REGIONAL TENSIONS: TEGUCIGALPA, HONDURAS, MAY 22, 1981. Ambassador Pezzullo was still grappling with ways to head off a confrontation between the United States and Nicaragua and ease regional tensions. He proposed a strategy to engage all immediately interested nations, not just those of Central America. Proposed participants, in addition to the five Central American states, were the United States, Mexico, Venezuela, Panama and, surprisingly, Cuba.[75] This was an innovative idea but one I thought a nonstarter. There was absolutely no possibility the Reagan administration would agree to Cuban participation. Beyond that, I felt Pezzullo failed to address the fundamental causative factor for the growing tension: Sandinista revolutionary evangelism.

I responded by pointing up these problems and suggesting a modified approach. The fundamental cause for concern among Nicaragua's neighbors, I argued, was its "training of and logistical support for insurgents and subversives in neighboring countries, actions against competing Nicaraguan influence centers and rhetorical excesses at home and abroad...coupled with its announced intention to build the strongest armed force in the region, [all of which] give substance to the fears of neighboring countries."[76] Their response, as long as these conditions existed, would be to increase their own military capability and encourage the anti-Sandinistas. Such behavior was entirely rational.

I argued that we should try to avoid military confrontation at all costs, citing some of the effects of the 1969 El Salvador/Honduras conflict. To build a regional approach, I suggested that we start by encouraging the proposed meeting of foreign ministers, followed by the chiefs of state summit. The immediate goal should be to develop economic incentives and arrangements to modify Nicaraguan behavior. Venezuela seemed a likely ally in such an approach, as did Panama.

Mexico, with which the administration was at daggers' point over Central America, did not seem a viable prospect, at least at the initial stage. Perhaps the Venezuelans could bring Mexico along later. Cuban participation was a bone that could not be swallowed. An immediate problem would be to engage Guatemala, already objecting to the foreign ministers and chiefs of state meeting proposals.[77]

Once a process of engagement and détente was underway, it might be possible to broaden support by bringing European countries in, as well as others in the hemisphere. In any event, an effort along these lines seemed worth essaying. Other embassies, notably San Jose, submitted their critiques of Pezzullo's proposal and suggestions for getting such a process off the ground.

There was never a response to Pezzullo's proposal or the related recommendations. In part, these ideas were preempted by the Central American chiefs of state meeting proposal. But the underlying reason was that the administration had little interest in pursuing diplomatic means to resolve regional conflicts.

7

Policy Vacuum Continues as Troubles Mount

SUMMARY—Consultations yield little insight—responses to military effort to block transition—military also plans more bizarre operations and requests armaments—a secret trip to Washington and more NSC deceit—political maneuvering—efforts to define priorities ignored—refugee survey leaves our posture unchanged—human rights abuses confirmed and State ignores our plea to deter repression—OAS observer mission to end—visit to El Salvador—relations with Nicaragua deteriorate as Contras found engaging in criminal activity.

WASHINGTON CONSULTATIONS: WASHINGTON, D.C., MAY 24–JUNE 5, 1981. My first order of business was to meet with John Blacken and his deputy, Rich Brown. They didn't seem to know any more about our policy direction than the embassies. That was a shocker. Both were soon replaced. They had set up an intensive round of meetings at State, AID, CIA, Defense and the NSC. I also had several appointments on the Hill, Dick McCormack of Helms's office among them. My substantive session with Enders was on Friday, near the end of my consultations.

None of these sessions were very informative from the policy standpoint.[1] Administration officials either didn't have their act together, weren't sharing anything with me, or both. Roy Gutman described, in compelling and amusing terms, the new administration's confusion and conflict regarding Central America.[2] And I later learned that I was being deliberately misled and excluded from the various competing policy loops.

At the CIA I met with Nestor Sanchez, who was about to become a deputy assistant secretary at Defense. We discussed the arms interdiction issue, the use of Honduras as a safe haven for Salvadoran insurgents and, very briefly, Nicaraguan exile groups. I stressed that the latter were mostly former National Guardsmen, had no following inside Nicaragua and had been penetrated by the Sandinista intelligence service. I thought the chances of their being able to overthrow the Sandinistas were nil. That was still the view of the agency's analytical side and the entire intelligence community. Sanchez didn't take issue with my judgment or indicate the agency was considering assisting the Contras. But they were gearing up to help the Hondurans interdict the flow of arms and improve their internal security.

I met with Schweitzer and others at the NSC. Although he mentioned meeting with Alvarez, he didn't breathe a word about supporting the Contras, Honduran war plans or their sharp armaments buildup. It would be some time before I realized the full extent of his duplicity. I urged that he try to get formal closure of the helicopter reimbursement case, which was still hanging fire, and suggested that he try to get a higher delivery priority assigned for equipment and materiel purchased by the Hondurans. He promised to try. I made the same pitch in meetings at Defense and with the Joint Chiefs of Staff. General Nutting happened to be in Washington, and we had an opportunity to review the *Halcon Vista* exercise, which he wished to hold in late October; I reiterated my reservations about Marine Corps participation.

The McCormack meeting was a farce. I was not aware of his efforts with Haig to have me replaced, but he made it clear that he favored my prompt departure. On the other hand, he didn't know how much I knew about his involvement in the aborted Paz visit. He was surprisingly well briefed on Honduras and recited to the letter Zuniga's arguments for delaying elections. He also spoke knowledgeably about Walters's visit and stressed the importance of getting Paz to Washington soon. I assured him we were still pushing but that Walters had taken the urgency out of that request.

In my meetings with AID I made a strong pitch for increased funding in the coming year based on the need to support the newly elected government and outlined our request for an Economic Support Fund (ESF) grant to spur badly needed private investment. ESF allocations were largely driven by political, as opposed to economic, factors. I made the same case with Enders, who seemed more sympathetic.

Ray Seitz confirmed that I was slated to be replaced, which was no surprise. There did not seem to be any great urgency attached to getting me out of Honduras, however, and as far as he was aware no one had been suggested as my replacement.

The session with Enders was a good one, although it didn't provide many clues as to where we might be headed. I opened with an assessment of the election outlook and the forces seeking to block that process. He was well informed and explicitly reaffirmed the importance of getting a democratically elected government in office: it remained a key element in our strategy for Central America. When I said that we needed high-level reaffirmations of that point, he promised to see if Haig would do so. Within a few weeks, he did just that. I also addressed the economic situation, including our ESF proposal, the planned Council of the Americas mission and the government's budgetary problems. I also reviewed my concerns about *Halcon Vista*. He listened closely and made a few helpful suggestions.

On regional topics we discussed both El Salvador and Nicaragua. He was most concerned about the Salvadoran insurgents' use of Honduras as a safe haven and as an arms-traffic route. The refugee situation was noted only in passing, and nothing conclusive came of that discussion. We chewed over Pezzullo's proposal for reducing regional tensions briefly. Enders agreed that we needed to make an effort in that direction: it was not enough to support Central American initiatives such as the pending chiefs of state and foreign ministers meetings. I repeated my very negative impressions of the Contras and their prospects, urging that we pressure the Hondurans not to support them. He took all this onboard, but offered no comment.

As the session was winding up, I broached the question of my replacement. Moving me out before the November 29 elections, I said, could lead to a coup that would frustrate the electoral process. Zuniga and some elements in the military were eagerly awaiting any sign that might be interpreted as a change in our position. I knew it sounded self-serving, but because I knew I was going to be replaced, extending my tenure for a couple of months really didn't make much difference to me. But it could very well cost us our primary foreign policy goal in Honduras, with collateral damage to our regional goals. Enders said he understood my point and didn't believe it would be a problem. There was no commitment, but I left feeling he had understood and accepted my line of reasoning.

The following year, after my replacement in Honduras, I landed in the European Bureau as director for Northern European affairs, with responsibility for ten countries, including the United Kingdom. Unexpectedly, I again found myself crossing bureaucratic swords with Enders. That time the issue was our policy in the aftermath of Argentina's attack on the Falkland Islands, where Argentine and British interests were in direct conflict. I was not then aware that the CIA had been using Argentina's military as our prime contractor to run the Contra operation. That arrangement had come to a quick end when we supported the British counterattack; the CIA assumed direct responsibility for that "covert" war.

Eighteen months later Enders was forced out as assistant secretary and assigned as ambassador to Spain. He asked me to be his DCM. It came as a surprise, but I accepted.

I had a few more anticlimactic days of consultation before heading back to Tegucigalpa little wiser.

SOVIET WHEAT FOR NICARAGUA: BLUEFIELDS, NICARAGUA, MAY 28, 1981. The first load of Soviet wheat arrived in Nicaragua two months after the Reagan administration canceled a $9.6 million grain contract.[3] The administration's "war party" became exercised, seeing this as an escalation of the cold war in Central America. In fact, it was an opportunity for the Soviets that we created. How had they expected the Sandinista government to respond? For those who predicted increased Nicaraguan reliance on the USSR, the prophecy fulfilled itself.

MISKITO EXODUS CONTINUES; LEADER ARRIVES: PUERTO LEMPIRA, HONDURAS, LATE MAY 1981. The flow of Miskito Indian refugees from Nicaragua increased steadily, with their numbers reaching over 2,000.[4] Honduran concerns about this influx were growing and were accentuated by the approach of the rainy season. Relief agencies, fortunately, had begun to serve this need.

Among the more recent arrivals was Miskito leader Steadman Fagoth. He had been arrested by Sandinista authorities in February and charged with plotting against the state. He was released in April, but harassment continued. So, he and his close associates sought refuge in Honduras, crossing near Puerto Lempira. Fagoth approached the embassy while I was in Washington, requesting assistance in arranging a visit and a meeting with administration officials. The embassy reported his request, urging that he be received.[5]

AMBASSADOR HINTON PRESENTS CREDENTIALS: SAN SALVADOR, EL SALVADOR, June 1, 1981. Deane Hinton presented his credentials as U.S. ambassador to junta president Napoleon Duarte.[6]

SANDINISTAS ALLEGED TO RECEIVE SOVIET TANKS AND AIRCRAFT: WASHINGTON, D.C., JUNE 2, 1981. The *Washington Post* reported that administration officials claimed Nicaragua had received several Soviet T-55 tanks, MIG jets and other weapons. This article also reported an increase in arms moving through Nicaragua to Salvadoran guerrilla groups, although the means of their transit was not specified.[7] The information about Soviet arms was largely spurious. Although arms shipments from the USSR were growing, the Sandinistas had received no tanks or jet aircraft. Indeed, the Soviets never transferred high-performance aircraft, although tanks did arrive later. Soviet restraint was at least partially the result of U.S. diplomatic representations making clear that such action would sharply alter the military balance in the region, would be unacceptable and could draw a swift response from the United States. And although the flow of arms to the Salvadoran rebels may have been on the upswing, there was no evidence that they were moving overland.

This was evidently U.S. disinformation designed to exaggerate Soviet involvement in Nicaragua and gain public support for our efforts against the Sandinista regime.

ALLEGATIONS OF ELECTORAL FRAUD RAISE CONCERNS: TEGUCIGALPA, HONDURAS, JUNE 3, 1981. Press reporting of allegations of electoral fraud by leading National Party figures, coupled with threats to withdraw from the process, were raising our concerns about Zuniga's intentions. He lost few opportunities to beat this drum in his meetings with embassy officers and visitors, official and unofficial. What was new was that other party officials had gone public with this threat.

According to all our sources, the jointly administered Electoral Tribunal was making progress in purging unqualified registrants, and the numbers that were likely to slip through would be marginal. There was little chance of partisan favoritism. Nonetheless, we suspected Zuniga might use this pretext to pull out, undermining the legitimacy of the result. Would he withdraw simply to discredit and frustrate the process rather than face up to losing what was almost certainly his last chance to be president? Based on his record, we thought he would.

We dispatched two political officers to sound out the Tribunal chairman, Ubdoro Arriaga. The dimensions of the problem, according to Arriaga, were modest: they had detected about 39,000 fraudulent registrations out of over 1.5 million registered voters, about 2 percent. Most of these cases had been in three provinces that were National Party strongholds. The screening process was continuing, but he did not expect to uncover large numbers of additional fraud cases. Arriaga was not especially worried about the National Party pulling out. He believed strong public support for elections would deter them from carrying out this threat. Support for the electoral process and the popular desire for an elected government indicated that there would be a strong backlash against any group or party that sought to frustrate the popular will. National Party leaders knew this and would prevent Zuniga from withdrawing.

Nonetheless, Arriaga and his colleagues on the Tribunal had scheduled an intensive round of meetings with private groups—civic, professional, unions, business—in an effort to generate additional nonpartisan pressure to keep the process on track.[8]

AN INVITATION TO VISIT EL SALVADOR: TEGUCIGALPA, HONDURAS, JUNE 5, 1981. Among the pending matters when I returned was a message from Ambassador Hinton, inviting me to his first private dinner with President Duarte. He knew that Duarte and I had been friends for many years and thought it might help break the ice if I were present. He had already cleared this proposal with State, so there would be no problem in my getting approval to leave the country.

I had known Hinton slightly some 10 years previously, when he had been AID director in Guatemala and I was stationed in El Salvador. I looked forward to renewing that acquaintance. We now had a number of common concerns, and closer cooperation would be very helpful. I accepted his invitation with alacrity.

AN INSIDE LOOK AT ZUNIGA AND THE NATIONAL PARTY: TEGUCI-
GALPA, HONDURAS, EARLY JUNE 1981. Arcos had an unusually candid luncheon conversation with National Party leader Armando Velasquez Cerrato.
An army colonel who claimed to be on active duty but had no official responsibilities, Velasquez was very active in the National Party and the Zuniga campaign. He had unloaded on Arcos, detailing the sad state of Zuniga's campaign, dissension within the National Party, Zuniga's poor standing with most
of the military and other facets of the Honduran political scene. Velasquez
substantiated much of what we had been hearing from other, less well placed
sources, and provided several new insights about Zuniga and others.

I asked Arcos to work with Walker and the Political Section to evaluate this information and produce a balanced report. The result was an unusually candid, inside look at the National Party, its presidential candidate and
his relations with the military and others. It was more colorful than our regular reporting because Velasquez had been so indiscreet.

Some of his more interesting points follow:

• Zuniga's campaign was in serious trouble. He was a poor candidate,
trusted no one other than his daughter, Elizabeth, insisted on exercising complete control of the party apparatus and was very low on campaign funds. He
would delegate only to Tita, whom Velasquez characterized as "politically
unsophisticated, given to intrigue [and] distrust and committing endless blun-
ders." Zuniga's threat to withdraw the party from elections was empty: other
party officials and candidates would not permit it. Zuniga was in regular contact with Guatemalan right-wing leader Mario Sandoval Alarcon, who was
closely linked with the death squads in that country. Zuniga hoped to receive
financial support from Sandoval and his friends.

• Zuniga's relations with the military were poor. FUSEP commander
Colonel Alvarez was contemptuous, and he had few friends on the Superior
Council. His best friend was probably President Paz, their relationship going
back to the Lopez Arellano period. Velasquez contrasted Zuniga's situation
with that of Suazo Cordova, whom he claimed was having some success with
cultivating the military, especially Alvarez. Suazo had assured the military
that, if elected, he would not meddle in their affairs. He was credible. No one
believed that Zuniga would refrain from trying to manipulate the military.

• Paz as wan incorrigible drunk and had nearly been ousted over Holy
Week. Air Force commander Lopez had learned that several senior officers
were planning to remove Paz and enlisted Alvarez's support to block this
move. (This was new information but was unsubstantiated.)

• Paz was completely reliant on Minister of Finance Valentin Mendoza
in the economic area. He made no move without Mendoza's approval. According to Velasquez, Mendoza had cultivated Paz by "helping him settle personal financial problems."

Velasquez also reported that Zuniga was "frustrated" at his inability to have me replaced. My sympathy was limited. He also offered a prescient observation about the junior officers and Alvarez, soon to become Armed Forces commander. He claimed junior officers detested Alvarez for his arrogant, overbearing demeanor and his cold, ruthless ambition.[9] We were skeptical of this report, but less than three years later junior officers forced Alvarez out of office and into exile at gunpoint.

REFUGEE OFFICE TEAM VISITS, EQUIVOCATES: TEGUCIGALPA, HONDURAS: JUNE 8–11, 1981. After months of prodding, urging and importuning, State's Office of Refugee Affairs sent a team of four officers to have a firsthand review of the situation. The office's slow response to the Honduran refugee problem was a striking contrast to its actions the year before when Costa Rica had been asked to help deal with the Cuban boat people. On that occasion, refugee affairs moved quickly and innovatively to help the Costa Ricans prepare for the planned influx of Cubans, providing real leadership. But when it came to Honduras coping with Salvadoran and Nicaraguan refugees, this office wanted to leave everything in the hands of the UN High Commission for Refugees (UNHCR). The rationale was both political and financial.

In the Costa Rica case Cuban refugees arriving in Florida had become a major domestic political issue. Consequently, we were willing to foot the bill for setting up refugee camps in Costa Rica to avoid the domestic political problem of more refugees. It was clear that the Salvadoran refugee situation impacted directly and negatively important regional foreign policy objectives. Domestic political consequences, however, were near the margin.

From where we sat, only the United States could provide the leadership to deal with this problem in ways that served, rather than damaged, those foreign policy ends. Leadership, however, implied financial burdens. At the time, we were spending massive amounts to support the Salvadoran government. Helping to fund resolution of the refugee problem would almost certainly reduce those costs in the longer term, as well as make it more difficult for the Salvadoran rebels and relieve very real human suffering. But no one wished to grasp this nettle.

We had arranged a full program for this team—meetings with virtually everyone involved plus a trip to the frontier. We briefed them on the problems of feeding and caring for the refugees and of controlling and accounting for the assets allocated to ensure they were not diverted to the rebels. In this regard there had been an important new development: refugees in Colomoncagua had been transferred to a new, consolidated site some 20 kilometers from the frontier. That step improved security and service delivery, and, we hoped, would reduce the diversion of refugee supplies. Most refugees, however, remained in the La Virtud area.

Our visitors had been instructed to avoid any commitments for additional U.S. aid. They recognized the problems we had identified, reviewed operations on the frontier with El Salvador and, based on their observations, made recommendations to the UNHCR to improve the situation. They also urged the Hondurans to set up new camps away from the frontier, while carefully offering no help.

Given these limits, this team accomplished what it had set out to do, and its members returned to Washington with a much better appreciation of the situation. That was not nothing. It would be some time before we finally screwed up the courage to address this problem, committing additional resources for the resettlement of refugees away from the frontier.

PROBLEMS WITH *HALCON VISTA* PROPOSAL: TEGUCIGALPA, HONDURAS, JUNE 8, 1981. At the first Political/Military group meeting after my return, I relayed the substance of separate conversations I had had with General Nutting and Enders on this topic and informed them of the tentative late-October exercise dates. The Political counselor and Colonel Goodwin immediately voiced concern over the timing. The former was worried that the exercise would occur just as the November 29 election campaign was reaching its peak, becoming a domestic political issue. The latter noted that these dates might conflict with the major overhaul of the Honduran Navy patrol boats, making it impossible for the Honduran Navy to participate. Because the exercise was supposed to have a naval element, that would be a problem.

I cabled these reservations to both State and Southern Command without a specific recommendation.[10] I was tired of fighting this issue. If State was willing to let these exercises become a political issue, why should I object? Similarly, if Nutting wanted to risk having an exercise in which the Honduran Navy couldn't participate, that was okay by me. Indeed, those concerns were among the least of my worries about this exercise. Of far greater concern was its likely impact on the region, Honduran military aspirations and behavior, and international perceptions.

HUMAN RIGHTS: HONDURAN BEHAVIOR TURNS AND CONTRAS EXPOSED: TEGUCIGALPA, HONDURAS, JUNE 11, 1981. We received a series of intelligence reports that signaled a clear, unequivocal change in the Honduran security forces' human rights behavior. The first provided answers to the mystery of the Barrillas and Navarro families, the Salvadorans who had been missing since April. It confirmed that this group had been detained by FUSEP's National Intelligence Directorate. That action had been taken at the request of Salvadoran authorities, who suspected that several family members were part of a guerrilla support network. The Hondurans had held and questioned them for several days, but their interrogators, some of whom had been trained by the CIA, had failed to produce useful information. At Salvadoran request, several of their interrogators were flown to Tegucigalpa to see what they could do.

The Salvadorans reportedly used extremely brutal techniques, which produced considerable data about the insurgent supply network. At the conclusion of this interrogation, members of the Barrillas/Navarro families were too brutalized to be released without serious political repercussions. The solution was to bring a Salvadoran Air Force plane to Tegucigalpa to repatriate them. Twelve members of the two families were loaded aboard. They were not, however, onboard when the plane landed at Ilopango airport, after a nonstop flight. They had exited the aircraft en route. Two small children and an aged grandmother were later turned over to Salvadoran immigration officials at the Pan American highway crossing point.[11]

The second report involved criminal acts carried out by Nicaraguan exile groups in Honduras to raise money for their fight against the Sandinistas. For several months we had been closely monitoring a steady increase in holdups of banks, supermarkets and payroll deliveries. These are often indices of preinsurgency, as subversive groups amass financial resources and test their planning, operational and safe-house networks. Based on this information— as well as the attacks on mission facilities, the Vinelli kidnapping and the SAHSA highjacking—our assessment of the Hondurans' security situation was sharply bearish. This intelligence report attributed many of those actions to the anti-Sandinista group ARDEN, which was led by former National Guard officers.

According to this report, Honduran security forces were aware of this but had decided not to intervene. That policy, however, changed abruptly when ARDEN kidnapped the son of a wealthy Nicaraguan exile, holding him for ransom. That was more than the Hondurans would tolerate. They brought ARDEN leaders in and read them the riot act. As a result, the boy was released immediately with no ransom paid. ARDEN was also told to rein in its other criminal activities or face active prosecution.

Based on this, it was hard to argue that ARDEN was anything more than a group of thugs who justified their activities on political grounds. But it seemed to me this might afford an opportunity to press the Hondurans to crack down on ARDEN, thus effectively countering Nicaraguan claims that they were abetting the Contras. It was worth a try.

But this was not all. Yet another intelligence report described a recent meeting in Panama involving senior military officials of that country, Honduras and Venezuela. The Hondurans described their plans to support the Contra operation and later launch a military attack on Nicaragua. The Venezuelans and Panamanians allegedly agreed to support this plan. This, I suspected, was an exaggeration of any commitments given by these officials. It was not credible. Nonetheless, this report too provided another opportunity to try to bring some clarity to our regional policy.

These three reports might be used to force the administration to think through and define its regional objectives. Did we wish Honduran human rights abuses to escalate unchecked and threaten our other interests? Did we really wish to support an insurgency in Nicaragua using a group that seemed little more than a criminal band? Did we want Honduras to deter attacks on Nicaragua from its territory, or did we wish to support a cockamamie scheme to attack that country? In sum, where did we really wish to go, and how did we propose to get there?

The stakes, however, were higher than I realized. In addition to the above concerns, Honduran actions had the potential to threaten goals, of which I was unaware, being pursued by other agencies:

• The CIA, under Casey's leadership, was busily planning its Contra operation, with Argentina as its cutout, even although there was no presidential finding or other legal basis for this action;

• Hard-liners within and without the administration were pushing for stronger action against the Salvadoran insurgents, Nicaragua and Cuba, with nearly all of their proposals involving Honduras;

• Elements within the U.S. military were unilaterally planning to gain access to Honduran bases as part of a larger "power projection" strategy to contain the communist threat in Nicaragua.

In an effort to ensure high-level attention to these intelligence reports, I sent a NODIS cable addressed to Enders assessing their significance.[12] Regarding the Barrillas/Navarro case, I wrote:

> I find [deleted] especially worrying because it suggests GOH (or at least FUSEP) may be in process of altering its traditional moderate, non-repressive but effective approach to the terrorist/insurgency problem.... I believe that the GOH's non-repressive behavior has been a major contributing factor to this country's relative tranquility and stability. The adoption of brutal, inhumane tactics could give our enemies precisely the kind of popular toe hold [*sic*] they now lack in Honduras.... These matters bear close watch in the coming weeks and may ultimately require some direct, candid talks to the Hondurans and others.

Regarding the Contras I wrote that: "the Nicaraguan exile group ARDEN...is prepared to engage in outright criminal and terrorist acts against innocent people and counts among it members some pretty stupid individuals. But it is an ill wind that blows no good: ARDEN's stupidity in this case could provide the incentive needed for the GOH to take some action against the anti–Sandinistas, thus strengthening its ability to rebut FSLN accusations of GOH support for the 'counter-revolutionaries.'"

Continuing, I had the following to say about the Panama meeting:

"While we believe [source] overstates the level and substance of agreements reached in Panama (witness other reports of the meeting), thereby reaffirming Honduran proclivity to hear what they wish to hear, it also indicates that anti-Sandinista activities will be increasing. If we could be confident that all of the actors were thoughtful, careful and prudent, this might be a good thing. I suspect, however, that it would be an error to underestimate their capacity for the ill-conceived and maladroit."[14]

In retrospect, it is not surprising that this cable brought a thundering silence from Washington. I was, unknowingly, raining on a planned parade and its several floats. Although there might have been some voices of reason within the administration, they were drowned out by others. Less than a week later, the time for U.S. action would be at hand. We would have to act to head off escalating Honduran human rights abuses.

SAN SALVADOR VISIT: SAN SALVADOR, EL SALVADOR, JUNE 12–13, 1981. After a 35-minute flight, the attache aircraft landed at Ilopango airport on the outskirts of San Salvador. As we debarked, we were met by the base commander, our Defense attache and an embassy officer. The latter and I headed for the chancery. We formed quite a procession. I was used to riding in an armored sedan followed by another car full of bodyguards. Here we had a caravan consisting of an armored personnel carrier (APC) with automatic weapons poking through gun ports, our sedan (armored), an armored follow car (sedan), and bringing up the rear, another APC with automatic weapons sticking out of gun slits. This was serious stuff.

I was unprepared for the chancery's appearance. Completed in 1967, it had been a striking architectural marriage of stone, glass and sharp angles, sited on a small city block and surrounded by a light, grilled fence. The grillwork had been replaced by solid steel, with concrete blockhouses built at each corner. The building had sandbag gun emplacements on all four corners of the roof and was draped in heavy steel nets as a defense against rocket-propelled grenade attack. A Salvadoran APC was stationed in front of the building, and several police cars were parked on side streets. And embassy security personnel seemed to be everywhere. There was no doubt we were in a war zone.

Hinton welcomed me and provided a quick overview of the political and military situations—neither were very good at the time—before turning to topics of more mutual concern: insurgent activities along the border, the refugee situation in Honduras, how intelligence exchange between El Salvador and Honduras might be improved, and the relationships between these issues. After an hour or so, we adjourned to his residence for lunch. This time the armored caravan was even larger and, if possible, more heavily armed.

Hinton and I continued our discussion during lunch and then returned to the chancery, where I met with the Political counselor, chief of station and others. Later, it was back to the residence for dinner.

Duarte arrived at the appointed hour, accompanied by an armed escorting column that was even larger than Hinton's. He looked tired, showing the strain of his difficult position and dependence on the Salvadoran military. When he was the appointed junta president, the military needed him and his Christian Democratic Party to legitimize the junta, and Duarte and his party needed the military for access to the political power that had twice been denied them in rigged elections. It was a marriage of convenience, with the generals being the final arbiters.

The main purpose of our dinner, however, was not substance. Hinton wanted me to help him establish an easy, informal relationship with Duarte. So Duarte and I talked about the old days: our families and mutual friends, some occupying senior positions in the junta government, others killed by death squads, still others who had aligned themselves with the insurgents and left the country. Hinton occasionally asked questions about our tales but mostly listened, picking up clues about Duarte, his perceptions of the United States and his perspective on the world.

Later, the conversation moved seamlessly to the political and security situations. Duarte described the tension between himself and his party on the one hand, and the military on the other. He and his associates walked a narrow and dangerous line, never certain of which opinion, decision or action might bring a midnight visit from a death squad; never knowing whether some family member might be killed or kidnapped as a result of a misstep on their part (his daughter was later kidnapped by the rebels); never knowing exactly which of the senior military might have ties with the death squads and be secretly plotting their elimination; and always knowing that the military could oust them at any time.

The only possible solution, Duarte believed, was elections. He had no doubt that the Christian Democrats would win free elections. Indeed, he hoped that Ungo's party, the National Revolutionary Movement, or the Democratic Revolutionary Front (FDR) could somehow be persuaded to participate in elections to help legitimize the outcome. He was willing to meet with Ungo and/or members of the Front at any time to work out their participation, even though such a meeting would undoubtedly cause him problems with the military and had little chance of success. He was convinced that even the "moderates" in the FDR were unwilling to accept accommodation or the popular will. They saw "negotiations" solely as a tactical ploy and wished to impose a totalitarian system. If there were any real democrats among them, they were entirely hostage to the "hard men" of the paramilitary groups.

Once a president was elected, Duarte believed the power equation would change. From that point forward, the military would become dependent on the politicians for legitimacy, without which they could not defeat the insurgents. By this point Hinton was carrying our side of the conversation, and I was mostly the listener.[13] Hinton, the next morning, told me that it had been a very valuable session for him.

In the morning we went back to the chancery, escorted by the light brigade. I had time for coffee, said good-bye to some of the embassy staff and extended an invitation to Hinton to come to Tegucigalpa anytime he felt he needed to get away from constant pressure in El Salvador. Colonel Miller and I were then off to the airport, his assistant having gone out earlier to prepare the plane. We were happy to be headed home.

POLICE AUTHORIZED TO KILL HABITUAL CRIMINALS: TEGUCIGALPA, HONDURAS, JUNE 15, 1981. In conversation with an embassy officer, a FUSEP official stated that the police had been "authorized" to kill habitual criminals. Elaborating, he said that when FUSEP picked up a suspect who had more than 25 previous criminal detentions, the individual was summarily executed. Over 150 persons had been so dispatched in the previous three months, he claimed.

We did not have independent confirmation. But press accounts of "known delinquents" being found dead in and around major population centers or killed in unexplained "shootouts with FUSEP agents" lent credence to it. We reported it, adding to the record of escalating human rights abuses in Honduras.[14]

HONDURAN SCHEME TO ATTACK SALVADORAN INSURGENTS: TEGU-CIGALPA, HONDURAS, MID–JUNE 1981. We received yet another intelligence report indicating the Honduran military were still dreaming up harebrained schemes. This time Colonel Alvarez had approached the station chief with the story. He reported that the Superior Council of the Armed Forces was considering a proposal by President Paz to recommend that the United States support an "all out surprise assault on Salvadoran insurgents" by the Honduran and Salvadoran armies. Moreover, the Superior Council reportedly believed that this operation could be completed, and the insurgents eliminated, in five days.

I was dumbfounded. This plan struck me at least as unrealistic as the scheme to attack Nicaragua. Paz seemed to be dreaming up these stratagems in a desperate effort to get the Reagan administration's attention. The other senior military, if not actually encouraging him as Alvarez seemed to be doing, certainly didn't seem to be exercising any critical judgment or restraining influence.

I added a somewhat understated comment assessing this report, as follows:

> General Paz' [sic] plans to broach the possibility of an all-out surprise assault on Salvadoran insurgents by Armed Forces of Honduras and El Salvador is noteworthy and problematic.... Since the topography in this [frontier] area is exceedingly

rough, the communications primitive to non-existent, the integral troop lift capability limited to one battalion (ground) and a couple of companies (air and helicopter), I have serious doubts that the Hondurans could move a significant number of troops in a manner that would preserve the element of surprise. As for the Superior Council's judgment that the insurgents could be eliminated in five days, I can express only wonderment.... An overt Honduran attack along the lines described by Alvarez would immediately destroy what remains of Honduran private sector confidence, triggering increased capital flight and recession...would intensify Nicaraguan fears about the intentions of the 'northern tier'...[and] might well precipitate direct Nicaraguan action against Honduras, especially if Honduras deployed and engaged its strategic reserve in El Salvador. In short, I believe the scheme outlined by Alvarez is a recipe for serious destabilization of the region.[15]

Were the Hondurans serious, or were they simply trying to get our attention? Was there really no one among the senior officers who could see that they lacked the logistic capability to support such an operation, or that five days to complete the operation was a pipe dream? The Salvadoran military— far better trained, better equipped and battle hardened—had been at it for two years without success. Was Alvarez using the station chief as a channel to get this proposal to Casey? Was it really Paz's idea? Was it a desperate bid to get to Washington? Goodness knows.

The following year the Hondurans collaborated with Salvadoran forces in several offensive operations and actually moved into and occupied one of the disputed pockets. Those actions were to little avail. Insurgents continued to use bases in the frontier area until the cease-fire of nearly a decade later.

ESCALATING HONDURAN REPRESSION DEMANDS ACTION: TEGUCIGALPA, HONDURAS, JUNE 17, 1981. In the early morning of June 11 the People's Revolutionary Union (URP) leader Tomas Nativi and an associate, Fidel Martinez, were abducted from Nativi's home by six armed, hooded men.[16] News of their abduction hit the local media the following day. Organizations on the extreme left were vocal and active in accusing the security forces of the abduction and demanding their release. The URP, in its statement, linked the disappearances to General Walters's visit and promised retribution. We had to take that threat seriously. Cuba's *Prensa Latina* news service and *Radio Havana* lost no time in airing charges against Honduran security services. FUSEP denied any knowledge of their abduction or whereabouts.

We quickly tightened our security, and once again I asked all CT elements to see what they could pick up. Nativi had a high public profile and, according to intelligence sources, was involved with clandestine terrorist units. Accordingly, he was a likely target for the Honduran military.

In short order sources confirmed that Nativi and Martinez had been arrested by National Intelligence Directorate agents, tortured, then killed. This represented a further escalation of officially sponsored human rights abuse.

The administration had equivocated on the human rights issue thus far, but I believed these abuses could no longer be ignored; we had to act. Failure to do so would only allow the spiral of violence to accelerate, triggering further unrest and instability. Thus, I sent a NODIS cable to Enders that began: "I am deeply concerned at increasing evidence of officially sponsored/sanctioned assassinations (reftels) of political and criminal targets, which clearly indicate GOH repression has built up a head of steam much faster than we had anticipated."[17] I went on to describe how such actions could destabilize the political situation and threaten our interests and policy objectives. Accordingly, I urged that we "try to nip this situation in the bud" by raising the issue with Paz and Alvarez, stressing that such activity would cause us to reconsider both our economic and military assistance. One of the keys to success of this strategy would be the degree to which they found my démarche credible. Mixed or equivocal signals from other sources would ensure its failure, although its success under the best of circumstances would be by no means certain. If this failed, I recommended a series of further actions applying steadily escalating persuasion and pressure.

There was no official response to this cable or to the strategy I had proposed. In fact, State and the Reagan administration continued to ignore Honduran human rights abuses, which increased steadily until Alvarez, then commander of the armed forces, was removed by a junior officers' coup in 1984.

HONDURAS/NICARAGUA TENSIONS RISE: TEGUCIGALPA, HONDURAS, JUNE 18, 1981. Foreign Minister Elvir called and asked that I come by his office. When I arrived, I found him quite agitated, in sharp contrast to his normal measured demeanor. The cause was the Sandinistas' arrest, trial and recent conviction of two hapless Honduran farmers on charges of spying. The Honduran government maintained, correctly as far as we could determine, that the Nicaraguans had engaged in a naked provocation.

Honduran leaders had raised this problem with their Sandinista counterparts in their earlier "tensions easing" meeting. The Nicaraguans had promised to look into the matter but had done nothing. The trial had gone ahead, and the accused were convicted. Moreover, the Nicaraguan government had firmly refused to provide evidence of their guilt and had even denied the Honduran embassy access to the alleged spies. Elvir had called in the Nicaraguan ambassador, who said that his government was considering turning the two over to Honduras rather than imprisoning them. Elvir was skeptical, because he did not believe the Sandinistas were dealing in good faith. I noted that the Nicaraguan ambassador had called on me the previous day—an unusual act in itself—and made the same point when I inquired about this case. Perhaps it was not just a ploy.

Elvir's principal worry, however, was his military colleagues. Most of them favored a strong, public response to the Nicaraguan action, and some were advocating military action. The first he thought ill-advised and the second mindless. He was arguing for, as a first step, a low-key diplomatic approach. He recalled that General Walters had cautioned President Paz to avoid any action that might give the Sandinistas an opportunity to consolidate their deteriorating domestic political situation. I encouraged him, noting that the diplomatic route he was suggesting would leave Honduras occupying the high moral ground and strengthen its case if it ultimately went public. It would also avoid giving the Sandinistas further justification for their continuing arms buildup. Elvir thanked me and repeated that his government had as yet made no decision on how to proceed.

Honduras's relations with its neighbor were nearing a flash point, and Elvir was worried. It also appeared that some of the military remained enamored with their two-phased plan for a preemptive attack on Nicaragua and thought this incident might provide an adequate pretext for its launch.

I reported this to Washington immediately, along with my intention to seek an early appointment with Paz to reiterate our hope that his government would exercise restraint in its dealings with Nicaragua.[18]

UNIVERSITY LEADERS ALLEGE UNITED STATES RESPONSIBLE FOR DISAPPEARANCES: TEGUCIGALPA, HONDURAS, JUNE 18–20, 1981. National University Rector Juan Almendares and leaders of various left-wing student groups and radical Marxist organizations held a press conference in which they denounced the recent disappearances and other repressive acts by the government. This was not surprising, but their linkage of these acts to the United States generally, and to Walters and me specifically, was troubling.

According to the wire service report, Almendares had specifically linked the United States with recent repression, mentioning Walters and me by name. We quickly decided that we could not let these allegations pass unchallenged, but we first needed to see how the media played them and verify that Almendares had made the statements attributed to him. I put in a call to Almendares, my first of many that went unanswered that day and the next. Arcos too tried unsuccessfully to reach him.

Although the conference received some radio coverage, it was ignored by television. Press coverage the following morning was thin: only *Tiempo* gave it significant space, but its treatment was sensational. "U.S. State Department Is Responsible" screamed the headline, with the subtext reading "for the recent bloody deeds, National University Rector affirms."[19] It reported that Almendares had been the principal speaker and asserted that the upsurge of repression followed the models of Guatemala and El Salvador—death threats, disappearances and the discovery of unidentified bodies. As to culpability, he was quoted as saying that "the U.S. Department of State recently sent its traveling ambassador, Vernon Walters, to bless the electoral process as a mask for the repressive models that the government is carrying out, with

Ambassador Jack Binns assuming a similar role." The other speakers attacked the Honduran government vigorously but apparently did not directly implicate the United States. Arcos checked with the wire service and the *Tiempo* editor to verify what had been said. Both stood by their stories, as reported.

Arcos prepared a draft response in the form of a letter from me to Almendares. Walker and I reviewed, parsed and honed it. In less than a page I expressed my surprise at the statements attributed to him, alluded to my own experience at being misquoted and denied the allegations leveled. I also asked that whoever had made these charges either retract or present evidence to support them. In closing, I affirmed our continued support for elections and the return to constitutional rule and concluded by saying that I was certain he would have no objection to my sharing the letter with the media.[20] We held off distributing it until I could speak with Almendares. As the day wore on, I became increasingly antsy. So we waited and Arcos's press staff deflected media calls.

By late afternoon, I decided that we had to proceed. It was evident that Almendares wasn't going to respond to our calls, so we sent the letter to his office by messenger. Copies were also released to the media.

DECEIT FOLLOWS SECRET TRIP TO WASHINGTON: WASHINGTON, D.C., JUNE 19, 1981. Colonels Gustavo Alvarez, Leonides Torres Arias and Hubert Bodden traveled to Washington to meet with General Schweitzer at the NSC, returning to Tegucigalpa the same day. Schweitzer provided State a memorandum purporting to detail the substance of the discussion on June 23. The meeting, he claimed, had been set up June 18 at the request of the Honduran Defense attache and with the active support of the American general who chaired the Inter-American Defense Board (IADB); they had not told him that anyone was coming from Honduras.[21] Present from our side, in addition to Schweitzer, were Roger Fontaine, also on the NSC staff, and representatives from the U.S. Army and U.S. Navy staffs and the IADB. That kind of turnout for a meeting with a resident military attache was highly implausible.

According to the memo, the principal topics were Honduran concerns about Nicaragua and El Salvador and their need for additional security assistance. They also reiterated their plea for an invitation to President Paz to visit Washington, endorsed elections and asked that the United States intervene in the dispute with Texaco. As regarded Nicaragua, they allegedly complained about Sandinista incursions, denied they had any intention of invading that country or "otherwise interfering with Nicaragua's revolutionary process" and expressed concern about the Sandinista arms buildup. Schweitzer commended them for their restraint and "stressed [the] absolute need to [continue to] do so."

This was not credible. At the time, the Hondurans had already broached their strategy to use the Contras—with Argentine and U.S. help—to provoke the Sandinistas into attacking them, to Schweitzer, Casey and others. According to that scheme, once they attacked, Honduras, the United States and others would defeat them militarily. We also knew from contemporaneous intelligence reports (and, later, investigative journalism) that they continued to push this strategy at every opportunity. And their concerns about Nicaragua were growing, as evidenced by my recent discussions with Paz and Elvir.

It defied belief that these officers traveled to Washington urgently and secretly to meet their pal Schweitzer and then didn't mention the Contras or their larger strategy. What was really agitating them, I believe, was our inaction on their proposals vis-à-vis Nicaragua and their requests for additional assistance. Those had to have been the principal topics discussed. And any counseling for restraint that Schweitzer might have offered was to keep them from getting too far out in front.

The El Salvador portions of the report were equally fictitious. The memo alleged they had focused mainly on the refugee camps and how to handle them and that Schweitzer suggested they consider joining with "El Salvador in combined military operations against the guerrillas." Of course we knew from Alvarez that Paz and the senior military wished to propose a major Honduran/Salvadoran offensive against the insurgents. Thus, on its face Schweitzer's account is incredible.

As to security assistance, Schweitzer's memo said merely that the Hondurans had presented an extensive list of materiel they needed, which they suggested "we might find excessive." Schweitzer promised to review it and made no reference to additional assistance. In fact, Alvarez later told us that he and Torres Arias had pushed hard for more assistance, asserting that this was the reason Paz was so anxious to get to Washington. According to Alvarez, Schweitzer said all fiscal year 1982 funds were obligated, but the administration had requested $200 million from Congress for a "special presidential fund"; once that was approved, we would respond favorably to their request.

Although not initiated by Schweitzer, this adventure was another example of the private agendas for Central America being pursued by administration officials. And his memorandum was a tissue of lies designed to screen his improper, uncoordinated dealings with the Hondurans and to deceive State and the embassy. Schweitzer was a cannon loose on the deck of our pitching foreign policy ship.[22]

HUMAN RIGHTS: RETURNING A BALL TO STATE'S COURT: TEGUCIGALPA, HONDURAS, JUNE 19, 1981. We received a routine cable from State forwarding an inquiry from an American citizen as to the whereabouts of her sister, Concepcion de Navarro, and other members of the Salvadoran group detained by Honduran security forces. This was a poser.[23] We were certain that we knew what had happened to Ms. Navarro. Senior officials at State and other agencies also knew. This information, however, was extremely sensitive and highly classified. We had no authority to release it, and it appeared that State was passing the buck to us for a response. That didn't make me very happy.

After thinking and consulting Walker and others, I sent a NODIS cable to Bushnell, pointing up the problem and telling him how I proposed to handle this hot potato. We would respond to the inquiry in an open channel, citing press reports and the public statements of the security forces denying knowledge of the group's whereabouts and indicating we had no further information.[24] Thus, I put the ball back in State's court, allowing Bushnell or someone else to decide whether to go further.

We deliberately misled an American citizen about what had happened to her sister, with the full knowledge of senior officials. State had the option of making the truth known, but it chose not to do so.

MAGAZINE OUTLINES ALLEGED U.S. STRATEGY ON NICARAGUA: WASHINGTON, D.C., JUNE 20, 1981. The *New Republic*, which was close to many neoconservatives in the Reagan administration, published an extensive article describing the administration's intentions regarding Nicaragua. According to authors Morton Kondracke and Nicholas Kotz, two options were under consideration. The first was a plan to mobilize former National Guardsmen, launch a Bay of Pigs–type invasion from Honduras and liberate the country. The second was longer term and marginally more realistic. It posited the termination of bilateral and multilateral assistance, triggering widespread popular unrest. At a strategic moment, CIA-trained exile armies would invade Nicaragua from neighboring countries and the United States, overthrowing the Sandinistas.[25]

The authors had been selectively briefed by administration sources. There was no mention, for example, of using the Argentines as cutouts, a central element in the plan carried out by the CIA. The strategy ultimately adopted embodied elements of both these options.

PRESS RAISES REFUGEE SUPPLY DIVERSIONS, CITES EMBASSY: TEGU-CIGALPA, HONDURAS, JUNE 22, 1981. In what appeared to be a planted story, *Tiempo* and *La Tribuna* asserted that the State Department was preparing another "White Paper"[26] on Central America, this time drawing heavily on reports from our embassy that substantial quantities of refugee relief supplies were being diverted to the insurgents. *Tiempo* claimed its story was the result of "investigations carried out by *Tiempo* reporters"; *La Tribuna* made no such claim. Both reported that the embassy had determined refugee-relief organizations—CARITAS, CEDEN and others—were responsible for these diversions. *Tiempo* concluded: "Thus far, the U.S. Embassy has said nothing to the

Honduran media about this report, but it is believed that this information will be part of a second State Department White Paper about CA guerrillas."[27]

It had to have been a deliberate leak or a plant, as our reports had been classified, usually with highly restricted distribution. These articles were certain to cause us trouble locally. I was sure that no one in the embassy had leaked the story, and it was even less likely that they had gotten it directly from Washington. Neither paper had overseas correspondents. Moreover, the "White Paper" references were nonsense. And how did they both get the story at the same time with the same angle? It smelled like a purposeful plant.

The UNHCR representative was aware of our concerns, which State had passed on to his headquarters and had been raised by our refugee office team. Thus, it was likely that the relief agencies knew of our suspicions. Yet it seemed implausible that they were the source. They had nothing to gain by going public. And why would they frame the story in the context of a White Paper? The Honduran government also was a possible source, but that theory too made little sense. The more likely source was Zuniga, who probably learned of our concerns from his Washington friends. Whatever the origin, Zuniga could see how this story might be used to create a problem for us. The White Paper wrinkle, too, smelled like the kind of thing he might dream up.

We decided to adopt a reactive posture. It was speculative and explicitly stated that the embassy had said nothing to the local media. We would see what happened and tailor our response accordingly. In the meantime, we would deflect questions.

ENDERS FINALLY CONFIRMED: WASHINGTON, D.C., JUNE 23, 1981. Thomas O. Enders was finally confirmed by the Senate and, on this date, sworn in as Assistant Secretary for Inter-American affairs.[28] He had in fact been running the bureau for several months.

LETTER TO RECTOR HITS PRESS: TEGUCIGALPA, HONDURAS, JUNE 23, 1981. All the dailies reprinted the text of my letter to Rector Almendares, calling for a retraction or evidence that the United States or its embassy was involved in the government's alleged repression. *El Heraldo*, my former nemesis, presented the letter most accurately, under the headline "Absolutely Slanderous Declarations Attributed to University Rector." The others were tendentious,[29] and most juxtaposed photographs of Almendares and me. They were hyping the story.

HINTON URGES JOINT SALVADORAN/HONDURAN OPERATIONS: SAN SALVADOR, EL SALVADOR, JUNE 23, 1981. Hinton transmitted an assessment of the outlook after four weeks at post.[30] It was addressed only to State, and he was very bearish. The overall situation was "bad," he said, going on to describe why he had reached this conclusion and what he recommended we do about it. When I later had the opportunity to review and comment on this cable and State's response thereto,[31] I was impressed. Hinton's exposition was comprehensive and trenchant, his recommendations generally sound and often innovative. It was the kind of document you read then wish you had written.

The portion dealing with Honduras, however, was of concern. One of the first imperatives Hinton mentioned was the need to choke off the supply of arms and munitions reaching the insurgents. To this end he recommended improved intelligence about air supply routes, establishment of a joint Salvadoran/Honduran intelligence operations staff to address the overland routes, and measures to reduce infiltration via sea routes. These recommendations seemed reasonable to me, and I indicated my support for them. Over the longer term, however, he urged that we push both countries to mount joint military operations against the insurgents. I had serious reservations about such an initiative.

State's response proposed a regional approach to arms interdiction, "preferably under SOUTHCOM's coordination." That too seemed like a mistake to me. The cable went on to identify several other priority objectives: moving the refugee camps away from the frontier, increasing Honduran military presence on the frontier, and intelligence sharing. We had been and would continue to advocate all these steps.

PAZ WORRIES ABOUT NICARAGUA AND ECONOMY: TEGUCIGALPA, HONDURAS, JUNE 23–24, 1981. I was finally able to meet with President Paz to follow up on my June 18 session with Elvir on relations with Nicaragua. Paz was lucid but downbeat. He described his busy schedule over the previous two weeks—various economic meetings with ministers, legislators and the private sector; negotiations with Texaco; problems with Nicaragua.

He confirmed that tempers were high as a result of Nicaragua's handling the alleged spy case. When I expressed our concern that his government might respond in a rash manner, he agreed that they had to avoid anything that made the Sandinistas appear the aggrieved. He added that he wanted to avoid at all cost anything that would draw attention away from the internal conflicts between the Sandinistas and other Nicaraguan institutions, which were reaching a critical stage. He had yet to decide how to respond but was leaning toward an initial low-key diplomatic protest. In that case later steps would be based on the Nicaraguan response. It seemed clear that Elvir had briefed him on our discussion and had urged restraint.

Paz also reiterated his concern over the Nicaraguan arms buildup and asked about the intelligence exchange mechanism Walters had proposed during his visit. I reported that I had followed up recently on that matter and had been told that it was still under study. Paz was disappointed. Another U.S. "promise" had not come to fruition. I took this opportunity to pass on to him our latest intelligence assessment of the Sandinista arms buildup: still no sign of heavy armor or high performance aircraft, but runways and other facilities were being improved, and Nicaraguan pilots were training in Cuba.

He went on to describe his ongoing difficulties with the legislature and private sector over taxation and the coming year's budget. I sensed Paz could feel power slipping from his hands almost daily as elections approached. He did not mention the Alvarez, Torres Arias and Bodden trip to Washington.

I reported this to State.[32]

REFUGEE RELIEF GROUPS RESPOND TO PRESS STORY: TEGUCIGALPA, HONDURAS, JUNE 23, 1981. The private refugee relief organizations were quick to act on the reported leakage of supplies to Salvadoran insurgents. Most wrote to me, asking that I set the record straight.[33] The Catholic relief agency, CARITAS, which we suspected was most heavily engaged in diversion of supplies, sent a copy of its letter to the press at the same time.[34] The UNHCR office made no public comment.

Our carefully crafted response began by stressing the important humanitarian work being done by relief organizations and our continuing financial and material support for their work. The latter gave rise to our desire to ensure these resources were properly handled and went only to those for whom they were intended. Based on our observations, we believed that small amounts of supplies had reached the hands of the Salvadoran insurgents. Acknowledging that total control of foodstuffs and other supplies was impossible, especially in the La Virtud area, and that the relief agencies were attempting to assure proper accountability, we believed improvements were possible. We had communicated our concerns to the UNHCR in official channels. We had not, however, raised this issue in public fora and were not in any way responsible for the press articles. Because of their requests that we clarify this matter publicly, the media were sent copies of this letter.[35] Copies were also sent to all Honduran government offices that had been copied on the relief organizations' letters to us.

The press dutifully reprinted our letter without further comment, laying this tempest to rest.[36] Foreign Minister Elvir later thanked me for having brought the issue of supply diversion into the open. I told him that he should thank the Honduran press.

RECTOR RESPONDS; REVERBERATIONS CONTINUE: TEGUCIGALPA, HONDURAS, JUNE 24–29, 1981. Rector Almendares's response to my letter hit the press and was reprinted without comment.[37] Its sarcastic tone—"I am sorry that you abandoned for some minutes the important business of your post to occupy yourself with this small matter" (allegations that the United

States was responsible for increased Honduran repression)—was surprising. Almendares had finally called me the day before, denying having made the statements attributed to him and implying that they had been made by others. He also offered to make a tape of the press conference available to me at his office. That was an opportunity I declined. He was nonresponsive, however, when I suggested that he simply make that statement in his public response and disassociate himself from the accusation. Nor did he indicate any reason for not having returned my calls earlier. It was a brief and cool conversation.

The letter said he had nothing to retract or to prove and repeated the invitation for me to listen to a tape of the press conference. It concluded with a reference to my statement of support for elections and installation of constitutional government by "having to advise you that this was a decision adopted firmly by the Honduran people, after 18 years in which they were obliged to live under an unconstitutional regime."

That would have ended the matter had it not been for an unsolicited editorial from *La Prensa* defending the embassy and my position. Entitled "New Campaign Against U.S. Embassy," it summarized the attacks that had been made on me from the left and right and the substance of my argument with Almendares, comparing him to Sancho Panza.[38] Its central theme was the existence of groups that wished to prevent elections and the link between those efforts and the attacks on me:

> There are too many forces striving to sabotage the political process in our country. Those of us who believe in democracy look on these gratuitous attacks against the United States with indifference. After all, an embassy like that of the United States has done nothing but stimulate and collaborate with the restitution of a legitimate, republican and popular system.
> Those who hurl invectives at Binns show that they don't understand where the enemies of the people really are. Or...they know clearly what the truth is, but nevertheless assume unjust and sectarian positions which can only lead us to the destruction of the relative peace in which we live. Eventually, this will lead to an explosion of destructive violence that daily tears at our brothers in Guatemala and El Salvador.

It caused Almendares to fire off an angry letter to *La Prensa* that was promptly published, keeping the dispute in the public eye a bit longer.[39] We kept our heads down.

FURTHER SCHEMES TO BLOCK ELECTIONS: TEGUCIGALPA, HONDURAS, JUNE 25, 1981. Reports that the military and Zuniga were plotting to block elections were again cropping up. As speculation began to near epidemic proportions among the political classes, I convened a skull session with the DCM, Political Section, CIA, our military and Arcos in an effort to reassess the threat. The product weighed these reports and concluded that they did not appear well founded.[40] One source appeared to be the Christian Democratic leader, who was alleged to have said that the USG had decided to support a delay in elections.

In an effort to counter its effect, I met with the Christian Democratic presidential candidate, who denied any knowledge of his colleague's alleged statements and promised to assure him such reports were without foundation. I did the same with leaders of the Liberal, the National and other minor party. In addition, all CT members were instructed to affirm the same point with all their contacts.

Several contacts had suggested that Zuniga was the ultimate source of these rumors. He was continuing to present himself as the Reagan administration's preferred candidate to all and sundry and, in his meetings with official visitors and embassy officers, constantly harped on the need to delay elections because of electoral fraud. Moreover, we discovered that National Party legislative leaders had approached one of the minor parties, requesting that it support an amendment to suspend elections indefinitely. Because the minor parties held the balance in the legislature, that party's two votes, combined with those of the Nationalists, would have been enough to pass the amendment. They spurned that approach.

Nonetheless, the situation was fragile enough to warrant continued close monitoring. Any number of events—a decision to replace Paz, a sharp deterioration in the economy, an armed confrontation with Nicaragua, increased civil unrest or terrorism—might be enough to tip the scales.

NICARAGUA RELEASES ALLEGED SPIES: MANAGUA, NICARAGUA, JUNE 26, 1981. President Paz phoned to report that the Nicaraguan government had agreed to release and return the two alleged Honduran spies.[41] That was good news and would lessen tensions somewhat. Paz, however, complained that the Sandinistas had only taken this action after completing a show trial to demonstrate "Honduran aggression."

TURNOVER IN THE DEFENSE ATTACHE OFFICE: TEGUCIGALPA, HONDURAS, JUNE 26, 1981. Our Defense attache and command pilot, Bill Miller, was retiring to Hawaii. He was replaced by Col. Dale Bollert, USAF.[42] In addition, within a few weeks our new Army attache would be at post, strengthening our collection capabilities with the Honduran Army.

LA PRENSA INTERVIEW: TEGUCIGALPA, HONDURAS, JUNE 26, 1981. Amilcar Santa Maria of *La Prensa*'s editorial board had requested an interview that would be published July 4, our national day. I quickly agreed, seeing this as another opportunity to reiterate our continuing support for elections.

Arcos and I met with Santa Maria for a wide-ranging hour-and-a-half review of our policies, which included an off-the-record discussion of the local political scene, alleged coup plotting and so forth. He was happy when he left, and Arcos and I were confident he would treat us fairly.[43]

AMERICAN HOSPITAL MANAGER KIDNAPPED: VALLE DE ANGELES, HONDURAS, JUNE 26–29, 1981. Two armed, masked men broke into the home of Ronald McBroom, business manager of the Seventh Day Adventist hospital in Valle de Angeles, in the late evening. They seized McBroom and, after threatening his wife and two hospital technicians, took him away in his own car. They left a crude note that condemned "Yankee imperialism," threatened to kill McBroom if the police or media were notified and indicated they would be in touch regarding ransom. It was signed "People's Guerrilla Command."

Less than an hour later, the kidnappers returned to the house with their hostage. McBroom's car had run out of gas, and they wanted another vehicle. This time they left in a hospital van. The hospital director, Dr. Frank McNeil, had been notified and was at the McBroom home when they returned. Once the kidnappers left the second time, be came directly to the chancery, and the Marine security guard called Walker. McNeil had not notified Honduran authorities.

Walker immediately went to meet McNeil. He urged that McNeil inform Colonel Alvarez immediately. McNeil agreed, but they were unable to reach Alvarez in the early morning hours. McNeil decided to delay further action until he could be sure of reaching Alvarez or another senior officer.[44] He met with Alvarez later in the day and was reassured by his interest and assurances that the case would be solved quickly.

When we met to assess this event, it was apparent that it had been the work of amateurs and not very skilled ones at that. We had no record of the "People's Guerrilla Command." But all we could do was to reassure McNeil and McBroom's wife, keep in touch with FUSEP and hope. We didn't wait long.

Before the day was out, McBroom was free, and one of the kidnappers was arrested while he drove around in the hospital van. McBroom had persuaded the kidnapper guarding him to allow him to walk away in return for a personal check for several hundred dollars. This "terrorist" was arrested the following day when he tried to negotiate the check at McBroom's bank.[45]

FUSEP confirmed that the perpetrators were common criminals who sought to mask their criminal endeavor as a terrorist act. This episode would have been something out of Looney Tunes were it not for the response of Honduran security forces. Both kidnappers were killed while "trying to escape." We reported their deaths as further examples of FUSEP's increasing repression and human rights violations.[46]

McBroom and his colleagues were upset over the elimination of the miscreants, especially the one who had allowed McBroom to escape.

OAS OBSERVER OPERATIONS WINDS DOWN: TEGUCIGALPA, HON-
DURAS, JUNE 29, 1981. In late June Foreign Minister Elvir told the OAS that
Honduras had decided to abandon its earlier request for another extension of
the OAS mandate. He had not apprised me. Elvir later explained that his
action had been the result of a discussion with Salvadoran Foreign Minister
Chavez Mena, who reported the Salvadorans were not going to request an
extension. The Salvadorans later changed their minds, renewing their request
without advising the Hondurans. Once Elvir learned that the Salvadorans
now wished the mission to continue, he reversed his position. It was too late.

I advised State of this situation and pushed for a six-month extension
of the mission.[47] State, Defense and the OAS, however, wanted to close the
operation, and the crossed wires provided sufficient pretext. Consequently,
the observer team began packing up and the USAF helicopters soon
returned to Panama. With the observers' departure, we lost our best intelligence about the frontier, as well as our best means of transportation to
and from the area.

SUAZO CORDOVA WISHES TO VISIT THE UNITED STATES AGAIN:
TEGUCIGALPA, HONDURAS, JUNE 29, 1981. Months earlier, before Paz became
fixated on going to Washington, we had arranged for Suazo Cordova to visit
Washington and offered the same courtesy to Zuniga. I urged him to accept
this offer. There are, of course, major differences between visits of candidates
and those of chiefs of state, the most obvious one being that the candidates
have no chance of meeting the president.[48] That, I suspect, accounted for
Zuniga's lack of interest. It would have been very difficult for him to sustain
his claimed closeness to the administration if he had gone to Washington and
not seen President Reagan.

Out of the blue I received a call from Suazo, who asked that we set up
a program for him in the latter half of July. Within that time frame he was
flexible. "Delighted," I said, while thinking of the problems his request would
cause me with Paz and Zuniga. Nevertheless, I was glad he had decided to
go. He was unknown to the administration, and Zuniga's friends were telling
everyone they could buttonhole that he was a crypto-Sandinista. In addition,
Suazo could only benefit from further exposure to Washington. I sent off a
request with a strong recommendation that he be given special treatment.[49]

I immediately phoned Zuniga to apprise him of Suazo Cordova's request
and again urge that he allow us to do the same for him. He was noncommittal, but I knew from his tone that there was no chance he would do so.
Next, in an effort to limit damage with Paz, I called Foreign Minister Elvir.
I stressed the distinction between Suazo Cordova's private travel and that of
a chief of state. He recognized the difference and appreciated the heads-up.
Whether Paz did is another question. There wasn't much more I could do.

A few days later I received a call from Rafael Callejas, a young politician and former AID employee, who was on Zuniga's ticket as candidate for first vice president.[50] He wondered if we could arrange a program for him in Washington. "Of course," I responded, knowing that he was Zuniga's stalking horse and a very presentable one at that.[51] We did, and Callejas, by all accounts, made a good impression.

U.S. MILITARY ADVISERS IN SALVADORAN COMBAT: LA UNION, EL SALVADOR, JUNE 29, 1981. Three members of a U.S. military mobile training team were at the La Union naval base when it came under a sustained insurgent attack. This was the first instance in which U.S. military were present during combat between Salvadoran military units and rebels.[52] Our embassy and other facilities, of course, had come under attack on several occasions, but these were terrorist attacks rather than combat.

8

Transition Crisis Reached as My Replacement Is Named

SUMMARY—More congressional visitors—a summons to Washington regarding human rights reporting—my replacement confirmed but not announced—further CIA deception—"emergency" Honduran arms purchases—conflicting regional policies and priorities ignored—new problems with Southern Command and adviser withdrawn—crisis point as military decide to postpone elections and we counter—Caribbean Basin Initiative—priests support Salvadoran insurgents—Soviet tanks in Nicaragua as refugees flee to Honduras—Enders negotiates tentative agreement with Sandinistas.

ANOTHER CONGRESSIONAL VISITOR: TEGUCIGALPA, HONDURAS, JULY 1, 1981. Congressman Steven Solarz (D-NY), a member of the House Foreign Affairs Committee, arrived with a single aide. His 48-hour stop was part of an extended trip to evaluate the Central American situation. Refugees were a key interest, and he had independently arranged several appointments with private relief groups.

I met Solarz at the airport and brought him directly to the chancery for a briefing. He was serious and knowledgeable about the region, leading personalities and the principal sources of conflict, and he asked penetrating questions. Our people had the answers. Solarz appeared to be one of the few congressmen to arrive with an open mind. In reviewing our policy goals, I stressed the critical importance of the transition process, the threats thereto and its significance in regional terms, asking that he emphasize U.S. support for the elections in all his meetings with Hondurans. He agreed willingly. In statements, public and private, Solarz stated flatly that the United States supported the election of democratic governments in Honduras and throughout the region and strongly opposed military coups.[1]

Although we had not set up his meetings with the refugee relief agencies, he graciously invited me or other embassy officers to attend those sessions.

We accepted, and I decided to attend the meeting with the Catholic relief group, CARITAS, because of our suspicions that this agency's workers were engaged in the diversion of foodstuffs and other supplies. When I arrived at Solarz's hotel room, I found the meeting with CARITAS representatives, an American couple, already in progress. I sat quietly for about twenty minutes, listening to this couple relate virtually all of the disinformation that the Coordinator for Solidarity with the Salvadoran People had been peddling over the past few months—Salvadoran military atrocities, à la babies on bayonets, a Honduran military buildup on the frontier, joint Honduran/Salvadoran military operations and Honduran attacks on refugees.

Solarz maintained a poker face, occasionally interrupting to ask a pointed question and glancing at me. When there was a pause in their presentation, I decided to put my oar in. I acknowledged that the Salvadoran military was perpetrating extensive and serious human rights abuses on their own people. There was no doubt about it, but there was also a substantial body of evidence that the insurgents were also guilty of serious violations, although apparently with less frequency. Their random terrorist bombings, kidnappings and assassinations were certainly serious human rights abuses. The rebels and their supporters were also engaged in a disinformation campaign attacking both the Salvadoran and Honduran governments and military establishments, as well as U.S. activities in support of the Salvadoran junta. I offered rebuttals to most cases alleged by the CARITAS representatives.

They had been unhappy with my arrival and were more so after my remarks. But they did not challenge them. When they left a few minutes later, Solarz expressed his appreciation for my comments, adding that was precisely why he had invited the embassy to have someone in attendance.

Two months later, after my replacement had been announced, Solarz planted an item in a Jack Anderson column to the effect that while in Honduras he had been "approached by representatives of several political parties, singing Binns' praises. The Ambassador has been quietly trying to get the ruling junta to hold free elections, and the civilian politicians don't want to see him go."[2] I appreciated the gesture.

A SUMMONS FROM ENDERS: TEGUCIGALPA, HONDURAS, JULY 2, 1981. I received a cryptic phone call from one of Assistant Secretary Enders's aides informing me that Enders wished to see me in Washington as soon as possible. The aide didn't know the purpose of the summons but said we would receive a cable authorizing my travel. As Independence Day was almost on us, and I had to host a national day reception for a large number of Hondurans and the diplomatic community, as well as an informal celebration for the embassy staff and families, the earliest I could go was the following week. We agreed that I would travel July 8.[3]

I suspected the purpose of this summons was to advise me officially of what had been circulating in the corridors of State for several weeks: that I was to be replaced by John D. Negroponte. I welcomed another opportunity to make my case for staying on until the elections now scheduled for late November.

VISAS FOR ARGENTINES TRIGGER INVESTIGATION OF VICE CONSUL: TEGUCIGALPA, HONDURAS, EARLY JULY 1981. Once again the station chief laid a bombshell on my desk. He asked if I was aware that our Consular Section had issued visas to five Argentine military intelligence officers. I was not and was appalled. He provided five names, pseudonyms used by military intelligence officers working in Honduras, saying that the passports in these names had been issued by Argentina's military intelligence directorate. They had traveled to Miami with the visas we issued, apparently to meet with Nicaraguan exiles. This placed us in the embarrassing position of having facilitated Argentina's work with the Nicaraguan exiles, which, as far as I was aware, remained a major U.S. policy concern.

Issuance of a visa to a citizen of the third country normally requires that the post receiving the visa request query the consular office in the individual's country of origin before issuing a visa. This preclearance practice is designed to keep people who do not qualify for visas in their home countries from shopping consular offices in neighboring countries for a more obliging consul. Exceptions can be made under special circumstances, but such cases are relatively rare. As usual, I asked Walker to find out what had happened. He reported that Sarah Horsey had checked the records and found that one of our vice consuls had issued these visas without preclearance or advising her of his action. The vice consul told Horsey that a Nicaraguan friend had come to the consular office with the five Argentines in tow. He said they were his employees and needed to travel to Miami immediately on urgent business. He claimed they could not wait for preclearance, which normally took at least 48 hours. Inasmuch as he was a friend, the vice consul issued the visas on the spot. He did not have authority to waive preclearance, however, and had not cleared his decision with Horsey.

It was the mention of the Nicaraguan, however, that really got our attention. A fairly prominent member of the anti-Sandinista exile community, he was also suspected of being a Sandinista mole. There were also other questions that needed clarification. Had the vice consul interviewed the Argentines before issuing the visas? If so, he might have some useful intelligence; if not, it would be another violation of standard procedures. Second, there was a question of the extent to which the vice consul had continued his social contact with the Nicaraguan, despite mission policy requiring that all officers avoid such relationships. Walker had to interview the vice consul.

Reporting back, Walker said the vice consul had not interviewed the five Argentines, having only spoken to them briefly in the consular offices. He freely acknowledged awareness of mission policy regarding Nicaraguan exiles, which he had earlier indicated in writing. But he hadn't believed the policy applied to friends. In fact, it turned out that his relationship with the Nicaraguan was closer than we had imagined: they were sharing the vice consul's house. We now had a possible Sandinista agent living with an embassy officer. This was a security risk of some significance, as well as a flagrant violation of mission policy. And the more deeply Walker delved, the worse the situation became. The vice consul was an avid gun collector, and his Nicaraguan roommate had given him several weapons that were allegedly taken from Sandinistas during Contra forays. This booty included an engraved Soviet presentation pistol, complete with an elaborate case, and a Kalashnikov assault rifle.

These items had significant monetary value, raising yet another question. It might appear that the visas had been issued in return for something of value. The appearance of serious impropriety was there, even if the vice consul's actions had not been influenced by these gifts. At this point we suddenly had a potential visa bribery case. We had no choice but to report this matter to State's Visa Office and to call RSO Sy Dewitt back to open an investigation. Walker advised Horsey and the vice consul of the investigation and directed that the vice consul not go into the office until the investigation was completed. He was also instructed to get his Nicaraguan friend to move out of his house immediately. We could take the latter step because the embassy leased the vice consul's residence, and we had the right to say who resided there.

In retrospect, another significant question jumps out. How did the station chief know that the passports in question bore pseudonyms and had been issued to Argentine military intelligence officers? A normal visa preclearance would not produce that type of information. The consular office receiving such an inquiry usually checks the records to see if the individual named has previously been refused a visa or is on a list of persons ineligible to receive one. That's it. The information about the false passports could have come from only a few sources: the Argentine officers themselves; the Hondurans or Nicaraguans who worked with them; or Argentina's military intelligence headquarters in Buenos Aires. All suggest that the CIA—nearly five months before the signing of a Presidential Finding authorizing covert support for the Contras—was pretty close to the operation, either participating in the Miami meeting or keeping close enough contact with Nicaraguan exiles or Argentine military intelligence officials to have them provide these details.

INDEPENDENCE DAY CELEBRATIONS: TEGUCIGALPA, HONDURAS, JULY 4, 1981. *La Prensa* published my interview with Amilcar Santa Maria the morning of July 4. It was nearly a full page under the banner "U.S. Support for Elections a Serious and Consistent Policy." Once again Santa Maria covered the points we had made accurately and sympathetically.[4] It was a great way to start our national day.

The big event was an afternoon reception in the residence gardens for government officials, political leaders, senior military, other Honduran friends of the United States and the diplomatic corps—over 200 people. Of the top level, only Foreign Minister Elvir, who was out of the country, didn't make it. We were only mildly surprised to see Zuniga—bold as brass—among the first to come through the door. He and I exchanged *abrazos* for a cameraman. After my short speech extolling the friendship between the United States and Honduras, and Acting Foreign Minister Fortin's graceful response, we had a champagne toast. Guests lingered for another half hour or so and then departed.

POPULAR SANDINISTA LEADER RESIGNS, LEAVES THE COUNTRY: MANAGUA, NICARAGUA, JULY 8, 1981. Eden Pastora, by far the most popular of the Sandinista leaders, resigned his positions as vice minister of defense and chief of the militia, departing Nicaragua for exile in Costa Rica.[5] This was a serious blow to the Sandinista leadership and hurt them politically. Pastora later joined the Contras.

WASHINGTON CONSULTATIONS: WASHINGTON, D.C., JULY 8–11, 1981. The first order of business on Enders's agenda was the human rights issue. He observed that the situation in Honduras appeared to be deteriorating. I agreed completely and referred to my action recommendations, to which State had yet to respond. After some discussion Enders came to the point. He was concerned that information about Honduran abuses would leak, creating obstacles to the realization of our other objectives in that country and in the region. That, he emphasized, would be a major problem. I shared his concerns and noted that that was why all my cables on that subject were in the most restricted distribution channel, NODIS.[6] However, I believed it was essential that State and administration policy makers have this information. Enders agreed, but to reduce the possibility of unauthorized disclosure, he asked that I send all communications on this subject outside official channels, using the so-called back channel.

These are State cables sent in CIA channels. On receipt at Langley or an overseas station, they are printed and hand-delivered to the addressee. There is no formal record of these communications: officially, they don't exist. They can, however, be traced in special circumstances, as was done in the Iran-Contra investigation. Enders's request seemed improper. I nodded but made no specific commitment to honor it. In fact, I had already decided that I would not. There was no doubt that Enders inferred from my lack of response that I would not comply.

That matter behind us, Enders told me that he had just sent a cable to

San Salvador, asking for Deane Hinton's comments on several suggestions for improving Salvadoran/Honduran cooperation. Since I was in Washington, he would like to have my views as well and handed me a copy of the cable, along with an earlier assessment from Hinton.[7] I promised to review both and get back to him before I returned to post.

Enders also said that we would shortly be launching a broad-gauged economic initiative for the Caribbean basin countries, hopefully with the support and collaboration of Mexico, Venezuela and Canada. He stressed that it would not be a program based on traditional development lending or social development programs. Rather, he envisaged a cooperative umbrella encompassing new incentives for private investment and new concessionary tariffs for regional products and manufactures, as well as our traditional development activities. It was also important, he believed, that this program not be viewed as just another scheme "made in the USA" and imposed on Latin America. To that end he was planning a consultative meeting of potential donors and recipients in Nassau in a few weeks. Talks with the Mexicans and Venezuelans were already well advanced, and our embassies would soon be receiving instructions to invite other potential participants. The plan was to be known as the Caribbean Basin Initiative (CBI).

This was an important, indeed visionary, initiative. Such an approach had long been a gleam in the eye of the Inter-America bureau, but never before had we been able to overcome political resistance in the building and at the White House, let alone in Congress. Official resource transfers would never be sufficient to meet the needs of these countries without strong private investment capital flows from international and domestic sources. Encouraging this was vital. I mentioned that we were working with the Honduran private sector to arrange a Council of the Americas mission designed to stimulate investment interest in Honduras. Enders thought this especially positive, as he had been in touch with the council regarding the CBI.

As our meeting seemed to be winding up without mention of my replacement, I broached the issue. Enders apologized, saying that he had thought I was aware of what had been going on. State, he said, had nominated John Negroponte to replace me. But objections had surfaced when Negroponte's name was sent to the White House for approval. Enders expected these would be overcome but had no sense of when the nomination might be announced, let alone confirmed by the Senate.[8]

I again made the pitch that my replacement prior to the elections would send the wrong signal to those wishing to block the transition process, possibly jeopardizing our overriding policy objective. If it sounded like special pleading, so be it. Enders again said he would keep that in mind. I was not reassured.

In reviewing Enders's cable to Hinton on relations between El Salvador and Honduras, I was impressed by its sense of realism. He suggested five principal goals, all of which made sense and, with deft handling and additional resources, were probably attainable:

- Confidence-building measures to bring the two governments and militaries together, beginning the process of creating a trusting and cooperative relationship based on mutual interests
- Relocating the Salvadoran refugee camps away from the immediate frontier area
- Increasing the number of Honduran troops deployed along the border
- Encouraging greater intelligence sharing
- Improving the Honduran capability to interdict illicit arms traffic

My memo response emphasized that each of these goals was realistic and that we were already pursuing them. But we needed to be realistic in our expectations, avoid pushing the Hondurans further than they wished to go (some, of course, were willing to go much further than we were) and come forward with additional resources to assist and encourage them. I thought there were three major factors to keep in mind. First, the Hondurans were deeply distrustful of the Salvadorans as a result of the 1969 soccer war (and as Salvadorans were of them). Those feelings could only be overcome with time and confidence building. Second, Honduran military and political leaders recognized their interest in seeing the insurgents defeated but feared that more direct involvement would damage their international standing, cause domestic political unrest and trigger terrorist and insurgent activity in Honduras. They were dead right. Third, the Honduran budgetary situation, absent additional resources, precluded a significant increase in military operational outlays.[9]

Following my return we received almost no further information about Honduran human rights abuses from the Station, although I did not notice it immediately. There can be no doubt that the station chief was directed not to share such information with me. His superiors had earlier complained about his reporting on human rights, but he had provided information on several serious incidents after that time. Years later, I discovered that it is not uncommon for CIA headquarters to instruct station chiefs not to share information with their ambassadors, a violation of its agreement with State. And Clarridge, according to the Iran-Contra Independent Counsel, frequently issued such instructions.[10] Final proof was provided by a CIA Inspector General's report on Honduran human rights abuses released in October 1998. It stated that much of the "information [regarding human rights abuses] was not reported at all [deleted] or was mentioned only in internal CIA channels and not disseminated to other agencies."[11]

Thus the Station ceased to report human rights violations, intentionally misleading the embassy and our government regarding Honduran abuses. An additional 29 "disappearances" were later documented between mid-July and the time I departed the country at the end of October.[12] Although the flow of inside information ceased, we routinely reported alleged violations that came to our attention through the media or other overt sources. I also continued to raise the issue in other contexts. However, Enders's desire to preclude further human rights reporting was largely met.

SANDINISTAS CLOSE OPPOSITION NEWSPAPER: MANAGUA, NICARAGUA, JULY 10, 1981. Upping its repression of the domestic opposition, the Sandinista government closed *La Prensa,* the leading opposition newspaper, for having criticized government interference in the media.[13] The paper later reopened but continued to face Sandinista harassment, such as restricting its access to newsprint.

SALVADORAN MILITARY ATROCITIES: CHALATENANGO DEPARTMENT, EL SALVADOR, JULY 10–11, 1981. In two separate operations, Salvadoran military units massacred nearly 100 peasants and their families from two rural villages. The victims were suspected of being guerrilla sympathizers.[14]

INVESTIGATION COMPLETED; VICE CONSUL DEPARTS: TEGUCIGALPA, HONDURAS, MID–JULY 1981. RSO Dewitt was quickly in Honduras to conduct the investigation of our errant vice consul. Our new JAS chief, George Clift, was the post security officer and became involved. Walker, Clift and I met with Dewitt to review the case and share the background information we had on the Nicaraguan and on the Argentine role in Honduras. Dewitt had to be fully aware of the context in which these events had occurred.

He began by examining the consular records and interviewing the vice consul. When Dewitt mentioned the impropriety of his having ignored normal operating procedures to issue the visas at the request of someone who had given him items of value, the vice consul adamantly denied any connection between the two. It apparently took some persuasion by Dewitt to convince the vice consul that an appearance of impropriety existed.

Evidence and statements Dewitt gathered left no doubt that the vice consul had improperly issued visas to the Argentine intelligence officers; accepted items of value, at the very least creating the appearance of impropriety; and knowingly violated embassy policy regarding relations with Nicaraguan exiles. Whether this constituted fraud was to me irrelevant. I had lost all faith in the vice consul's judgment and in his ability to administer visa law and regulation. I no longer wanted him in the country. Walker, Clift and Dewitt agreed with my judgment and believed there was enough evidence to justify his immediate transfer back to Washington. Dewitt reported his findings to State, and I sent a cable to the Consular Affairs Bureau and director general of the Foreign Service explaining my decision and requesting authority to order the vice consul's immediate transfer. It was promptly granted.

TEXACO DISPUTE REMAINS DEADLOCKED; HONDURANS RESTIVE: TEGUCIGALPA, HONDURAS, JULY 13, 1981. The dispute with Texaco remained deadlocked, and the government was coming under increasing attack for failing to resolve the conflict. Expropriation was again coming to the fore. We continued to hew the line that it was a sovereign decision but that the United States always insisted on prompt, adequate and effective compensation. I repeated this to President Paz and Foreign Minister Elvir several times and to other officials as well, secure in the knowledge that the government's financial position would not allow timely compensation. I also reiterated that the refinery was covered by a political risk insurance policy issued by the Overseas Private Investment Corporation (OPIC), with attendant implications. If Honduras failed to compensate Texaco properly and OPIC settled the claim, the dispute would become a government-to-government issue.

The CT was concerned that many Honduran officials didn't realize the full implications of expropriation, despite our efforts to educate them.[15] We were convinced that once government leaders recognized the consequences of expropriation, they would discard it as a possible solution. And that meant they would be more apt to get down to serious negotiations with Texaco. Accordingly, we recommended that OPIC send a team to Honduras to brief officials on Texaco's investment risk coverage and how it might become a major obstacle in our bilateral relations. State and OPIC, however, seemed to regard this suggestion as encouraging rather than deterring expropriation, so it came to naught.[16] We redoubled our local efforts.

SOVIET TANKS ARRIVE IN NICARAGUA: TEGUCIGALPA, HONDURAS, JULY 14, 1981. Arcos called to alert me that the *Los Angeles Times* had reported that a Sandinista leader publicly confirmed the arrival of Soviet tanks. This was not unexpected news, but it was sure to cause new problems with the Hondurans. First, General Walters had promised President Paz that we would pass them any intelligence we received about Soviet weapons deliveries, and he had specifically cited tanks and high-performance aircraft as sensitive items. And General Schweitzer had reaffirmed this commitment to Alvarez when he visited Washington. If the *Los Angeles Times* was correct, the Hondurans could only conclude that our commitments meant nothing or that our intelligence collection was lousy.

Second, this development was likely to drive the Honduran military's fear of a Nicaraguan attack to hysterical levels. That could have all sorts of repercussions, from renewal of Paz's backdoor efforts to visit Washington, to even greater dissatisfaction with security assistance levels, or to a preemptive attack on Nicaragua in an effort to force U.S. intervention.

I fired off an urgent cable reminding State of Walters's commitment to Paz and requesting detailed information on this shipment that we could pass to the Hondurans.[17] Two days later, before State had responded to my request, Colonel Alvarez told us he had confirmation the Nicaraguans received 28 Soviet T-55 tanks. Alvarez's source had been shown the tanks by a Sandinista official and had counted 28. I reported this to State, telling them to disregard my earlier request.[18]

ANOTHER NICARAGUAN LEADER SEEKS ASYLUM: MANAGUA, NICARAGUA, JULY 14, 1981. Following the example of Eden Pastora, Fernando Chamorro, leader of the Social Democratic Party, fled Nicaragua and sought asylum in Costa Rica. After arriving in San Jose, he announced the formation of the "Internal Front," an organization dedicated to "the liberty of Nicaragua."[19]

HONDURAN ARMS ACQUISITIONS RUN AMOK: TEGUCIGALPA, HONDURAS, JULY 15, 1981. Colonel Goodwin received a formal request from the General Staff for a lengthy list of additional equipment they wished to acquire under the FMS program, despite the fact those funds were already fully obligated by previous orders. And they had been told repeatedly that there were no additional FY 1981 funds available. The Milgroup's rough estimate of the cost of the new items exceeded $10 million. The new request included anti-tank weapons ($2 million), four used light helicopters with parts and armaments ($1.25 million) and individual equipment items ($1.3 million). None of these items had appeared on previous lists but now were apparently being given a higher priority than $10 million worth of unfunded "urgent needs" that had previously been identified and were to be ordered if additional funds became available.

Goodwin was to meet with the General Staff today and needed guidance. We agreed that he should try to persuade them to realign priorities and bring the total of the material on order down to the actual funding level. I was skeptical he would succeed, but he had to try. Beyond that, I instructed him to deliver the following messages: there was no chance of additional current year funding; the projected over expenditure of current and coming fiscal year accounts had to be resolved because we could not accept orders in excess of actual funding levels; yesterday's request, in its original form, might prejudice their case for additional FY 1982 funds, but we would forward it as submitted, if that is what they wished; and we were very concerned over their failure to observe the priorities that they previously worked out with Milgroup assistance.

This was another example of their lack of discipline in the military procurement process, if it could be dignified with that term. A short time later we learned that they had spent several million dollars to purchase two new communications systems from different suppliers, both of which were incompatible with their existing systems, and an Israeli executive jet.[20] These were hardly priority items. Still later, we learned they had made major antitank weapon and munitions purchases totaling several more millions on the international market. Much of the ammunition turned out to be overage and unusable. It was difficult to avoid the suspicion that kickbacks or other forms of corruption were involved in these transactions.

I reported these developments to State, Defense and Southern Command, reiterating my customary appeal that we avoid anything that would excite the Hondurans' already exaggerated security assistance expectations and requesting guidance to deal with the most recent dustup.[21]

LA TRIBUNA STRONGLY ENDORSES ELECTIONS: TEGUCIGALPA, HONDURAS, JULY 17, 1981. Quoting heavily from my July 4 *La Prensa* interview, *La Tribuna* ran a half-page editorial strongly supporting the transition and democratic elections. Although it is unusual for a newspaper to base an editorial on another paper's exclusive story, the most noteworthy aspect of *La Tribuna*'s piece was its direct references to a possible preemptive coup and to Zuniga's claim that the United States favored his candidacy.[22]

This was a strong and very welcome endorsement of the transition and our policy. Unfortunately, it also suggested growing concern about moves to block the elections.

REPORTED SALVADORAN INCURSION INTO HONDURAS: VALLADOLID AREA, HONDURAS, JULY 18, 1981. According to the Honduran press, Salvadoran forces entered Honduran territory on the outskirts of Valladolid while on an anti-insurgent sweep in Chalatenango Department. Although these reports had little domestic impact, they were picked up by the wire services and were receiving considerable coverage elsewhere. Our review of this incident indicated that it occurred in or very near a disputed area—the Zagalapa "pocket"—that began about one mile south of the Valladolid town center.[23] A slight map-reading error could easily have brought the Salvadorans into Honduran territory, so we felt the report was credible. The media, of course, overlooked that fact in their reports.

We subsequently learned that General Chinchilla and his Salvadoran counterpart had agreed the Hondurans would turn a blind eye to any Salvadoran incursion during this particular operation. Foreign Minister Elvir later shared with me his "deep concern" over coverage of this incident, fearing that they would trigger popular demonstrations against the government domestically and terrorist attacks on facilities abroad. Ambassador Pujol in Washington had already reported threats against Honduran consulates in San Francisco and New York, and Elvir feared an even stronger reaction in Europe. Nothing in Elvir's remarks indicated that he was aware of the "blind eye" agreement reached by the two chiefs of staff. Had they decided not to advise their respective foreign ministers? Was Elvir testing my knowledge? I suspected the former but really didn't know. In any event I suggested that he might wish to lodge a pro forma diplomatic protest with the Salvadoran government. That way he could at least say that he had defended Honduran sovereignty.

Elvir's fears, happily, were not fulfilled. There was no local reaction, nor were there attacks on Honduran embassies or consulates. This incident, however, suggested that Elvir was not always cut in on military decisions and that increased Honduran cooperation with Salvadoran operations could carry a political cost. We would do well to keep both in mind.[24]

EFFORT TO EASE TENSIONS WITH NICARAGUA FUELS CONCERNS: MANAGUA, NICARAGUA, JULY 19, 1981. Foreign Minister Elvir, Chief of Staff Chinchilla and several other senior officers visited Managua, continuing efforts to ease tensions. They were warmly and courteously received, met with the ruling junta and military commanders, and had an extended session with Minister of Defense Humberto Ortega. They also met with the papal nuncio, other diplomats and a few private sector representatives.

Elvir believed the visit had been positive and would help to ease tensions in the near term. Ortega had apologized for mistreatment of the alleged Honduran spies repatriated in June, stressed the need for a continuing dialogue, and suggested the two governments improve communications between military units along the border. Nonetheless, Elvir and his colleagues were bearish about the longer term.

The Sandinistas had not flaunted their military buildup, but neither had they tried to hide it. They claimed that they wished to live in peace with their neighbors and had no aggressive intentions but were increasing their forces to defend themselves against an anticipated U.S. invasion. Their goals were a 50,000-man army and a 200,000-man militia, with tanks and armored vehicles (this compared with combined Honduran forces of about 17,000 men— see appendix 2). Naturally, the Hondurans viewed this with trepidation.

Of even greater concern was the Sandinistas' sympathy for insurgent movements in El Salvador and Guatemala, about which they were quite open. Ortega had acknowledged that some Sandinistas were providing "unofficial" material support for these movements but said they were receiving no "official" support. The government, he asserted, lacked the capacity to prevent this "unofficial" traffic. Elvir was contemptuous of this official/unofficial distinction and disbelieved Ortega's claim. He and his companions were convinced that the Sandinistas would have no compunction about supporting extremists in Honduras.

Elvir believed the Nicaraguan economy was a shambles and would collapse if it weren't for foreign aid. The principal donors cited by Ortega were

Mexico, Venezuela, France, East Germany, West Germany, Iraq, Algeria and Canada. Elvir thought it interesting that Ortega had not mentioned Libya.

Acknowledging that their visit had been brief, Elvir said they had seen no signs of a meaningful opposition and suspected the revolution was indeed irreversible. Concluding the briefing, Elvir asked me two questions: how did we see the situation in Nicaragua and how did we plan to respond to the growing Nicaraguan military threat? I had no basis to respond and told him so. What I couldn't tell him was that the Reagan administration had no answers to his questions and had no coherent policy addressing them.

I did offer some personal observations based on my recent discussions in Washington and from what I could glean from cable traffic. From what I could see, we did not believe the game was over. There were still a number of countervailing institutions in Nicaragua—the Church, the private sector, organized labor, some agriculture groups and the opposition newspaper, *La Prensa*—that had not given up. West Germany and Venezuela, for example, were trying to help these pluralistic forces, and I was under the impression that we were still exploring ways in which we could aid them.

On the military side I reiterated that the Rio Treaty remained in force and that I did not believe the Sandinistas would be foolish enough to risk overt offensive moves. To deal with subversion, we were helping Honduras and the other Central American countries improve their capabilities, as well as strengthen their defense establishments.

Elvir stated flatly that these efforts were insufficient to meet the threat. Honduras, he said, had to increase its army, improve its logistic capability and build its strategic-arms stockpile. When I noted that a Honduran effort to match the Sandinistas man for man, weapon for weapon would be self-defeating, he agreed that Honduras could not bear the burden alone, implying that we should make up the shortfall. He then questioned whether Honduras's civilian political leaders recognized the threat and would be able to strengthen the armed forces. Sometimes, he confessed, the decision to return to democratic rule seemed a mistake.

That was a shocker. Elvir had always been forthright in his support for the transition. He may have been signaling a shift in the Superior Council's position on elections. More likely he was merely voicing doubts that were increasing among the military and others. In response I suggested that stopping the electoral process would be an even greater mistake. Elvir agreed. Continuing, I said it seemed obvious that Honduran law had to be changed to provide for legal punishment of kidnappers, hijackers, arms traffickers and their ilk. What, I asked, was the status of the proposed national security law?

He said it was stalled in the assembly, which did not wish to deal with the issue before the elections. On the other hand, he was no longer sure that this legislation was a good idea: enactment of such a law in El Salvador had actually precipitated violence, and he anticipated a strong reaction from the

Honduran left if it were passed. I opined that the two countries were hardly analogous and observed that it might well be greater folly not to address this matter.[25]

This was one of our most extended and candid discussions, and I had never seen Elvir so downbeat. Because he was the most reflective and restrained of the senior officers, I could only assume that his colleagues were highly exercised. There was much to digest: heightened fears of Nicaragua, doubts about the civilian political leadership, a growing feeling that the transition had been a mistake and the retreat from attempting to deal with recognized shortcomings in the legal system. In reporting this discussion to Washington, I noted that many of the concerns Elvir had expressed were widely shared. The behavior of the two principal political parties was not reassuring. Of almost equal concern was the national security law. This issue seemed to be too important to the military and security forces to be allowed to languish, yet it was. Alvarez and, presumably, others were probably happy to continue "disappearing" suspected subversives, a practice faster and more certain than any legal system. That, however, was an atypical Honduran attitude.

I made two action recommendations. To attempt to allay Honduran concerns about Nicaragua and try to undo some of the damage resulting from our failure to meet our repeated commitments to keep them informed (e.g., the Soviet tank delivery), I urged that I be given our comprehensive assessment of the situation in Nicaragua, which I could share with senior leaders. Several months earlier, I had been given such information and instructed to brief Paz and others. That had been appreciated. The Hondurans might, I thought, find an updated assessment somewhat reassuring.

Second, I recommended that I be authorized to urge President Paz, other senior military officers and civilian political leaders to move promptly to address the vexing legal aspects of the subversion/terrorism challenge.[26] There was no substantive response to either recommendation.

PUSHING THE CARIBBEAN BASIN INITIATIVE: TEGUCIGALPA, HONDURAS, JULY 19, 1991. We received instructions to explain the Caribbean Basin Initiative to President Paz and key government leaders and to invite Honduran participation at the initial meeting in Nassau.[27] By the time I confirmed my appointments, Elvir had received invitations from Mexico and Venezuela. This paved the way for our representations and underscored that it was a multilateral effort.

The Honduran response was positive, if unenthusiastic. The first question from both Elvir and Finance Minister Mendoza was "what are the proposed resource transfer levels?" Once we explained the concept behind this plan, they became skeptical. Elvir, however, warmed when the consultative process was explained, seeing the possibility of the Central American states developing a common position prior to Nassau. The scheduled regional foreign ministers conference, he thought, would afford an opportunity to do this, although admittedly it would be difficult to find a formula acceptable to Nicaragua.

Finance Minister Mendoza, who was briefed by AID director Oleson, diverged from Elvir. Although essentially supportive, Mendoza argued that the proposed consultative process would take too much time. "Honduras needs greater assistance in the immediate future," he said, citing balance of payments and direct budget support as pressing needs. He was also skeptical that Mexico would provide much beyond the oil facility. And finally, Mendoza opposed anything that might limit the bilateral relationship. Accordingly, he said that Honduras would not support Central American nations negotiating en bloc.[28] This internal division became irrelevant when the Central American governments could not agree on a common approach.

The press caught me leaving the Foreign Ministry. Because the CBI had already been announced, I explained the purpose of my visit, outlining very briefly the scope and intent of the program. The first question was whether this new plan included military assistance. I said that it did not. That statement, not surprisingly, is what made the headline.[29]

SUAZO CORDOVA'S WASHINGTON VISIT: WASHINGTON, D.C., JULY 20–23, 1981. Suazo Cordova met with State and AID officials, called on congressional leaders and had a brief meeting with Vice President Bush. It was a great program, thanks to the work of the Honduran desk. Substantively, his American interlocutors emphasized all the right points: support for elections, the need to reform the legal system, our commitment to continued economic and security assistance.[30]

Feedback was positive. Most of those who met with Suazo Cordova had been impressed by his apparent seriousness and moderation. That was pleasant news.

SOUTHERN COMMAND FRONTIER SURVEY GROUP ARRIVES: TEGUCIGALPA, HONDURAS, LATE JULY 1981. Southern Command's second (and much larger) arms interdiction survey team arrived to assess the cross-border clandestine traffic problem and review ways to improve Honduran communications and primary intelligence collection. I was determined to keep this group on a very short rein and directly accountable to Colonel Goodwin. On their arrival I arranged to meet with all of the officers—there were eight to ten of them, as I recall—and the Milgroup staff to review and approve their plans and to ensure they understood our ground rules.

The frontier survey unit would be divided into three or four subgroups that would visit the Honduran detachments on the border. Their mission was to improve Honduran effectiveness and identify civic action projects that

Southern Command might undertake in collaboration with the local units.[31] Their operations would be coordinated by a small team working out of the Milgroup offices. The communications/intelligence team, under direct Milgroup supervision, would visit various field and base units throughout the country, working to improve existing communications facilities and networks. It was agreed that the CT would review the recommendations of both teams before they were presented to the Honduran General Staff. I was, in sum, satisfied with our oversight and coordination mechanisms.

My principal worry was political—how the presence of uniformed personnel, particularly on the frontier, would be perceived by the public, the media and our adversaries. Most of the participants were Special Forces troops, Green Berets. Their presence could not be hidden, but I wanted them to keep as low a profile as possible. And much to their dissatisfaction, I also directed that they not carry fire arms.[32] I did not believe the situation in Honduras, even along the frontier, warranted their being armed. They were assigned to Honduran units, and the Hondurans were responsible for protecting them. Given that our military advisers in El Salvador were prohibited from carrying arms, there was certainly no reason for those in Honduras to be armed. I made it clear, however, that I would be willing to review this policy at any time if the situation changed. But until that time, anyone violating that ban would be subject to immediate return to Panama. In addition, these teams were instructed to avoid the press, the border areas when military operations were underway on either side and the refugee camps.[33]

They grumbled but had no option but to accept.

FURTHER REACTIONS TO TENSIONS-EASING EFFORTS: TEGUCIGALPA, HONDURAS, JULY 23, 1981. The anxiety voiced by Foreign Minister Elvir about Sandinista intentions did not take long to spread. The alarm evidenced by those who visited Managua reached the working level with exaggerated force and new, specious, embellishments. For example, it was widely believed that Sandinista officials had "confirmed" they would receive high-performance aircraft. That and other allegations stoked Honduran paranoia. As a result, Goodwin's second arms procurement meeting with the General Staff degenerated into an extended critique of U.S. security assistance policies and practices and our perfidy. Goodwin and his officers believed that our relations with the Honduran military had reached a new low. They may have been correct.

We decided to advise Washington and Southern Command of this latest downward twist and suggest possible actions, short of a massive increase in security assistance funding, that might help restore a measure of equilibrium. I cautioned against granting the additional military sales credit or other sharp increases in assistance, but acknowledged that a modest, carefully targeted increase might make sense. But the most effective thing we could do to allay Honduran concerns was to remove their other sources of complaint (e.g., speed up deliveries of materiel on order, provide lower interest rates on FMS credits, resolve long-pending legal disputes) on which we had been seeking action for months.

Colonel Goodwin was not happy with these recommendations. He believed that we had to up our FMS by an additional $10 million to save the relationship. I certainly sympathized with him, but didn't share his view. The Honduran fears were exaggerated, and we should not reward them by granting additional credit that would only worsen the government's budgetary crunch and fuel the military's appetite for even more. But I did ask that he append an extended comment to this cable, making the best case he could for a marked increase in FY 1981 funding. He did so.[34]

I continued to believe it essential to bring such diverging views out into the open so that Washington could have the benefit of the full range of opinions in arriving at a decision. This practice also reinforced cohesion and reduced the likelihood of dissenting "unofficial" communications among various agencies and their headquarters. Perhaps as a result of this cable, we soon made progress on the delivery and other issues. Although there was no significant change in FY 1981 funding, Goodwin's plea for more prevailed in the longer term.

COUNCIL OF THE AMERICAS VISIT: TEGUCIGALPA, HONDURAS, JULY 24–28, 1981. The Council of the Americas mission turned out to be quite a success, at least from the private sector's standpoint. And it was helpful for us in that mission members stressed the importance of the transition process in their meetings with their hosts, emphasizing how important it was for elections to be held on schedule. Paul Vinelli and COHEP president Fernando Lardizabal believed that seeds for future investment had been planted and were very pleased with the result.

ASSESSING NICARAGUAN REFUGEE SITE: PUERTO LEMPIRA, HONDURAS, JULY 28, 1981. Miskito Indian refugees continued to move into Honduras. According to government data, their numbers had reached 3,000, and the conditions under which they were living were, by all accounts, abysmal. We needed a firsthand look at the situation. Accordingly, I set out with Colonel Bollert in the attache aircraft, accompanied by the AID disaster relief officer and the refugee affairs officer.[35]

Puerto Lempira proved to be the most isolated, impoverished place I had seen in Honduras. Located on an estuary in a wide, low-lying savannah, the land appeared suitable for little other than cattle grazing. However, there was no practical or economic way to get cattle to market; the only links with the rest of the country were by air or sea, and the shallow harbor limited sea lift to small boats. And during the rainy season, due shortly, the whole area became waterlogged, if not actually underwater.

The air base was located several miles outside the town. It was macadam, but the three or four buildings sited around the field were ramshackle indeed. We found the air base commander, a slovenly, middle-aged captain, in his small, sparsely furnished (a desk and two chairs) office. A faded photo of the Honduran flag, a fly-specked map and a commercial calendar adorned the walls. The ensuing discussion was not particularly illuminating. He confirmed what we already knew then said he didn't have a vehicle that could take us to town. He offered to find someone who would drive us around, however, and shortly a vehicle was on its way to pick us up. Colonel Bollert and his copilot elected to stay with their aircraft. The central part of Puerto Lempira consisted of no more than 30 buildings, all of which were in need of paint or more substantial repairs, and a lot of palm trees. The streets were packed earth. We stopped in what appeared to be town center, and the town clerk appeared. He turned out to be far more communicative than the base commander.

The refugees were scattered between Puerto Lempira and the Nicaraguan border, with 600 to 700 in or near the town; the clerk later took us to visit two of the "camps." There were no regular refugee relief workers in the area nor any medical professionals. Every week or so CEDEN flew in supplies and sometimes brought a nurse or doctor to treat the sick. The town clerk controlled the food stocks and managed distribution with the help of several refugees. He was very concerned about sanitary conditions in the camp areas and expected serious health problems once the rains came. We soon saw first-hand the grounds for his concern.

The refugee sites were pitiful. These people were essentially living in the open. They had no tents, no sanitary facilities, no regular water supplies. Each site had a few plastic tarps, strung between trees and poles, that provided a modicum of shelter. Most of the inhabitants seemed to sleep in string hammocks strung between trees. They cooked over open fires and sat on the ground. We spoke with several of the refugees who uniformly despised and feared the Sandinistas, preferring to live in these dire conditions than to return to Nicaragua. They too were concerned about their health and sanitary conditions and also about adequate food. The men all wanted to work, but there were no jobs available. It was a sad situation.

During our return to Tegucigalpa we discussed ways we could help. There were a number. First, AID would make additional food commodities available and try to persuade the relief agencies to devote greater attention to the area. It would also see if we could acquire tents and other basic supplies from disaster relief stores in Panama. Second, we would make representations to the UNHCR's office about doing more for these people, stressing the need for medical services, and ask State to make a parallel approach to the high commissioner's office in Geneva. Finally, I would raise the issue with the foreign minister and suggest that the military provide air lift and other services.

These efforts produced some results, although the Miskito refugees never received the level of assistance provided those from El Salvador.

A SHOE DROPS: OFFICIAL NOTICE OF MY REPLACEMENT: TEGUCI-GALPA, HONDURAS, JULY 29, 1981. I received a personally addressed cable from the director general of the Foreign Service, instructing me to request *agreement* for my replacement, John D. Negroponte. Aside from the communicators who deciphered and printed this message and Amy, who brought it to me, I shared its contents only with Walker and Martha. It would serve no purpose to have this information on the streets before the White House made the official announcement. As for the CT, I wanted to tell them before the public announcement. As yet, however, I felt it would be premature, even though everyone had heard reports that I would soon be replaced.

I met with Elvir the following day, delivering the formal request.[36] I told him that there was normally a lapse of a week or two between granting *agreement* and public announcement of the nomination; confirmation could take several months more, depending on the press of other Senate business, recess periods and so forth. I had no basis to speculate on how long Negroponte's confirmation might take or when I would actually depart Honduras. I also undertook to obtain advance notice of the White House announcement, so the Honduran government would not be taken by surprise.

Elvir expressed his personal regret that I was being replaced. His comments seemed sincere but were most certainly not shared by Paz or most other senior military. A couple of weeks later Elvir called me to the Foreign Ministry to give me the letter granting Negroponte's *agreement*. I immediately cabled the text to the director general. Walker and I speculated that within the week the news would be out and Zuniga would be gloating publicly. We were pleasantly surprised. There were no local leaks.

REFUGEE RELIEF WORKER ADMITS SUPPLY DIVERSIONS, IS DEPORTED: TEGUCIGALPA, HONDURAS, JULY 30, 1981. The Honduran police reported the arrest of a CARE refugee relief worker for suspicion of diverting food supplies to the Salvadoran insurgents. This individual, falsely documented as a Honduran, was believed to be a Salvadoran national. During interrogation he admitted to having turned over refugee food supplies to Salvadoran insurgents and also to having acted as a channel for the transfer of two weapons to the rebels. He was deported to Costa Rica.[37]

This was further confirmation that refugee supplies were reaching the insurgents. Further investigation, however, revealed that CARE was not involved. It had never employed this individual; rather, the UNHCR's local office identified him as having been employed by CARITAS. The warehouse he managed, however, had once been used to store CARE food stocks, which apparently accounted for FUSEP's confusion.[38] We advised FUSEP, hoping in that way to preclude further dissemination of false information about CARE.

Neither the arrest nor expulsion of the individual involved were made public.

CONCERNS ABOUT REGIONAL POLICIES AND OBJECTIVES: TEGUCI-GALPA, HONDURAS, JULY 31, 1981. I had become increasingly troubled by the apparent drift in our regional policy, and the lack of an overarching ratio-nale. Enders had been confirmed nearly two months earlier and had actually been running the bureau for a couple of months before that. Yet from where I sat, little had changed, the CBI apart. Although a positive development, the CBI did not address what I believed to be the central problems and the conflicts emerging from our several discrete bilateral policies. We had no defined hierarchy of interests or policy priorities. At the time, I had no real appreciation for the Reagan administration's internal conflicts and disorga-nization, but I could recognize policy stasis. And since I was on my way out, there was no risk involved in inquiring about the emperor's nudity.

Ambassadors Hinton and Pezzullo had recently sent comprehensive sets of policy and action recommendations for their respective countries to State in the NODIS channel.[39] Pezzullo's were his final attempt to influence the administration's direction; less than three weeks later he left Managua. Many of their proposals, if adopted, would directly involve or affect Honduras. I had a legitimate interest in commenting on those matters. But beyond that, I felt impelled to broach the larger issue of the conflicts inherent in our pur-suit of uncoordinated bilateral policies. After discussing this situation with Walker, the only one with whom I had shared my two colleagues' cables and my concerns, I drafted a message that sought to address these issues con-structively.[40] The complete text is found in appendix 3.

I summarized our principal objectives in the three "core" countries as follows:

• Honduras: Continued social and political stability through successful conclusion of the transition to democratic government, and Honduran sup-port for our objectives in El Salvador and Nicaragua.
• El Salvador: Preventing the collapse of the junta and the possible installation of a radical regime by assisting in the defeat of the insurgency and in needed socioeconomic reforms.
• Nicaragua: Preventing consolidation of a hostile Marxist government by supporting pluralistic forces and deterring the Sandinistas' support for rev-olution in neighboring countries.

On their face they were largely complementary and without inherent contradiction. The rub came when we began to frame subgoals and specific courses of action to achieve them.

El Salvador provided the simplest example. It was in our interest to close off supply routes through Honduras and limit the flow of refugee supplies to the insurgents. Actions to realize those goals, if pushed too far, could have unintended consequences that prejudiced our principal objective in Honduras. For example, our actions could provoke counterstrokes by the Salvadoran insurgents—more terrorist attacks in Honduras, the launching of an insurgency there—that might cause the military to foreclose the elections. All things considered, this risk was probably worth taking, but we had to recognize it and be sensitive to Honduran concerns. Most important, we had to be alert to possible consequences.

Similar potential conflicts arose from other proposed actions as well. Increased cooperation between the two armies in the frontier area, pushed hard by Hinton, was especially risky. My colleague was eager to see joint Salvadoran/Honduran operations that would draw Honduras directly into the conflict. Strategically, I felt Hinton exaggerated the importance of controlling the border area in the overall conflict. The outcome of the Salvadoran civil war did not hinge on the insurgents' use of safe havens along the border but on their ability to operate clandestinely in most parts of the country, to maintain regular supply routes and to increase or sustain their popular support. If the Hondurans became directly involved in combating the rebels, the insurgency was almost certain to spread into Honduras, possibly ending the transition or, if after the elections, bringing a military coup.

Ambassador Pezzullo was urging that we continue trying to deal with the Sandinistas and encourage the internal opposition. Escalating hostility and support for covert military operations against them, he argued, would be counterproductive. I agreed. But we also had to find effective ways to curb the Sandinistas' revolutionary evangelism and their material support for insurgents and subversives in neighboring countries. To that end Pezzullo continued to urge that we encourage the Hondurans to "build bridges" with the Sandinistas. The latest attempt to defuse tensions, however, had only left the Hondurans more frightened than before. From my vantage point, we had to ensure the Sandinistas focused on the regional consequences of their exaggerated arms buildup and then did something about it. Building bridges was not enough. Enders's ill-fated effort to persuade them to abandon their export of revolution was a positive step.

Conversely, we couldn't expect the Sandinistas to ignore the activities of the Contra forces operating out of Honduras. Although these groups were no threat to the regime, they were a nuisance and were costing lives. They also fueled Sandinista paranoia about a U.S. invasion. I was, of course, unaware of the full extent of Honduran support for the Contras' cause but knew that some elements in the administration were enamored with the notion of a covert war against Nicaragua. I believed that a major Contra effort backed by the United States would threaten the stability of Honduras.

Were the Sandinistas likely to sit idly by if the United States used Honduras to mount a covert war against them? Not a chance. They would increase their support for Honduran dissidents and make every effort to foment an insurgency there. What would that mean for the maintenance of stability and a democratic government? The answers seemed a no-brainer.

My cable did not pretend to be an exhaustive listing of potential conflicts in our bilateral policies, nor did I offer solutions to the many dilemmas they posed. I stressed the need to get our priorities sorted out and our ducks lined up. To that end I recommended the convening of a meeting of the Central American ambassadors with the Washington policy-making establishment to hash out these issues.

There was never a satisfactory response to these suggestions. Within a few weeks Pezzullo was gone; within three months I would be replaced; and within two years Enders would be out. Our policy in the region would not begin to make sense for nearly a decade.

HALCON VISTA EXERCISE: DISAGREEMENTS CONTINUE: TEGUCIGALPA, HONDURAS, LATE JULY 1981. The scope and nature of the joint U.S./Honduran military exercise *Halcon Vista* provoked a running debate. We had lost the argument over whether it would actually involve deployed Honduran and U.S. military units. It would. The possible participation of U.S. Marine Corps units remained a contentious issue. I opposed their presence, even if only on board the U.S. Navy ships involved. Instead, I suggested that they be off-loaded at the Guantanamo, Cuba, naval base for the duration of the exercise. Our embassies in Nicaragua, Costa Rica, El Salvador and Guatemala shared my position and so advised State.[41]

Southern Command and the U.S. Atlantic Fleet commander, Admiral Harry Train, insisted that the amphibious ship, which had a logistics support role, carry its full complement of Marines during the exercise. Moreover, Southern Command wanted the Marines to participate in the actual exercise, landing them on Honduran beaches as part of the "aggressor force" that would be opposed by joint Honduran and U.S. forces. Ultimately, a State compromise allowed the Marines to remain aboard their ship but not to participate in the actual exercise.

To reduce the political fallout, State and the embassy also supported the idea of inviting Nicaragua to send observers to the exercise. President Paz was concerned about the possible political consequences and so supported tendering the invitation. We were all fairly confident the Sandinistas would not accept. Southern Command agreed, and the invitation was issued. The Sandinistas declined to come, preferring to exploit the issue for political ends.

Despite this compromise, tensions between the embassy and our military colleagues in Panama were running pretty high, and Colonel Goodwin was feeling pressure from both sides.

WASHINGTON REVISITS ARMS INTERDICTION PLANS: WASHINGTON, D.C., JULY 31, 1981. State and Defense were continuing to worry the arms interdiction bone. A special interagency committee chaired by retired General Gordon Sumner, at the time an assistant to Enders, had finally been established to review the problem. This group was supposedly addressing the issues of improved intelligence, regional cooperation and security assistance support, but its output looked more like second-guessing our recommendations.

It also seemed fixated on a harebrained scheme to establish a *cordon sanitaire* in the air and on the ground along the border between El Salvador and Honduras. Recognizing the importance of moving refugees back from the frontier, the Sumner group theorized that, once the refugees were moved, "...numerically augmented Honduran and Salvadoran forces, both ground and air, could establish a coordinated program of continued presence and interdiction that should make it difficult for the enemy to move unimpeded and undetected." Alarmingly, they advocated a "free fire zone" in the area.

Committee members had either skipped or forgotten the parts of our reports dealing with the substantial numbers of Hondurans living and farming along the border; the area's topography; the limited Honduran troop lift, logistic and financial capabilities; and commercial and humanitarian ground and air traffic.

On receipt of a State cable outlining these ideas and calling for comments,[42] I asked Walker to convene the political-military committee to prepare our response.

REGIONAL MEETING PROPOSAL AND UNWANTED PUBLICITY: TEGUCIGALPA, HONDURAS, AUGUST 9, 1981. As we were responding to General Sumner's cable, we received a Southern Command proposal for a meeting of the ministers of defense and the intelligence chiefs of Honduras, El Salvador and Guatemala, to be hosted by General Nutting in Panama. Its stated purpose was to facilitate increased cooperation on arms interdiction and improve intelligence sharing. The embassies were not invited.[43]

Nutting's proposal was vexing. Being familiar with that command's modus operandi, I saw the proposal as a transparent effort to map out action plans with the military establishments of these three countries without input from the respective embassies. I was not prepared to let that happen. Just as Walker and I were discussing this matter, I received a call from State's Operations Center advising that the *New York Times* had published a long article about the presence of U.S. Special Forces troops in Honduras along the frontier with El Salvador.[44] The article appeared to be based largely on indiscreet statements of a Southern Command officer working in La Virtud, a Capt. Michael Sheehan. Its principal thrust was that U.S. troops were there to "support a military effort against the insurgents," help the Honduran army patrol the border, and control the Salvadoran refugees. From the sound of it, this was precisely the kind of coverage I had hoped to avoid.

I asked the Ops Center to cable the full text and then alerted Colonel Goodwin. I asked that he be in my office first thing the following morning with the head of the Southern Command survey team. Walker alerted Arcos of the story so that he would not be blindsided by media calls. He was to withhold comment but to take specific questions to which we might respond.

DEALING WITH U.S. MILITARY INDISCRETIONS AND INITIATIVES: TEGUCIGALPA, HONDURAS, AUGUST 10, 1981. The *New York Times* article was even more damaging than the Ops Center had described. What jumped out at me was the allegation that Sheehan and his enlisted men were carrying M-16 rifles, a clear violation of our ground rules. Moreover, the comments attributed to Sheehan included such gems as these: "the National Security Council has approved the use of Special Forces units in Honduras to support the military effort against the Salvadoran guerrillas...[and] a Special Forces unit will soon be based in La Virtud"; "this dump (La Virtud) is the center of the world"; the refugees were providing food to the insurgents; and "they [the refugees] have no human rights...[they] have a right to food and a roof" and medicine. It could hardly have been worse, and I was fulminating. I was certain this story would continue to plague the mission and U.S. policy for months.

Both Goodwin and the team commander were aghast when they read the article and rightfully so. They immediately questioned reporter Raymond Bonner's veracity. They could not believe Sheehan and his team had violated our weapons policy or that Sheehan made the statements attributed to him. I knew Bonner and, although the thrust of much of his reporting seemed to me sympathetic to the insurgent cause, I doubted that he would have fabricated this story. Regardless of the truth—which none of us knew—Bonner's article had destroyed Sheehan's ability to carry out his mission, making him a liability. Beyond that, I wanted to know what had actually occurred. If Sheehan and his team violated our weapons policy, they would be out of the country *pronto*.

I directed Goodwin to have Sheehan in my office the following morning. I didn't care how he traveled, I just wanted him in my office the next day. Once I had a chance to hear his side of the story, I would decide how to proceed.

That matter disposed of, I turned to Southern Command's proposed defense ministers meeting. In my cable I argued against it on several grounds while endorsing our encouragement of increased intelligence exchange and cooperation within the region. From my particular standpoint, I feared this initiative would reinforce Honduran belief that Southern Command was more sympathetic to their concerns and more effective in securing additional security assistance for them, further undermining the mission. But most important, it would set in train plans about which we would know nothing. Alternatively, I urged General Nutting to take his show on the road, visiting the three countries and making bilateral presentations. This, I thought, would produce better data (e.g., the Hondurans would not be inhibited by having the Salvadorans at the table), and the Command could also draw on the knowledge and experience of mission agencies—State, CIA, Defense attache and Milgroup—in each country, as well as the host country military. State and Defense representatives from Washington might also attend.[45]

It was essential to prevent Southern Command from imposing its preferred outcome without embassy input or knowledge, because the embassies would ultimately be responsible for implementing any plan. It was far better to have a role at the outset than trying later to overturn or alter plans Southern Command had worked out unilaterally. Gratifyingly, Ambassadors Pezzullo and Fred Chapin, only recently arrived in Guatemala, agreed. This meeting did not occur during my tenure.

REGIONAL ARMS INTERDICTION PROPOSALS: TEGUCIGALPA, HONDURAS, AUGUST 10, 1981. Walker and the Political-Military group had done an excellent job in preparing responses to the Sumner group's questions. Their cable parsed the interdiction problem geographically and by mode of transportation. The geographic areas were the Pacific Ocean sector, the Gulf of Fonseca, and overland from either Honduras or Guatemala. The means of transport were air, sea and land. Embassies were asked to address a number of possible options in each of these problem subsets. We were asked to focus on surface and air infiltration routes. By that time it was clear that air routes had become the most significant. They also sought our opinions on general means to help with the task (e.g., increasing security assistance and establishing "free fire" zones along the border).

We underscored that the Hondurans saw the principal threat as coming from Nicaragua, not El Salvador. Although they would cooperate in trying to stem the illicit flow of arms to the insurgents, their main focus and allocation of resources would probably be toward the Nicaraguan flank, not the Salvadoran. Beyond that, their capabilities were extremely limited. Honduras had no blue water maritime capability and could not contribute to closing the Pacific sea routes. Their shallow water capability in the Gulf of Fonseca was very limited, all three of their 65-foot patrol boats at the time being inoperative, nor did they have any useful radar capacity. Although it would be possible, through provision of additional patrol craft, radars and training, to enhance their contribution in the Gulf, this would entail considerable lead time and increased operational costs. The Honduran government had no prospect of being able to fund such outlays.

If we were serious about closing off the Pacific route, the quickest and most effective way would be to have the U.S. Navy deploy a ship off El Salvador to monitor sea and air traffic, communicating suspicious movements to the Salvadorans. They would then be responsible for intercepting the suspected traffickers. We could also help the Salvadorans improve their intercept capability.

Honduras had a theoretical air intercept capability, but it lacked radar or other means to identify air traffic and its aircraft. And under international law, it had no right to shoot down suspicious aircraft even in its own airspace, although it might try to force rogue aircraft to land. Moreover, increased Honduran Air Force operations too would run into budgetary constraints. Finally, we threw cold water on the aerial free-fire zone notion by pointing out that the El Salvador/Honduras frontier area lay under regular international flight corridors and that refugee relief organizations frequently flew light aircraft in this area on medical evacuation or critical resupply missions. It was a nonstarter.

Overland traffic was another matter. Here Honduras could make an important contribution without busting its budget. This discussion allowed us to reiterate our view that resources and manpower should be concentrated on stopping arms traffic as it entered Honduras, not as it moved out of Honduras into the hands of the guerrillas, that is, the wholesale/retail rationale. It also gave us a chance to complain about the CIA's glacial pace in moving on its part of the interdiction program.[46] The agency's principal interest, of course, was in the Contra operation; the arms interdiction program was largely cover. That was probably the reason the CIA was not represented on the Sumner panel.

We also tried to spike the ground *cordon sanitaire* scheme. It was even more mindless than the aerial free-fire zone. We pointed out that even if the 20,000-plus Salvadoran refugees were moved away from the frontier, an estimated 80,000 Hondurans would still live there. There was no way they could be moved away from their homes and farms, and a free-fire zone wouldn't work with them there.

In sum, we concluded that there was not much the Hondurans could do to interdict the illicit arms flow beyond what we had already proposed. If the United States thought it essential to disrupt maritime and air routes, then our military resources, coupled with improved Salvadoran capabilities, were the most promising options.[47] It was not a message Washington wished to hear, but I was pleased with our group's work.

HALCON VISTA: INITIAL PLANNING: TEGUCIGALPA, HONDURAS, AUGUST 10–14, 1981. The Southern Command planning group met with the Honduran General Staff to plan the joint exercise. Colonel Goodwin and Milgroup members participated to ensure they conformed with the agreed parameters. The exercise scenario posited a situation in which insurgents in neighboring countries were using Honduran waters and frontier areas to resupply their forces. The Honduran government had requested U.S. assistance. The first actions would be the deployment of U.S. staff and logistics support followed by the formation of joint task forces at the Honduran Air Force base in San Pedro Sula and at the Naval base in Puerto Cortez. Once these were set up, the operational portion of the exercise would begin.

On the first day, U.S. Navy small craft would act as an "aggressor force" seeking to land supplies and men surreptitiously on the north coast. The Honduran Navy and Air Force would attempt to intercept this force and prevent it from landing. A second day would involve landing Honduran "aggressor" troops on the shore from Honduran small craft. The Honduran Army, supported by Honduran Air Force helicopters, would then try to locate and neutralize the landing force.

About 140 U.S. military personnel would be involved, excluding the ship crew and embarked Marines, who would play no role in the exercise. Fewer than 1,000 Hondurans were expected to be involved.[48]

SALVADORAN INSURGENTS CAPTURE FRONTIER GARRISON: PERQUIN, EL SALVADOR, AUGUST 10–15, 1981. Insurgent forces encircled and besieged the garrison town of Perquin, located near the Sabenetas disputed area. After several days of hard fighting, the guerrillas seized the town, capturing a number of government defenders. Although little more than a village, capture of this strategically located garrison was an important rebel victory.

The rebels later offered to release 34 Salvadoran National Guardsmen and civil patrolmen captured in this operation to the Red Cross. A government counterattack, however, prevented the prisoner transfer.[49]

MEETING WITH SHEEHAN AND COPING WITH THE FALLOUT: TEGUCIGALPA, HONDURAS, AUGUST 11–13, 1981. Walker and I met with the Milgroup's Army Section commander and Captain Sheehan midmorning. He was shaken by the *New York Times* article and concerned about how it would affect his career. He vigorously denied that he or any members of his team had carried M-16s, as alleged. He claimed they had avoided the press but ran into Bonner accidentally when they went to dinner at the French physicians' residence. I could understand why anyone in La Virtud would jump at a chance to dine with the French. The team had also avoided the refugee camps, as instructed, and delayed its visit to La Virtud for several days because of an earlier Salvadoran army operation in that area. Sheehan pointed out that I had specifically approved their visit to La Virtud to assist in setting up a community relations program.

Similarly, Sheehan denied the provocative statements attributed to him. He claimed to have hardly exchanged any words with Bonner. He theorized that Bonner's quotations were either second hand misinterpretations of things he may have said to French and Honduran medical personnel and refugee relief workers or were fabricated out of whole cloth.

I was inclined to accept that Sheehan and his team had not intentionally violated our standing instructions regarding carrying arms. I was somewhat skeptical of his denials of the statements attributed to him but had myself been the victim of misquotation on more than one occasion. Clearly, Sheehan had been naive and indiscreet, a not infrequent occurrence with our military when they enter a new and foreign environment. Just as clearly, I could no longer allow him to work on the frontier. As his team's work in that area was complete, I allowed him to remain on the job with the understanding that under no circumstances would he return to the frontier.

I reported the results of this interview and my decision to State, with an information copy to Southern Command.[50] Walker, however, was skeptical of Sheehan's protestations of innocence generally and his denials of the comments specifically. Walker knew Bonner fairly well and thought it extremely unlikely that he had fabricated the story. His skepticism turned out to be well placed. The following week, in the face of continuing fallout and questions we couldn't answer, Walker persuaded me to send an embassy officer to La Virtud to try to ascertain what had actually occurred. I should have done that sooner.

State's press guidance concerning the incident covered Honduran security assistance levels, a short description of our military assistance activities in Honduras (denying assignment of Special Forces units, but acknowledging the presence of individual members of that organization because of their specific professional capabilities), denials of statements attributed to Sheehan and the allegation that team members had been armed, and an explanation for the team's presence on the frontier. Most important was an explicit denial that the NSC had approved the use of Special Forces units in Honduras.[51]

Although the local press had ignored the Bonner story, the article had been read on a morning news program. Arcos had also received a number of calls from media in Mexico City. To respond, and to be ready for local inquiries, we consulted with the ministry of defense to work out a coordinated statement based on the State guidance.

We had not heard the last of this incident.

ENDERS MEETS WITH SANDINISTAS, COMES UNDER FIRE FROM RIGHT: MANAGUA, NICARAGUA, AUGUST 11–12, 1981. Assistant Secretary Enders visited Managua for the first high-level meeting between U.S. officials and the Sandinistas since President Reagan's inauguration. It was to be the last serious U.S. attempt to reach an accommodation with the Nicaraguan government for nearly a decade. The irony was that Enders's effort might have succeeded had it not been for opposition from within the administration.

After acrimonious meetings on the first day, a private session between Enders and Daniel Ortega the second day was productive. Enders took a hard line but acknowledged that the Nicaraguan revolution was irreversible, noted our opposition to many of the Sandinistas' policies, and stated that Somoza's overthrow was not only a fact but also necessary. Essentially, he offered Ortega a trade-off.

The United States would provide formal assurances not to attack Nicaragua directly or by "other means," close exile military training facilities in the United States, and consider renewing economic assistance. In return, the Sandinistas would end their support for revolutionary movements elsewhere (specifically, their support for the Salvadoran insurgents was to end within two weeks) and agree to as yet undefined limits on the size of the Sandinista army and weaponry. Ortega accepted this proposal and Enders's suggestion that they meet again in late September to review progress and work out details of this quid pro quo. Ambassador Pezzullo believed the deal struck would achieve our essential objectives.[52]

Unfortunately, the agreement was effectively dead before Enders returned to Washington. The administration was not prepared to accept a diplomatic solution, period.

The hard-liners—William Clark, Bill Casey, Jeane Kirkpatrick, Cap Weinberger, Bud McFarlane and others—went berserk when they learned the details of Enders's proposal. Not only were they able to block his efforts to flesh it out, but this initiative probably marked the point at which they resolved to oust him.[53] The agreement staggered on for a few weeks, being revised, hardened and changed almost beyond recognition, ultimately dying a death of a thousand bureaucratic cuts.

I believe that this initiative was in part designed to preempt the Contra operation, which the CIA was by then advocating. If an agreement securing our priority interests had been struck and we were committed not to use "other means" against the Sandinistas, there would be no reason to mount a covert paramilitary operation. The death of this framework agreement forced Enders to adopt the so-called two-track approach, which rationalized the Contra operation as a lever to force the Sandinistas to the negotiating table and to accept more punitive terms. But this strategy too was rejected by most players apart from State.

Later, the administration mounted two further efforts to reach a negotiated agreement with the Sandinistas, led respectively by former senator Richard Stone and career ambassador Harry Shlaudeman. Although State supported these initiatives, they were in reality little more than fig leafs to help assuage congressional opposition to the Contra war. Former secretary of state George Shultz, in his memoirs, provides a detailed and acerbic description of the administration's conflicts over these initiatives and how they were frustrated.[54]

GUATEMALAN PRESIDENT PAYS A SURPRISE VISIT: TEGUCIGALPA, HONDURAS, AUGUST 11, 1981. General Garcia Lucas, president of Guatemala, visited Tegucigalpa briefly and unannounced to meet with President Paz. It was just four days before the scheduled Central America and Panama foreign ministers' meeting, in which Guatemala's participation was still in question. The official explanation for Lucas's visit was that it concerned long-standing bilateral trade issues. That story fed Honduran rumor mongers' appetite for conspiracy theories.[55]

CONTRA GROUPS UNIFY: GUATEMALA CITY, GUATEMALA, AUGUST 11, 1981. Two Nicaraguan opposition groups, the September 15 Legion and the Nicaraguan Democratic Union, announced their unification under the name of the Nicaraguan Democratic Force (FDN). This merger had been pushed by the Argentines and Hondurans, who argued that it would facilitate covert assistance from the United States.[56] Their operations in Guatemala were closed and moved to Honduras.

MORE DECEIT: CIA REGIONAL OPERATIONS CHIEF VISIT: TEGUCI-GALPA, HONDURAS, MID–AUGUST, 1981.[57] I had agreed to a visit by the CIA's new Latin America operations chief, Duane "Dewey" Clarridge, for the purpose of meeting his Honduran counterparts concerning the arms interdiction program. I wished to do everything I could to accelerate that effort. The most memorable aspect of my session with Clarridge was Clarridge. He was singularly conspicuous in Tegucigalpa. Having previously been attached to our Rome embassy, he looked like a fugitive from *La Dolce Vita:* dark shirt and tie, beautifully tailored light suit, Italian shoes and a marvelous sun tan. Beyond his flamboyance, I found him polished, intelligent and glib. Some covert operator, I thought.

He and the station chief, who would accompany him on his rounds, were to meet with Colonel Alvarez, National Intelligence Directorate chief Lopez Grijalva, other senior FUSEP officers and perhaps military intelligence chief Torres Arias to discuss details of the agency's proposed arms interdiction program. That sounded reasonable to me. Clarridge had a lot more on his mind than he shared with me, however. His principal purpose was to discuss the Contra operation. But disguising his aims was not the only deception. Unbeknownst to me, they also met with President Paz,[58] a major no-no in terms of ambassadorial oversight. This was another deliberate deception.

Clarridge assured the Hondurans that the United States was prepared to back the Nicaraguan exile opposition in its struggle against the Sandinistas. Gutman reported that he told Paz that President Reagan personally had directed him to come and advise him that we would support action to "liberate" Nicaragua from the Sandinistas.[59] Although the CIA may not have accepted all elements of Alvarez's original scheme, the Hondurans believed that Clarridge was committing the United States to overthrowing the Sandinista regime.[60] Later that month, according to Gutman, Clarridge returned to Honduras on a private aircraft, bringing with him Col. Mario Davico, the vice-chief of Argentine military intelligence. Their purpose was to work out an operational structure: essentially, the United States would finance the Contra operation, the Argentines would train and direct their forces, and Honduras would provide the safe haven out of which they would operate. The Nicaraguan exiles would provide the bodies.[61]

I was not apprised of Clarridge's second visit or of his agenda. It should also be emphasized that these activities occurred nearly four months before the Presidential finding for Contra support was issued and Congress notified, as required by law.

HONDURAS AND THE IMF: ECONOMIC SABOTAGE? TEGUCIGALPA, HONDURAS, AUGUST 13, 1981. The IMF's extended fund facility (EFF) agreement called for the assignment of a representative to Tegucigalpa to monitor compliance. That had been one of the conditions demanded by the private sector in return for its support of the government's tax package, and President Paz had agreed to it. The private sector did not believe the government could be trusted to meet its economic commitments, a judgment we shared. Others, however, felt that this precondition encroached on Honduran sovereignty.

Consequently, we were surprised to learn from State that the IMF had decided not to send a representative to Honduras, an apparent breach of the accord. We feared the absence of a representative would increase the likelihood of Honduran backsliding and would certainly erode the private sector's confidence in both the economy and government. Raising these points, State advised that IMF's regional director had interposed an objection to the original agreement. That seemed curious.

Looking into the matter locally, we found that the IMF director's objection had apparently been inspired by Finance Minister Valentin Mendoza. According to Central Bank President Martinez, he had received a phone call from the regional director, suggesting that a resident representative was unnecessary. Martinez then cabled the Fund, reiterating the government's position that the resident representative was an integral part of the agreement and must be honored, emphasizing President Paz's pledge. The following day, in the absence of Paz, who was "indisposed," Mendoza called a special meeting of the economic cabinet and, after an acrimonious debate, persuaded its members to revise the Honduran position because it was "damaging to national dignity." Mendoza advised the Fund of the government's new position.[62]

Private sector leaders were outraged and appealed to Paz. They were not successful. We were confused. This step seemed to make no sense at all. It undermined the business community's confidence in the government and economy, as well as its future willingness to accept governmental commitments.

It also meant that the government was more apt to violate the terms of the IMF agreement, which would only make future cooperation with that body more difficult. To us it seemed deeply detrimental to Honduran interests.

Later events indicated that this action served a political end. Mendoza was closely allied with senior military officers who wished to block the electoral process and probably took this step to provide further grounds to postpone the elections. If that was the motive, it was self-defeating, making future revitalization and management of the economy more difficult even if Paz should remain in office.

SALVADORANS JOIN PARADE OF SURPRISE VISITORS: TEGUCIGALPA, HONDURAS, AUGUST 14, 1981. Salvadoran junta President Napoleon Duarte, Vice President Jaime Abdul Gutierrez and Foreign Minister Fidel Chavez Mena popped in to meet with President Paz, Chief of Staff Chinchilla and Foreign Minister Elvir. The stated purpose of the meeting was also to deal with bilateral economic issues. That announcement shifted the rumor mills into overdrive. The favored theory, especially on the left, was that the three chiefs of state—Paz, Lucas Garcia and Duarte—were planning a joint military attack on Nicaragua.

I received a very general debriefing on both meetings from Elvir, who said they had dealt at least in part with trade issues. He also said the Salvadorans had discussed their domestic political situation, including efforts to persuade Ungo and the Democratic Revolutionary Front (FDR) to participate in elections.[63] Paz later told me that the meeting with the Salvadorans dealt mainly with Nicaraguan threat and the situation on their common frontier. The variations in their stories seemed curious.

Salvadoran foreign minister Chavez Mena later provided Walker and me with a more detailed account. It had been triggered by an August 13 phone call from Paz asking Duarte to come to Tegucigalpa, the "sooner the better," but without specifying a purpose. Concerned about what Paz and Lucas might have cooked up the day before, Duarte said he could come the following day. When the Salvadorans arrived they were met by their Honduran counterparts and ushered to the Air Force officer's club. Chavez Mena characterized the meeting as unfocused. Paz was poorly informed on economic issues and the agenda for the CAP foreign ministers' meeting. One of the more memorable parts, according to Chavez Mena, was Paz's litany of complaints about the assembly, the civilian politicians and the private sector. It sounded, he remarked, as although the military were already justifying the future overthrow of the elected government. Chavez Mena flatly denied any discussion of security issues or the Sandinistas.[64]

This difference was probably explained by the fact that Colonel Gutierrez remained behind in Tegucigalpa when Duarte and Chavez Mena returned to San Salvador. That is no doubt when the security-related discussions occurred. We concluded that whatever purpose Paz may have had in mind, these meetings had not been worth the negative fallout they generated.

POSSIBLE MAJOR MINING INVESTMENTS EVAPORATE: TEGUCIGALPA, HONDURAS, AUGUST 14, 1981. At least three major mining investments—one American and two Canadian—were still pending, awaiting changes in the mining code. We had been pushing for action on the mining code because we thought these investments, aggregating several hundred million dollars, would have a very favorable impact on the economy, generate other investment and improve business confidence. We estimated that they would create 2,000 new jobs directly, and an equal number indirectly, and increase Honduras's foreign exchange earnings, a constant source of concern.

As a result of the Council of the America's mission, which urged expedited revision of the mining code, the Ministry of Finance invited Rosario Mining to submit its recommendations for changes in the code. Rosario responded quickly. The government's response was both fast and unexpected. Rather than presenting a counterproposal, offering to negotiate differences or even identifying the problems it had with the proposal, the ministry simply advised Rosario that the proposal was unacceptable; no reasons given .[65]

When I met with Rosario officials, they related their story and conclusion that there was no chance the transition government would enact the needed revisions. They also reported that one of the Canadian firms had reached a similar conclusion, so there would be no new investments for a while. This was another lost opportunity for Honduras.

FOREIGN MINISTERS' MEETING AND JOINT DECLARATION: TEGUCI-GALPA, HONDURAS, AUGUST 15, 1981. The Central America and Panama (CAP) foreign ministers meeting came off with a hitch; Guatemala, which had sought to block it, was represented only by its ambassador to Honduras. The main goal of the meeting was to revitalize regional economic cooperation and integration, moribund since the 1969 El Salvador/Honduras conflict. Secondarily it was an effort to ease tensions in the region. We also saw it as an opportunity to engage the participants in the fledgling Caribbean Basin Initiative (CBI). All of our CAP embassies had been instructed to urge that the final declaration include a reference to the CBI.

To the surprise of few, the meeting fell well short of achieving these goals. The Declaration of Tegucigalpa, as the joint statement was known, emphasized the importance of regional economic cooperation, trade and investment and called on the international community to collaborate in reducing barriers to the area's exports. It contained no reference to the CBI.[66]

Nicaragua had blocked specific mention of the initiative, although there was a side agreement that the six participating countries would invite the four principals—the United States, Canada, Mexico and Venezuela—to a

September meeting scheduled for San Jose, Costa Rica. Guatemala also blocked a stronger commitment to regional integration. Over the longer term, the conflict in El Salvador, the covert war against Nicaragua and the lack of Guatemalan enthusiasm would preclude significant economic cooperation.

CONGRESSIONAL STAFF DELEGATION ARRIVES: TEGUCIGALPA, HONDURAS, AUGUST 15, 1981. A delegation of three congressional legislative assistants—representing Congressmen Gerry Studds, Mickey Leland and Ron Dellums, Democrats all—came to town to inquire about the refugee situation. And they wished to visit the refugee camps. Their interests, however, turned out to be broader. The earlier visit of Representatives Studds, Mikulski and Edgar was not among my happiest memories, but I thought our subsequent exchange of correspondence had contributed to Studds's having a more balanced understanding of the region and the challenges we faced. That, at least, is what his letters suggested.

We provided the customary embassy briefing, set up meetings with Honduran officials and refugee relief agencies, and arranged for their transportation to the frontier. Our briefing touched on a number of sensitive matters, including human rights. I also pitched them on our effort to obtain $20 million from the Economic Support Fund (ESF) for Honduras. They seemed quite responsive in that regard. They also agreed to meet with us before returning to Washington to share their impressions, thus providing an opportunity for us to try to place in context their observations and conclusions.

DEFENSE DEPUTY ASSISTANT SECRETARY VISITS: TEGUCIGALPA, HONDURAS, AUGUST 15–17, 1981. We received a cable requesting country clearances from embassies in Honduras, El Salvador and Guatemala for an orientation visit by the Defense Department's new deputy assistant secretary for Inter-American affairs, Nestor Sanchez. He was due to arrive in Tegucigalpa the following day, a Saturday, and remain until Monday. Some advance notice; it was a fait accompli.[67] That wasn't the only problem I had with the request. Sanchez had been the CIA's chief of Latin American operations until his replacement by Dewey Clarridge, and I really didn't want him in town on Clarridge's heels because I thought it would send the wrong signal. But I couldn't think of an acceptable reason to withhold clearance, and I didn't need another conflict with Defense. It was just as well that I concurred in his visit.

Sanchez's program was straightforward: a session with our Milgroup, followed by meetings with President Paz and Colonel Alvarez, in my company. He would then go on to El Salvador in the attache aircraft. His principal purpose, it turned out, was to brief the Central American heads of state on Enders's recent trip to Managua and our effort to reestablish a positive relationship with the Sandinistas. He did not, however, mention the framework accord Enders and Ortega had reached. It struck me as curious that a

Defense official was carrying out this essentially diplomatic mission. I had no idea why someone from State was not chosen, but the purge of the Inter-America bureau left Sanchez far better known in the region than any of Enders's aides.

Paz sincerely appreciated this briefing and Sanchez's promise to keep him apprised of developments regarding the Enders initiative. Not surprisingly, he was skeptical that Enders's efforts would come to much but agreed it was important to show we were making an attempt to reach accommodation. Sanchez ran through the same briefing with Alvarez, but his reaction was direct and critical. That was not unexpected. Alvarez believed there was no chance the Sandinistas would stop exporting revolution or ease their repression of the domestic opposition. All the United States was doing, he asserted, was giving them more time to consolidate power. Shifting the discussion to the Salvadoran frontier, Alvarez said the Hondurans had just cracked a major insurgent support network, in part as a result of information provided by the Salvadorans. Several prisoners were still undergoing interrogation, but the warehouses they had uncovered contained few weapons or other material. Alvarez speculated that the insurgents were preparing for a new offensive and had moved nearly all materiel to the front. Although the government had made no announcement, he said they would probably agree to our using it publicly, if that would be helpful.[68]

This information had not been reported to me or in official channels. I assumed the Hondurans had not shared it with the CIA. Now, however, I suspect this may have been another example of my being cut out of the information loop because of human rights implications. The Honduran Human Rights Commission's report reveals that 21 people—Salvadoran, Honduran and other—were arrested in early August and then vanished without trace.[69] The timing of these detentions suggests they were part of the operation described by Alvarez. I reported Alvarez's statements, but had no information about the human rights abuses.

SHEEHAN AFFAIR: MORE QUESTIONS AND A FINAL DECISION: TEGUCIGALPA, HONDURAS, AUGUST 17–23, 1981. State reported that congressional and media interest in the Sheehan case was unabated. The visiting congressional staff delegation had also spoken with local officials, foreign physicians, refugee workers and newsmen in La Virtud. Based on their discussions, its members were convinced Sheehan had carried an M-16 in the town and made most, if not all, of the statements attributed to him.[70] They were certain to carry those views back to Capitol Hill.

We had to make a better effort to determine the facts. Walker and I decided to send a junior officer to La Virtud to interview the French physicians and others. This officer had visited the frontier several times previously, was familiar with the area and knew a number of people in La Virtud. She

returned August 19, the same day we debriefed the congressional staff delegation, having interviewed French, German and Honduran physicians and a
Dutch photographer. All had been in La Virtud during Sheehan's visit. Only
one, the photographer, claimed to have seen Sheehan carrying an M-16. His
description of the event seemed credible to her. The staff delegation reported
that several of their sources said Sheehan had carried an M-16 to dinner at
the French physicians' residence, yet none of those at the event would confirm
that to our officer. Who was telling the truth? Those at the dinner, however,
reported they had heard Sheehan make most of the remarks attributed to him
in the article and that he had done so in Bonner's presence.[71]

It now seemed that Sheehan had lied. The allegations that he had carried a weapon, however, were not conclusive. But there was no doubt he violated embassy guidelines and displayed poor judgment. He had also become
a lightning rod for public and congressional concerns and was a liability. I
knew that if I expelled him I would trigger another confrontation and generate still more ill will with Southern Command and General Nutting. I did
not want or need either. I decided to ask Nutting to recall him, rather than
for me to direct his departure. That would allow Nutting to avoid the indig-
nity of having me direct Sheehan's return. But, if he wouldn't recall him, I
could still order him back to Panama. I phoned Nutting personally, explaining the reasons for my decision before advising Sheehan.

Nutting was extremely unhappy with my request. He defended Sheehan, denying that he would have said the things attributed to him or have
lied to me. Nor did Nutting believe that the statements of others were credible, suggesting instead that they were "out to get" Sheehan. This line of
argument left me unmoved, so he shifted to another. My action, he said,
would ruin the career of a fine young officer. That was nonsense. I knew
enough about the Army personnel system to know that the fitness report prepared by Sheehan's unit commander, not my request that he be recalled, would
affect his career.

I told Nutting that my decision to request Sheehan's recall was being
made "without prejudice," thus leaving it to the Army to decide whether the
incident would reflect on his career. Nutting accepted that recall was the best
option and agreed. Sheehan departed Honduras August 24.[72]

I hoped that Sheehan's recall would serve as an object lesson for other
advisers on temporary assignment, establishing that we meant business with
our operational and behavioral guidelines . It also allowed us to respond to
subsequent inquiries by saying that Sheehan was no longer in the country.

PEZZULLO LEAVES NICARAGUA: MANAGUA, NICARAGUA, AUGUST 18,
1981. Disappointed with the Reagan administration's policy toward Nicaragua,
and despite Secretary Haig's request that he remain at post, Ambassador Pezzullo left Managua after tendering his resignation. He accepted a "Diplomat

in Residence" appointment at the University of Georgia, retiring from the Foreign Service the following year.[73]

SALVADORAN ARMY RECAPTURES PERQUIN: PERQUIN, EL SALVADOR, AUGUST 18–20, 1981. Salvadoran army units recaptured Perquin after airlifting an airborne company north of the town, allowing for a coordinated attack from two directions.[74] There were heavy casualties on both sides, but many of the insurgents escaped.

CONGRESSIONAL DELEGATION DEBRIEFING: TEGUCIGALPA, HONDURAS, AUGUST 19, 1981. Walker, our human rights officer and I met with the staff delegation to hear its report. The delegation's impressions of the refugee situation seemed far more balanced than those of the earlier Studds/Mikulski/Edgar mission. In that sense our work appeared to have paid off. The delegation was also concerned about the Barrillas/Navarro case because of inquiries from the American citizen relative of Navarro. We could not, however, divulge what we knew to them without revealing the source. But their greatest concern was the issue of U.S. military advisers, particularly Sheehan's actions. This was to become the subject of later correspondence with Studds and his staff.

Sometime later we learned from State that Studds's aide had secretly recorded all or part of our initial briefing. I was outraged. I regarded this clandestine recording to be a gross violation of trust and one that could only poison relations between an embassy and visiting congressional and staff delegations. That the recording may also have included sensitive classified information, the release of which might prejudice our relations with the Honduran government, only stoked my anger. Consequently, I wrote to both Studds and his aide, voicing my concerns and displeasure candidly.[75] I received no response or acknowledgment.

PROBLEMS WITH PROPOSED NATIONAL SECURITY LAW: TEGUCIGALPA, HONDURAS, AUGUST 19, 1981. I met with Suazo Cordova to discuss the proposed national security law. Although we had not seen the text, we expected its passage would provide a legal basis for prosecution of a number of serious offenses (e.g., kidnapping, aircraft hijacking, arms smuggling) not covered by the existing penal code. We also believed approval would lessen the security forces' growing reliance on extralegal means to deal with subversion, thus easing the human rights problem. With the department's approval, I honored President Paz's request that I ask Suazo Cordova to support enactment.

Our discussion proved enlightening and very worrisome. Suazo Cordova said his party was, in principle, well disposed toward this legislation. But there were practical problems. First, they had yet to see the text. It had been read to them several months earlier, but despite repeated requests, the president's office had still not provided it. Suazo Cordova, however, was certain that the National Party had received a copy. I was dumbfounded. Continuing, he said that several provisions, as read to them, conflicted with the constitution the assembly was drafting. For example, the proposed law would allow security forces to enter private dwellings between the hours of 6:00 P.M. and 6:00 A.M. without a court order. There was also a potential conflict with the draft constitution on maximum prison sentences, with the security law providing up to 70 years for some offenses, exceeding limits in the draft constitution. Although concerned at the lack of evenhandedness on the part of Paz and the military, Suazo Cordova said the Liberals would support a new national security law if the constitutional issues were resolved and the National Party also did so.

After further discussion, Suazo Cordova agreed that I should advise Paz of his position and urge that he give the Liberals the text of the draft legislation posthaste.[76] I was uneasy. Paz and the military were not dealing squarely with the Liberals. Moreover, they appeared to be pushing draconian legislation and had asked me, in effect, to urge the Liberals to buy a pig in a poke. Nonetheless, I was prepared to continue as an intermediary as long as State agreed. But Paz and the military would also have to understand that our support was strictly in principle and that we took no position on the substantive parts of this legislation. Those were matters for the Hondurans to work out among themselves.

I reported this to State and told Paz of the Liberals' position. For whatever reason, the push to enact this legislation had ended, and no more was heard of it during my time in Honduras.

MORE SALVADORAN ATROCITIES AND MORE MILITARY ASSISTANCE: SANTA ANA DEPARTMENT, EL SALVADOR, AUGUST 20–25, 1981. Over this five-day period, 83 decapitated bodies of young men were found, most of them in the relatively peaceful province of Santa Ana. Death squads using a makeshift guillotine were responsible.[77] On August 25 the United States, without publicity, authorized the transfer of four helicopters to El Salvador.[78]

HONDURAN PRIESTS INVOLVED IN GUERRILLA SUPPORT NETWORK: TEGUCIGALPA, HONDURAS, AUGUST 21, 1981. A member of the Catholic hierarchy provided detailed information on the activities of several priests in the Santa Rosa de Copan diocese in support of the Salvadoran insurgents. Most of this information only confirmed what we had heard from other sources, but it provided important details and insights.

The principal activists were two Salvadoran "guerrilla priests" active in the frontier area, working with refugees and developing insurgent support networks. Their names were Trinidad Nieto and Porfilio Martinez; the latter reportedly carried false Mexican identification papers. A group of Spanish Passionist priests assigned to the Santa Rosa diocese provided direct support for these two. The Spanish group also directed an American priest, Robert Gallagher, the mouthpiece of the Committee for Solidarity with the Salvadoran People.

Father Fausto Milla, the Honduran priest earlier arrested entering the country with $36,000 in cash, maintained a bank account in Santa Rosa with a balance of $50,000. When church authorities confronted him about these funds, he claimed they were donations from his parishioners, a story our source described as "absurd." Milla was known by Church authorities to have a direct link to the insurgent coalition propaganda apparatus based in Mexico and was believed to use these funds to disseminate propaganda, pay couriers and carry out other activities in support of the guerrillas.[79]

This source also reported that the Auxiliary Bishop of San Rosa de Copan had met with a visiting American religious delegation, finding most of its members well intended but naive. They were heavily influenced by a Mexican religious leader traveling with them and known to be close to the insurgents' Mexico City propaganda office. That person had been in touch with members of the Honduran Communist Party (PCH), and the latter were assisting the American delegation. For that reason Archbishop Santos had declined to meet with the Americans.[80] We reported this to State.

LIBERAL LEADER REBUFFS PRESIDENT PAZ: TEGUCIGALPA, HONDURAS, AUGUST 21, 1981. President Paz had been invited to make an official visit to Venezuela August 24–26. In addition to cosponsoring the CBI and the Central American oil facility with Mexico, Venezuelan president Luis Herrera Campins was our strongest and most effective ally in seeking to keep the Honduran election on track. I met fairly frequently with my Venezuelan colleague to exchange information and, occasionally, coordinate actions. The principal purpose of the Venezuelan invitation was to give President Herrera an opportunity to emphasize the importance Venezuela placed on the success of the transition.

In an uncharacteristic effort to reach out to the political parties, Paz had invited all four presidential candidates to accompany him. I thought this an excellent move, as did most of the civilian political leaders. There was, however, a very important exception: Suazo Cordova had declined Paz's invitation.

When I learned of this, I was once again dumbfounded. By snubbing Paz, Suazo Cordova would only intensify the military's suspicion of his party, and he risked irritating the Venezuelans as well. And they were providing important economic support. I was reluctant to raise the issue directly with him, since he had not mentioned it in our meeting of the previous day.

My Venezuelan colleague, I learned, was so incensed with Suazo Cordova that he refused to approach him without instructions from Caracas. I cabled State, asking Enders to suggest that Venezuela direct its ambassador to ask Suazo Cordova to reconsider.[81] I also telephoned one of Suazo Cordova's key aides, Carlos Flores, to express my surprise at this decision and suggest that Suazo Cordova might wish to reconsider. These efforts were to no avail.

CRISIS POINT: MILITARY REPORTEDLY DECIDE TO DELAY ELECTIONS, TEGUCIGALPA, HONDURAS, AUGUST 21, 1981. A usually reliable source reported that the Armed Forces Superior Council had decided to delay the November 29 elections until February 1982. The level of detail in this particular report enhanced its credibility. I was very concerned, but at least it wasn't a surprise. The rationale was to allow time to complete the new national identity card system, thereby purging the electoral rolls of 200,000 fraudulently registered voters. It was specious, and the cited numbers were nonsense. The chances of completing the national identity card system in less than three months was far closer to none than to slim. I was convinced that delay meant the military would remain in power indefinitely. If implemented, this was certain to provoke major popular and political unrest and to seriously damage our interests in Honduras and the region.

I quickly convened the Political/Military group to review the likely consequences and work out a strategy to frustrate the reported plan. After evaluating the threat as very serious, this cable described the potential implications as follows:

> Delay or frustration of electoral process is likely to be seriously destabilizing at a time when we are seeking to contain spread of violence and uncertainty in the region...[and] be detrimental to both our bilateral and regional interests and be perceived as a sign of USG backsliding, weakness or irresolution. As yet, however, we have not seen any signs that GOH or military have done anything to implement their decision, although we should expect that they will make some move shortly. If we are to avoid this challenge to our interests, we should act with dispatch, bearing in mind that by opposing a change in the election date we risk placing ourselves at cross purposes with the armed forces. It will be a high stakes game, and whatever the outcome there will be a legacy of resentment; but we have considerable leverage—in the form of our own assistance, Honduran dependence and popular support—on our side.[82]

Our proposed strategy to defeat this initiative included the following specific steps:

• I meet with Paz on his return from Caracas to deliver a personal high-level (e.g., Secretary Haig or President Reagan) message expressing our serious concern about reports that elections might be delayed;
• Enders (or Haig) call in Honduran ambassador to make the same points;

• State or the White House issue a strong public endorsement of the Honduran transition process and elections, avoiding mention of a specific election date to give us "wiggle room" in case the military goes ahead with this scheme; we will also have "if asked" press guidance saying that the assembly had fixed the elections date and, unless it should change that date, we support elections as scheduled;
• I visit leaders of all political parties to assure them that the United States continues to support November 29 elections, and to urge the Liberal and minor parties to stand firm against any change;
• I call on key military leaders—Alvarez, Torres Arias and Chinchilla— to reaffirm our commitment and concerns (we also suggested a high-level military emissary to strengthen this message); and
• if the above actions fail to have the desired effect, we should approach major Honduran interest groups (media, business, labor), assuring them of our position and urging them to oppose any delay.[83]

I didn't await State's approval to start the ball rolling. My first contact was with a leader of the Christian Democrats; he shared our concerns and stated flatly that Honduras "simply cannot tolerate an extra month of this transition government." His party would oppose any change in the election date.[84] When State did not respond to the cable, I phoned to spur action. I was told that Enders was out of town and no one was willing to make a decision in his absence. But another visit by General Walters was under consideration. Beyond that, I was encouraged to continue our local efforts without specific guidance. I did so.

Approaching Liberal Party leaders, I found them solidly behind the scheduled election and, because the military could not change the date without an assembly vote, confident that they could block it. The leaders of the other minor party said they too would oppose a change: there was no chance of a majority in favor of a new election date. All were confident that the military would draw back from a coup d'état[85]

9

Efforts to Block Elections and Conflict with U.S. Military

SUMMARY—Paz seeks counsel on delaying elections—we advise against and General Walters makes another visit—assurances on elections prove false, as Paz and senior military continue delaying efforts—differences with Southern Command reach a crescendo—military advisers machine-gunned by terrorists—policy speech and press conference reaffirm U.S. support for elections—my replacement announced, spurring speculation of U.S. policy change—*Halcon Vista* plans—other statements of support for elections—exposure of military corruption adds to uncertainty—France and Mexico "recognize" Salvadoran insurgents—Sandinistas cope with growing unrest and protest joint military exercises—Enders backs away from earlier agreement

STATE ADDRESSES MY REGIONAL POLICY CONCERNS: NOT! WASH-INGTON, D.C., AND TEGUCIGALPA, HONDURAS, AUGUST 25–26, 1981. State finally responded to my July 31 cable voicing serious concerns about conflicts in our various bilateral policies and the need for improved policy and program coordination.[1] At least the cable carried the same subject line. In fact, it did not address any of those issues. Instead, it announced an additional $3.4 million in fiscal year 1981 FMS credit was being allocated to Honduras as a result of reprogramming.[2] This news might be welcome, if paltry, to the Hondurans, but it really had nothing to do with my concerns. This response struck me as a classic bureaucratic kiss-off, indicating that there was no chance the concerns I raised would receive interagency consideration.

At the practical level I was worried about what this unexpected largess might imply. And it also made the mission and me look like fools because pursuant to instructions we had repeatedly told the Honduran military that no such funds were available. Nor did it seem to me to be a propitious time to tell the Honduran military we were increasing FMS funding. They were planning to block the transition. Consequently, I cabled State, requesting authorization to link this increased funding directly to our concerns about postponement of elections.[3] It was granted.

FRANCE AND MEXICO RECOGNIZE SALVADORAN INSURGENTS: MEXICO CITY, MEXICO, AUGUST 28, 1981. A joint Franco-Mexican communiqué recognized the Salvadoran Democratic Revolutionary Front (FDR) as a "representative political force" entitled to negotiate a political solution to the conflict in that country. The United States joined the Salvadoran junta government in denouncing this declaration and rejecting negotiations in favor of promised elections. Nine other Latin American nations issued a joint rebuttal communiqué condemning the Franco-Mexican statement and accusing the two countries of intervening in the internal affairs of El Salvador, favoring "subversive extremes."[4]

This was a setback for our policy, underscoring the concerns of allies. Fortunately, no other allies were willing to go public with their differences.

SALVADORAN COURT ORDERS MURDERER FREED: SAN SALVADOR, EL SALVADOR, AUGUST 28, 1981. A Salvadoran judge, citing "inconsistent" evidence, ordered the release of Ricardo Sol Meza, one of the two oligarchs responsible for the January 4 slaying of American advisers Mike Hammer and Mark Pearlman. This decision was subsequently sustained by the Supreme Court. He was released October 22 and never reindicted.[5]

ANOTHER CONGRESSIONAL DELEGATION COMES TO TOWN: TEGUCIGALPA, HONDURAS, AUGUST 29–SEPTEMBER 1, 1981. Another "unofficial" congressional delegation sponsored by the Unitarians, who had arranged the earlier Studds/Edgar/Mikulski program, arrived Saturday afternoon. It was led by Tom Petri (R-WI). John McAward was again the director. As with the Studds group, this delegation's program was split between that arranged by the embassy and that set up by McAward.

When the delegation deplaned, it was apparent that there would be problems. There were about 15 delegates, one of whom was a representative and two who were his staffers. The others had been invited by the Unitarians and had no official standing. We had arranged several high-level meetings, including a session with President Paz, and I had no intention of traipsing into those meetings with a large, unofficial retinue. Accordingly, I told McAward and Petri that we would have to separate the official visitors from the rest of the group for several of the meetings. McAward wasn't happy.

The presence of unofficial visitors also meant that our CT briefing would have to be circumspect to avoid sensitive information and issues. Nonetheless, I reviewed our concerns about possible frustration of elections and asked Petri if he would stress their importance in his meetings and when speaking to the media. He agreed and did a superb job.

The group's Sunday program included visits to a training center run by some of Petri's missionary constituents and several Peace Corps sites, as well as group meetings. Among the latter were sessions with the Liberal Party's dissident ALIPO faction, labor and *campesino* union leaders and the local UNHCR representative. That evening Wackerbarth hosted a reception that gave the visitors an opportunity to meet some Hondurans. Our program the following day included group meetings with leaders of both the major parties (Zuniga had begged off, so they only met the National Party's two vice presidential candidates) and a dinner at the residence with the minor party presidential candidates, media representatives and university professors and administrators. We had not been able to set up meetings with military leaders, despite considerable effort. I suspected they were tired of hearing visitors endorse the electoral process.

Arcos, acting as interpreter, and I escorted Petri and his aides to the meeting with Paz and the later call on the legislative assembly. The press awaited us at both stops. Petri forcefully and effectively endorsed the electoral process, reaffirming our position on this issue.[6] And he had said essentially the same thing in all his meetings with Hondurans. This was especially useful coming from a Republican. During the Paz meeting Petri pressed repeatedly for a firm commitment that elections would be held on schedule, but he didn't get it. Paz bobbed, weaved and evaded. Our intelligence report appeared to be on the mark.

I was impressed by Petri's seriousness and intelligence. That, however, did not hold true for the rest of McAward's merry band. The size of the group, which we had not expected, made it unwieldy and difficult to support logistically. Beyond that, I was troubled by persistent and often confrontational questions posed by the unofficial members. On at least two occasions I felt obliged to intervene when questions to Hondurans were inappropriate, rude or blatantly biased. I was not present at all of their meetings, however.

Based on our two experiences with McAward's groups, I recommended that embassies draw back from direct involvement in such "unofficial" programs and asked that State brief potential congressional participants about the inherent difficulties.[7]

ENDERS BACKS AWAY FROM EARLIER DEAL WITH SANDINISTAS: WASHINGTON, D.C., AUGUST 31, 1981. Reflecting administration opposition to his framework agreement, Enders wrote Ortega, noting that continued Sandinista support for the Salvadoran and other revolutionary groups was creating an insuperable barrier to normalizing relations. There would be no further dialogue unless that support was terminated.[8]

Although there were some later exchanges, Enders's letter effectively drove a stake through the heart of the proposed agreement with Nicaragua.

PAZ REQUESTS URGENT MEETING, BROACHES ELECTIONS DELAY: TEGUCIGALPA, HONDURAS, SEPTEMBER 1, 1981. President Paz wished to see me right away. I already had an appointment with him scheduled for the following day, so this request had to be important. After a cursory description of his recent meetings with Presidents Lucas, Duarte and Herrera Campins, Paz said that he planned official visits to Mexico and Canada in the near future (a not very subtle hint for us to get aboard the bandwagon). He then moved to his main topic: delaying elections.

At that point I interrupted, saying that I wished to give him some good news before discussing the elections issue. We would increase Honduras's current year FMS credit line by $3.4 million and, more important, the Defense Department had upgraded Honduras's FMS delivery priority from 8 to 3. That was a big jump and would sharply shrink delivery times. Paz seemed as genuinely pleased as I had ever seen him. I hoped this news would temper the impact of what I would be saying about elections.

Paz then detailed the case for postponing the elections. It was the Superior Council's rationale with two significant changes: the number of fraudulently registered voters he cited was only 100,000, not the Council's asserted 200,000; and he added a new concern, a possible violent backlash from the 100,000 people who would be purged from the electoral roll. He claimed he faced a tough decision. If the electoral council succeeded in purging those fraudulently inscribed, there would be a strong reaction. Yet if he proceeded with elections knowing so many voters were bogus, the losing party would protest the outcome, bringing political turmoil. Consequently, he was leaning toward postponing elections until completion of the national identity card system, then using the resulting lists as the new electoral roll. That, he thought, was the only way to preserve the integrity of the electoral process. Concluding, he asked for my views.

As State had not responded to my cable urging a proactive posture on this issue, I was without specific instructions. So I hewed to the previous policy line. I agreed that he faced a tough decision. The embassy, I noted, had been following the problems he described very closely since the visit of General Walters. Although the decision to delay elections belonged to the Honduran people, he had asked my opinion and I would give it.

Friendly governments such as the United States and Venezuela strongly supported the transition. But most important, the Honduran people had endorsed it overwhelmingly in the April 1980 assembly elections. Recent embassy soundings, I stressed, indicated strong, broad popular support for elections in November. All of the political parties publicly supported that schedule, although the Nationalists had added some caveats. The private sector, unions, *campesino* groups (except for those on the far left) and media were solidly behind November elections. A delay in this process, it seemed to me, would be extremely destabilizing.

Continuing, I listed the likely consequences of delay:

• It would trigger an all-out international propaganda campaign against the provisional government and military, and extremist calls to arms would have far greater resonance. If he feared the backlash from 100,000 fraudulent voters excluded from the rolls, he should be worried indeed about the reaction of the entire electorate feeling that its wishes were being ignored.

• I had specifically asked private sector contacts what consequences it would have. Overwhelmingly, they thought that postponement would seriously weaken international and domestic confidence in Honduras, with a disastrous economic impact.

• Honduras's image with friendly countries would suffer severely, and economic and security assistance might be reduced or suspended.

• Finally, I suggested that political turmoil would seriously jeopardize both Honduran and U.S. interests in the region.

Paz indicated awareness of all of these points but was equally fearful of the consequences of elections. What, he asked, would I advise him to do? I acknowledged that neither of the options were good, so he had to choose the least bad. To me, delay of the elections was clearly the worst option. Because voter registration, the central problem, was the responsibility of the parties, I urged that he call the party leaders together, describe his concerns and tell them to agree on a solution that would allow the elections to go forward on schedule. He appeared unpersuaded but thanked me for my counsel and said he would keep in touch.[9]

I surmised that the Superior Council had not yet made a firm decision to delay elections, although Paz and others were pushing for that outcome. This raised some question about our source's reliability, but the forewarning he provided was more valuable than advice of an actual decision after the fact. I also inferred that Paz had advanced our appointment as a result of Representative Petri's insistence on an assurance that elections would proceed as scheduled. He had felt the heat and wished to sound me out anew.

We were dealing with a matrix of conflicting and convergent interests. Paz, as was clear from his international travel program, enjoyed his position and was increasingly unwilling to give it up. Colonel Alvarez, already selected to succeed Paz as commander of the armed forces, wanted to move up. Other senior officers, however, saw Alvarez's advancement as a threat to their ambitions and were supporting Paz in delaying elections. That group included Colonels Torres Arias, Bodden, Montoya and Bueso Rosa.

Election defeat would end Zuniga's control of the National Party, so he supported delay. His near-term interests coincided with those of Paz and his supporters, but over the longer term they diverged. The anti-Zuniga faction, and even some of Zuniga's own supporters who liked the money, influence and perks of the legislature, opposed delay. The Liberals and two minor parties were also opposed, although the Liberals' dissident ALIPO faction was seeking to leverage concessions from Suazo Cordova by threatening to support postponement. I thought ALIPO was bluffing but couldn't be certain.

The private sector, labor, the media and other institutions were supporting elections but were not yet directly engaged. They all had influence that could be brought to bear. We needed to increase our efforts with the public and the proelection groups. The Petri visit had been very helpful, but more was required. I had a pending invitation from the San Pedro Sula Rotary Club to speak at one of their monthly dinners, and that seemed an excellent opportunity to get our message out. Not only did Rotary afford an important private sector audience in Honduras's commercial center, but my speaking there would also assure extensive media coverage.

I accepted the invitation, and charged Walker, Arcos and Wackerbarth with developing an appropriate speech. The principal theme would be the return to democracy and the private sector's critical role in its success, but I also wished to speak out on government corruption. My stock was already low with the military, and I was on my way out, so this seemed like an ideal opportunity to address the corruption issue in front of a sympathetic audience.

HALCON VISTA PRESS GUIDANCE: TEGUCIGALPA, HONDURAS, SEPTEMBER 2, 1981. Our proposed press guidance described the exercise scope in general terms and noted the presence of a U.S. Navy amphibious ship in Puerto Cortez to provide logistic support for the participating U.S. small craft. It stressed that the ship would not participate in the actual exercise. We also prepared responses to expected questions, to be used on an "if asked" basis. The principal issues they dealt with were the possible perceived threat to Nicaragua (denied, based principally on the size of forces involved) and the presence of Marines aboard the amphibious unit. We emphasized that the Marines were part of the normal crew of such ships, that they would play no part in the exercise and that U.S. forces would not be involved in any landings on Honduran shores.[10] The latter point would be important later. We sent it to State, Defense, Southern Command, the Central American embassies and other military addressees for clearance. Later we would have to coordinate the approved text with the Hondurans.

The statement and responses to questions underwent some revision during the clearance process, but their substance was unchanged.

ALLEGED HONDURAN PARTICIPATION IN PERQUIN OPERATION: TEGUCIGALPA, HONDURAS, SEPTEMBER 2, 1981. Rebel spokesmen alleged that Honduran forces participated in the Salvadoran Army's recapture of Perquin. Allegedly, one or more companies from the Honduran Tenth Battalion, stationed in Marcala, had joined the attack. This unit supposedly entered the disputed territory and attacked Perquin from the north, coordinating its operations with Salvadoran forces attacking from the south. These reports were soon echoed by the Coordinator for Solidarity with the Salvadoran People and picked up by the local media. As usual, the government and the military ignored the allegations, making no public comment.

We were dubious and curious. If the Hondurans had participated in a joint operation, they had broken new ground. Defense attache and Milgroup officers could find nothing to substantiate these reports. Moreover, one of our visiting training groups had been with the Tenth Battalion for several days immediately following the Perquin operation and had seen no indication that its units had been mobilized or seen recent action. One Tenth Battalion officer, however, claimed to have led a five- or six-man patrol into the Sabanetas disputed area several days before the Salvadoran operation.

A Defense attache report from San Salvador provided an explanation, confirming that the entire operation had been conducted by Salvadoran forces. They had airlifted an airborne company into the area north of Perquin, allowing a coordinated attack from both directions.[11] We speculated that the airborne company's distinctive uniforms may have confused the guerrillas, causing them to think Hondurans were involved.[12]

ELECTIONS DELAY REPRISE WITH PAZ: TEGUCIGALPA, HONDURAS, SEPTEMBER 3, 1981. I was instructed to get back to Paz posthaste and to let him know, in strong terms, that we believed delaying the electoral process would be a serious mistake.[13] I called his office immediately, and he agreed to see me that afternoon. Just before our meeting I received a phone call from the new director of Central American affairs, Craig Johnstone, advising that another trip by General Walters was under consideration to underscore our concerns. He wanted my views; I promised to get back to him after meeting with Paz.

Paz was subdued, probably having a good idea of what I would say. I told him that I had relayed his concerns to Washington and been instructed to discuss this issue further. Specifically, he should understand that my government greatly appreciated his willingness to share these concerns with us. Beyond that, Washington supported elections as scheduled, had specifically endorsed the arguments I had raised with him earlier and asked that I give him several additional points he should take into account:

• We believed any delay in elections would represent a serious blow to our mutual efforts to resolve Honduras's economic and social problems;
• Secretary of State Haig and Assistant Secretary Enders, on repeated occasions, had stressed the importance we attach to the electoral process in Honduras and Central America; and

• Our economic and military assistance had been justified to Congress on the basis of Honduras's progress toward democracy; a delay would prejudice continued congressional support for that assistance.

I also added that Secretary Haig was considering sending General Walters back to Honduras to emphasize our concerns. Perhaps exceeding my instructions, I offered to consider any suggestions he might have as to how we could assist him in ensuring elections were held on schedule.

Paz had become more downcast by the minute but took careful note of each point, interrupting on several occasions to ensure that he recorded them accurately. Regarding our possible help with elections, he said he would give it some thought and get back to me, adding that he planned to assemble the party leaders, as I had earlier suggested. In reporting this meeting to Washington, I was overly sanguine:

> "Paz evidently anticipated the message I was bearing...and [was] perceptibly downcast upon my departure.... From his standpoint we have just put paid to what may have been his last scheme for remaining in a power position after January 1981.... Nevertheless, I believe we can count on Paz to report accurately to the Superior Council on USG position. At this point I believe we have pretty well spiked the idea of postponing the elections. The next key date will be September 29, when electoral tribunal is due to conclude review of electoral lists; after that date no one can be added to or taken off the rolls. If we can get past that date without a crunch, there appear to be few obstacles (other than pre-emptive *coup*, which I would currently judge as highly unlikely) to elections.... On basis of above assessment, proposed Walters visit is not as urgent as it was, but I still believe it would be helpful to reinforce our message."[14]

Despite this upbeat assessment, I asked the CT to keep its collective ear to the ground for any further indications that this plan might be gaining support and to continue repeating our mantra of support. The results of our soundings confirmed near unanimous support for elections on schedule, the only dissenting views coming from senior officers and Zuniga's band. This too we reported to State.[15]

Nonetheless, General Walters would return to reemphasize our position.

LABOR PROBLEMS SURFACE IN NICARAGUA: MANAGUA, NICARAGUA, EARLY SEPTEMBER 1981. The Sandinistas' earlier declaration of a state of "economic and social emergency," which made strikes and work stoppages a crime, met with resistance from workers and unions, including those affiliated with the Sandinista front. In a meeting with our chargé d'affaires, Roger Gamble, Sandinista leader Bayardo Arce accused the American Institute of Free Labor Development, which was still active there, of engaging "in subversive activities against our government."[16]

ANOTHER ROTARY INVITATION: TEGUCIGALPA, HONDURAS, EARLY SEPTEMBER 1981. Apparently not wishing to be upstaged by its San Pedro Sula counterpart, the Tegucigalpa Rotary called to invite me to speak at its October meeting. This offer was also too opportune to refuse. I again charged Walker to take the lead in drafting a speech that would pour the old wine of our support for the transition to democracy and the private sector's critical role therein into a new bottle. Wackerbarth, Higgins and Arcos all contributed to this effort.

MILITARY REQUESTS RIOT-CONTROL TRAINING: TEGUCIGALPA, HONDURAS, SEPTEMBER 8, 1981. The Honduran General Staff asked that we provide crowd- and riot-control training for army units in Tegucigalpa, San Pedro Sula and La Ceiba. They were assigned to back up FUSEP in case of large-scale civil unrest and were wholly unprepared for that role. Historically, Honduran elections had provoked extensive civil disorder. Although the previous year's elections had been orderly, President Paz and other senior officers now feared the extreme left would seek to provoke rioting, hence this request. And because the elections were less than three months away, the request had some urgency.

It was in our interest that the army be able to deal with large, unruly crowds effectively and with a minimum of violence, if elections were held. That was a big if, given what we knew of the high command's intentions. On the other hand, if the military delayed or otherwise foreclosed the promised elections and popular protest ensued, we would find ourselves in the position of having recently trained the forces being used to repress citizens protesting the military's antidemocratic action. We would be helping the military defeat our overarching policy goal.

We parsed this conundrum extensively in the political-military committee and decided to go ahead. I authorized Colonel Goodwin to pass the request to Southern Command and advised State of our decision.[17]

WALTERS VISITS AGAIN, URGES ELECTIONS AS SCHEDULED: TEGUCIGALPA, HONDURAS, SEPTEMBER 9, 1981. General Vernon Walters arrived appearing tired and grumpy. He was not pleased to be back in Tegucigalpa. We proceeded directly to President Paz's office at General Staff headquarters for an extended discussion. With no anecdotes and little introduction, Walters moved directly to the point. Honduran elections, he said, were a fine example for the world and Latin America especially. The United States, he continued, was delighted that the Honduran government was encouraging its people to express their political will and hoped they would cast their votes on schedule: the electoral process was a critical political safety valve.

Paz, obviously uncomfortable, agreed but then recited the familiar problems that caused him to consider delaying the vote. There was an extended discussion, with Paz rationalizing and Walters reiterating the same point: the United States wanted a solution to the registration problem so that elections could go ahead. If they should be postponed, Walters added, he would have to try to explain what had happened to our Congress, an extremely difficult task. Paz was getting the message, and he didn't like it. Finally, he said he would convene the party leaders before going to Mexico September 13 to resolve the electoral rolls problem. After more than an hour, Paz ushered us into another room where four Colonels—Alvarez, Torres Arias, Bonilla and Bueso Rosa—were waiting, then departed.

They opened by citing the growing threat posed by the Nicaraguan arms buildup and the possibility that the "communists" would take over in El Salvador. The longer we waited to do something about Nicaragua, they opined, the higher the cost would be in terms of Honduran blood. Regarding El Salvador, they repeated Salvadoran military complaints about the inadequacy of our assistance—the insurgents were allegedly getting more arms and equipment than they were. Of course that was nonsense. Having let them ventilate, Walters stated flatly that the United States would not let the insurgents win in El Salvador, period.

As for Nicaragua, he said the Sandinistas were at a crossroads, and once they chose their path, we would respond appropriately. But he had come to talk about Honduras.

It was essential, Walters emphasized, that elections go forward on schedule. Citing Paz's plan to meet with party leaders, Walters asked Alvarez if there was time to solve the questionable voters problem before the November election. Alvarez said there was, and the others seemed to agree. With that admission in hand Walters reiterated the importance of holding to the elections schedule. The discussion then shifted to the military's unhappiness with Liberal Party candidate Suazo Cordova, who had again declined to accompany Paz on his official visit to Mexico, and their need for greatly increased military assistance. Walters ignored the first point and made reassuring noises about the second but no commitments.

We went directly to the chancery, where Walters quickly drafted a cable. He concluded that the military had already decided to postpone the elections but might not implement their decision, writing as follows: "In my own personal opinion, they have decided to postpone the elections, perhaps for six months, to try to work out the voter registration problem, although this decision may not be implemented for one reason or another."[18]

Not, I thought, a very risky assessment. I told Walters that we believed the voter registration issue was a specious rationalization for stopping the electoral process. Nor was I as certain that a decision had in fact been made, but it was his cable. I then took him to the airport, his mission in Honduras completed. There was no publicity about his visit, but he had laid it on the line with Paz and the colonels.

ELECTIONS WILL GO FORWARD, ALVAREZ SAYS: TEGUCIGALPA, HONDURAS, SEPTEMBER 10, 1981. The station chief and I had a meeting with Colonel Alvarez to deal with the arms interdiction program. Those matters disposed of, I raised the elections question. They were, Alvarez replied, an important factor in the overall security equation. The left—including Honduran subversives, the Sandinistas and the Salvadoran insurgents—wished to block them and exploit the ensuing unrest. For its part, the United States had made it clear that delay of elections could prejudice continued economic and military assistance; Paz had read back my earlier talking points verbatim to key senior officers, and Walters had reaffirmed that position unequivocally. So despite their very real concerns about irregularities in the electoral rolls, the military would ensure elections went forward on schedule. But they did not want to be blamed for irregularities or other problems if the process turned sour. Party leaders would have to agree to purge the rolls by a certain date. Otherwise, the military would issue a public statement: describing what they saw as electoral irregularities and the shortcomings of the parties; "guaranteeing" that the elections would be held November 29; and disavowing any responsibility for the outcome and aftermath. In sum: elections would go ahead as planned, but the military institution would not accept responsibility for the consequences unless the party leaders cleaned up their act.

I told him that what he had described was a wise and prudent decision and that I would report his assurances to Washington. In that report, I stated that the electoral process seemed to be back on track, and that the embassy would be in touch with key leaders of all parties, urging that they cooperate fully in what appeared to be a good-faith effort to ensure elections were held on November 29.[19] I was pretty certain, however, that Paz, Zuniga, and the others seeking to block the process had not thrown in the towel.

RECONSIDERING RIOT-CONTROL TRAINING: TEGUCIGALPA, HONDURAS, SEPTEMBER 10, 1981 Despite Alvarez's assurances, I was having second thoughts about the riot-control training. Elections were still far from certain, and if they were postponed, there was likely to be widespread rioting and disorder. After reopening this issue with Walker, Goodwin and our political staff, I became convinced that provision of this training could lay the groundwork for a moral and public relations disaster. We couldn't allow ourselves to be placed in the position of helping repress those who supported our principal policy goal.

Accordingly, I cabled State conditioning my earlier approval of this training.[20] Should elections be delayed or blocked by extralegal means, the training would be canceled. That effectively placed the training, which Southern Command planned to launch in October, in suspense until the elections picture cleared. Goodwin was distressed by my decision, and Southern Command was outraged.

TIME FOR A GETAWAY: TEGUCIGALPA, HONDURAS, SEPTEMBER 11, 1981. Martha and I decided to get away by ourselves for a few days. Elections seemed to be back on track, and I was confident Walker could handle whatever came up with skill and aplomb. I obtained permission to be absent from post and made a couple of phone calls to friends in London. We would be welcome there and were on our way, to return September 20.

SALVADORAN ARMY TAKES THE OFFENSIVE: PROVINCIAL AREAS, EL SALVADOR, SEPTEMBER 14, 1981. The Salvadoran Army launched major search-and-destroy operations against the insurgents in eight of the country's fourteen provinces. These attacks represented the Army's largest offensive operation up to that time; there was heavy fighting.[21]

SOUTHERN COMMAND QUESTIONS HOLD ON RIOT-CONTROL TRAINING: TEGUCIGALPA, HONDURAS, SEPTEMBER 17, 1981. Colonel Goodwin received a very testy message from Southern Command regarding the riot-control training that accused the embassy of damaging our relations with the Honduran military. As the Honduran military's desire to postpone elections and our efforts to dissuade them from this course were highly sensitive, Southern Command had not been fully informed of those developments and so was in the dark as to my reasons for blocking this training. But they correctly assumed this action would be resented.

After consultation, Walker and Goodwin decided an embassy response could await my return. Goodwin, however, sent an interim reply that described the Honduran military's negative reaction to our blocking of the riot-control training but without contextual background.[22] That intensified the command's dyspepsia.

DEFENSE DEPARTMENT ANNOUNCES *HALCON VISTA* EXERCISE: WASHINGTON, D.C., SEPTEMBER 18, 1981. The Pentagon spokesman announced that U.S. and Honduran forces would hold a three-day joint military exercise in Honduras October 7–10, 1981.[23] To no one's surprise, the Sandinista government protested, charging that it was an aggressive act. The Sandinistas characterized it as "aggressive and warlike," a "provocation," an "imperialist ambush" and a threat to Nicaragua. And they lost no time trying to exploit it to their advantage. Daniel Ortega led the charge in his regular September 18 radio broadcast and was quickly joined by others. The answer, they claimed, was for Nicaragua to strengthen its defenses. Our embassy reported that the government was "principally using *Halcon Vista* to rally Nicaraguans to the militias."[24] Later, Nicaragua raised the issue at the UN General Assembly.

DUARTE VISITS WASHINGTON, SEEKS MORE AID: WASHINGTON, D.C., SEPTEMBER 20–22, 1981. Salvadoran junta president Napoleon Duarte began his first official visit to Washington, meeting with President Reagan, Vice President Bush and Secretary Haig, among others. He requested additional military assistance, with communications equipment the highest priority, and $300 million in new economic aid.[25]

SOUTHERN COMMAND AND ANOTHER VISITOR: TEGUCIGALPA, HONDURAS, SEPTEMBER 21, 1981. On my return from London, I learned of Southern Command's dyspepsia over the riot-control training issue and decided to send a personal cable to General Nutting, laying out the background of the election postponement issue and the reasons for my decision. Goodwin was not optimistic that it would do much to calm the waters, and he was probably right.

I explained how the Honduran military had tried to block elections, the concerns that effort raised in Washington, my instructions, the Walters visit, and the possible consequences of postponement. Therefore, I had reconsidered my earlier support for riot-control training. That many Honduran military officers deeply resented our efforts to frustrate their plans was not surprising, but our overriding consideration was the broader interests, not pleasing the Honduran military. The maintenance of good relations was not an end in itself but a means to serve our national interests.[26] I had no difficulty deciding that the notional benefits of good relations with the military were far less important than keeping elections on schedule.

Our new ambassador to the OAS, William Middendorf, was due to arrive late in the afternoon and would be in town until the following evening. He would stay at the residence, and would tie me up much of the next day. A Reagan crony, Middendorf was a neophyte in Latin American affairs and spoke no Spanish. Walker had set up a CT briefing at the residence, beginning at 6:30 P.M., to be followed by dinner at the Chico Club. The next day I was scheduled to take Middendorf to meet the acting foreign minister (Elvir was traveling) and the local OAS representative.

Middendorf displayed little interest in the substance of our policy in Honduras or in what was happening there. He was, however, extremely interested in Honduran primitive art, buying a couple dozen paintings, some of which cost several thousand dollars.

When I suggested that he affirm to the press that the United States continued to support the transition process and elections on schedule, Middendorf demurred. He preferred not to address internal political matters. I was astounded: he was the first official visitor to refuse to publicly endorse this policy goal. The next day, when the press caught up with us at the Foreign Ministry, Middendorf stuck to his resolve. His failure to endorse elections was noted: "The diplomat did not wish to opine [on the electoral process when asked], which left journalists surprised, since such an attitude is unusual for American diplomats."[27] It was not helpful.

NEW RIGHT-WING PARTY IN EL SALVADOR: SAN SALVADOR, EL SAL-
VADOR, SEPTEMBER 21, 1981. Roberto D'Aubuisson, a cashiered army major,
announced the formation of a new ultra right-wing political party, the
National Republican Alliance (ARENA). D'Aubuisson had a long history of
involvement with rightist death squads, masterminded the assassination of
Archbishop Oscar Romero and was involved in plotting against the junta
government. His new party was to enjoy substantial support from the Salvadoran oligarchy and private sector.[28] It also had some support in ultra-conservative American circles.

TERRORISTS MACHINE-GUN AMERICAN MILITARY TRAINERS: TEGU-
CIGALPA, HONDURAS, SEPTEMBER 22, 1981. The CT meeting started without Colonel Goodwin, who had not shown up. About a half hour into the
meeting Amy interrupted to tell me Goodwin was on the phone. When I
answered, he advised me that a vehicle with five members of a Southern Command training team had been machine-gunned: two men had been seriously
wounded, but the other three were unharmed. The attack occurred about an
hour earlier, as their vehicle entered the drive to Milgroup headquarters.
Goodwin was calling from the Honduran military hospital, where our
wounded had been taken, and reported that a medical evacuation aircraft was
en route from Panama to pick them up. The assailant had been standing at
a nearby bus stop, pulled a submachine gun from a bag and riddled the vehicle before jumping on a motorcycle and escaping. He had not been caught.

This was devastating news. I asked Goodwin to keep me or Walker
informed of developments and hung up. I briefed the others and told them
to return to their offices immediately, advise their personnel of this development and tighten security as best they could. The meeting was over. Walker
advised State's Operations Center and set up an emergency response team,
drawing on other staff as needed. He would serve as the central coordinating point until this crisis was put to rest. The station chief went off to FUSEP
to find out what they were doing to locate those responsible and to set up a
coordinating channel. Clift alerted the Marine guards and the civilian guard
contractor, advised the regional security office in Panama and stepped up
security at our facilities. We expected USIS would be inundated with press
inquiries, so Arcos needed to prepare press guidance.

I still had to worry about Middendorf, then at the residence waiting for
me to pick him up. I sent my car and security detail to the residence to bring
him to the chancery. I called Martha to tell her what was happening, ask that
she advise Middendorf of the change in plans, and remain at home. When
Middendorf arrived, we went directly to the Foreign Ministry. Surprisingly,
he revealed little comprehension of basic protocol. On our way to the Foreign Ministry he repeatedly demanded to stop the car so that he could be
photographed against various backdrops. Consequently, we were over a half

hour late. I don't recall how we got Middendorf to the airport, but I wasn't sorry to see him go.

In retrospect, I should probably have tried to reschedule the Foreign Ministry appointment and gone directly to the military hospital to visit our casualties. That would have been the right thing to do. By the time we finished at the ministry, the wounded were being loaded on the evacuation aircraft.

Back at the chancery Walker had things well in hand. FUSEP, however, had no clues as to who was responsible, and the assailant had gotten away without a trace. Off-duty Marines and civilian guards had been recalled, increasing guard presence at all our facilities; FUSEP had stationed a vehicle and guards in the chancery and annex area; and the Honduran military had posted armed guards at the Milgroup compound. All agencies had advised their employees of the incident, instructing them to vary their times and routes to and from work and take other precautions.

I had a meeting with a joint American/Honduran business group scheduled in our auditorium, and they were beginning to show up. Once assembled, I joined them long enough to explain what had happened and excuse myself from further participation, leaving the meeting in the hands of Wackerbarth and Higgins.

Shortly thereafter Enders phoned to check on the situation and suggest that I cancel my San Pedro Sula trip and speech. I demurred, pointing out that I did not wish to give the terrorists the satisfaction of having forced me to change my plans. Moreover, I believed the speech was important in terms of our policy objectives and would receive even greater media coverage in the wake of this incident. He accepted these arguments. His call, however, did cause me to focus on the need for security precautions in San Pedro, since my visit and program had been widely announced. I pulled Walker, the station chief, Clift and Arcos (because he would be accompanying me) together to make the required arrangements.

I had also scheduled an American businessmen's meeting in Tela the morning before the speech, which meant that Wackerbarth and Higgins would fly with us to Tela in the morning. Arcos and I would be dropped off in San Pedro Sula after that meeting, and the rest of the group would return to Tegucigalpa. The Defense attache would fly back to San Pedro Sula the following morning to pick us up.

Late in the afternoon FUSEP reported that the Lorenzo Zelaya Popular Revolutionary Command, the URP's paramilitary arm, had claimed responsibility for the attack. This group had earlier attacked our facilities and carried out other terrorist actions, including the airliner hijacking. But there were still no good leads as to who had actually carried it out.

We determined that the Southern Command trainers had failed to take even the most rudimentary security precautions. They had traveled to and from work at the same time every day, using the same vehicle and taking the same route. And they were always in uniform. They had made the terrorist's job easy. As a result of these findings, which were passed on to all mission officials as an object lesson, we reviewed basic security precautions with all staff members. Moreover, Milgroup changed its operating procedures to ensure that visiting military alternated arrival and departure times and rotated vehicles; armed Honduran military escorts would also be assigned; all our military personnel, including visitors, were instructed to wear civilian shirts or jackets over their uniforms when driving around the city. After considerable reflection, I declined to lift my prohibition on our military carrying weapons. There was no doubt that this incident raised our collective security consciousness, but two men had paid a very high price for that lesson.

In addition, Clift saw this incident as an opportunity to force faster action on our various and long-pending security enhancement projects. Had our vehicles been armored as promised, it is unlikely that attack would have produced casualties. State had been dragging its feet in implementing plans for both the chancery and annex, despite earlier promises of expeditious action. He urged that I again request State to speed up action, citing the attack as further justification for priority treatment. I agreed to do just that.

It had been the kind of a day one never forgets.[29]

FDR LEADER REJECTS ELECTION PARTICIPATION: MEXICO CITY, MEXICO, SEPTEMBER 22, 1981. Rebel political leader Guillermo Ungo, also head of the National Revolutionary Movement, rejected Duarte's call for an "electoral dialogue," alleging it was an attempt to divide the opposition.[30]

SAN PEDRO SULA SPEECH AND PRESS CONFERENCE: SAN PEDRO SULA, HONDURAS, SEPTEMBER 23–24, 1981. Reaching the hotel in San Pedro Sula, Arcos and I phoned our offices. Because of intense media interest in the events of the previous day, we decided to hold a press conference the next morning before returning to the capital. I left Arcos to make those arrangements while I reviewed my speech.

The Rotary had a full house for the dinner, and the media (which had advance copies of my text) were in attendance. Emphasizing the importance of the transition to democracy, I described the structure, reasons for and purposes of the recently announced Caribbean Basin Initiative (CBI) and outlined the role and responsibilities of the private sector. The lines that drew the most sustained applause were those dealing with corruption.[31] The audience seemed to like the overall message, giving me a standing ovation.

Following dinner, Arcos and I hung around to chat with Rotary members. Several of them congratulated me for having broached the corruption issue publicly but were dubious that things would be much better under an elected government. They also offered condolences for our wounded military. After a suitable time, we retired behind our security cordon.

Our press conference the following morning drew a sizable number of journalists who, for the most part, addressed subjects not covered in the speech. I opened the session with a brief statement reaffirming our support for elections as scheduled and stating that the attack on our military trainers would not weaken our resolve to continue economic and security assistance programs. Most of the questions addressed the terrorist attack and the *Halcon Vista* exercise, but our alleged efforts to make Honduras "our policeman" for the region and our support for the Nicaraguan Contras also received appreciable attention.

Responding to terrorist attack questions, I noted that it seemed to have been an "isolated" event, apparently carried out by the same group that had shot up our annex building the previous year. I also opined that the extreme left was not a growing force in Honduras. As to *Halcon Vista*, anyone who considered the forces involved—three U.S. patrol vessels, a small USAF contingent and some Honduran forces—would conclude that this event did not represent a threat to Nicaragua or anyone else. We had invited Nicaragua to send observers to witness the exercise, but the invitation had been rejected. The press would also be invited to observe and could draw its own conclusions based on what it saw. I flatly denied the "regional policeman" canard, as well as allegations of U.S. support for the Contras. I firmly denied the embassy had links with these exile groups. After about 40 minutes Arcos wound it up, and we headed for the airport.

POPULAR PROTEST OF GOVERNMENT REPRESSION: TEGUCIGALPA, HONDURAS, SEPTEMBER 24, 1981. A major popular demonstration against increasing government repression organized by left-wing groups brought several thousand people out to march in central Tegucigalpa. This was one of the largest demonstrations in years, and it was entirely peaceful.[32]

SENATE REQUIRES CERTIFICATION FOR SALVADORAN ASSISTANCE: WASHINGTON, D.C., SEPTEMBER 24, 1981. The Senate voted to require President Reagan to certify biannually that the Salvadoran government was making progress on human rights and political reforms as a condition for continued U.S. assistance. The House Foreign Affairs Committee approved a similar requirement.[33]

SOUTHERN COMMAND URGES APPROACH TO HONDURANS FOR "JOINT USE" BASE: TEGUCIGALPA, HONDURAS, SEPTEMBER 25, 1981. Shortly after my return, I met with Walker and Goodwin for a debrief on the latter's visit to Southern Command the previous week. The terrorist attack and my travels prevented our meeting earlier. While in Panama, he had been approached by a senior officer who asked that he "unofficially" inquire if the Hondurans would be receptive to a proposal for a "joint use" air base. To make such a deal attractive, he was told that the United States would fund completion of the Honduran air base at Comayagua, then under construction, in return for an agreement allowing the USAF use of that facility. This officer had stressed that Goodwin should avoid any implication that his inquiry represented a commitment; it was simply an "unofficial" request for information. Goodwin had taken no action on this, wanting my concurrence before doing so.

By the time he finished, I was livid. Such an inquiry would suggest a major change in our regional policy and could have far-reaching implications in Honduras and beyond. There was no indication that Washington was even aware of this idea, let alone had approved it; indeed, the nature of the request suggested that it was a purely Southern Command brainstorm. Establishment of a joint-use air base would be unprecedented in peace time and represent a major financial obligation.[34] There was no doubt that it would be viewed by the Sandinistas and their supporters as proof the United States was preparing to attack Nicaragua and would complicate our relations with allies in the hemisphere and Europe. Finally, it would whet Honduran military appetites for action against Nicaragua, which certainly needed no encouragement.

I was not about to allow Southern Command to take (or perhaps continue) such policy initiatives in Honduras. And there was no way, given the Honduran penchant for constructive interpretation, that such an approach could be made without implying a willingness on our part to commit. I thanked Goodwin for informing me, explained my reservations and directed him to refrain from raising this matter unless he heard further from me.

I immediately cabled State, with an information copy to General Nutting, describing the approach to Goodwin, setting out my concerns and requesting guidance.[35] To my amazement, State's reply came the same day. It said that Washington agencies were unaware of this proposal and, therefore, we should take no action. I so advised Goodwin, noting that this cable had also been sent to Southern Command.[36]

This raised the friction between the embassy and Southern Command to a new level. It was, however, an initiative that wouldn't die and one that we revisited during the following month. It should also be noted that within eight months the United States and Honduras signed a joint-use agreement for the Comayagua and other air bases at considerable cost to us.[37] These bases became the principal loci of later U.S. military operations in Honduras.

PAZ RENEWS PUSH TO DELAY ELECTIONS; DISSIDENT LIBERALS SEE OPPORTUNITY: TEGUCIGALPA, HONDURAS, SEPTEMBER 25, 1981. While I was in San Pedro Sula, a leader of the Liberals' dissident ALIPO faction advised me his group had met with President Paz a few days earlier. Paz asked that they support a "coup to prevent elections" in return for several cabinet positions in the successor government. Colonel Bueso Rosa had arranged the meeting. The *Alipistas* had asked Paz if he had a commitment to the United

States or other governments to hold elections November 29. He said not, leaving them with the impression that there would be no international obstacles to the delay. They told him they would think about his offer and, hence, wished to hear my views. Like Dracula, Paz's effort to postpone elections simply wouldn't die.

I told the ALIPO leader flatly that we were making every effort to ensure elections were held on schedule and that we had made that point very clear to Paz and senior officers on repeated occasions. There would, I stressed, be very serious repercussions if elections were not held on November 29.

He thanked me and said that ALIPO believed the delay of elections would provoke a political crisis. However, ALIPO had "documentary proof" that Suazo Cordova's faction had engaged in "serious fraud" in the party's recent candidate selection process. Unless Suazo Cordova and his allies were willing to give ALIPO "a fair shake and share of power," they would be tempted to support Paz's preemptive coup. Accordingly, he wondered if I would suggest to Suazo Cordova that he seek accommodation with ALIPO.

This was thinly disguised political extortion, and it got up my nose. But I didn't wish to do anything that might damage the transition process. I said that on several occasions I had offered private counsel to Suazo Cordova and his advisers but without much success. Because of the critical importance of elections, I would be willing to speak to Suazo Cordova about an accommodation with ALIPO, but I would not recommend any specific terms or actions. And I certainly could make no promises about how Suazo Cordova might react. In return, I would expect ALIPO to avoid anything that might jeopardize the electoral process. I did not get a firm commitment, but I had little choice but to proceed.

This information, which I reported,[38] had significance beyond ALIPO's political extortion effort. Foremost, it proved that Paz had not given up on postponing elections. Second, in the light of Alvarez's earlier assurances to me, Bueso Rosa's involvement as Paz's agent suggested a division within the military high command. That was critical information. A struggle among the senior officers could change the power equation dramatically, perhaps even preserving the transition. Unless I received instructions to the contrary, I told State, I planned to broach the ALIPO problem with Suazo Cordova. That would place me, and by extension the United States, more deeply in Honduran factional politics than was proper or desirable. I did not receive instructions to desist and so proceeded.

MEDIA COVERAGE OF SPEECH AND PRESS CONFERENCE: TEGUCIGALPA, HONDURAS, SEPTEMBER 25, 1981. *La Prensa* and *Tiempo* reprinted the complete text of my speech under headlines emphasizing the critical role of private enterprise and trade unions in democracy and the corrosive effects of governmental corruption. Two radio stations also broadcast the speech, one live and the other the following day. Moreover, two days later *La Prensa* followed with an editorial elaborating on both themes and then revisited these topics the following week.[39] We couldn't have done better ourselves.

Coverage of the press conference was also extensive, but it stressed the sensational over the substantive. The attack on our military advisers and my denial of U.S. plans to make Honduras the regional "policeman" were the main headline themes, but nearly all accounts repeated my principal points evenhandedly. Unfortunately, none highlighted my reaffirmation of our support for elections, although that point was included in the body of most articles.[40]

We had accomplished our goals. Indeed, I even imagined that I could hear the gnashing of teeth coming from the General Staff and Zuniga's house. I had received congratulations from many business leaders and a few trade unionists; it seemed that my cautionary words on corruption had struck an especially responsive chord. Much of the credit for this public diplomacy success was due to Arcos's excellent relations with all the media, as well as his contribution to the speech itself.

NEW DAS PLANS VISIT, ADVISES OF ANNOUNCEMENT OF MY REPLACEMENT: TEGUCIGALPA, HONDURAS, SEPTEMBER 25, 1981. I received a phone call, followed by a cable, from Enders's new deputy assistant secretary, Everett "Ted" Briggs, who was responsible for the Central American region. Briggs would be in El Salvador and wondered if it would be convenient to stop in Honduras September 30 on his way back to Washington. I said we would welcome his visit.[41] It would, I thought, give the CT and me an opportunity to get a better understanding of where our policy was headed. Things at the time were still extremely opaque, at least to me. And it would give us another shot at President Paz along with one more chance to get our message to the public.

Briggs also told me that State expected the White House to announce the nomination of John Negroponte during the coming week. He had no idea how quickly the Senate would act to confirm but assured me that Enders was aware of the possible political impact of the announcement and of my desire to remain at post until the elections. Later Enders would ask that I leave by October 31.

I immediately passed this news on to Foreign Minister Elvir and advised the CT at our next meeting. No one was surprised. I also initiated preparations for a comprehensive briefing book to bring Ambassador-designate Negroponte up to speed on our program and the issues he would be confronting. This book, I emphasized, would be Negroponte's first impression of the mission and its leadership; accordingly, it behooved them all to do the best job they could. And they did.

Every agency submitted a description of its organization, operational goals and the strategies it was pursuing to realize the desired ends. Other background papers were prepared describing the major Honduran institutions; the political, economic and security environment; and specific problem areas, such as corruption in government. As part of this process, the CT also identified nine critical issues the new ambassador would have to deal with early in his tenure and mapped out recommended strategies. My goal was to give Negroponte the basic information he would need to hit the ground running.

I asked Walker to ramrod this effort and assigned a junior officer to assist him. We needed to send the completed book to Washington posthaste. Initial drafts had to be completed by October 5. Walker and I would review them, suggest changes as appropriate and return them for final revision as quickly as possible. Our deadline for completion of the book was October 7. Walker and others would be burning some midnight oil.

PROMISES, PROMISES: SECURITY PROGRAM STASIS: TEGUCIGALPA, HONDURAS, SEPTEMBER 28, 1981. I was finally able to complete the cable demanding expeditious action in our security enhancement projects that Clift had suggested. The most dramatic recent examples of the escalating threat were the attack on the Southern Command training team and the mass protest of growing government repression. But the problem was greater than these incidents. I was concerned with the potential consequences of the U.S. military presence along the Salvadoran frontier, leftist allegations that we were responsible for Honduran human rights abuses and for "regionalizing" of the Salvadoran conflict, and the growing assertiveness of the unified Contras. Any of these could provoke further terrorist actions against the U.S. mission and personnel.

State's lack of urgency on our security enhancement program—which had been undertaken on a "crash" basis in February—was unconscionable. Our repeated pleas for faster action had little result. In view of my impending replacement I had nothing to lose by raising the failings of the security bureau and foreign buildings office at a high level and in forceful terms, so I did.

With input from Clift and Walker, the cable was a detailed critique of promises made but not fulfilled, juxtaposed with the growing threat to all our employees, American and Honduran. If this negligence should result in more casualties, I wanted the blood to be on State's hands. The principal complaints were these:

• Eight months after plans were developed and approved for the annex building accommodating over one hundred employees, absolutely nothing had been accomplished.

• The vehicle armoring program—which could have prevented injuries to the two wounded Southern Command officials—was far behind schedule, four armoring kits (weighing over 2 tons) had simply disappeared en route to Tegucigalpa, and State had unilaterally decided that the AID director's new car need not be armored. Neither Oleson nor I agreed with that decision.

• Bulletproof glass (Lexguard) for the executive offices, which overlooked the street and were the venue for senior staff meetings several times a week, had not been shipped, despite repeated requests.[42]

The cable drew a defensive reaction and more promises, but it didn't result in notable progress during the month I remained in Tegucigalpa. Extensive work was completed later, substantially strengthening the physical security of our facilities.

SUAZO CORDOVA ON ELECTIONS AND ALIPO COMPLAINTS: TEGUCIGALPA, HONDURAS, SEPTEMBER 28, 1981. I opened my meeting with Suazo Cordova by asking how the electoral rolls negotiations were proceeding. He was confident a workable plan had been agreed to for purging the rolls and that elections would go forward on schedule. The two minor parties were totally in agreement with the Liberals, but the National Party continued to be ambivalent. Publicly, its leaders supported elections on November 29, but privately they were equivocal.

When I inquired about negotiations with ALIPO, he responded with the candid opinion that full accommodation would not be possible. ALIPO, he said, was demanding six or seven "safe seats" in the legislature in return for full support of the Liberal ticket. Candidate slates had already been selected by provincial conferences, and there was no way to reopen that matter under party bylaws. If he tried to do so, he would split the dominant Rodista faction, as well as violate the bylaws and democratic norms. Nonetheless, he was willing to negotiate other issues with ALIPO—party organization, the party platform, and even cabinet and subcabinet posts. As to ALIPO's threat to challenge the allegedly fraudulent internal proceedings before the Electoral Tribunal or the courts, Suazo Cordova did not believe they had a leg to stand on. The tribunal's mandate specifically excluded matters of internal party governance, and previous attempts to involve the courts had been unsuccessful.

I left the meeting persuaded that Suazo Cordova would not accommodate ALIPO on candidates. He regarded their threats as minimal, and he was probably right. On the other hand, he seemed to indicate some flexibility on other issues, and I so advised my contact. Beyond that, I avoided further engagement in this internal dispute.[43]

REPORTS OF MY REPLACEMENT FUEL CONCERNS: TEGUCIGALPA, HONDURAS, SEPTEMBER 28, 1981. Over the previous weekend Carlos Roberto Reina, president of the Inter-American Human Rights Court and ALIPO leader (and later president of Honduras), told Walker that he had heard that I would soon be replaced. Didn't the State Department realize, he asked, "that the Ambassador's replacement during the delicate pre-election period would send a strong and negative signal" to Honduran political leaders? Walker said he was not aware of plans to replace me but agreed that my replacement before the elections would send the wrong signal.

Arcos had also been approached with the same question and a similar observation. In his case it was the leader of one of the minor parties who asked for confirmation (which he didn't receive) and observed that a change at this juncture would be "very, very unfortunate." News of my impending departure was clearly on the streets because Suazo Cordova too had raised the subject with me in our meeting. He said he had been told by National Party leader Mario Rivera Lopez that I would be replaced "within the next couple of weeks." If true, Suazo opined, the United States would be making a serious mistake.

I decided to come clean with Suazo Cordova. I confirmed that I was being replaced, although it certainly wouldn't be within the next two weeks. The timing would be dictated by the speed with which the Senate confirmed my successor. I also asked Suazo to honor my confidence on this matter until the official announcement was made, which I expected in the next few days. He agreed, but we both knew he would have a hard time doing so. I also stressed that regardless of the timing, our position on elections remained unchanged: they should be held as scheduled.

I reported these observations without comment.[44]

BASE PROPOSAL DRAWS SOUTHERN COMMAND "EXPLANATION" AND RIPOSTE: HOWARD AIR FORCE BASE, PANAMA, AND TEGUCIGALPA, HONDURAS, SEPTEMBER 29, 1981. My cable on the joint-use air base notion, and State's unequivocal reply thereto, finally produced a response from the Southern Command's U.S. Air Force element commander.[45] As best I recall, it was a pretty lame effort, explaining how a member of his staff had approached Colonel Goodwin on this subject and maintaining that the conversation was private and should not have been passed on to me. Most ironically, at least in my view, it concluded with a rather snide comment that in the future he would appreciate advance coordination on issues concerning his command. That was too rich to ignore.

I fired back a cable indicating that I shared his preference for coordination of issues involving Honduras and, indeed, had a statutory basis to demand it. In this case the embassy had not been consulted and would have objected to raising this issue with the Hondurans. I went on to explain that position.

Should the Hondurans raise this idea on their own initiative, I suggested that, based on State's instructions, the proper response would be to say the matter had to be referred to Washington for consideration.[46]

This did not put an end to Southern Command's efforts to advance its agenda behind our back.

WHITE HOUSE ANNOUNCES NEGROPONTE NOMINATION, MY RESIGNATION: WASHINGTON, D.C., SEPTEMBER 29, 1981. The White House announced the nomination of John D. Negroponte as ambassador to Honduras and the acceptance of my resignation. This story was picked up from the wire services and hit the local airwaves that afternoon. The following day it made front-page headlines in two papers and was covered by all.[47]

El Heraldo, often Zuniga's mouthpiece, gloated that this announcement confirmed its report published six weeks earlier, which the embassy had characterized as speculation. The weekly *La Republica* also published an editorial criticizing the "form, not the content" of my support for the electoral process and hoping that the new ambassador would be more respectful of Honduran "dignity." *Tiempo* was more generous, judging somewhat hyperbolically that I had "had very great success" in my mission and that I was "highly respected in all political, economic, social and cultural circles." Other papers were more evenhanded, limiting themselves to reporting the facts.

LAND SCANDAL RAISES CORRUPTION CONCERNS: TEGUCIGALPA, HONDURAS, LATE SEPTEMBER 1981. The press broke a story detailing the sale, for several million dollars, of land actually owned by the government, back to the government. Minister of Finance Valentin Mendoza was directly implicated. He quickly resigned and left the country. What had happened to the money was not clear, but the whole affair seemed a bit blatant, even for Honduras. A tidal wave of speculation and rumor about corruption within the military and the two major political parties followed.

As details emerged, this incident seemed to suggest an internecine military struggle. The initial report of this transaction was conveyed to the Superior Council of the Armed Forces by Central Bank president Martinez, a confidant of Colonel Alvarez. The first public mention of it was by a radio newsman who had often been used by Colonel Torres Arias to float spurious stories or otherwise serve his interests. The upshot, on which virtually all observers agreed, was that Paz had been severely damaged; it seemed problematical that he could last in office until January, when the newly elected government was due to take office.[48] Reverberations would echo for some time.

DEPUTY ASSISTANT SECRETARY BRIGGS'S VISIT: TEGUCIGALPA, HONDURAS, SEPTEMBER 30–OCTOBER 1, 1981. The attache aircraft delivering

Briggs in Tegucigalpa landed shortly after noon. We went directly to the residence for lunch. I pressed him to lay out precisely what our regional policies were and where we expected them to take us. His responses were uninformative, so I pushed harder. Finally, he answered, leaving me astonished. He simply didn't know and was as much in the dark as I was. Enders, he said, played his policy cards very close to his vest and had not shared much about his intentions with others.

My immediate thought was that Briggs was conning me. The situation he described, in which an assistant secretary did not share his plans and strategies with his principal deputy for a region, seemed incredible. In retrospect, however, I suspect what Briggs told me was pretty accurate. It seems clear from other accounts of Enders's tenure that he was indeed playing a very careful and sometimes independent foreign policy game. In part, this was dictated by his awareness that others in the administration wanted nothing less than unremitting hostility toward Nicaragua and would seek to block anything that smacked of a more traditional diplomatic approach. Moreover, my own later experience as Enders's deputy in Madrid confirmed his preference for not sharing all his plans with others.

After lunch, we went to the embassy, where Briggs was briefed and had an opportunity to visit with several State officers. That evening I hosted a buffet dinner in his honor, inviting the presidential candidates and other political and private sector leaders. The next morning I took him to see Foreign Minister Elvir and President Paz. During the session with Paz, Briggs once again emphasized the importance of holding elections as planned, a message that he reiterated when speaking with the press as we left the Foreign Ministry.[49] From there it was to the airport to catch his plane.

10

Coup Attempt Fails as I Wind Up

SUMMARY—Our support for the transition continues—planned coup collapses when Air Force commander and others defend elections—military imposes "conditions" on party leaders—efforts to prevent election continue and we counter—new data reveal economy is in critical shape—further conflict over joint military exercise—demonstration against embassy—key issues facing new ambassador defined—some Salvadoran rebels favor negotiations and begin to target infrastructure—Sandinistas protest *Halcon Vista* and repress opposition—I depart Honduras.

SALVADORAN MEDIATION EFFORT FOUNDERS: PANAMA CITY, PANAMA, OCTOBER 2, 1981. The Salvadoran insurgent coalition accepted in principle Panama's offer to mediate between them and the Salvadoran junta government. The junta rejected this initiative.[1]

DOCUMENT REVEALS FDR/DRU NEGOTIATING STRATEGY: SAN SALVADOR, EL SALVADOR, OCTOBER 4, 1981. A captured rebel coalition analysis and strategy document favored seeking a negotiated solution to the conflict.[2] Its premise was that negotiations were essential to avoid direct U.S. military intervention, which the rebels believed would provoke an extended and unwinnable war, with an enormous loss of civilian life. The preconditions for negotiations, however, seemed like the demands of a military victor.

It was never clarified if this document represented rebel policy or was merely a discussion paper. But it indicated that part of the coalition believed the war might be unwinnable, even at that early date.

PLANNING MY DEPARTURE AND IMMEDIATE FUTURE: TEGUCIGALPA, HONDURAS, EARLY OCTOBER 1981. Once my October 31 departure was fixed, I advised the foreign minister and the dean of the Diplomatic Corps, as both customarily hosted farewell dinners. The balance of the month would be something of a social whirl.

I also phoned the Director General of the Foreign Service to inquire about onward assignment. She was aware of nothing on the horizon other than a "Diplomat in Residence" position.[3] I was able to arrange an assignment to the University of California's Institute of International Studies. With that issue resolved, the world seemed much brighter.

HALCON VISTA PLANS VIOLATE GUIDELINES: SAN PEDRO SULA, HONDURAS, OCTOBER 5, 1981. I flew to San Pedro Sula to meet with General Nutting and senior Honduran officers for a final briefing on the exercise set to begin in two days. We gathered at the Honduran Air Force base. As the Southern Command briefers described the scope of the exercise I realized that it had been expanded beyond what had been agreed to in the "Letter of Intent." Even more troubling, the planned activities of the U.S. units exceeded what we had announced in our press statements and outlined in the carefully crafted exercise guidance. Southern Command planners had ignored the agreed-upon exercise parameters, reached only after agonizing interagency debate.[4]

I could scarcely believe what I was hearing. I was seated between Nutting and Goodwin and quickly asked the former to suspend the briefing. He was not enchanted but agreed. Our Honduran hosts were surprised by the interruption, but at that point I was beyond caring what they might think. Nutting and I went to an adjoining room, accompanied by his chief of staff and his senior exercise director and Colonels Goodwin and Bollert. I expressed my surprise and anger over what appeared to be a unilateral expansion of the exercise scope and the planning group's failure to consult with the embassy on these changes. As a result, I noted, we found ourselves in the compromising position of having issued a press statement and guidance that U.S. forces would not be involved in landing the infiltrating units, yet we would be doing just the opposite. Our Air Force had also expanded its role from logistic support to actual operations. In addition to making us liars, these changes would give the Sandinistas another stick with which to beat us in international forums. Both were unacceptable.

The exercise director said he had agreed to these changes at Honduran request. He had no explanation for the failure to consult. Nutting said that he too had been unaware of these changes, having learned of them in the briefing. He agreed that both he and I should have been consulted before such changes were accepted. But because we had already committed ourselves to the Hondurans, he did not believe we should change the exercise at that juncture. I was not prepared to accept a fait accompli. Reaffirming my unwillingness to be placed in a position where we would appear to have lied in our press statement, I said that if we couldn't agree on how to deal with this matter, it would have to be referred to Washington for interagency resolution, even if that meant delaying the exercise. That got their attention and left them fuming.

After some hard bargaining, it was agreed that Honduran patrol craft, not U.S., would be used to land the infiltrating forces. Because the Hondurans did not have enough helicopters to meet exercise troop lift requirements I reluctantly agreed to that change. The briefing was resumed, and the briefers announced the alteration in landing plans and finished the briefing.

By the time we returned to Tegucigalpa, I had cooled off. I was tired of fighting with Nutting and his minions. I also had plenty of other things to worry about, as it was apparent that coup pressures were again building. I decided against cabling State about the *Halcon Vista* problems because it would do no good and only trigger another round of recriminations. A week later, after the first public demonstration against the embassy in many years, I wrote Enders informally to relate my experiences and assess the exercise.[5]

CHANTING THE MANTRA: TEGUCIGALPA SPEECH: TEGUCIGALPA, HONDURAS, OCTOBER 6, 1981. My speech to the Tegucigalpa Rotary was essentially a rehash of that in San Pedro Sula. One of the few noteworthy passages was a critique of the import substitution development model favored by many Latin American governments and which had historically been supported by U.S. development programs.[6] It had been lifted from one of Enders's recent speeches and received considerable attention. The Rotary provided a full house, with the business and commercial sectors represented by heavy hitters. The message was well received. Advance copies of the speech were sent to all media outlets, but coverage was far less than it had been for the earlier event. Only *La Prensa* gave it significant space, focusing almost exclusively on the development policy issue and the role envisaged for the private sector.[7] Nonetheless, it was worthwhile to have reiterated our "elections on schedule" message to this audience and to explore further how our development priorities were changing.

JOINT EXERCISE TRIGGERS ANTI–U.S. DEMONSTRATION: NORTHERN HONDURAS AND TEGUCIGALPA, HONDURAS, OCTOBER 7–8, 1981. *Halcon Vista* got underway the early morning of October 7, with Honduran patrol boats seeking to locate and stop the "infiltrating force" composed of three U.S. Navy patrol craft. The infiltrators were dutifully intercepted and neutralized by Honduran Air Force units. The second day saw the Honduran Navy land the infiltrating force on an isolated beach, while Army units tried to locate and neutralize it. From later accounts of our Milgroup officers, the exercise achieved most of its desired ends, providing the Hondurans with badly needed field operations and coordination experience. Other shortcomings—especially in communications—were also identified. This experience, we hoped, provided

With U.S. General Wallace Nutting (*far left*) and Honduran Chief of Staff Mario Chinchilla (*second from left*), receiving honors on arrival at the Puerto Cortez naval base during preparations for *Halcon Vista* exercise, October 1981. Honduran Navy commander Col. Ruben Montoya is visible over Gen. Chinchilla's shoulder.

a useful object lesson. I certainly hoped it would put a damper on their plans to attack Nicaragua.

From my vantage point, I didn't find it especially helpful to be seen collaborating closely and publicly with the Honduran military at a time when senior commanders, including the provisional president, were trying to block the transition to democracy. And because all the major political players were aware of the gyrations of Paz and his colleagues, their efforts could hardly be regarded as covert. There was another substantive reason for my displeasure as well.

On October 8 there was a major popular demonstration against the embassy and U.S. "imperialism." Several thousand people, mostly students and left-wing trade unionists, marched from city center to the chancery, waving signs, howling protests against *Halcon Vista*, jeering at Uncle Sam and demanding that "Yankees go home." It was an orderly march and smaller than that of two weeks earlier. FUSEP was out in force, so there had been no real danger to our installations or personnel. But it was the first time in at least five years that there had been a significant public demonstration directed against the U.S. embassy.[8]

Some of my colleagues suspected that this demonstration had been orchestrated by military officers seeking to block elections, but I thought not, because of the students and leftist union leaders involved. The pro-coup faction, however, stood to gain, being able to cite the demonstration as an example of the kind of "disorder" a new civilian government would bring. It also suggested there were limits to what the United States could do in Honduras without provoking popular backlash.

KEY ISSUES FACING THE NEW AMBASSADOR: TEGUCIGALPA, HONDURAS, OCTOBER 7–9, 1981. The CT members completed drafts of their respective portions of Negroponte's briefing book quickly, swamping Walker and me. Several of the issues papers also required extensive revision and rework, which necessitated a series of ad hoc meetings to clarify points and think through proposed implementing actions.[9] The book identified key policy issues addressing keeping elections on track, relations with the elected government, coping with the economic crisis and structuring our assistance program accordingly, managing Honduran external and internal security concerns, deterring human rights abuses and the Honduran role vis-à-vis Nicaragua and El Salvador. The strategies recommended for dealing with these issues were, I thought, sound, although several went further than I would have liked. But I wanted to give Negroponte the benefit of the CT's views rather than my own. Not surprisingly, those recommendations concerning human rights, security assistance and the Nicaragua and Salvadoran issues were at sharp variance with the path chosen by the Reagan administration.

The book was completed by our deadline and sent to State via diplomatic courier. Our American secretaries, who had typed nearly 200 pages of classified briefing papers, some several times, were frazzled. And so was Walker. I was very pleased with the book and the CT's performance in putting together a high-quality document in very short time. In retrospect, I believe we did a pretty good job identifying the issues, if not the strategies for dealing with them. Once the covert war against the Sandinistas became our central interest, it drove our Honduran policy. In addition to large-scale, supposedly clandestine, operations, this led to a dramatic increase in our military assistance levels, establishment of a substantial U.S. military presence and complicity in growing human rights abuses.

LAND SCANDAL FALLOUT THREATENS ELECTIONS: TEGUCIGALPA, HONDURAS, OCTOBER 8–9, 1981. As the land scandal continued to unfold, it became clear that military officers wishing to block the transition had not given up and were now using the corruption issue to create uncertainty. One of our private sector contacts estimated the probability that elections would not be held at 80 percent. I thought that overstated, but it may have reflected general expectations. I had charged all CT elements to be alert for anything that would shed some light on what was going on, and they were producing a lot of data. I was meeting frequently with senior staff, individually and collectively, in an effort to make sense out of what we were turning up.

As we analyzed developments, it appeared that one of the principal purposes of the planned coup was to constrain Colonel Alvarez's power, if not actually block his advancement to commander of the armed forces. The pro-coup faction was venal and considered Alvarez a threat. They had earlier used Paz as a cat's paw, playing on his desire to remain in office and citing electoral irregularities as the rationale to block elections. That strategy had failed. And after the land scandal broke, Paz had become a liability. It was hard to justify a coup in order to keep him in power. It seemed that the best way those threatened by Alvarez could neutralize him was by overturning the transition government, ousting Paz and installing a military junta. That would not prevent Alvarez's rise, but it would force him to share power with several other officers.

One loose end in this theory was Zuniga. He had to know what was going on and was no doubt a player at some level. Yet his hand was not visible. A coup would assure his continued domination of the National Party, provide renewed access to power and offer the prospect of gaining the presidency in a future election. He had worked closely with several of the pro-coup group previously, including Torres Arias, and was no doubt confident of his ability to manipulate any new junta government to his advantage.

Who was leading the pro-coup group? Torres Arias appeared to be the primus inter pares, but Colonels Bueso Rosa, Bodden and, we thought, Montoya were also key players. Bueso Rosa and Bodden, not coincidentally, happened to command the San Pedro Sula and Tegucigalpa military garrisons, critical positions in the event of a military putsch.

Drawing on this theory, I cabled State that we saw an increasingly dangerous situation and suggested several steps we should take in an effort to keep elections on track: "In view of the apparent deterioration in political environment, I believe some further action on the part of USG is merited, especially in view of widespread perception that my replacement signals some change in USG policy toward Honduras generally and the elections specifically. While I am not sanguine that anything we do will dissuade key actors from their plans, we do have the capability to influence those—including military officers—who may be hesitating or who believe USG is shifting its position. And these people could well determine which way the balance swings."[10]

I described what we were doing locally and urged two additional actions for Washington to make our influence felt: Enders would soon be traveling to Cancun, Mexico, for a Caribbean Basin Initiative (CBI) meeting and should stop in Tegucigalpa to reaffirm our position to President Paz and the media; and State's press spokesman should make a strong statement endorsing elections, with advance notice to the embassy so that we could ensure maximum coverage in the local media.

These weren't dramatic steps, but we had very little time. If the military were going to block the elections, they had to move relatively quickly. Taking these actions was better than sitting on our hands and watching our overarching policy objective go down the drain. But there was even less time than we anticipated.

KEY MILITARY LEADERS MEET, APPROVE COUP PLAN: TEGUCIGALPA, HONDURAS, OCTOBER 9–10, 1981. All military units were placed on full alert beginning 12:01 A.M. October 10, which meant that officers and men were restricted to their respective bases. No reason was given for this action, of which we became aware only after the fact. Once we learned of it, we recognized that it was a clear preparatory step for a coup.

A meeting of key senior military unit commanders was also convened at General Staff headquarters the evening of October 9.[11] According to reports from several sources, the purpose of this meeting was to gain approval for a military coup to preempt elections. Those assembled were told that the country was in a state of acute political and economic crisis, a growing threat from Nicaragua, irregularities in electoral rolls and the possibility that the recent land scandal would spread, directly implicating several senior military officers. Torres Arias then asked those present if they would support a coup to oust the provisional government, block elections and leave Paz in place.

Alvarez, whose promotion would have been threatened by Paz's remaining, was present but reportedly took no active role in the discussion that followed. The only dissenting voice was that of Air Force commander Col. Walter Lopez, who posed several objections. First, he felt duty bound to defend the political transition and believed its frustration would be seriously destabilizing and threaten relations with the United States. Second, he did not want the blood of fellow citizens on his hands. Finally, he objected to taking such action to protect corrupt colleagues. The latter point led to a major row with Torres Arias. According to our sources, there was no visible support for Lopez among the officers present. At the conclusion of this heated debate, Lopez stated flatly that he would not support a coup and that all Air Force pilots shared his position.

He left the meeting, going directly to the Tegucigalpa air base. He directed his command, including San Pedro Sula, to fuel and arm all aircraft, and to go on full alert. In addition, he began contacting less senior Army officers in command positions whom he believed supported elections, advising them of the senior officers' plans and seeking their support. In this way he was able to obtain Army troops from the Fifth Artillery Battalion to reinforce the Tegucigalpa air base defenses.[12]

Following Lopez's departure, the other officers reportedly agreed to proceed with the coup, provided their subordinates would support it. By the time these officers returned to their units, early October 10, they discovered a singular lack of enthusiasm among their subordinates, and in some cases out-right opposition. Lopez and his allies had been busy and managed to divide the armed forces; a coup was not possible without the support of those who actually commanded the troops, and they didn't have it.

This situation, coupled with Lopez's apparent willingness to fight, forced Torres Arrias and the others to reconsider. Further meetings ran throughout October 10. Ultimately, the coup scenario was abandoned. They had little option but to support elections. Once that decision was made, they decided to try to impose certain conditions on the successor government. Both Zuniga and Suazo Cordova were summoned separately to meet with Paz and the Superior Council. They were told that the military remained concerned about the election process and was placing responsibility for its success or failure directly on the parties. They would support the outcome only "so long as it is carried out freely, honestly and in accordance with the law." None of this was new. But they also distanced the institution from anticipated cabinet changes, which would be the sole responsibility of President Paz. This step was apparently designed to insulate the military from any new corruption scandals.

These points were incorporated in a formal pronouncement that was signed by the party leaders and Paz. Regular radio and television program-ming was preempted repeatedly during the evening of October 10 to read this statement to the public.[13] We learned later, however, that the military had imposed further conditions that were not addressed in the formal announce-ment.

Once our officers spotted unusual activity at military bases early Octo-ber 10 and learned that forces had been placed on alert, we braced for a coup. The radio and television bulletins came later, indicating just the opposite. We were puzzled. Except for the cryptic reference to cabinet changes, all of the points in the armed forces' declaration had been made public earlier, so why the fuss? We redoubled our efforts to find out what was going on.

THE MIST CLEARS: RECENT EVENTS CLARIFIED: TEGUCIGALPA, HON-DURAS, OCTOBER 13, 1981. We had a regular CT meeting first thing and spent most of the time trying to assess recent events. We were still unaware of what had happened at the October 9 meeting, Colonel Walter Lopez's valiant and pivotal confrontation with his peers, and much of the other behind-the-scenes maneuvering. Several embassy officers, however, had picked up reports that the military had come close to overthrowing the gov-ernment but little more. These reports didn't make much sense in the con-text of the subsequent declaration assuring that elections would go forward, so we considered them unconfirmed rumors.

Suazo Cordova phoned immediately after the meeting, urgently wish-ing to see me at the residence. He could not discuss the matter on the phone.

I told him that he could come to the residence directly, and left the office. He arrived alone and in an agitated state. He then provided the contextual details, described previously, that gave substance to the coup reports. Suazo Cordova had obtained this information from Colonel Lopez, who asked that he pass it on to me to ensure the embassy was informed. Lopez, he said, remained concerned about his own future but was fairly confident he would be safe in the near term, if only because of the solidarity shown by the other Honduran Air Force (HAF) officers. All pilots had submitted resignations, to become effective if Lopez should be replaced. Thus, if the commander of the armed forces dismissed Lopez, they would have an Air Force with no pilots. And Lopez had strong support among middle- and lower-grade army officers.[14]

Nearly everything Suazo Cordova reported was later substantiated by other sources, each of whom shed further light on this murky affair. Some accounts, however, smacked of ex post facto rationalization by the senior military. One such version alleged that the senior officers' meeting had only considered a coup as a "contingency" in the event the politicians did not accede to the conditions they wished to impose.[15] But that version was belied by concurrent reports—later substantiated by actions—that even after Suazo Cordova and Zuniga accepted the conditions, some officers were still attempting to block elections. Still another version had the senior officers making a tentative decision to oust the provisional government, subject to the reaction of their subordinates.[16] I believe Suazo Cordova's account, largely supported by other military and civilian sources, to be the most accurate.

One of the most interesting of the tidbits we picked up involved Zuniga. According to a well-placed military source, Zuniga had earlier assured the putative coup leaders that they need have no fear the Reagan administration would withhold recognition of a new military government or interrupt the flow of military and economic assistance. That had then been passed on to the unit commanders at the October 9 meeting.[17]

There was, however, one critical piece of information Suazo Cordova failed to share with me: the substance of the secret conditions he had agreed to. And I failed to inquire because I assumed that meeting dealt only with matters covered in the military's proclamation. We later learned the military had demanded, as a quid pro quo, agreement on several steps that sharply restricted a civilian government's ability to oversee and direct the military establishment. These conditions, which will be described later, established the "rules of the game" for Honduran democracy for the next decade and have still not been entirely reversed. Even in retrospect, it is difficult to blame Suazo Cordova for having accepted them because at the time he was unaware of the split in the Armed Forces and did not realize the military could not move to block elections without triggering a military-against-military conflict. They had bluffed and carried the day.

We later acquired a document that cast clear, if somewhat prolix, light on the pro-coup faction's intentions and plans. It had reportedly been considered by the Superior Council in late September and allegedly represented the members' views at that time. Its operative portion stated:

> The actual provisional government, due to the precarious circumstances and inherent limitations, has not developed a true approach or defined its objectives, which we consider essential to modify immediately by forming an new provisional government, preserving the actual president [in office], and finding the true national interests, establishing a clear policy toward our political and economic future, with a democratic conception, without qualifying objectives, and through commercial and economic relations with those friendly countries that can help us effectively. The November 29 elections do not constitute a solution to the political problem of this country; it is believed that responsible, aware people that are interested in Honduras and not in public positions, would agree that, given the existing internal and geopolitical circumstances, it is preferable to extend in office the provisional government over which General Policarpo Paz Garcia presides, *for at least two more years*. In this way the restructured bases for a truly democratic electoral process, first within the parties and later within the country, can be established;...*in order to realize the above it is very important to: plan a true program tending to orient national and international opinion in a favorable direction; it is therefore essential to centralize official news and that Honduran ambassadors, consuls and other international officials end their isolation and initiate action that reflects the national realities.*[19] [Emphasis added.]

Although the Superior Council may have considered this document, I very much doubt that it had been endorsed as reported. Whatever its standing, the document suggested that many senior officers were bent not only on blocking elections but also on establishing a strong, authoritarian regime.

RESPONDING TO THE ALMOST COUP: TEGUCIGALPA, HONDURAS, OCTOBER 13, 1981. I returned to the chancery and convened key officers to share Suazo Cordova's information and discuss actions we could take to calm disquiet and keep the elections on track. Several of the others had by then acquired information confirming parts of Suazo Cordova's report. There was a consensus that we needed to reaffirm our support for the transition and elections, as well as demonstrate our displeasure with the coup attempt, but there weren't many ideas for how we might accomplish those ends.

The first thing that came to mind was the pending riot-control training request. Although in suspense, Southern Command was ready to send a team on very short notice. I instructed Colonel Goodwin to be prepared to tell the Hondurans that the training had been canceled but to provide no official explanation. Privately, he could tell key contacts that the ambassador had made this decision with State Department concurrence, nothing more.

I did not plan to advise Southern Command of my decision until I had State's approval in hand. I was confident that the Honduran military, who were quite gifted at reading signals (even when they didn't exist), would figure this one out very quickly. I also planned to find an early opportunity for a high-profile affirmation of our continuing commitment to the transition. After some discussion, I decided to hold a farewell press conference for that purpose.

Beyond those steps, the best we could come up with was to renew with urgency our recommendation that Enders visit Honduras soon to deliver this message in unmistakable terms. If he was not available, then perhaps General Walters could make yet another visit. We would, I noted in my cable, particularly welcome any suggestions State might have to accomplish our purpose.[20] There were none.

VENEZUELAN CONCERN OVER ELECTION THREATS: TEGUCIGALPA, HONDURAS, OCTOBER 14, 1981. My Venezuelan colleague phoned to ask for an appointment. He said he wished to discuss the events of the previous weekend and the corruption scandal. He was deeply concerned. Specifically, he wanted my assessment whether the military might again try to stop elections and my views on possible Venezuelan efforts to keep the process on schedule.[21] Discussion of these topics over the phone was extremely indiscreet because the Honduran military controlled the phone company and might well be tapping our respective phones. I assumed that he hoped they were. When we met, he confirmed my assumption.

He wished to recommend that his government send a high-level emissary to emphasize its concern and suggest that the oil facility and other Venezuelan support would be endangered if elections were postponed. He also wanted his Foreign Ministry to call in the Honduran ambassador to make the same points. Did I think this would be useful? I did indeed. I told him that we had recently had a special high-level representative here to go over this same ground with Paz and senior military officers. A similar effort by Venezuela would provide invaluable support. I also noted that although the immediate crisis had passed, the situation remained very fluid and another crisis could arise at any moment.

"WRONG SIGNAL TO CENTRAL AMERICA": LOS ANGELES, CALIFORNIA, OCTOBER 14, 1981. The *Los Angeles Times* published a lengthy article noting that "The impending departure of U.S. ambassador Jack Binns, just before the first presidential election here in more than a decade, is casting doubt on U.S. policy toward this Central American country." The article, based largely on reporter Juan Vasquez's interviews with local political leaders, was an apt description of Honduran opinion and uncertainty. Not surprisingly, it linked my replacement with the departures of White, Pezzullo, Bowdler and Cheek, suggesting a "purge" was underway.[22]

I had met briefly with Vasquez at Arcos's suggestion. He accurately quoted me as having denied any link between my replacement and U.S. support for the elections, but added that "you have to admit there's [*sic*] a lot of people with active imaginations around here." Arcos also helped Vasquez with other appointments and gave him a backgrounder. The article went on to describe some of Zuniga's efforts to undermine me and his claims to have influenced my removal. Vasquez also quoted a Foreign Ministry official who affirmed that my replacement "was causing anxiety among Honduran politicians and diplomats."

SALVADORAN INSURGENTS DESTROY VITAL BRIDGE: CENTRAL EL SALVADOR, OCTOBER 15, 1981. Insurgent forces dynamited the Puente de Oro bridge over the Lempa River, leaving it beyond repair and effectively isolating the eastern third of the country.[23] This attack on a key infrastructure element had a devastating impact on the economy and seemed to indicate a change in the insurgents' strategy. Attacks on infrastructure targets increased.

A temporary span was installed shortly, but it would be years before a replacement bridge was built.

STATE OKAYS OUR ACTION PROPOSALS: TEGUCIGALPA, HONDURAS, OCTOBER 15, 1981. Deputy Assistant Secretary Briggs phoned to say that State concurred in canceling the riot-control training and in our local efforts to reaffirm the importance of elections. The possibility of a high-level visitor was still under consideration. That was all I needed. I immediately advised Goodwin to tell the Hondurans that these trainers would not be coming and to let Southern Command know of my decision. Arcos had already set up the press conference for that afternoon.

GOING OUT WITH A BANG: FINAL PRESS CONFERENCE: TEGUCIGALPA, HONDURAS, OCTOBER 15, 1981. We had decided to hold the press conference in my chancery office. Following the event we would serve wine and I would work the room, thanking them for their attentions over the previous year. We had a packed house. All the papers, both Tegucigalpa TV channels and several radio stations were present.

The floor was open to questions after my brief opening statement, which reiterated U.S. support for elections in the following terms:

> There has been no change in our policy toward Honduras: we will continue to collaborate with the government and people of Honduras on political, social, economic and security matters. In this context, my government—the White House, the Congress, the Department of State and this mission—continues to support the transition to democracy and the electoral process. Any suggestion that there has been a change in U.S. policy in this regard is, at best, simply false. At worst, it is an attempt to frustrate the will of the Honduran people. It is my belief and that of my government, based on our consultations and conversations

With Honduran journalists at final press conference in chancery office, October 1981.

with representatives of nearly all Honduran institutions—the government, the political parties, the private sector, the unions, the Armed Forces, the church and others—that elections will be held November 29, as scheduled. I hope this statement will end, once and for all, speculation about the U.S. position."[24]

Questions covered a wide range of subjects, with the electoral process and the U.S. reaction to a hypothetical coup being revisited several times, with variations. Other topics included our economic and military assistance levels; the apparent Central American "arms race" and risks of war; the alleged alignment of Honduras, Guatemala and El Salvador against Nicaragua; and whether National Party leader Zuniga had been responsible for my replacement.

The conference received considerable TV and radio coverage that evening and the next day, and my comments made front-page headlines in all the papers the following morning, with full accounts of the conference inside.[25] The editorial decisions of two papers, *La Prensa* and *La Tribuna*, to headline my coup comment reflected concerns about the events of the previous weekend. My carefully chosen words to the effect that such contingencies could not be ignored, gave them an opportunity to address a normally taboo topic. Our message was out in clear and unequivocal form, thanks to the media.

And, for the last time, *La Prensa* followed up with a supportive editorial. It condemned the Honduran penchant for rumor mongering, conspiracies and imaginary coups, but its primary aim was to refute the theory that my departure implied a change in U.S. policy regarding elections. The theory that my replacement was "the fruit of the 'sympathy' Reagan feels for one of the two traditional parties and demonstrates the 'influence' that the more conservative of the two enjoys in Washington" it labeled nonsense. It went on to define U.S. regional policy goals as "support for democratic governments; backing moderate reforms that promise greater social justice in freedom; and increasing the level of security in the region."[26]

Reaction was uniformly and strongly favorable, except for the military. Most of them were tight-lipped, but one senior officer ventured the opinion that my remarks were "not helpful." As an apparent sign of disfavor, very few military officers turned up at farewell functions hosted by the Foreign Ministry, my diplomatic colleagues and mission officers.

CONDITIONS ON ELECTIONS: CODIFYING THE STATUS QUO: TEGUCIGALPA, HONDURAS, OCTOBER 18, 1981. The embassy finally acquired a document entitled "General Considerations Prior to the Initiation of a Constitutional Government" detailing the conditions imposed by the Superior Council on October 10. It stated that the Central America situation and threat of "international communism" were such that the next government had to "accept, recognize and obligate itself to carrying out the following postulates." Several were benign, but the effect of others was to codify what was already widely assumed: the military would remain the ultimate arbiter of national policy, despite having passed the baton of governance to an elected, constitutional government.

The key clauses limiting the elected government's freedom of action included:

• granting the Superior Council veto power over the nominations for ministers of defense, interior, public works, finance, and transportation and a number of noncabinet positions, including heads of the central bank, the electric power grid, the telecommunications agency, and the port authority;
• agreeing that government officials who "distort or compromise the political future of the nation must be separated immediately from their posts" (presumably the Superior Council would decide when such distortions or compromises occurred);
• assuring the Superior Council that it would be consulted on all subjects that might "affect our republican forms and national sovereignty"; and
• agreeing that the armed forces "will remain vigilant and watchful of events in order to avoid chaos and destruction of the Honduran family" (whatever that meant).[27]

Not explicitly mentioned, although apparently subsumed under the "national sovereignty" catchall, was the exemption of military funding from normal budgetary appropriation and oversight.

These conditions were a bad deal for the parties and the Honduran people. Codifying and committing to what previously had been accepted only tacitly made change—and meaningful democracy—more difficult. To Suazo Cordova, who at the time was unaware that a coup attempt had failed, acknowledging these realities to ensure the process of democratizing Honduras was the "least bad" option. Zuniga may have been a horse of a different color, but it's hard to imagine him advocating a reduced role for the military. Today it may be easy to criticize the party leaders for having accepted this accord. But Suazo Cordova, at least, thought he was choosing between accepting a variation of the status quo and a coup. And it was far better for Honduras than a new military government.

AN IDEA THAT WON'T DIE: EFFORTS TO BLOCK ELECTIONS CONTINUE: TEGUCIGALPA, HONDURAS, OCTOBER 19, 1981. We were still picking up credible reports that Torres Arias and others were continuing efforts to block elections. With the coup route foreclosed, they were again attempting to persuade, buy or coerce sufficient votes in the assembly to change the elections date by amending the electoral law. If the National Party under Zuniga supported a delay, they needed only three additional votes to realize their goal.

In addition, several newspapers published articles questioning the legality of members of the Constituent Assembly standing as candidates in the November 29 elections. In the unlikely event that this thesis should prevail, one presidential candidate, several vice presidential candidates and most congressional candidates would be disqualified, making elections virtually meaningless. We suspected Torres Arias was behind this.

The ALIPO faction of the Liberal Party had also gone public with a decision to challenge legally their party's selection of congressional and municipal candidates, alleging violation of party bylaws. It was not clear whether that initiative was sponsored by the pro-coup bloc, but there was no doubt the *Alipistas* were trying to use uncertainty about elections to lever concessions from Suazo Cordova. In so doing they too cast a shadow on the legitimacy of the process.

Concurrently, the military had moved to address the problem of disaffection among the junior officers. Paz, as commander of the armed forces, had convened a series of meetings with the lower grade officers in which he stressed the need to maintain institutional cohesion and solidarity. We thought it highly improbable that these sessions would breathe new life into the failed coup plot.

In reviewing the situation our Political/Military group was unanimous in believing there was still a good chance the electoral process would be frustrated. The probability range of their views ran from 60 percent against elections occurring, to 60 percent that elections would be held.[28] The possibility that the military might find the needed votes to change the election date was most troubling. I asked the Political Section to keep in touch with leaders of the two minor parties regarding their positions and to see if there were any signs that some of the Liberal legislators might be drawn into the Torres Arrias plan.

U.S. STUDY URGES AVOIDING CONFRONTATION WITH NICARAGUA: CARLISLE, PENNSYLVANIA, OCTOBER 20, 1981. The Army War College, in a specially commissioned assessment of policy options regarding Nicaragua, counseled against a direct paramilitary confrontation with that country. It concluded that "it is still too early to challenge the Sandinistas. Based on their role in the overthrow of Somoza, the Sandinistas are still supported by a wide spectrum of the Nicaraguan populace. A well-organized opposition has yet to develop inside Nicaragua. Somocistas are unlikely to gather sufficient support within Nicaragua to manage a successful counterrevolution."[29]

This assessment was consistent with intelligence community evaluations and, like them, was ignored.

SANDINISTAS CRACK DOWN ON PRIVATE SECTOR: MANAGUA, NICARAGUA, OCTOBER 21, 1981. The Nicaraguan government arrested businessman Enrique Dreyfus, president of the business group COSEP, and several other private sector leaders. They were accused of violating the "socioeconomic emergency" and maintenance of public order laws.[30]

This action triggered a letter to the Nicaraguan government, signed by 22 members of the House Foreign Affairs Committee, expressing their serious concern over the arrest of these leaders.[31]

HELMS'S QUESTIONS AND ALLEGATIONS REQUIRE RESPONSE: TEGU-CIGALPA, HONDURAS, OCTOBER 22, 1981. Negroponte's Senate hearing had afforded Senator Helms an opportunity to allege that the Liberal Party was closely linked with the Sandinistas and had received $2 million from Libya's Mu'ammar Qadhafi. If elected, Helms suggested, the Liberals would represent a serious threat to U.S. interests. This canard was pure Zuniga.

I received an urgent phone call from State, requesting an analysis of the foreign policy differences between the two major parties. This request was followed by a cable listing questions Helms wanted answered by October 26.[32] Two of Helms's specific queries implied I was biased in favor of the Liberal Party and had poor relations with President Paz. The cable also asked for both unclassified and classified answers, the latter for use in closed session.

The comparative foreign policy analysis was something of a poser. Neither party had meaningful platform statements dealing with foreign policy, nor had either candidate addressed the subject in formal speeches. Accordingly, there was no research to be done, just a great deal of guesswork. The bottom line was that we did not expect significant divergences from the policies of the Paz government. A Nationalist government might be a bit more xenophobic than a Liberal one and more likely to seek closer relations with Argentina. In Central America we expected that both would pretty much follow the military's lead vis-à-vis Nicaragua, the Liberals being a bit closer to the Salvadoran and Costa Rican governments and the Nationalists forging closer relations with Guatemala. Both would continue close cooperation with the United States. From the foreign policy standpoint it was largely a case of choosing between Tweedledum and Tweedledee.[33]

The specific questions raised by Helms left no doubt he was being driven by information from Zuniga. We prepared the two sets of factual, accurate answers that generally took issue with the premises underlying his questions. In concluding our response, I appended the following:

> It is evident that most of these questions originated from information—much of it totally without foundation—which Senator Helms' office received from Zuniga or his family and close associates. It is also clear that questions 5, 6 and 7 are designed to discredit me. I hope that the Department will ensure that the record of the hearings does not lend substance to that effort. While it is true that my relations with Paz have been strained for some time (although that stress has in no way affected our ability to communicate) the principal sources of his irritation have been U.S. policy decisions which I have sought to carry out. The point is that these policy decisions—especially the one on the need for elections—were in direct conflict with his interests and ambitions.[34]

The ultimate irony in Zuniga's successful manipulation of Helms was that, once in office, the Suazo Cordova administration became our firm ally in the covert war against the Sandinistas and our increased military presence; Zuniga and his family, on the other hand, came to oppose and speak out against both.

ANALYSIS DISCLOSES DETERIORATING ECONOMIC SITUATION: TEGUCIGALPA, HONDURAS, OCTOBER 23, 1981. An AID economist from the Regional Office for Central America and Panama visited Honduras to project balance of payments, foreign exchange and budget deficits for 1981 and 1982. The data he developed working with Honduran central bank and finance ministry technicians was alarming. Earlier projections prepared by the IMF and World Bank officials in May now had to be revised downward, in some cases sharply. The 1981 balance of payments deficit, for example, had grown from $35 million to $97 million; for 1982 it had been projected at zero, but was now expected to be in deficit by at least $76 million. As net foreign reserves were only $110 million at the beginning of 1981, we anticipated they would be exhausted early in 1982, placing the new government in serious straights.

The budgetary outlook was equally distressing, if not worse. The 1981 deficit was estimated at $85 million, and the 1982 deficit was already projected at $129 million. The latter figure probably understated the problem because the new year would certainly bring new, unbudgeted, expenditures and commitments. This suggested the new government would face a nearly unmanageable fiscal situation early in its first year.

We reported these data to State, underscoring the critical nature of the economic problems the new government would face and urging prompt action to approve and implement the Economic Support Fund (ESF) program we had recommended earlier.[35]

LAND SCANDAL PAYOFFS TO SENIOR OFFICERS: TEGUCIGALPA, HONDURAS, OCTOBER 23, 1981. A well-placed Honduran banker approached me about the earlier land scandal that had panicked the senior officers corps. Several officers, he reported, had received $25,000 each from the proceeds of this fraudulent transaction. Finance Minister Mendoza, who handled the transaction, apparently received nothing, although he may have been slated to receive his payoff after the proceeds were transferred to banks in the United States. Once the nature of the scandal became known, the public prosecutor had frozen the accounts containing most of the proceeds, blocking the planned transfers.[36] No wonder some officers were worried.

We also learned that the military had made a concerted effort to put a lid on the corruption issue. Editors and publishers of all the newspapers had been spoken to, as had the owners of television and most radio stations. This type of pressure was by no means unusual in Honduras, and this time it worked. Political leaders were also asked to cooperate in curtailing public discussion, which they did, probably because they had their own corruption skeletons. The upshot was that we heard little more on this topic.

ELECTIONS OUTLOOK BRIGHTENS: TEGUCIGALPA, HONDURAS, OCTOBER 23, 1981. The question of a high-level visitor to reinforce our elections message was still alive. Our most recent information, however, suggested the crisis had passed. Our soundings of assembly leaders indicated efforts by the Torres Arias group to suborn or coerce legislators had failed: the votes to postpone elections were not there. Perhaps of even greater significance, a recent National Party poll indicated Zuniga was now leading Suazo Cordova. Although we had doubts about the reliability of that poll, it was helpful, making it less likely that Zuniga would support delaying elections. And our most recent information about the Superior Council was that most members were resigned to the elections. We therefore concluded that a high-level visit was unnecessary.

However, I urged that State approach the Venezuelan government to send an emissary, as recommended by my Venezuelan colleague.[37]

REJECTING ENDERS'S REQUEST TO DELAY MY DEPARTURE: TEGUCI-GALPA, HONDURAS, OCTOBER 23, 1981.[38] Deputy Assistant Secretary Briggs phoned to say that Negroponte's arrival had been delayed, so Enders wanted me to stay on for another 10 to 14 days. I was dumbfounded. After regaining my voice, I reminded Briggs that I had argued long and hard to stay until after elections but had lost that argument. We had agreed on an October 31 departure, and I had so informed the Honduran government and others. I was engaged in a round of farewell ceremonies predicated on that date. To announce a change now would make us all seem like fools. Moreover, Walker was a strong, effective officer, and I was confident that he could handle anything that might arise. Thus, I saw no substantive reason to remain and would not unless directed to do so.

Briggs seemed taken aback and got a bit huffy. I was past caring.

SOUTHERN COMMAND DOES IT AGAIN: AIR BASE RIGHTS REVISITED: TEGUCIGALPA, HONDURAS, OCTOBER 26, 1981. The station chief advised me that Colonel Alvarez had expressed concern about an approach made to a senior Honduran Air Force officer by a Southern Command official. The latter had requested that the Honduran representatives to the Central American Air Force Commanders' conference—an annual clambake sponsored by Southern Command and being held in Panama October 26–28—and to the Army Commanders of the Americas conference in Washington, D.C., November 3–5, suggest that the United States and Honduras establish a joint air base at Puerto Lempira. That isolated site on the north coast near the Nicaraguan frontier possessed an improved runway that had been built by the United States during WWII.

According to Alvarez, the Southern Command representative said it was critical that the Hondurans present this idea as their own, not the Command's. The Hondurans, he said, were enthusiastic about the proposal because they wished to develop a closer security relationship with the United States but thought this a curious way to do business. Alvarez wondered if the station chief knew anything about this subject. He did not but said he would check.

This was another egregious example of Southern Command's attempting to drive policy outside normal channels and seeking to avoid being caught violating statute and the earlier injunction to refrain from such action. In the process they had excited Honduran expectations and my bile. I was furious. I was also unhappy that the station chief had taken several days to advise me of Alvarez's approach but assumed he had wanted his headquarters' approval before actually informing me. At that point there were many things going on that I was not privy to. I decided to ignore his delay, as there wasn't much I could do about it. But I was certainly going to blow the whistle on Nutting's boys. They just didn't know how to play by the rules.

Honduras Country Team. Front row (L to R): Col. Dale Bollert, USAF (Defense Attache); Cresencio Arcos (Public Affairs Officer); William G. Walker (Deputy Chief of Mission); author; John Oleson (AID Director); Col Willard Goodwin, USAR (Military Group commander): back row: Robert Higgins (Commercial Attache): George Clift (Chief, Joint Administrative Section); Paul Wackerbarth (Chief, Economic Section); Station Chief; Sarah Horsey (Chief, Consular Section); Peter Lara (Peace Corps Director); and David Shaw (Chief, Political Section); Drug Enforcement Agency representative was absent. October 1981.

I fired off a quick cable to Enders, explaining what had happened and the Honduran reaction. I followed it with another to Nutting, pointing out that this action seemed to be another violation of statute and specific instructions. I also informed him that I had advised State separately and concurrently because the Central American Air Force Commanders' conference was by then underway.[39]

As best I recall, there were no replies to either message prior to my departure. However, I was to send another cable on this topic to State.[40]

FINAL FAREWELLS: TEGUCIGALPA, HONDURAS, OCTOBER 30–31, 1981. Martha and I had experienced an outpouring of goodwill and well-wishes from our many friends, American, Honduran and diplomatic, at a round of farewell parties, dinners and lunches. On Friday, my final day at the chancery, the entire mission staff gathered in our employee cafeteria for a farewell ceremony. It was, for me, a moving moment, not least because I was able to present Arcos with a sustained Superior Performance award for his truly outstanding service over the preceding year. This was the highest award an embassy could authorize, and even it required approval of USIA in Washington. Walker and I had worked hard to secure that approval, and Arcos was nearly floored with surprise.

The next morning, after a tearful good-bye to the residence staff, we left for the airport, where we met all agency heads, many other staff members and most of their spouses, in the airport's VIP lounge. That was exactly where our adventure had begun 13 months before.

It was handshakes and hugs all around before we boarded the Air Florida flight to Miami.

11

Tying Up Loose Ends: Some Important Later Events

A metaphorical storm had hit Central America and continued to gain strength after my departure, raging for another decade. The United States did not create this torment, but for most of the decade we seeded its clouds relentlessly, fueling the death and destruction that it wrought.

In Nicaragua, our ill-conceived and ultimately illegal Contra operation was a failure. The anti-Sandinista forces never realized a significant military success, developed no popular following within Nicaragua, and wasted many lives. And our mindless pursuit of this misadventure damaged our nation internationally and provoked a constitutional crisis domestically. Arguably, the Contra operation helped persuade the Sandinistas to accept a negotiated settlement and elections. But that thesis requires two important caveats. First, Nicaragua's collapsing domestic economy and the Sandinistas' conviction that they could win a popular election—both products of their hubris—were the principal factors that drove them to accept the Arias plan in 1989. Second, there is a substantial body of opinion that something very close to what was finally agreed on could have been realized years earlier through more active American diplomatic engagement. Ambassador Larry Pezzullo is the most compelling advocate of that thesis, but he is by no means alone.

Neither case, of course, can be proven. But it is a fact that the Reagan administration never supported the Arias process or the other Central American peace initiatives, although it sometimes went through the motions for domestic political purposes. Indeed, the administration often strove mightily to discredit these efforts. The 1989 accord between the Sandinista government and the other Central American states, which led to the 1990 elections, began to disperse the Nicaraguan storm cell. With Violeta Chamorro's inauguration in April 1990 the storm was spent.

In El Salvador it took a year and a half to blow itself out. But without Sandinista material and moral support, the rebels had no hope of defeating the popularly elected and U.S.-supported Salvadoran government. Our support for democratic processes and our economic and military aid were critical for the Salvadoran government's survival and the eventual negotiated end to that conflict. The storm in El Salvador finally dissipated in late 1992, thanks to the Sandinista collapse, American steadfastness and UN negotiating efforts.

Although our policies and actions ultimately helped to end that conflict, they were not above reproach. Most egregiously, we failed to exercise our overwhelming influence—economic and military—to force the Salvadoran government and military to correct their human rights abuses. It beggars the imagination to suppose that we could not have had greater influence on their behavior, possibly saving thousands of lives.

We were also seriously remiss in failing to support the various Salvadoran peace or mediation efforts until very late in the game. It was not until 1989—after the Sandinistas had agreed to free elections—that the Bush administration agreed to support the Arias plan and later UN efforts to negotiate a settlement in El Salvador. No one can say whether skilled diplomacy might have yielded an earlier settlement to that conflict. My friend and colleague Bill Walker, our ambassador in El Salvador at the time and whose judgment I respect, argues that it was not. He makes a good case, but I am still not persuaded.

The whirlwinds that raked Nicaragua and El Salvador did not leave Honduras untouched. Terrorism, an unsuccessful insurgency sponsored and supported by the Sandinistas, and increased human rights abuses were all fed by our actions. Another casualty was our relations with Honduras and its people. Our policies and behavior—particularly the "secret" Contra operation and the overwhelming U.S. military presence—gave rise to serious anti-American sentiment, shaking the democratic forms that we sought to encourage and nurture. Nonetheless, democracy took root. The Honduran people spoke in 1981, 1985, 1989, 1993 and 1997, successively electing Roberto Suazo Cordova (Liberal), Jose Azcona Hoya (Liberal), Raphael Callejas (National), Carlos Roberto Reina (Liberal) and Carlos Flores Facusse (Liberal) to the presidency.

The following chronology describes some later developments that place the events in which I participated in a larger framework, tying up some loose ends. It also provides contextual fabric useful in understanding the arguments detailed in the final chapter.

1981

November 23. President Reagan signed National Security Decision Directive 17, authorizing the creation of a 500-man paramilitary force composed of Nicaraguan exiles, and allocating $20 million to that end. On December 1 Reagan signed the covert operations finding, authorizing the CIA to begin this operation, even though Latin America Division chief Duane Clarridge had been setting it up since at least August. CIA director Casey later told Congress that this operation was designed to interdict the flow of arms from Nicaragua to the Salvadoran rebels.[1]

November 29. The Liberal Party and Suazo Cordova won the Honduran elections with 54 percent of votes cast; nearly 80 percent of registered voters turned out. There were no significant charges of fraud or disorder during the electoral process.[2] It had been a success.

Mid-December. In Honduras the CIA began funding, arming and training Nicaraguan exile forces, using the same Argentine military personnel that had been working with the Contras as trainers and operational advisers.[3]

1982

March 31. The U.S. initiated negotiations to acquire military base rights in Honduras.[4] An amendment to the existing Bilateral Military Assistance Agreement was concluded May 6, 1982. It provided U.S. access to air bases at Palmerola, Goloson and La Mesa, and "other aerial ports that the two governments may subsequently agree upon." In return the U.S. agreed to improve facilities at these bases, "as well as the construction of new facilities and installation of equipment as may be necessary."[5] At that time the base at Palmerola was less than 50 percent complete; the United States financed its completion at a cost of more than $13 million.[6]

April 2. Argentina invaded the Falkland (Malvinas) Islands, a British colony. After a period in which Secretary Haig attempted to mediate a settlement, the U.S. condemned Argentina's action and threw its full support behind the United Kingdom. That effectively ended the CIA's relationship with Argentine military intelligence for the direction of the anti-Sandinista operation, forcing the CIA to assume direct responsibility. The Argentine pullout, however, was slow and messy.[7]

Early July. Honduran army forces moved into one of the disputed areas on the frontier with El Salvador in an effort to preclude its use by Salvadoran insurgents.[8] This was the first significant Honduran military operation against Salvadoran rebel forces.

August 30. Col. Leonidas Torres Arias, in a Mexico City press conference, charged that Honduran armed forces commander General Alvarez was leading Honduras into military confrontation with Nicaragua and called on the Honduran Congress to dismiss him.[9] Torres Arias had been ousted as head of Honduran military intelligence the previous May and assigned abroad, along with Colonel Hubert Bodden.

September 17. Honduran guerrillas attacked a Chamber of Commerce meeting in San Pedro Sula, taking over 200 hostages, including the ministers of finance and economy and the president of the Central Bank.[10] The government rejected the guerrillas' demands, but extended negotiations resulted in the release of all hostages and the safe passage of the guerrillas to Panama and, later, Cuba.

December. President Reagan signed the first Boland amendment, prohibiting the expenditure of funds "for the purpose of overthrowing the Government of Nicaragua." The administration rationalized its continued support for the Contras on the grounds that they were not trying to overthrow the Sandinistas.[11]

1983

January 8–9. The Contadora peace process for Central America, sponsored by Mexico, Colombia, Venezuela and Panama, was launched. The United States showed pro forma interest, but administration hard-liners opposed it. It was later endorsed by other Latin American nations, engaging most Central American governments. It made some progress but produced no settlements. Later initiatives built on its accomplishments.[12]

January–February. U.S. and Honduran military forces held joint exercises involving 4,000 Honduran troops and "hundreds" of Americans in the Puerto Lempira area.[13]

May 27. Secretary of State George Shultz announced that Enders would be replaced by Langhorne Anthony Motley, ambassador to Brazil. The hard-liners had won.[14]

Late May. The United States and Honduras reached an agreement to increase the number of U.S. military advisers sharply and establish a regional training center at Puerto Castilla.[15] The Honduran Congress approved this accord in late June.

July. Unidentified Reagan administration spokesmen described a strategy to use Honduras as a platform to project military power against Nicaragua and Cuba. According to the *New York Times,* this announcement caught both the Defense Department and the Honduran government by surprise,[16] despite the fact that U.S. military presence in Honduras had been steadily expanding.

August 28. The *New York Times* reported that joint military exercises in Honduras would involve 4,000 U.S. troops and cost between $10 and $30 million; the public response in Honduras was mixed.[17]

1984

January 11. The pilot of a USAF helicopter was killed when he inadvertently entered Nicaraguan airspace and was shot down.[18] This was the first reported death of a U.S. serviceman as a result of the buildup in Honduras.

January. The United States, increasingly concerned about Honduran human rights violations, urged restraint; the chief of the Honduran intelligence directorate was transferred to another position.[19] These actions had little effect, as disappearances and other violations continued. The Honduran Human Rights Commission documented 18 disappearances in 1984, most occurring after replacement of the military intelligence chief and the March ouster of armed forces commander Alvarez; 26 in 1985, most of which have been attributed to the Nicaraguan Contras; 4 in 1986; 22 in 1987; and 12 in 1988.[20]

Mid–March. The CIA mined several Nicaraguan harbors; the Contras quickly warned the international maritime industry of that action. Several ships, including British and Soviet vessels, were damaged, triggering an international outcry and a major brouhaha in Congress. New efforts were made to limit CIA operations, and Nicaragua filed a case against the United States in the World Court.[21]

March 23. The Department of Defense announced that joint exercises planned for April in Honduras would involve Army, Navy, Air Force and Marine elements totaling 33,000 U.S. personnel.[22]

March 30. In a barracks coup, junior Army officers forced armed forces commander Alvarez out of office at gunpoint, sending him to Costa Rica on an Air Force plane; also ousted were chief of staff General Jose Bueso Rosa, Navy commander (and now General) Ruben Montoya and FUSEP commander Daniel Bali Castillo.[23] Alvarez later moved to Miami and became a Department of Defense consultant. Bueso Rosa was sent to Chile as military attache.

April 4. The Honduran Congress confirmed General Walter Lopez, commander of the Honduran Air Force, as the new commander of the armed forces.[24]

May 27. General Lopez, in a public statement designed to allay growing public concern and stop mass rallies opposing U.S. military presence, announced that the United States must train increased numbers of Honduran troops and fewer Salvadoran military at the Puerto Castilla center.[25]

September 28. Faced with U.S. foot dragging in its efforts to renegotiate conditions for the Puerto Castilla center, Honduras directed the suspension of all training activities there, pending conclusion of a new bilateral security agreement.[26]

September/October. Common Cause, in a special report on the U.S. military buildup in Honduras, described ten "temporary" U.S. bases.[27]

October 1. The second Boland amendment entered into effect. It provided that "During Fiscal Year 1985 no funds available to the CIA, DOD or any other agency or entity involved in intelligence activities" could be used to support the Contra operation.[28]

November 1. The FBI arrested several individuals in Miami, charging them with plotting to assassinate President Suazo Cordova; the operation was to have been financed with funds raised by smuggling cocaine. The Honduran military attache in Chile, General Jose Bueso Rosa, was directly implicated and indicted.[29]

November. The Honduran government officially requested 12 F-5 fighter aircraft as part of the renegotiated bilateral security assistance agreement.[30] The United States had opposed the transfer of high-performance aircraft to Central American nations.

1985

September 28. Ricardo Zuniga Jr., who had retired from the Honduran army and become a prominent critic of U.S. policy and military presence in Honduras, was killed by persons unknown.[31]

November 21. General Bueso Rosa was arrested in Miami for conspiring to assassinate President Suazo Cordova.[32] Drug smuggling charges against him were dropped in a plea bargain. The Defense Department sought, unsuccessfully, to persuade the Justice Department not to prosecute. Bueso Rosa pled guilty to two RICO murder-for-hire counts; General Robert Schweitzer testified on his behalf at the sentencing hearing. Later, Lieutenant Colonel Oliver North and Assistant Secretary of State Elliott Abrams sought to persuade Justice and the FBI to agree to release and deport Bueso Rosa because of fears that, in North's words, he would "start singing songs nobody wants to hear" about our efforts to arrange Honduran military to support the Contra operation after the Boland amendment entered into effect. Current and former senior officials joined this effort, including Admiral John Poindexter, Duane Clarridge, retired General Paul Gorman (former commander-in-chief, Southern Command), and Defense Department undersecretary Fred Ikle and Deputy Assistant Secretary Nestor Sanchez.[33] They were unsuccessful.

December. Congress eased the ban on Contra assistance, authorizing the United States to provide them with intelligence information, communications equipment, training and food, medicine and other "humanitarian" supplies.[34]

1986

January 31. Under pressure from his military colleagues, General Walter Lopez resigned as commander of the armed forces; he was replaced by General Humberto Regalado.[35]

February 14. The *New York Times,* citing unnamed U.S. officials, reported that the CIA was fully aware of Honduran human rights abuses during the 1981–84 period.[36]

July 13. The General Accounting Office reported that the Defense

Department had violated the law in establishing a permanent military presence in Honduras without congressional authorization.[37]

October 30. The State Department announced the United States would provide Honduras with F-5 aircraft, overturning its previous policy on advanced jet aircraft in the region.[38]

December 30. Defense announced a four-month exercise in Honduras involving 3,000 U.S. troops.[39]

1987

January 6. The U.S. Senate voted to create a special committee to investigate the Iran-Contra affair.[40] The House followed suit.

February. Costa Rican president Oscar Arias proposed a framework for negotiated solutions to the conflicts wracking Central America. This built on the Contadora process and led to a negotiated end to the Sandinista/Contra conflict and elections in Nicaragua. Although this initiative did not succeed in the case of El Salvador, it provided a basis for later UN mediation that led to resolution of that conflict. Arias received the 1987 Nobel Peace Prize for his efforts.[41]

May 1. A former Honduran military interrogator, Florencio Caballero, charged that the CIA trained and advised those responsible for Honduran human rights abuses and was aware of the security forces' secret prisons and abductions.[42] Caballero subsequently testified before the Inter-American Human Rights Court, in San Jose, Costa Rica.[43]

August 8. The five Central American presidents signed a peace plan following the earlier Arias proposals. The United States, which had not been enthusiastic about these proposals, was taken by surprise and questioned the action.[44]

August 9. A restaurant near the Palmerola air base was bombed, injuring six U.S. servicemen and six Hondurans.[45] The Honduran responsible was granted asylum in Mexico; the United States protested to the Mexican government to no avail.[46]

1988

January 18. The Inter-American Human Rights Court began hearing charges that the Honduran government was responsible for human rights abuses and the disappearance of Angel Manfredo Velasquez.[47]

April 7. A Tegucigalpa demonstration protesting the irregular extradition of an alleged Honduran drug trafficker turned into a mob attack on the U.S. embassy annex. The building was torched, and five demonstrators were killed, apparently by Honduran police. This was the largest ever Honduran demonstration against the United States, and most observers considered the extradition case was merely a flash point for deeper resentment over U.S. policies, the Contra operation and U.S. military presence.[48]

July 29. The Inter-American Human Rights Court ruled that the Honduran government was responsible for the disappearance of Velasquez and ordered it to pay restitution to his family; President Azcona accepted the court's verdict. This was the court's first verdict finding a government responsible for such abuses.[49]

1989

January 25. Former General Gustavo Alvarez, who had returned to Honduras in 1988 as an evangelist, was assassinated by five unknown assailants. They were never identified.[50]

February 14. The Central American presidents, pursuing the Arias plan, agreed to disarm the Contras and to close their bases in Honduras and Costa Rica in return for a Sandinista agreement to hold free elections in 1990.[51] The United States did not support this accord.

February 18. A U.S. military bus was bombed near Comayagua, injuring three American servicemen.[52]

March 24. The Bush administration agreed to support the Arias plan for disarming the Contras and holding elections in Nicaragua.[53]

July 13. A bomb exploded outside a discotheque patronized by American servicemen in La Ceiba on the northern coast, wounding seven servicemen, three seriously.[54]

1990

February 25. The Sandinista government held free elections, with international observers attesting to their openness and fairness.[55] Opposition presidential candidate Violeta Chamorro won a landslide victory.

March 30. Leftist snipers shot and wounded "at least 6" U.S. servicemen near Tela on the northern coast.[56]

April 20. The Sandinista government, President-elect Violeta Chamorro and Contra leaders signed an accord establishing a cease-fire and procedures for disarming of Contra forces by June 30.[57] Five days later Chamorro was sworn in as president, ending nearly 11 years of Sandinista rule.[58]

1991

September 25. UN Secretary General Javier Perez de Cuellar announced that the Salvadoran government and rebel leaders had signed a UN-brokered agreement outlining the steps to end the conflict in that country; further negotiations were needed to finalize the details.[59]

September 26. The United States announced that it would write off $431 million in official debt owed by Honduras as part of its contribution to an economic reform program.[60] The write-off included $325 million in loans and $106 million in Food for Peace debt, about 15 percent of Honduras's total foreign debt.

November 15. Salvadoran insurgents, complying with the UN peace agreement, announced a unilateral cease-fire, effectively ending combat in that nation.[61]

1992

January 16. A final agreement between the Salvadoran government and the insurgent coalition was signed in Mexico City; a formal cease-fire entered into effect February 2.[62]

June 8. Honduras created the National Commission for the Protection of Human Rights; one of its tasks was the investigation of disappearances and other abuses that occurred during the 1980s.[63]

December 15. The Salvadoran ceremony marking the formal conclusion of that conflict drew statesmen from the hemisphere and beyond. Vice President Dan Quayle headed the U.S. delegation.[64]

1995

July 25. The Honduran government charged 11 current and former military officers with kidnapping and torturing suspected subversives during the 1980s. They refused to surrender and took refuge at military bases; the armed forces asserted that civilian courts did not have jurisdiction and that the accused were also covered by an earlier amnesty law.[65]

1996

January 18. The Honduran Supreme Court, in a rare unanimous decision, found that military officers accused of human rights violations could be tried in civilian courts.[66] They remained at military bases and to this date have not been tried.

12

Summing Up

Identifying and Examining Foreign Policy Pathologies

U.S. policy in Honduras 1980–81, which Roy Gutman aptly labeled "banana diplomacy," was a study in foreign policy pathology. It was dysfunctional in the extreme, and the fault lay primarily in Washington, with State, the NSC, other foreign affairs agencies and, ultimately, with the president. There can be no doubt that this pathology worsened in later years, particularly with respect to Nicaragua. That story, however, is beyond the scope of this work.

Examples of foreign policy dysfunction are described, repeatedly and in detail, in the preceding chapters. It is, however, useful to review some of the more significant before examining how they might be avoided.

The Reagan administration's lack of adequate policy coordination mechanisms or processes in the early years, with the attendant proliferation of uncoordinated activities, was one of the most critical of the several dysfunctions. The CIA and Defense (usually acting through the Joint Chiefs of Staff's Southern Command) carried out unilateral activities, sometimes without the knowledge of other agencies, often without coordination. The NSC, too, had separate lines of communication and acted independently, in some cases deliberately misleading other agencies. The latter practice, of course, grew worse in the later years when the NSC became an operational entity in the effort to circumvent the Boland amendment and other restrictions on the Contra operation.

This dysfunction was in part the result of the administration's deliberate decision to weaken the NSC. Other agencies quickly grasped the opportunity for independent action this implied. The CIA and Defense purposely ignored, deceived and sought to marginalize the embassy, as illustrated by the CIA's dealings with Colonel Alvarez and President Paz, its initiative to take over the Contra operation even before the presidential finding was signed, and its efforts to cloak related actions under cover of the arms interdiction program; and Southern Command's unilateral actions with regard to joint exercises, security assistance funding and acquisition of base rights. The weakened NSC also got into the act: witness General Schweitzer's dealings with Alvarez and other senior officers. This unilateralism, for example, precluded our being able to develop a coordinated interagency approach to the arms traffic problem.

Concomitantly, the CIA, Defense and the NSC deliberately misled and ignored the ambassador (and, on occasion, State) in carrying out their unilateral activities, as evidenced by the CIA's handling of human rights violations, Southern Command's unilateral initiatives and General Schweitzer's misleading report of his meeting with Alvarez and others. These actions were in direct violation of Public Law 93-475, which provides that the ambassador has "full responsibility for the direction, coordination, and supervision of all United States Government officers and employees" in his or her country. To an extent State was a witting collaborator in this dysfunction in that some officials were aware of the plans of these agencies and made no effort to advise me or ensure compliance with the law.

The State Department also repeatedly failed to provide clear, timely policy guidance in response to our requests. This failure was in part attributable to the stasis of the Carter–Reagan transition and the absence of effective policy coordination mechanisms described previously. But there were other factors, such as a lack of leadership, at work as well. Examples of neglected issues include escalating Honduran human rights abuses, problems related to Salvadoran and Nicaraguan refugees, the deteriorating Honduran economy, and, most critical, the emerging conflicts in our uncoordinated bilateral policies in the region.

State was also derelict in not keeping the embassy apprised in a timely fashion of important events, actions and decisions that affected Honduras. That led to a policy disconnect between Washington and the field, the emergence of parallel lines of communication and divergent messages and, ultimately, the embassy's marginalization. The most striking example of this self-inflicted wound was the failure to advise the embassy or me of the direction the administration was moving with regard to Nicaragua and the role envisaged for Honduras. Other notable examples were the inordinate delay in advising the embassy of President Paz's March 1981 attempt to arrange an unofficial meeting with President Reagan, the establishment of direct, unilateral communication links with Colonel Alvarez and other senior officers by both the CIA and NSC, and Southern Command's secret plan to station troops on the border with El Salvador. A part, but by no means all, of this dysfunction can be attributed to the lack of policy coordination.

State was unwilling to recognize or address real and potential conflicts in our various bilateral policy objectives. Unless such conflicts and possible trade-offs are examined, clear priorities cannot be established. And they were not. For instance, our efforts to persuade the Hondurans to do more to control their frontier with El Salvador and to support the Contra operation led to increased terrorism and subversion in Honduras, which threatened the transition to, and stability of, democratic government. Similarly, as the Honduran military perceived that they were becoming an increasingly important element in our regional policy, their concerns about our reaction to a coup blocking the transition diminished.

The proliferation of voices—official, congressional and private—purporting to represent the new administration and describing varying versions of our policy was another dysfunction. This cacophony arose from the independent activities of various agencies and Senator Jesse Helms's staff and other self-appointed spokespeople. It forced the embassy to offer a nearly constant stream of policy clarifications and restatements, as well as giving rise to exaggerated expectations and perplexity among our foreign friends. It was an important factor in the Honduran military's aborted coup decision.

Senior officials—Haig, Casey, Clark, Weinberger, Kirkpatrick, Walters and, indeed, the president himself—shared an ideological outlook that caused them to disregard factual data and analyses or recommendations that did not conform to their perceptions. This led them to embark on ill-conceived operations and, later, to ignore or evade legal and other constraints in their pursuit of specious and phantasmic goals. This dysfunction, clearly visible during my tenure, was the most serious of the various dysfunctions, and it worsened in later years.

Congress also played a role in this mess. A number of representatives were very helpful in keeping elections on track. Others sought to persuade their colleagues to exercise greater and more effective oversight of the activities of the CIA and the U.S. military, but they were largely unsuccessful until late in the game. The administration strove mightily to frustrate such review, employing a variety of tactics, including perjury. Congress is often understandably reluctant to intrude too far into the foreign policy formulation thicket. Ultimately, however, accountability cannot be established without effective congressional oversight, and I believe it is fair to say that Congress failed in that task.

Finally, there is the matter of trust, a critical element in the successful conduct of foreign policy. Its antithesis, distrust, is seriously dysfunctional and has a pernicious effect on other pathogens. The Reagan administration did not trust me from the outset. I was seen—correctly—as a strong supporter of Carter's policies in Honduras and the region. And it was assumed that I could not or would not carry out the policies and instructions of the newly elected administration. I was given no opportunity to prove or disprove that assumption.

The raison d'être of the Foreign Service is to provide a corps of skilled professional diplomatists sworn to serve their country and Constitution, regardless of the party in power. Most officers take that role and their oath of office very seriously. Many political leaders, however, seem to have a problem with the part about the Constitution, believing that the Service should owe its primary allegiance to the incumbent president. Analysis, advice and recommendations within official channels that do not conform to an administration's conceptions are often seen as acts of disloyalty. The pernicious effect of this was demonstrated repeatedly during the Reagan administration but perhaps most graphically by Bud McFarlane's later observation that if he had expressed his doubts about our Nicaragua policy, he would have been branded a communist and removed.[1] What chance did a career officer have in such an environment?

The politicization of the Foreign Service—the tendency to consider career officers who served as senior department officials or ambassadors in the previous administration as either "Republican" or "Democratic" officials— did not begin with the Reagan administration. But it certainly grew during that time. Although the administrations of Presidents Bush and Clinton were less ideological, they did not reverse this practice. If unchecked this trend will destroy professionalism, opening the system to a host of abuses. Over time we will lose expertise, and objective analysis will be stifled. Discontinuity in our policies will increase. These are hardly preconditions for the successful conduct of our foreign relations.

Foreign Service officers, including career ambassadors, must provide their best advice on proposed policy directions. Their counsel, of course, may be disregarded or overridden, but it should not be suppressed by fear of political retribution. And once decisions are taken by lawful authority, these same professionals must carry out the resulting instructions scrupulously. With very rare exceptions they do so, despite the politicization that has occurred. If Foreign Service officers—whether at the ambassadorial or lower level— cannot carry out a stated policy in good conscience, they should resign from either their post or the Service. There is extensive precedent, much of it fairly recent, to show this ethos is still functioning.

I certainly sought to follow my instructions and guidance (when I had them), although at times I pursued goals that had been changed without my knowledge. Enders's request that I discontinue reporting human rights violations in official channels was improper, if not unlawful, and we both knew it at the time. There was no way he would have put that request in writing, hence my summons to Washington. My unwillingness to cooperate, however, fed the existing mistrust and led directly to my loss of access to intelligence on Honduran human rights abuses, as documented by later CIA investigations.[2]

A decade and a half ago, the late Philip Habib observed that the senior career officers helping to manage the transition between the incoming and outgoing administrations bear a special obligation to defend the integrity of the Service. Part of that is to insist that the new administration reward those who loyally served the latter. And these leaders must be willing to sacrifice their own professional futures for this principle, if necessary. It is a truism to say that the interests of a new administration are best served by loyal, professional support from the Foreign Service and that the most effective way to ensure that this occurs is to reward such service to the prior administration. That is a point that needs to be reiterated and perhaps relearned with every change in presidents. And it falls to the leaders of the Service to deliver the message.

Prophylaxes and Cures

The preceding list of dysfunctions is substantial. Some of them—e.g., the willingness of zealots to engage in extensive deception and felonious activity, the failure of Congress to exercise adequate oversight or to challenge a popular government that was clearly circumventing, if not breaking, the law—do not lend themselves to facile solution. Indeed, they may defy solution. Others, such as the discontinuities arising from changes in administrations, are largely structural and unavoidable, given our political system. Nonetheless, most arose at least in part from the absence of a foreign policy process and discipline. Both are critical for the successful conduct of foreign relations and are the president's responsibility. The buck comes to rest in the Oval Office.

Process, though vital, is not an end in itself nor a panacea for foreign policy woes. Rather it is an essential starting point that enables or facilitates the definition of goals and the thoughtful consideration of options and strategies for achieving them. Without it there can be little hope of avoiding many of the dysfunctions that arose in Honduras and the region during the 1980–81 period and foreshadowed the Reagan administration's later excesses.

No set of mechanisms or procedures, however well honed, can entirely offset human frailties, any more than they can replace, for example, vision and understanding of the forces at play. Yet even human factors can be attenuated by effective process: policy review, formulation and coordination mechanisms tend to discourage independent or ill-formed actions, dampening the effects of individual personality and interpersonal chemistry. Process also allows accountability to be fixed.

How might an effective policy process have impacted the specific shortcomings identified above? Its mere existence would not have guaranteed that requested guidance was forthcoming, but it would have made timely consideration and response more likely. A second dysfunction—the failure to keep the embassy apprised of important developments—is a State Department responsibility only tangentially related to the process issue. In some of the cases cited, however, State itself was unaware of specific developments; effective process would have reduced, although not eliminated, such instances.

Adherence to process cannot prevent uncoordinated policy actions, but it does increase the likelihood that independent initiatives will come to light, be addressed in an interagency context and, if unresolved, referred to higher authority. In this way process can help to create an environment more conducive to careful consideration, coordination and cooperation. Process deters unilateralism.

There are no procedural mechanisms I know of that would ensure other agencies honor an ambassador's oversight responsibilities absent political will at State and the White House to ensure compliance. Presidents routinely reaffirm the ambassadorial role but usually do little to enforce that mandate. Part of the problem lies with the secretary of state. If he or she fails to support the ambassador, to bring breaches to the president's attention, then other agencies can be counted on to ignore the ambassador. When violations have no consequences, statute and regulation will be disregarded.

If operating effectively, process should also sharply reduce the divergent voices phenomenon. The capacity of such mechanisms to restrict congressional or private foreign policy initiatives—like those that plagued us in Honduras—is limited, but the coherent and consistent iteration of a single policy line, partially a product of process, would diminish the credibility of freelancers of whatever origin.

Can process alone overcome the determination of senior officials to engage in the deliberate deception of other agencies and Congress; casuistical argument, dissembling and perjury; blatant disregard for congressional oversight and statute; and direct law breaking, in order to carry out their vision of a higher good? No. Process can never overcome zealots who are willing to ignore law and reason in pursuit of their notional holy grail. The principal defense against this kind of excess is the president. Unless a president is prepared to carry out his constitutional mandate, acknowledging the constraints that implies, and recognize that effective process is the only means to ensure a cohesive, coordinated foreign policy, there can be little hope.

Although a president must bear responsibility for establishing policy coordination mechanisms, ensuring they function effectively and demanding conformity with their findings and conclusions, he cannot do it alone. The support of others is essential. A foreign policy "vicar," as Secretary Haig liked to style himself, could not perform that function absent forthright presidential support, which he lacked. Nor, for that matter, can an NSC adviser fulfill a similar role without such support. The importance of process was known and understood by some in the Reagan administration, as Bud McFarlane's February 27, 1981, memorandum to Secretary Haig so ironically illustrated: "...we must assure that our political, economic, diplomatic, propaganda, military and covert actions are well coordinated."[3] Later, as NSC adviser,

McFarlane failed conspicuously to achieve that goal. And it's probably safe to say that as far as Central America was concerned, the Reagan administration never came close.

Why, then, were not appropriate mechanisms put in place? And why was Reagan's first NSC adviser, Richard Allen, intentionally rendered bureaucratically impotent? Part of the reason lay in the new administration's belief that the NSC under Nixon and Carter had been divisive, and it wished to avoid those problems. But whatever the cause, the result proved a serious mistake.

Foreign policy dysfunction did not spring fully developed at Reagan's inauguration. The November 1980 elections in the United States marked the onset of a policy paralysis arising within the outgoing Carter administration and was mainly a structural condition. The bitter legacy of campaign differences over our policies and mutual distrust, coupled with Carter's overwhelming rejection at the polls, left his foreign policy team dispirited and unwilling to address new problems or make decisions. That was understandable and largely unavoidable.

A final question needs to be examined. Would effective foreign policy process have precluded the events—misguided operations, intentional deception of Congress, single-minded pursuit of independent agendas—that led to the Iran-Contra affair? There is no simple answer. Given the personalities involved, probably not. But on the other hand, effective process might have deterred some of those actions and led to their earlier disclosure.

Assessing Our Honduran Policy

Many of our policies toward Honduras were quite successful, despite the cited dysfunctions. The foremost success was the completion of the transition process and installation of a constitutional, democratically elected government. That achievement has turned out to be far more durable than Honduran history suggested or than anyone anticipated. Since 1981 there have been four more elections and successful transfers of power; in two cases, the reins of government were turned over to the opposing political party.

Admittedly, Honduras is not a model of democracy, and corruption remains a problem, but its record is substantially better than that of many other nations. And perhaps most heartening, successive civilian governments have been able to claw back some of the powers ceded to the military, gradually circumscribing that institution's political influence.

The United States cannot claim most credit for the success of the 1980–82 transition, but we did play an important role. That advance was attained primarily by the Honduran people and institutions wishing to see an end to military rule. They supported the transition process, made their voices heard and took their chances with untested civilian leadership. Colonel Walter Lopez and other Honduran military officers who opposed the attempted October coup played the most pivotal role in allowing elections to go forward. And in 1984 they later played a vital part in safeguarding democracy when they ousted armed forces commander General Gustavo Alvarez, who had become increasingly contemptuous of the constitutional rule.

A couple of points need to be made about the U.S. role in the transition. First, there is no doubt in my mind that the embassy's constant iteration of our central message—the United States favored the transition process and the right of the Honduran people to choose their leaders—encouraged public support for elections and helped to dissuade many military officers from accepting the proposed coup. But we could not have succeeded in getting that message out absent the cooperation of the Honduran media. The embassy and the media produced a synergy that helped keep elections on track. It was a case of public diplomacy paying off in a big way. It is also fair to say that our more traditional diplomatic efforts—whether my formal démarches and private pressure, or the statements of congressional and other visitors, including General Walters—failed to persuade Paz and key military leaders that elections were essential. The military leaders who felt threatened by the transition were not swayed by our importunings, incentives or implied threats. They were bent on pursuing personal interest above all else.

Nearly all of the dysfunctional aspects of our foreign policy reviewed herein hindered successful conclusion of the transition. That they did not cause it to fail completely was nearly miraculous. Especially damaging were the conflicts inherent between our elections aim and other goals in the region—e.g., overthrow of the Sandinista regime, the establishment of U.S. military bases in Honduras, defeat of the Salvadoran insurgency—that were being independently pursued by the CIA and Defense largely without embassy knowledge. These encouraged the Honduran military to believe that they were too important to the United States for us to react vigorously in the event of a coup. Zuniga's assurances to the military that they need not worry, partially the product of his unofficial lines of communication with Washington, underscored that perception. The lack of timely responses to our requests, uncoordinated actions, poorly articulated policies, mistrust of me and other factors also had a negative impact.

Overall, our accomplishments can be measured against the specific policy goals outlined in my original instructions (appendix I), which remained essentially unchanged. The realization of our principal goal subsumed attainment of two related objectives: ratification of a new constitution and the legal registration of all political parties wishing to participate in elections. We had less luck with another related aim, encouraging the parties to develop meaningful programs of government. Their platform statements were long on rhetorical flourish and short on content.

Similarly, our efforts to ensure continuation of ongoing reform programs during the transition period and their acceleration once the elected government was in office were only partially successful. The pace of reform actually slowed during the transition, although it picked up again once Suazo Cordova took office. The peace treaty between Honduras and El Salvador was concluded, and our efforts to ensure its ratification may have been useful at the margin. Although the treaty yielded the normalization of relations between the two countries, progress toward increased regional cooperation was blocked by other factors, principally the conflict in El Salvador, the Sandinista regime in Nicaragua, and our efforts to undermine the latter.

There were two objectives where we had a notable lack of success: denial of the use of Honduran territory to forces hostile to El Salvador and Nicaragua and the continued containment of subversion, with due consideration given to human rights. Although our instructions were never amended, there were major changes in our policy. With respect to Nicaragua, instead of seeking to deny anti-Sandinista groups' use of Honduran territory, we began the covert financing and direction of their operations out of bases located in Honduras. The thrust of our policy changed from one of trying to contain the Sandinistas' leftward drift through incentives for cooperation and support of countervailing forces, to one of unrelenting hostility. Some progress was made in controlling the frontier with El Salvador, but our failure to take a timely role in addressing the refugee problem prevented significant improvement for several years longer than necessary.

Containing domestic subversion and protecting human rights was the area of conspicuous failure. Domestic subversion increased sharply, fueled by popular resentment of government repression and U.S. activities and military presence, as well as Sandinista sponsorship and support. Honduran human rights practices took a sharp turn for the worse in early 1981. We knew about this and did nothing. Our human rights interests were definitely subordinated to all other goals, period.

The latter policy change suggests two speculative questions. First, would a vigorous U.S. effort to persuade Honduran security forces to refrain from serious human rights abuses have succeeded? And second, would such efforts have adversely affected the attainment of other objectives?

I fear that the answers to both questions are discouraging to those who believe, as I do, that human rights constitute an important element in our foreign policy. In retrospect, it seems to me unlikely that we could have prevented those abuses or had more than a marginal effect on Honduran security forces' practices, given Alvarez's personality and position. And even a marginal effect would have required some pretty strong steps, for example, the temporary suspension of security or economic assistance. Such actions would surely have increased the likelihood that the October coup would have succeeded, thus defeating our principal policy goal. Measures such as those likely to have been required would also have severely damaged the CIA's liaison connection and our relations with the Honduran military.

Nevertheless, I still believe I was right to urge that we take a firmer position on Honduran human rights violations. That view may be a triumph of faith over reason.

On balance, I must conclude that the foreign policy dysfunctions described had seriously adverse, but not devastating, affects on Honduras and our interests there. That they made attainment of our main goal more difficult and encouraged repression and human rights abuses seems undeniable. Over the longer term, they encouraged policies that had very corrosive effects on Honduras—e.g., the covert Contra operation, the large and extended U.S. military presence—and produced high levels of anti-American sentiment.

But the Honduran people and their evolving institutions have shown extraordinary and unexpected resilience. Democracy has taken root and thrived. The military's political power is being steadily diminished. Honduran society is trying to come to terms with the uncharacteristic human rights violations of the 1980s, to find ways to establish some kind of accountability for those acts and to prevent their recurrence. Social and economic development have been slower than hoped, but progress has been made. None of these struggles is complete, nor can anyone be certain as to their outcome.

Notes

Chapter 1

1. A variety of CIA assessment memoranda recently released to the National Security Archive clearly point up heavy Cuban involvement. An interagency intelligence memorandum, "Growth and Prospects of Leftist Extremism in El Salvador," January 1980, notes that Cuba secretly purchased a small Costa Rican airline in 1979 to use for shipment of arms to the Salvadorans. This memo also states that there was a major shipment of arms through Honduras in December 1979; the Honduran Communist Party (PCH) was to be the principal support apparat for the insurgents; and the PCH had agreed to establish safe havens for the Salvadoran groups. A February 19, 1980, National Foreign Assessment Center (NFAC) memorandum stated that "Cuban assistance to Salvadoran insurgents continues to be channeled largely through the PCH. PCH special apparat agreed early last month to furnish 40 Cuban-trained military instructors to the Popular Liberation Front (FPL) of El Salvador in March." Another NFAC memo of June 20, 1980, describes three Cuban supply routes into El Salvador: overland from Nicaragua through Honduras; by sea via small boats crossing the Gulf of Fonseca; and by air, using light aircraft that stage through or transit Nicaragua.

2. Garst File, a number of documents sent to me by David Garst, a member of the mission, plus material that Garst had forwarded to Secretary of State Edmund Muskie that was later given to me. These documents span the May–September 1980 period. This file includes correspondence among Garst, York, Ortiz and others, April–June 1980, which clearly shows their opposition to the administration's human rights and land reform policies, as well as to my appointment.

3. U.S. Embassy San Jose cable 2535, "Visit to Costa Rica of Presidential Mission on Agriculture and Agro-Industrial Development," May 6, 1980. Release of this cable was not requested.

4. The State Department's restricted distribution communications, known officially as "Special Communications Channels," are designed to handle especially sensitive messages and limit access based on a reasonable need to know. At the time, the principal channels were, in ascending order of confidentiality, STADIS (no distribution outside the State Department, which was used to block distribution to other agencies); LIMDIS (usually reserved for substantive policy matters and distributed on strict "need to know" criteria, although distribution to other agencies was allowed); EXDIS (highly sensitive information, having even stricter need-to-know criteria and lesser distribution; lateral transmission to other embassies was allowed, provided the State Department is also an addressee, but not to be sent to other agency addressees);

and NODIS (the most restrictive of these channels, normally reserved for communications between the chief of mission and the secretary or president, and covering subjects of extreme sensitivity; no lateral transmission to other embassies allowed; Department determines distribution to other agencies on a case-by-case basis). There were a number of other special distribution channels not germane to this narrative. The cable in question was sent in the EXDIS channel.

5. U.S. Embassy San Jose cable 2242, "Presidential Mission on Agriculture," April 23, 1980. Release of this document was not requested, but the full text is included in the Garst File, op. cit.

6. Documents in the Garst File indicate that York received the text of my message when transiting Guatemala; a copy of the text, on plain paper, is included in the file. An officer who was in the Guatemalan embassy at the time, and in a position to know, confirmed to me that Ortiz had, in fact, passed the text to York. However, in an April 1997 telephone conversation I sought reconfirmation, but this individual had no recollection of the incident. Ortiz denied having given York a copy of my cable.

7. The Committee of Santa Fe, "A New Inter-American Policy for the Eighties," May 1980. The Committee included retired Gen. Gordon Sumner, Prof. Lewis Tambs, Professor David Jordan and Roger Fontaine, all of whom later had roles in the early Reagan administration. See also Roy Gutman, *Banana Diplomacy* (Simon & Schuster, New York, 1988), p. 21.

8. Foreign Service officers are entitled to a leave period in the United States after two years of service overseas; its purpose is to allow them to become reacquainted with American society and consult in the Department prior to resuming their overseas duties.

9. Gutman, pp. 19–20.

10. National Security Archive, *Nicaragua: The Making of U.S. Policy, 1978–1990*, guide and index, p. 54.

11. General Schweitzer also holds the dubious distinction of having chosen Lt. Col. Oliver North to serve on Reagan's NSC staff. See Robert Timberg, *The Nightingale's Song*, p. 281.

12. *Baltimore Sun*, "Unearthed: Fatal Secrets," by Gary Cohn and Ginger Thompson, June 11–18, 1995, a special report on human rights abuses in Honduras, 1980–88. Cohn and Thompson quote former Assistant Secretary of State Thomas O. Enders as confirming the Argentine role as CIA contract agents for mounting and directing the Contra operation out of Honduras. Also, see Gutman, pp. 49–57, for an extensive and interesting discussion of efforts by American right-wingers to secure Argentine involvement. Gutman, however, errs in attributing Argentina's eventual involvement in the Contra operation to the efforts he describes, in fact, the Argentines were already involved without USG knowledge or support and had been working with the Contras since at least mid-1980.

13. Department of State cable (EXDIS) 270099, "Updated Strategy for Period of Interim Government," October 9, 1980. The complete text of this document may be found in Appendix 1.

14. General Accounting Office (GAO) report, "Applicability of Certain Laws That Pertain to U.S. Military Involvement in El Salvador," July 27, 1982.

15. For a period during the Carter administration, the U.S. Information Agency (USIA) was known as the U.S. International Communications Agency (USICA). It later reverted to the USIA designation; overseas, USIA is known as the U.S. Information Service (USIS). For clarity, the traditional USIA/USIS designations are used throughout.

16. U.S. Public Law 93-475 states, in part, that ambassadors have "full respon-

sibility for the direction, coordination and supervision of all USG employees" in their country of accreditation. Presidents, in their private instructions to ambassadors, routinely reaffirm this mandate. The Carter letter added: "I expect you to provide positive program direction, assuring that all USG activities under the authority of your mission reflect and support current policy, are effectively coordinated and are economically administered."

17. Central Intelligence Agency, Inspector General's Report, "Selected Issues Relating to CIA Activities in Honduras in the 1980s", August 27, 1997; Walsh, Lawrence E., *Iran-Contra: The Final Report,* (Times Books, New York, 1994).

18. Department of State cable 213020, August 12, 1980. Unpublished National Security Archive holding.

19. National Security Archive, "Nicaragua," p. 54.

20. Letter to Amb. Jaramillo of that date, forwarding a copy of Garst's letter to President Carter; also Garst letter of September 8, 1980 (Garst File).

21. The Honduran press later reported as follows. *La Prensa,* San Pedro Sula, February 7, 1981, "Opinion" column entitled "Jack Binns: An Anguished Equilibrium," which dealt with statements made by members of a congressional delegation headed by Gerry Studds (D-MA) asserting that I had tried to prevent the delegation members from speaking out on alleged atrocities occurring in the frontier area and Honduran refugee camps, implying that I supported the extreme right. This column also reported the earlier efforts to depict me as a dangerous leftist as follows: "...when Binns was about to arrive in Tegucigalpa, a representative of an American state, whose name we omit because the subject has not previously been aired publicly, wrote in Guatemala an extensive letter that informed then President Carter that Binns and Robert White (then Ambassador in El Salvador) were men of the left...this letter which the most conservative elements of Guatemala printed in the thousands and brought to Honduras in the days prior to Binns being named Ambassador...." See also *La Prensa* editorial, March 23, 1981, entitled "The Campaign Against Binns."

22. National Security Archive, "Nicaragua," p. 54.

23. Department of State report, "DAS Cheek Meeting with FSLN Political Committee," September 27, 1980. National Security Archive holding.

24. *New York Times,* September 15, 1980.

25. CIA San Salvador Station report 271810Z, September 1980; from National Security Archive collection not yet included in published material.

26. National Security Archive, "Nicaragua," p. 55.

Chapter 2

1. National Security Archive, "El Salvador," p. 35.

2. Jack R. Binns, notes from first Country Team meeting, October 6, 1980.

3. National Security Archive, "Nicaragua," p. 55.

4. USCINCSO cable 081507Z, October 8, 1980. The exact title of this cable is not known, nor has this document been released. However, its purpose was to request ambassadorial concurrence in the proposed *Halcon Vista* exercise.

5. U.S. Embassy Tegucigalpa cable 6295, "Planned US-Honduran Exercise: *Halcon Vista,*" October 9, 1980. Paragraph 6 sets out four arguments presented during the Country Team's deliberations in support of the original Southern Command proposal.

6. Department of State cable 274568, "*Halcon Vista* Exercise," October 14, 1980.

7. U.S. Embassy Tegucigalpa cables 6522, "*Halcon Vista,*" and 6532, "*Halcon Vista* Exercise," October 21 and 22, 1980, respectively.

8. U.S. Embassy Tegucigalpa cable 6276 (NODIS), "Reported Coup Plans," October 7, 1980.

9. U.S. Embassy Tegucigalpa cable 6312, "FonMin Elvir on Border Dispute and Other CA Topics," October 10, 1980.

10. National Security Archive, "El Salvador," p. 35.

11. National Security Archive, "Nicaragua," p. 54.

12. My certainty about events has been shaken by subsequent revelations of the CIA's extensive involvement with Honduran countersubversive units. That information has caused me to ask myself whether our station could actually have been unaware of the activities of the Argentine advisers, given the latter's close involvement with these same units in the same time frame. I don't have a satisfactory answer. It is certainly possible but doesn't seem very likely, especially since the station engaged in an extensive pattern of deception and misinformation in its dealings with me following the change of administrations.

13. National Security Archive, "Nicaragua," provides extensive details of the escalating Contra activity during this period and the steady ratcheting up of Sandinista government repression against dissidents.

14. U.S. Embassy Tegucigalpa cable 6489, "Arms Smuggling and Somocista Activity in Southern Honduras," October 17, 1980.

15. U.S. Embassy Tegucigalpa cable 2558, "Ricardo Zuniga, a Rascal for All Seasons," April 13, 1981. This cable, which has not been released, detailed Zuniga's often nefarious history.

16. U.S. Embassy Tegucigalpa cable 6415 (EXDIS), "Liberal Party May Oppose Treaty with El Salvador," October 15, 1980.

17. U.S. Embassy Tegucigalpa cable 6444 (EXDIS), "Visit of Liberal Party Leader to U.S.," October 16, 1980.

18. *La Tribuna,* "Honduran Road to Democracy a Wise Decision," *El Heraldo,* "Honduran Democracy Will Spring from the Assembly," both October 15, 1980.

19. U.S. Embassy Tegucigalpa cables 6312 (EXDIS), see note 9 above; 6415 (EXDIS), see note 16 above; and 6445 (EXDIS), "Peace Treaty with El Salvador: Tactical Considerations and Recommendations," October 16, 1980.

20. National Security Archive, "El Salvador," p. 36.

21. U.S. Embassy Tegucigalpa cable 6490 (EXDIS), "Meeting with President Paz," October 17, 1980.

22. National Security Archive, "El Salvador," p. 36.

23. U.S. Embassy Tegucigalpa cable 6544 (EXDIS), "Reported Coup Plans," October 22, 1980.

24. U.S. Embassy Tegucigalpa cable 6766 (EXDIS), "Updated Strategy for Period of Interim Government," October 30, 1980.

25. Although I was at the time certain we had little information regarding the activities or plans of the Nicaraguan exile groups in Honduras, and even less about what the Argentines were doing, the CIA's later involvement with both groups has shaken my confidence in that regard. What is clear, as will be described, is that following the change in administration the CIA engaged in a wide range of covert activity in Honduras that was not shared with me or, perhaps, the State Department. And the Tegucigalpa station was an active player. There can be no question that during my tenure the station actively (and successfully) engaged in an extensive pattern of deliberate deception, in violation of both law and specific interagency agreements. Specific examples will follow in the narrative. But these were not the agency's only or most serious violations of law and policy during that period.

26. U.S. Embassy Tegucigalpa cable 6767, "Embassy Annex Hit by Gunfire," October 30, 1980.

27. U.S. Embassy Tegucigalpa cable 6803, "Additional Terrorist Incidents in Tegucigalpa," October 31, 1980. The complete text of the flyer may be found in U.S. Embassy Tegucigalpa cable 6853, "Translation of Pamphlet Sent by Group Claiming Credit for Attack on Embassy Annex," November 3, 1980.

28. U.S. Embassy Tegucigalpa cable 6958, "Physical Security Enhancement," November 11, 1980, describes the regional security officer's recommendations, all of which were implemented.

29. U.S. Embassy Tegucigalpa cable 6905 (STADIS), "Issue of Reimbursement for Leased Helicopter," November 5, 1980.

30. *Tiempo,* "University Repudiates Jack Binns"; *La Tribuna,* "University Bathes Car of Ambassador Binns in Paint"; both November 6, 1980.

31. As there were no State Department documents concerning this matter, I cannot be sure of the date, but I believe I was first approached in the indicated time frame. I could, however, be mistaken as to the approximate date but not about the substance.

32. Gary Cohn and Ginger Thompson, "Unearthed: Fatal Secrets," the *Baltimore Sun,* June 11–18, 1995.

33. Leo Valledares Lanza, *Honduras: The Facts Speak for Themselves,* the preliminary report for the National Commission for the Protection of Human Rights, July 1994, translated and published by Human Rights Watch/Honduras and The Center for Justice and International Law. Chapter 4, "Testimonies," contains the transcript of sometimes contradictory testimony by Florencio Caballero, one of the original trainees who was a member of Battalion 316 and predecessor organizations. See especially pp. 179–83. Other testimony is also of interest.

34. National Security Archive, "Nicaragua," p. 55.

35. Jack R. Binns, personal diary and notes.

36. U.S. Embassy Tegucigalpa cables 6992, "Nicaraguan Military Helicopter Seized in Honduras," November 11, 1980; 7065, "On-the-Spot View of Border Incidents," November 13, 1981.

37. Jack R. Binns, "Speech for American Association Luncheon," November 11, 1980.

38. Text of Honduran press clippings, various newspapers, November 12, 1980; *El Mercurio,* Santiago, Chile, November 13, 1980; unattributed clipping, Bogotá, Colombia, November 13, 1980.

39. As reported to me by Richard McCormack, then a member of Sen. Jesse Helms's staff, during a December 1980 meeting in Tegucigalpa.

40. National Security Archive, "El Salvador." Undated transition team memorandum from Sanjuan to Robert Neumann, entitled "Interim Report on the Bureau of Inter-American Affairs and Related Bureau and Policy Areas, Department of State." This memo also contained a number of structural and policy recommendations based on wildly inaccurate representations of the Carter administration policies, which are even more notable for their ideological content.

41. Ibid.

42. National Security Archive, "Nicaragua," p. 55.

43. U.S. Embassy Tegucigalpa cable 7314, "ARDEN-Nica Exile Group," November 19, 1980.

Chapter 3

1. U.S. Embassy Tegucigalpa cable 7468 (EXDIS), "Assessment of Continuing Coup Rumors and Policy," November 26, 1980.
2. National Security Archive, "El Salvador," p. 36.
3. National Security Archive, unpublished files: Department of State cable 137640, November 29, 1980; U.S. Embassy San Salvador cable 8332, November 30, 1980, reporting that Foreign Minister Chavez Mena indicated the National Police were responsible; CIA San Salvador Station report 041941Z, December 1980, which reports the National Police carried out these murders, confirming their responsibility. See also CIA San Salvador Station report 011823Z, December 1980.
4. National Security Archive, "El Salvador," p. 36.
5. CIA San Salvador station report 011823Z, December 1980.
6. *El Heraldo*, November 14, 1980, "The Ambassador Jack Robert Binns Ought to Shut Up."
7. U.S. Embassy Tegucigalpa cable 7572, "Honduran Ratification of Peace Treaty with El Salvador," December 2, 1980.
8. U.S. Embassy Tegucigalpa cable 7549, "Visit of Senate Staffer Richard McCormack," December 2, 1980.
9. Much later—after the November 1981 elections, I believe—we received confirmation that the Liberals had received a million dollars from the Sandinistas. They had taken this money, won the election, and ignored their Nicaraguan benefactors. The Suazo Cordova government promptly acceded to virtually every U.S. request to increase pressure on Nicaragua: support for the Contra operation, operational access to Honduran air bases, joint U.S./Honduran military exercises, and support for U.S. positions in international fora. This behavior was vintage Suazo Cordova. The irony was that Zuniga was right about Sandinista support for the Liberals, but, as Senator Helms's former aide, McCormack, later said to me, "You were right. Suazo Cordova turned out to be very pro-American." And, piling irony on irony, Zuniga, his son and his supporters were to become leading critics of U.S. policy and military presence in Honduras.
10. U.S. Embassy Tegucigalpa cable 7550 (NODIS), "Coup Plotting," December 2, 1980.
11. U.S. Embassy Tegucigalpa cable 7850, "Press Comment on Private Visit of SFRC Staffer McCormack," December 16, 1980.
12. National Security Archive, "El Salvador," p. 37.
13. Ibid., pp. 36–38, provides detailed chronology of events related to the murder of these churchwomen.
14. National Security Archive, "El Salvador," p. 37.
15. U.S. Embassy Tegucigalpa cable 7699 (EXDIS), "National Party Leader on Political/Economic Situation," December 8, 1980.
16. Later we learned that part of the surge in bank, supermarket and payroll robberies was the result of Nicaraguan anti–Sandinistas in Honduras trying to bankroll their crusade, not the extreme left.
17. U.S. Embassy Tegucigalpa cable 7685, "Security Threat Analysis—Further Update," December 8, 1980.
18. U.S. Embassy Tegucigalpa cable 7816, "Tegucigalpa: Capital of the Americas," December 12, 1980.
19. The description of this incident, unknown outside the small number of officials who were actually involved or advised of it, is based largely on my recollection of events. This information was closely held within our government at the time.

It was an extraordinary event and was indelibly etched in my mind, permanently shaping my attitudes toward U.S. Military Groups. I found the actions of these officers, one a graduate of West Point, mind-boggling; had I not lived through it I would find it unbelievable. To help ensure accuracy, I asked William G. Bowdler to review my narrative. He acceded to my request and suggested several corrections. I am confident it is an accurate overview of a complex matter. After so many years and absent documentation, however, there may be inadvertent errors. If so, they are unintentional and my responsibility alone.

20. Although each bilateral agreement governing Milgroup operations is unique in its details, they generally require host governments to provide office space, support vehicles and personnel housing allowances, as well as other related expenses.

21. U.S. Embassy Tegucigalpa cable 7979 (NODIS), "Vinelli Kidnapping: Carried Out by Salvadoran FPL," December 1980. The State Department has refused to release most of the cables on this subject, even although the incident and Vinelli's later release, are matters of public record in both the United States and Honduras. However, another cable on this subject that was released, Tegucigalpa 8094, "Update on Vinelli Kidnapping," December 30, 1981, clearly indicates that the FPL was responsible.

22. U.S. Embassy Tegucigalpa cables 7942, "Request for Assistance on Local Security Situation," December 19, 1980; and 8007, "Another Look at The Honduran Security Situation," December 1980. The State Department was unable to locate the latter cable.

23. National Security Archive, "Nicaragua," p. 55.

24. U.S. Embassy Tegucigalpa cable 7848 (EXDIS), "Situation on the Honduran Side of Frontier," December 15, 1980.

25. Jack R. Binns memorandum "The Frontier Problem," December 29, 1980. The Pol/Mil group consisted of the DCM, chief of the Political Section, station chief, Defense attache, Milgroup commander and Arcos. For these meetings we added the AID director and AID officer responsible for food programs, the head of the Economic Section and the regional labor attache.

26. National Security Archive, "Nicaragua," p. 55.

27. National Security Archive, "El Salvador," p. 37.

28. Carpio had been a leading trade unionist and head of the Salvadoran Communist Party when I served in El Salvador. He was repeatedly brutalized by Salvadoran authorities and was a dedicated Marxist. He broke with the Communist Party in 1970, establishing the Popular Liberation (FPL), the first guerrilla group, and taking up arms.

The military wing of the Faribundo Marti National Liberation Front (FMLN) dominated the opposition decision-making structure and was composed of Carpio's FPL; the People's Revolutionary Army (ERP), another Salvadoran Communist Party breakaway founded by Roque Dalton in 1972, which was reputedly even more violent than the FPL; the Armed Forces of the National Resistance (FARN), formed by dissident ERP members in 1975 following Dalton's murder by his own associates and considered the least doctrinaire of the paramilitary groups; the armed wing of the Communist Party, Armed Forces of the Liberation (FAL), which did not enter the insurgent struggle until 1980; and the Central American Workers Revolutionary Party, a small Trotskyist group. Under pressure from Cuba in 1980 these disparate groups formed the FMLN, which later joined with the FDR to form an umbrella Unified Revolutionary Directorate (DRU). The DRU, at least in theory, was the body that had to approve the good offices proposal. Herein the term FDR is used to represent both the FDR and the FDR/DRU.

29. U.S. Embassy Tegucigalpa cable 8025 (EXDIS), "Reina on a Negotiated Solution to Salvadoran Situation," December 24, 1980. This account is based on that cable, plus my recollection of phone conversations with Bowdler at the time; I do not recall having received an official report of the original meeting.

30. U.S. Embassy Managua cable 6100 (NODIS), "Meeting with FDR Leader Hector Oqueli," December 23, 1980. I had forgotten this cable until 1996, when I came across it in the National Security Archive's unpublished holdings.

31. Department of State cable 339182 (NODIS), "Meeting with FDR Leader Hector Oqueli," December 24, 1980. This cable too surfaced in the National Security Archive's unpublished holdings.

32. National Security Archive, "El Salvador," p. 38.

33. Ibid.

34. U.S. Embassy Tegucigalpa cable 8094 (EXDIS), "Update on Vinelli Kidnapping," December 30, 1980. This document has been withheld.

35. U.S. Embassy Tegucigalpa cable 8080 (NODIS), "Reina on Salvadoran Dialogue," December 30, 1980.

36. U.S. Embassy cable 8118, "Support for El Salvador/Honduras Border Observers," December 31, 1980.

37. National Security Archive, "El Salvador," p. 38.

38. National Security Archive, "Nicaragua," p. 56.

39. U.S. Embassy Tegucigalpa cable 0077 (LIMDIS), "Salvadoran Refugees in Honduras: Need for Refugee Camps and Strategies to Achieve Them," January 6, 1981.

40. Department of State cable 3027, "Helicopters for OAS Observer Group," January 8, 1981.

41. U.S. Embassy Tegucigalpa cables 0178, "Helicopter Support for OAS Border Observers," January 9, 1981; and 0284, "Extension of U.S. Support for OAS Observers," January 15, 1981.

42. U.S. Embassy Tegucigalpa cable 0201 (NODIS), "Reina Meets with FDR/DRU," January 12, 1981.

43. U.S. Embassy Tegucigalpa cable 0138, "Most Recent Estimate of Salvadoran Refugees," January 8, 1981.

44. National Security Archive, "El Salvador," p. 38.

45. *Diario las Americas,* "Cuba Trains Central American Guerrillas," January 13, 1981. Also, *El Heraldo,* "Cuba Prepares Armed Invasion of Central America," January 10, 1981; *La Tribuna,* "Cuba Incites and Trains People to Destabilize CA," January 10, 1981; *La Prensa,* "Cuba Trains CA Guerrillas," January 10, 1981, and "Cuba and CA Subversion," January 13, 1981.

46. U.S. Embassy Tegucigalpa cable 0184, "Letter of Resignation," January 10, 1981.

47. Although it is generally accepted that the Sandinistas ousted Somoza by force of arms, that was not the case. They were merely one element of a very broadly based anti-Somoza coalition that effectively closed down the country by means of a general strike, ultimately forcing Somoza to turn power over to an interim president and leave the country. After Somoza's departure, National Guard forces, for the most part, stopped fighting. In the chaos that followed, the Sandinistas, who were by far the best armed and organized of the opposition coalition, were able to seize power. It was the general strike and united opposition of nearly all Nicaraguans, together with pressure from the United States and other hemispheric nations, not Sandinista military prowess, that forced Somoza out and created the situation that they were able to exploit. The Salvadorans tried to use the same general strike strategy but were unsuccessful because they lacked the requisite popular support.

48. U.S. Embassy Tegucigalpa cable 0201 (see note 42 above).

49. U.S. Embassy Tegucigalpa cable 0248, "Proposed Meeting with Ungo," January 13, 1981.

50. National Security Archive, "El Salvador," p. 39.

51. U.S. Embassy Tegucigalpa cables 0348, "Codel Studds: Message for the President and President Elect Reagan From Codel"; 0362, "Text of Codel Studds 'Outline of Major Findings'"; 0389, "Codel Studds"; 0413, "Codel Studds"; 0439, "Codel Studds/Edgar/Mikulski in Honduras"; all late January 1981. The copy of 0413 is of poor quality and illegible in several spots.

52. *Tiempo,* "U.S. Ambassador Tried to Silence Salvadoran Army Atrocities," February 6, 1981; story was based on UPI coverage of their February 5 press conference in Washington, D.C.

53. Department of State cable 011455, "Honduran Views on Events in El Salvador," January 16, 1981.

54. U.S. Embassy Tegucigalpa cable 0329 (EXDIS), "Paz on Border Situation: 'What Does the U.S. Want Me to Do,'" January 16, 1981.

55. U.S. Embassy Tegucigalpa cable 0336 (LIMDIS), "Enhancement of Honduran Armed Forces, Especially on Salvadoran Border," January 16, 1981.

56. U.S. Embassy Tegucigalpa cable 0343 (LIMDIS), "Honduran Views on Events in El Salvador," January 16, 1981.

57. National Security Archive, "Nicaragua," p. 56.

58. U.S. Embassy Tegucigalpa cable 0335 (NODIS), "Press Query Re FDR/DRU Approach," January 16, 1981.

59. U.S. Embassy Tegucigalpa cable 0337, "IMF and IBRD Programs in Honduras," January 16, 1981.

60. Department of State cable 009168, "Salvadoran Refugees in Honduras," January 15, 1981. Release of this document was not requested.

61. U.S. Embassy Tegucigalpa cable 0346, "Salvadoran Refugees in Honduras," January 16, 1981.

62. U.S. Embassy Tegucigalpa cable 0345, "FonMin Elvir on Salvadoran Situation," January 16, 1981.

63. Central Intelligence Agency, "CA Arms Trafficking: The Comayaguela Case," February 20, 1981. Arms seized by the Hondurans included M-16 rifles and ammunition that were traced to U.S. Army stockpiles in Vietnam in the 1970s, rocket-propelled grenades and launchers of Chinese manufacture and other items.

64. U.S. Embassy Tegucigalpa cable 0390, "GOH Seizure of Clandestine Arms Shipment," January 19, 1981.

65. U.S. Embassy Tegucigalpa cable 0502 (EXDIS), "Possible Exchange of Arms Smuggler for Kidnapped Banker," January 23, 1981.

66. I am indebted to Bill Walker, who as U.S. ambassador in El Salvador played a crucial role in negotiating the final peace accords in that country, for this commentary about Guardado's later years. Would things have turned out differently if Guardado had been imprisoned by the Hondurans or had been turned over to Salvadoran authorities?

67. National Security Archive, "El Salvador," p. 39.

68. Bowdler, William G., in a letter to the author dated November 14, 1995.

69. Gutman, *Banana Diplomacy,* pp. 26–27. Gutman describes the transition and negotiations between Newsom and Allen. He may, however, have given Carbaugh too much credit for Bowdler's dismissal. Bowdler was an anathema to much of the far right, and Carbaugh's description of his role may have been exaggerated. Nor was Gutman aware that Bowdler had applied for retirement before Newsom's phone call.

70. Bushnell had been slated to be ambassador to Chile. Although he served the new administration loyally for nearly four months as acting assistant secretary, as any Foreign Service officer should have done, that nomination was not renewed, nor was he offered another position of comparable importance. In a very real sense he too was a victim of the Reagan administration's retribution for loyal service to the previous administration. And in some ways his treatment was even more egregious.

71. Gutman details the wild, often bizarre and uncoordinated, efforts of various insiders and outsiders to influence U.S. foreign policy in Central America; all too often the know-nothings prevailed.

Chapter 4

1. Several years earlier Congress had put an end to AID's public safety activities designed to provide professional police training. This prohibition followed exposure of CIA involvement in these programs. Some police units in recipient countries had engaged in serious human rights violations, and we were being tainted by these activities, even if we had not actually sponsored them. The Reagan administration never really tried to overturn that ban, so I suppose Paz's information was just another example of the misinformation spawned by the disorderly Reagan transition process. The risk of being tainted by client state actions, of course, is inherent in any assistance activity involving foreign police or military organizations. We cannot control their behavior and, if they begin repressing their own people, we invariably suffer from our association with them. There is no easy solution to this conundrum. Without help to develop more professional, less-abusive practices, change is likely to come at a glacial pace. Yet when security forces engage in traditional repressive behavior, those providing technical and other assistance are blamed.

2. U.S. Embassy Tegucigalpa cable 0457, "Honduran Request for Police Training," January 21, 1981.

3. *La Prensa*, "Salvadoran Marxists Wanted to Win the Diplomatic Battle in Tegucigalpa," January 22, 1981.

4. See, for example, the *Miami Herald*, "2 Salvadoran Coalition Leaders: We Were Near Talks with U.S.," January 29, 1981; and "Binns' Meetings: Same Set of Facts, Two Interpretations," January 31, 1981. The latter story was based on another backgrounder we gave Guy Gugilotta of the *Miami Herald*.

5. National Security Archive, "Nicaragua," p. 56.

6. U.S. Embassy Tegucigalpa cable 0443, "Reported Honduran Military Operations on Border," January 21, 1981.

7. National Security Archive, "Nicaragua," p. 56.

8. Department of State cable 020773, "Press Guidance—January 26," January 27, 1981.

9. Jack R. Binns, my written statement for the January 28 press conference and anticipated questions, undated.

10. U.S. Embassy Tegucigalpa cable 0615 (EXDIS), "Request for Guidance in Dealing with Nicaraguan Exiles," January 28, 1981.

11. A partial listing of front-page headlines follows: *La Prensa*, "US Does Not Plan Armed Intervention in El Salvador or Other Country in Area"; *La Tribuna*, "Cuba Sent Arms Decommissioned in Comayagua"; *Tiemp*, "Hidden Arms Were for Salvadoran Guerrillas"; *El Cronista*, "North American Ambassador Denies Charges"; all January 29, 1981.

12. U.S. Embassy Tegucigalpa cable 0697 (STADIS), "Proposed Visit of Gen. Nutting," January 28, 1981. Release of the cable was not requested.

13. U.S. Embassy Tegucigalpa cable 0622, "GOH Refugee Commission

Recommendations," January 28, 1991. The Department of State has withheld this cable.

14. National Security Archive, "El Salvador," p. 39.

15. Ibid. and National Security Archive, "Nicaragua," pp. 56–57.

16. Texaco's manager in Honduras was the sole representative of a major U.S. investor who was not enthusiastic about the embassy/U.S. business group meetings, and he was not a regular participant.

17. U.S. Embassy Tegucigalpa cable 0641, "Texaco/GOH Negotiations Continue Deadlocked," January 28, 1981. This document has one major excision.

18. My experience with several such disputes in other countries suggested that OPIC expropriation guarantees (insurance) were ill advised, precisely because they created a situation in which commercial disputes can become direct intergovernmental conflicts, overriding many other interests we might have in the offending country. This leaves the United States with little discretion in the conduct of our relations with countries involved in these disputes.

19. *La Prensa,* "Nationalization of Refinery Gets Serious"; *Tiempo,* "Binns Doesn't Wish to Comment on Texaco Blackmail"; *El Heraldo,* "The Problem Between Texaco and the Government is Purely Commercial"; all February 4, 1981.

20. U.S. Embassy Tegucigalpa cable 0724, "IMF Position on Honduras," February 2, 1981.

21. Department of State, cable 030214, "Memorandum of Secretary Haig's Conversation with Honduran Foreign Minister," February 5, 1981.

22. U.S. Embassy Tegucigalpa cable 0991 (EXDIS), "Impressions of Col. Gustavo Alvarez," February 11, 1981.

23. U.S. Embassy Tegucigalpa cable 0883 (EXDIS), "Costa Rican Role in Honduran Arms Seizure," February 6, 1981. This document has been excised in several places.

24. Foreign Broadcast Information Service Chiva Chiva, Panama, cable 120320Z, February 1981.

25. U.S. Embassy Tegucigalpa cable 1069, "Alleged Honduran Troop Build-up on Salvadoran Border," February 12, 1981.

26. U.S. Embassy Tegucigalpa cable 1212, "Pro-Guerrilla Priest Arrested," February 19, 1981.

27. U.S. Embassy Tegucigalpa cable 1144, "Elections, Ambassadors and National Party Leader Zuniga," February 17, 1981. This cable was drafted by Arcos, with input from Walker, hence its third person reference to "the Ambassador." Outlining the Liberal Party viewpoint, it also describes actual events that substantiated the theory they advanced. It proved prescient.

28. *Tiempo,* "Ambassador Binns Has Not Conversed with Salvadoran Marxist Leaders"; also "Political Labyrinth" column and cartoon; both February 21, 1981.

29. Richard McCormack, memorandum to State Department Counselor Bud McFarlane, "The Visit of President Paz," with enclosed Honduran news clips and translations, March 24, 1981. These documents were given to me some years later by a friend who had come across them in files in the counselor's office. This disclosure did not come as a surprise. In conversations with me at the time, McCormack was quite candid that he opposed my continuation in Honduras "because I was not the right man for that time." Nor was I surprised by Zuniga's ability to manipulate McCormack.

30. Virginia Prewett Associates, "Hemisphere Hotline—The Private New World Intelligence Service," January 30, 1981, p. 3.

31. U.S. Embassy Tegucigalpa cable 1133, "Honduras and the IMF," February 17, 1981.

32. U.S. Embassy Tegucigalpa cable 1146, "President Paz on Economic Situation and IMF," February 18, 1981.

33. Jack R. Binns, to Thomas M. Tracy, Assistant Secretary for Administration, March 5, 1981.

34. U.S. Embassy Tegucigalpa cable 1333 (EXDIS), "Possible Release of Arms Traffickers," February 24, 1981.

35. National Security Archive, "Nicaragua," p. 57.

36. U.S. Embassy San Salvador cable 1368, "OAS Consultations On El Salvador," late February 1981. This cable has not been released.

37. U.S. Embassy San Jose cable 1117, "OAS Consultations On El Salvador," late February 1981. This cable has not been released.

38. U.S. Embassy Tegucigalpa cable 1310, "Proposed OAS Consultations on El Salvador," February 24, 1981.

39. National Security Archive, "El Salvador," p. 39.

40. Tegucigalpa Defense Attache Office cable of February 15, 1981; National Security Archive holdings.

41. U.S. Embassy Tegucigalpa cable 1335 (NODIS), "Possible Assignment of U.S. Military Personnel in Honduras," February 24, 1981.

42. National Security Archive, "El Salvador," p. 40.

43. U.S. Embassy Tegucigalpa cable 1355 (EXDIS), "Socialist International Meeting in Panama," February 26, 1981. This cable is not available.

44. National Security Archive, "El Salvador," p. 40.

45. National Security Archive, "Nicaragua," p. 57.

46. National Security Archive, "El Salvador," p 40.

Chapter 5

1. U.S. Embassy Tegucigalpa cable 1448, "The Honduran Church: An Overview," March 2, 1981.

2. U.S. Embassy Tegucigalpa cable 1644, "A Cancer in the Vitals: Government Corruption in Honduras," March 7, 1981.

3. U.S. Embassy Tegucigalpa cable 1679, "Arms Infiltration Problem," March 11, 1981. The State Department refused to release this document.

4. U.S. Embassy Tegucigalpa cable 2558, "Zuniga: A Rascal for All Seasons," April 13, 1981. The State Department refused to release this document.

5. National Security Archive, "Nicaragua," p. 57.

6. U.S. Embassy Tegucigalpa cable 1584 (EXDIS), "Private Sector Leader on Possible Coup," March 5, 1981.

7. *Tiempo,* "Director of AID in Honduras," March 6, 1981.

8. U.S. Embassy Tegucigalpa cables 1795 (EXDIS), "Arms Infiltration and Military Assistance," and 1800 (EXDIS), "Arms Infiltration and Military Assistance," both March 13, 1981, detail our strategy and specific recommendations. They reflect the results of our meeting with Southern Command.

9. Department of State cable 82952 (EXDIS), "Arms Infiltration and Military Assistance," March 2, 1981.

10. National Security Archive, "Nicaragua," p. 57.

11. Department of State cable 56460 (EXDIS), "Honduran and Guatemalan Military Assistance to El Salvador," March 6, 1981.

12. U.S. Embassy Tegucigalpa cable 1673 (EXDIS), "Honduran Military Assistance to El Salvador," March 9, 1981.

13. U.S. Embassy Tegucigalpa press release, "U.S. Military Assistance to Honduras," March 9, 1981.

14. National Security Archive, "Nicaragua," p. 57.

15. Ibid.

16. U.S. Embassy Tegucigalpa cable 1802 (LIMDIS), "Reported Diversion of Refugee Relief Supplies to Guatemala [*sic*]," March 13, 1981. The title should refer to El Salvador, not Guatemala.

17. *La Prensa*, "U.S. Will Recognize Whatever Government Hondurans Elect Democratically," March 14, 1981; *La Tribuna*, "Honduras Not Being Converted into Gendarme of CA," March 14, 1981.

18. Jack R. Binns, to *La Prensa* and *La Tribuna*, March 16, 1981; both papers published the complete text March 18.

19. U.S. Embassy Tegucigalpa cables 1758, "GOH and Private Sector Reach Accord on Tax Package"; and 1804, "Liberal Party Leader on Financial Problem/Tax Package"; both March 1981. These documents are not available.

20. U.S. Embassy Tegucigalpa cable 1842 (EXDIS), "Honduran Military Disquiet Over U.S. Assistance Levels," March 17, 1981.

21. U.S. Embassy Tegucigalpa cable 1872 (EXDIS), "Honduran Military Disquiet Over U.S. Assistance Levels," March 18, 1981.

22. *New York Times*, "For Costa Rica, 2 Bombs Bring a Taste of Fear," March 22, 1981, p. 14. The *Times* reported that the embassy vehicle carrying the Marines was hit by a rocket-propelled grenade; in fact, it was damaged by a remote-controlled bomb that was exploded as the vehicle slowed to cross a speed bump.

23. National Security Archive, "El Salvador," p. 40.

24. Ibid.

25. Ibid.

26. *La Tribuna*, "Honduras: A Development Model for the Region," March 21, 1981; *Tiempo*, "Honduran Political Situation Is Best in CA," March 21, 1981.

27. U.S. Embassy Tegucigalpa cable 1962, "Codel Long Visit to Tegucigalpa," March 20, 1981.

28. Richard McCormack, memorandum to Bud McFarlane, March 24, 1981.

29. *El Heraldo*, "Binns Will Be Fired for His Intervention in Honduran Politics," March 20, 1981.

30. Richard McCormack, memorandum, March 24, 1981.

31. U.S. Embassy Tegucigalpa cable 1959, "Local Newspaper Attacks U.S. Ambassador," March 20, 1981; cable 1988, "*La Prensa* (Mar. 23) Editorial 'Campaign Against Binns,'" March 23, 1981; cable 1991, "Further Reverberations From Attack on Ambassador," March 23, 1981. Only cable 1988 is available.

32. Jack R. Binns, to Francisco Morales Calix, March 20, 1981.

33. Coverage was too extensive to cite in its entirety. See, for example, *Tiempo*, "What the Herald Says Is Slanderous and False: Binns"; *La Tribuna*, "They Try to Discredit My Country and Me: Binns"; *El Cronista*, "There Was No Meeting of the PDCH with Binns"; all March 21, 1981.

34. *El Heraldo*, various stories, pp. 4–5, all March 21, 1981. See particularly "Allegations of Binns' Intervention Follow Zuniga Thesis."

35. *URP*, "Jack Binns: Interference and Repression," March 21, 1981.

36. Valladares, "*Honduras: The Facts Speak for Themselves*," pp. 19, 130–33.

37. *La Prensa*, "The Campaign Against Binns," March 23, 1981.

38. U.S. Embassy Tegucigalpa cable 1991 (see note 31 above).

39. National Security Archive, "Nicaragua," p. 57.

40. This description of events is based on documents relating directly to this

matter, as well as my quite fallible powers of recall. Specific documents are my letter warning the technician of my intent to reprimand him officially for his actions (March 30, 1981); his memorandum to Colonel Goodwin reporting on the Superior Council meeting (March 24, 1981), in which he describes what he told that body; and my official letter of reprimand (April 6, 1981). I also met with Goodwin and the individual concerned prior to writing the March 30 letter in an effort to determine exactly what had happened and to explain to them where they had erred.

41. Department of State cable 77984 (EXDIS), "The Almost Visit of General Paz," March 27, 1981. That was the first notification I received of what was going on—four days after the fact. That delay, for whatever reason, was an extraordinary and inexcusable breach of practice. The State Department has refused to release this cable.

42. Richard McCormack to Bud McFarlane, memorandum, March 24, 1981.

43. Rich Brown (Deputy Director, ARA/CEN) to Jack R. Binns, March 27, 1981.

44. Ibid.

45. John Blacken (Director, ARA/CEN) to Jack R. Binns, official-informal letter, March 26, 1981.

46. Department of State cable 77984 on Paz visit (see note 41 above).

47. U.S. Embassy Tegucigalpa cable 2325 (EXDIS), "Aborted Paz Visit, Its Implications and Strategy Recommendations," April 2, 1981.

48. Brown to Binns (see note 43 above).

49. National Security Archive, "Nicaragua," op. cit., p. 57.

50. Robert Timberg, *The Nightingale's Song*, p. 424.

51. It was accepted practice to make seats on the C-12 available to mission personnel on all routine or logistic flights. Preference was normally given to military members and their dependents, and Panama was a popular destination for them because of the commissaries and post exchanges. On this flight the other seats were taken up by military and dependents.

52. Department of State cable 77984 on Paz visit (see note 41 above).

53. Based on the technician's memorandum of March 24, 1981, describing what he told the Superior Council.

54. *New York Times*, "Three Injured in Honduras as Assembly Is Bombed," March 27, 1981, p. 5.

55. U.S. Embassy Tegucigalpa cables 2142, "Demands of SAHSA Hijackers"; 2144, "SAHSA Hijacking: GOH Position and Strategy"; 2151, "SAHSA Hijacking"; 2164, "SAHSA Hijacking"; and 2182 (LIMDIS), SAHSA Hijacking"; March 30–April 1, 1981. Also see U.S. Embassy Managua cables 1448, "Hijacking of SAHSA 414, Chronology"; and 1452, "Hijacking of SAHSA 414," March 28 and 29. These latter cables are from National Security Archive, "Nicaragua Collection."

56. U.S. Embassy Tegucigalpa cables 2443, "SAHSA Hijacking"; 2987, "SAHSA Hijacking: Demarche to GOH"; and 3223, "SAHSA Hijacking: Approach to Col. Torres Arias"; all April 1981.

57. Quotations are from the technician's memorandum of March 24, 1981.

58. National Security Archive, "El Salvador," p. 41.

Chapter 6

1. U.S. Embassy Tegucigalpa cable 1800 (EXDIS), "Arms Infiltration and Military Assistance"; U.S. Embassy Tegucigalpa cable 2248 (EXDIS), "Arms Infiltration and Proposed Interdiction," April 1, 1981; Department of State cable 82952 (EXDIS),

"Arms Infiltration and Military Assistance," and U.S. Embassy Tegucigalpa cable 2300 (EXDIS), "Arms Infiltration and Military Assistance," April 2, 1981.

2. U.S. Embassy Tegucigalpa cable 2309 (LIMDIS), "Honduran Military Desire for Additional Assistance," April 3, 1981.

3. National Security Archive, "Nicaragua," p. 58. See also Gutman, p. 37.

4. Department of State cable 77984, (see chapter 5, note 41).

5. See chapter 5, notes 43, 44, and 45.

6. U.S. Embassy Tegucigalpa cable 2325 (EXDIS/STADIS), "Aborted Paz Visit, Its Implications and Strategy Recommendations," April 2, 1981.

7. U.S. Embassy Tegucigalpa cable 1800, "Arms Infiltration and Military Assistance," (see note 1 above).

8. *New York Times*, "Rightist Exiles Plan Invasion of Nicaragua," April 2, 1981.

9. U.S. Embassy Tegucigalpa cable 2342 (EXDIS), "Apparent Misuse of AID Funds," April 3, 1981.

10. National Security Archive, "El Salvador," p. 41.

11. *La Tribuna*, "Honduras Occupies Third Place in U.S. Military Assistance," April 10, 1981.

12. U.S. Embassy Tegucigalpa cable 2506 (EXDIS), "Arms Infiltration and Military Assistance," April 11, 1981. Also see Embassy Tegucigalpa cable 2448 (EXDIS), "Arms Infiltration and Military Assistance," April 8, 1981.

13. U.S. Embassy Tegucigalpa cable 2558, "Ricardo Zuniga, a Rascal For All Seasons," April 13, 1981. The State Department has withheld this cable.

14. U.S. Embassy Tegucigalpa cables 2543 (LIMDIS), "Honduran Military Leaders to Visit Washington," April 13, 1981. I drafted this cable on April 10, but it was not transmitted until April 13.

15. U.S. Embassy Tegucigalpa cable 2632 (LIMDIS), "Honduran Military Leaders to Visit Washington," April 20, 1981.

16. Department of State cable 113419 (EXDIS), "Colonels Alvarez and Lopez Grijalva," May 2, 1981.

17. Gutman, pp. 47–49.

18. *New York Times*, "Ally of Honduran Army Expects U.S. Right-Face," April 15, 1981.

19. National Security Archive, "El Salvador," p. 41.

20. Ibid.

21. State Department cable 93666 (EXDIS), "Message to President Paz," April 11, 1981. The State Department has withheld this cable.

22. One of the leaders of the Committee for Solidarity with the Salvadoran People was an American Catholic priest, Father Earl Gallagher, who worked in the Santa Rosa de Copan diocese. Another American priest, Father James Carney, was also active with the refugees; Carney was subsequently expelled from Honduras, joined a Honduran insurgent group in Nicaragua and was killed by the Honduran military in December 1983 while accompanying a guerrilla column infiltrating Honduras from Nicaragua. The circumstances of Carney's death are unclear and in dispute.

23. *New York Times*, "Salvadorans Deny Killings," April 10, 1981, 3:3.

24. U.S. Embassy Tegucigalpa cable 3253, "1981 World Refugee Report to Congress," May 11, 1981.

25. Jack R. Binns, daily diary, April 1981.

26. U.S. Embassy Tegucigalpa cables 2795 (EXDIS), "General Walters Visit"; 2968 (EXDIS), "General Walters Visit to Honduras"; 3254 (EXDIS), "General Walters Program for Honduras"; April 24, April 30 and May 11, 1981, respectively.

27. National Security Archive, "El Salvador," p. 41.

Notes: Chapter 6

28. U.S. Embassy Tegucigalpa cable 2835 (NODIS), "Honduran Scheme to Attack Nicaragua," April 27, 1981. There are a few excisions in this cable.

29. For further details, see Gutman, pp. 19–57. Gutman describes, often in the words of the players themselves, the harebrained efforts of self-appointed administration spokesmen, as well as the uncoordinated actions of some of those in official positions.

30. U.S. Embassy Tegucigalpa cable 2835 (NODIS), (see note 28 above).

31. Department of State cable 113419 (EXDIS), "Cols. Alvarez and Lopez Grijalva," May 2, 1981.

32. Ibid.

33. Ibid.

34. Gutman, pp. 46–48.

35. Sanchez, soon replaced by Duane "Dewey" Clarridge, moved over to Defense, where he served as deputy assistant secretary for international security, responsible for the Latin American region. In that capacity he was a frequent visitor to Central America, especially El Salvador. On several of those trips he transited Tegucigalpa. I suspect that he met privately (i.e., without my knowledge) with Alvarez and others. At that time Sanchez represented Defense on the "Core Group" set up by Enders to coordinate policy and activities in Central America. It was heavily tilted toward the CIA. Members, in addition to Enders, were Sanchez (Defense); Duane Clarridge (CIA); former CIA analyst Al Sapia-Bosch (NSC); and Lt. Gen. Paul Gorman, who also had served previously with the CIA (Joint Chiefs of Staff). This body later evolved into the Restricted Inter-Agency Group (RIG).

36. As was often the case, Schweitzer was speaking without authorization and was in no real position to direct U.S. policy, although he could on occasion influence it. He was very much on the periphery of our Central American policy and was generally regarded as a loose cannon. He was removed from the NSC in November, about the time I was replaced as ambassador, for repeated unauthorized public statements.

37. The story of the Barrillas/Navarro disappearance was described in greater detail in an article I wrote for the *Baltimore Sun*. See the *Baltimore Sun,* "Departing Honduras to Where?" by Jack Binns, October 29, 1995.

38. U.S. Embassy Tegucigalpa 2936 cable (EXDIS), "Possible Honduran Attack on Nicaragua," April 30, 1981. Pezzullo's cable, Managua 1949, is not available.

39. U.S. Embassy Tegucigalpa cable 2988, "Further Information on Border Situation," May 1, 1981.

40. U.S. Embassy Tegucigalpa cable 2971, "Proposed Halcon Vista Exercise," April 30, 1981.

41. U.S. Embassy Tegucigalpa cable 3089, "Constituent Assembly Passes Emergency Economic Plan," May 6, 1981.

42. U.S. Embassy Tegucigalpa cable 3015, "Press Guidance for SOUTHCOM Survey Team," May 4, 1981.

43. U.S. Embassy Tegucigalpa cable 3064 (EXDIS), "Paz on Nicaraguan Situation," May 5, 1981.

44. U.S. Embassy Tegucigalpa cable 3086, "Reported Nicaraguan Attack on Honduras," May 6, 1981.

45. Jack R. Binns, daily diary and notes.

46. *Washington Post,* "Honduran Military Girds for War with Nicaragua," May 5, 1981.

47. U.S. Embassy Tegucigalpa cable 3225 (LIMDIS), "Honduran/Nicaraguan Problems," May 8, 1981.

48. *La Prensa,* "The *Washington Post* Has Lied: Binns," May 9, 1981, which carried my verbatim comment under this sensational and inaccurate headline.

49. Front-page headlines were: *El Heraldo,* "USA Will Support Democratic Process in Honduras"; *La Tribuna,* "USA Ratifies Support of Honduran Political Process"; *La Prensa,* "US Doesn't Want War"; *Tiempo,* "Binns Confident of Pacific Solution With Nicaragua"; *El Cronista,* "US Supports Pacific Solution With Nicaragua"; all May 9, 1981.

50. U.S. Embassy Tegucigalpa cable 3205, "Request for Consultations," May 11, 1981. Release of this document was not requested.

51. U.S. Embassy Tegucigalpa cable 3291 (LIMDIS), "National Party Leader on Elections," May 12, 1981

52. Jack R. Binns, daily diary.

53. U.S. Embassy Tegucigalpa Issues Paper, "What Role, If Any, Should the USG Play in the GOH/Texaco Dispute?" October 12, 1981.

54. U.S. Embassy Tegucigalpa cable 3074 (EXDIS), "Reported Misuse of AID Resources," May 5, 1981.

55. U.S. Embassy Tegucigalpa cable 3333 (EXDIS), "Apparent Misuse of AID Resources," May 13, 1981.

56. U.S. Embassy Tegucigalpa cable 3336 (EXDIS), "Meetings With President Paz, FonMin and Military Leaders," May 14, 1981; this cable was drafted by Walters and details the first day's meetings.

57. *La Prensa,* "Reagan's Special Envoy Unreachable for Journalists"; *Tiempo,* "Ex of the CIA Spoke with Paz Yesterday"; *El Heraldo,* "US State Department Envoy Met with Paz"; all May 14, 1981.

58. Binns, Jack R., daily diary.

59. U.S. Embassy Tegucigalpa cable 3368 (EXDIS), "Meeting with President Paz," May 14, 1981. This cable was drafted by Walters and included the following comment about Paz's elections commitment: "While President Paz reaffirmed his and the Armed Forces commitment to the November elections, I sensed a growing concern on his part at his ability to carry through on this promise. This may well be connected to his desire to retain the post of commander of the armed forces after the new president is sworn in."

60. Ibid.

61. This incident was not included in Walters's cable describing the meeting (see note 59 above). Indeed, Walters's version of these events specifically stated "Only Ambassador Binns and I were in the room with him," which was untrue. Presumably, Walters covered the substance of the private meeting in a separate report to Haig.

62. Secretary Haig offered a similar theory at a March 18 Senate Foreign Relations Committee hearing and was challenged by committee members. State issued a clarification of Haig's comment two days later, saying these women "may" have run a roadblock, which led to an "exchange" of gunfire, but that Haig had not wished to imply the women had engaged in a gun battle. National Security Archive, "El Salvador," p. 40.

63. This incident was not included in the embassy reports of Walters's visit. As far as I am aware, there is no written record of it. This account is based principally on my recall (it was certainly one of the most memorable events in my 25-year career). To ensure its accuracy, I asked Bill Walker to review this account and offer any corrections, additions or amendments he thought necessary. He acceded to my request and suggested several changes, which were incorporated. Although there were several minor differences in our respective recall of details, we agreed that the general substance of the account is accurate. Any errors of omission or commission, however, are my responsibility.

64. This account is based on press reports and a USIS transcript of the conference. See *La Prensa,* "20 Million Lempira Increase in US Military Assistance for Honduras"; *Tiempo,* "Reagan Will Fill 'Oasis' with 20 Million in Arms"; both May 16, 1981. This was not what we had hoped would be emphasized about Walters's visit; the media's presentation of the military assistance levels was also incorrect.

65. Jack R. Binns, to editors of all major newspapers, clarifying the military assistance issue, May 18, 1981. Verbatim question and answer were taken from a USIS transcript of the press conference.

66. National Security Archive, "Nicaragua," p. 58.

67. See note 64, above, for press headlines.

68. *Tiempo,* "US Has Not Increased Military Assistance to Honduras"; *La Prensa,* "About US Military Assistance for Latin America"; *El Heraldo,* "North American Military Assistance Remains at Announced Levels"; all May 20, 1981.

69. U.S. Embassy Tegucigalpa cable 3456 (EXDIS), "Assessment of General Walters' Visit," May 18, 1981.

70. U.S. Embassy Tegucigalpa cable 3574, "Visit to Salvadoran Refugee Sites," May 22, 1981.

71. U.S. Embassy Tegucigalpa cable 3427, "Survey Team Recommendations on Arms Infiltration," May 18, 1981.

72. U.S. Embassy Tegucigalpa cable 3674, "Arms Interdiction Training Proposal," May 27, 1981.

73. Jack R. Binns, daily diary, program notes and correspondence with the Council of the Americas, various dates.

74. U.S. Embassy Tegucigalpa cable 3572 (EXDIS), "CA Chiefs of State Meeting," May 22, 1981.

75. U.S. Embassy Managua cable 2178 (EXDIS), "Regional Approach to CA Security," May 21, 1981. This cable has not been released.

76. U.S. Embassy Tegucigalpa cable 3610 (EXDIS), "Honduran/Nicaraguan Conflict: Regional Considerations," May 22, 1981.

77. Ibid.

Chapter 7

1. Office of Central American Affairs memorandum, "Ambassador Binn's [*sic*] Appointments"; and Jack R. Binns, notes.

2. Gutman, *Banana Diplomacy,* pp. 26–38 and 46–120.

3. National Security Archive, "Nicaragua," op. cit., p. 58.

4. U.S. Embassy Tegucigalpa cable 3253, "1981 World Refugee Report to Congress," May 11, 1981.

5. National Security Archive, "Nicaragua," p. 58.

6. National Security Archive, "El Salvador," p. 42.

7. National Security Archive, "Nicaragua," p. 58.

8. U.S. Embassy Tegucigalpa cable 3910, "Conversation with Chairman of National Electoral Tribunal," June 4, 1981.

9. U.S. Embassy Tegucigalpa cable 4057, "State of National Party and Military in Politics," June 9, 1981.

10. U.S. Embassy Tegucigalpa cable 4036, "Additional Thoughts on Proposed *Halcon Vista* Exercise," June 8, 1981.

11. *Baltimore Sun,* "Departing Honduras to Where?" provides a more detailed account of this incident.

12. U.S. Embassy Tegucigalpa cable 4127 (NODIS), "Potential Problems with GOH and Exile Groups," June 11, 1981. Portions deleted are references to intelligence reports.

13. U.S. Embassy Tegucigalpa cable 4289 (EXDIS), "Views of Junta President Duarte," June 16, 1981.

14. U.S. Embassy Tegucigalpa cable 4300 (EXDIS), "Possible Appearance of Death Squad Type Justice," June 17, 1981.

15. Jack R. Binns, draft text of "Ambassador's Comment," undated.

16. Valladares Lanza, *Honduras,* pp. 20–21.

17. U.S. Embassy Tegucigalpa cable 4314 (NODIS), "Reports of GOH Repression and Approach to Problem," June 17, 1981. See also U.S. Embassy Tegucigalpa cable 4409, "Disappearance of Revolutionary Leaders," June 19, 1981, for further details on the Nativi/Martinez case.

18. U.S. Embassy Tegucigalpa cable 4368 (EXDIS), "Possible Deterioration in Honduran/Nicaraguan Relations," June 18, 1981.

19. *Tiempo,* "U.S. State Department Is Responsible," June 19, 1981.

20. Jack R. Binns to Rector Juan Almendares, June 19, 1981.

21. This section is based on the text of a memorandum of conversation of this meeting that was prepared June 26 by Schweitzer's office at the request of the Honduras desk officer. The text of that memorandum was incorporated in a draft cable, "Honduran Military Delegation Visit with NSC Staff Members, June 19, 1981," to be sent to Tegucigalpa June 29; that cable was never transmitted. It was my understanding that State—Enders or one of his deputies—refused to authorize its transmission. A "bootleg" copy was then sent me by someone who questioned its accuracy, which was presumably why the bureau had declined to approve its transmission. I had earlier been advised by telephone of this meeting on June 23. This is another example of the Hondurans' desire to work outside official channels and Schweitzer's freewheeling approach to foreign policy.

22. Jack R. Binns, official-informal letter to Assistant Secretary Enders, July 17, 1981.

23. Department of State cable 16004, title not known, on or about June 18, 1981. Release of this cable was not requested.

24. U.S. Embassy Tegucigalpa cable 4395 (NODIS), "Allegations of Abduction by Honduran Security Forces," June 19, 1981.

25. National Security Archive, "Nicaragua," p. 59.

26. This is an allusion to the February 23 "White Paper" that described Cuban and other support for the Salvadoran insurgency and was subsequently found to contain numerous errors.

27. *Tiempo,* "U.S. Embassy Preparing Second 'White Paper'," June 22, 1981; *La Tribuna,* "Aid for Refugees Given to the FMLN," June 22, 1981.

28. National Security Archive, "El Salvador," p. 42.

29. In addition to the cited article, see *Tiempo,* "Jack Binns: Almendares Declaration Slanderous"; *La Tribuna,* "U.S. Continues Supporting Return to Constitutional Government"; *El Cronista,* "Amb. Jack Binns Writes to National University Rector"; all June 23, 1981.

30. U.S. Embassy San Salvador cable 4743 (EXDIS), June 23, 1981. This cable, which was Hinton's initial assessment of the situation in El Salvador and a comprehensive set of policy recommendations for the USG, carried special indicators for Secretary Haig, CIA director Casey, Defense Secretary Frank Carlucci and others. Only those portions dealing directly with Honduras are addressed. Release of this document was not requested.

31. Department of State cable 170597 (EXDIS), "Assessment of Salvadoran Situation," June 27, 1981.

32. U.S. Embassy Tegucigalpa cable 4496 (EXDIS), "President Paz on Nicaragua and Tax Problem," June 23, 1981.

33. National Evangelical Committee for Development and Emergency (CEDEN) letter, June 22, 1981; CARITAS of Honduras letter, June 23, 1981; also sent to media outlets.

34. *La Tribuna,* "CARITAS Attends to the Needy without Distinction of Creed or Color," June 23, 1981.

35. Jack R. Binns, to CEDEN executive director, Noemi de Espinoza, June 24, 1981.

36. *La Tribuna,* "Impossible to Control All Help for the Refugees," June 25, 1981; *El Cronista,* "U.S. Does Not Criticize CEDEN and CARITAS," June 26, 1981; *Tiempo,* "Binns Writes CEDEN Director," July 1, 1981.

37. *La Tribuna,* "Won't Retract and Invites Ambassador to Listen to Tapes," June 25, 1981; "I Have Nothing to Retract: Almendares to Binns," June 25, 1981; *La Prensa,* "He Won't Retract, Almendares Says to Binns," June 26, 1981.

38. *La Prensa,* "New Campaign Against U.S. Embassy," June 24, 1981. Translation of text may be found in U.S. Embassy Tegucigalpa cable 4545, "La Prensa Editorial Entitled 'New Campaign Against American Embassy,'" June 24, 1981.

39. *La Prensa,* "Will of Honduran People Ended 18 Years of Unconstitutional Rule," June 29, 1981.

40. U.S. Embassy Tegucigalpa cable 4601, "Speculation About Delay or Frustration of Elections," June 25, 1981.

41. U.S. Embassy Tegucigalpa cable 4625, "Paz Reports GRN to Return Alleged Honduran Spies," June 26, 1981.

42. Jack R. Binns, daily diary.

43. Ibid.

44. U.S. Embassy Tegucigalpa cable 4637, "American Citizen Kidnapped by Alleged Political Terrorists," June 27, 1981.

45. U.S. Embassy Tegucigalpa cable 4710, "Second Kidnapper Arrested by Police," June 30, 1980.

46. U.S. Embassy Tegucigalpa cable 4822, "Another McBroom Kidnapper Killed by Police," July 3, 1981.

47. U.S. Embassy Tegucigalpa cables 4696, "GOH Decides," June 29, 1981; and 4823, "Chief of Staff on OAS Observers," July 3, 1981.

48. In most cases presidential candidates from Latin America would be received at the assistant secretary level; in exceptional cases, they might see the secretary of state or the vice president. Suazo Cordova, as president of the legislature, had courtesy meetings with the Speaker of the House and president pro tem of the Senate. Zuniga, however, held no office that would allow him such access, perhaps another reason for his reluctance to visit Washington.

49. U.S. Embassy Tegucigalpa cable 4653, "Proposed Visit By Assembly President," June 29, 1981.

50. In addition to the president, the executive branch in Honduras includes three vice presidents. Curious as this may seem to Americans, the practice of having multiple vice presidents is fairly common in Latin America.

51. U.S. Embassy Tegucigalpa cable 4815, "Visit of Vice Presidential Candidate," July 1, 1981. Document not available.

52. National Security Archive, "El Salvador," p. 42.

Chapter 8

1. *Tiempo,* "American Congressman Visits on Mission of Peace," July 2, 1981; *La Prensa,* "American Congressman Arrived Yesterday," July 2, 1981.

2. *Washington Post,* "Poland's Plight Prompts Two to Try to Flee," Jack Anderson, September 4, 1981.

3. Jack R. Binns, daily diary.

4. *La Prensa,* "U.S. Support for Elections a Serious and Consistent Policy," July 4, 1981.

5. National Security Archive, "Nicaragua," p. 59.

6. See chapter 1, note 4. NODIS is reserved for matters of extreme sensitivity. At that time only 20 copies of NODIS messages were made, and their distribution was handled directly by the Department's executive secretariat.

7. U.S. Department of State cable 170597 (EXDIS), "Assessment of Salvadoran Situation."

8. Later I learned that Senator Helms and others had objected to Negroponte because of his association with Henry Kissinger. Ironically, Negroponte left the NSC because he disagreed with Kissinger on Vietnam.

9. Jack R. Binns, memorandum for Assistant Secretary Enders, "Improved Honduran/Salvadoran Cooperation," July 9, 1981.

10. For the findings of the Iran-Contra Independent Council regarding Clarridge, see Lawrence E. Walsh, *Iran-Contra: The Final Report,* Times Books, New York, 1994, pp. 247–262.

11. Central Intelligence Agency Inspector General's Report, "Selected Issues Relating to CIA Activities in Honduras in the 1980s," August 27, 1997, p. 3.

12. Valladares Lanza, *Honduras,* pp. 21–38. According to this report, 29 individuals vanished between August and November after being detained by Honduran security forces. Of that group 15 were Salvadorans (presumably members of a suspected insurgent support group), 11 were Hondurans and 3 were other nationalities.

13. National Security Archive, "Nicaragua," p. 59.

14. National Security Archive, "El Salvador," p. 42.

15. At the time Texaco received OPIC coverage, the Honduran government had been fully informed about all aspects of the coverage and its potential implications. Indeed, host government agreement to these arrangements is a precondition for extension of insurance coverage. Texaco's coverage, however, had been agreed to many years previously, and the then-current political leadership did not seem to grasp how expropriation might prejudice the whole range of relations with the United States.

16. U.S. Embassy Tegucigalpa cable 5056 (STADIS), "Texaco/Honduras Negotiations," July 13, 1981.

17. U.S. Embassy Tegucigalpa cable 5168 (EXDIS), "Soviet Tanks in Nicaragua," July 14, 1981.

18. U.S. Embassy Tegucigalpa cable 5179 (EXDIS), "Soviet Tanks in Nicaragua," July 17, 1981.

19. National Security Archive, "Nicaragua," p. 59.

20. U.S. Embassy Tegucigalpa cable 5167 (LIMDIS), untitled, July 14, 1981.

21. Ibid.

22. *La Tribuna,* "The U.S. and Our Electoral Process," July 17, 1981.

23. U.S. Embassy Tegucigalpa cable 5617, "Alleged Salvadoran Incursion into Honduras," July 31, 1981.

24. U.S. Embassy Tegucigalpa cable 5325 (LIMDIS), "Honduran Foreign Minister on Border Situation," July 22, 1981.

25. U.S. Embassy Tegucigalpa cable 5352 (EXDIS), "FonMin on Nicaragua and Outlook in Honduras," July 22, 1981.

26. Ibid.

27. U.S. Department of State cable 189539, "Nassau Conference on Caribbean Basin," mid-July 1981. Release of this document was not requested.

28. U.S. Embassy Tegucigalpa cable 5420, "Nassau Conference on Caribbean Basin," July 21, 1981.

29. *El Heraldo,* "Assistance Plan for CA and Caribbean Does Not Include Military Aid," July 22, 1981.

30. U.S. Embassy Tegucigalpa cable 5199, "Suggested Talking Points for Honduran Liberal Party Visit," July 17, 1981.

31. "Civic action" is a phrase used by the U.S. military to describe small civil engineering (e.g., improving roads, drilling wells, repairing buildings), preventive health (e.g., inoculations, basic health care) and similar projects carried out by military units in order to enhance the military's popularity, while serving legitimate economic and social development ends. These activities are designed "to win the hearts and minds of the people." Although the developmental impact of these activities is often near the margin and they rarely engage the communities that benefit, they do some good.

32. The only American members of the U.S. mission allowed to carry weapons were the Marine Security Guards (normally only while on embassy property) and the DEA agents when actually on a narcotics operation. Exceptions were occasionally made for others, e.g., the Regional Security Officer, but these were rare. Several military members had advised me that they often carried handguns in their cars. They were aware of our policy and knew the likely consequences if implicated in a public incident involving use of a weapon. I chose not to make it an issue.

33. U.S. Embassy Tegucigalpa cable 5940, "*New York Times* Story on Green Berets," August 12, 1981.

34. U.S. Embassy Tegucigalpa cable 5373 (LIMDIS), "GOH Request for Increased FMS Credit for FY 81," July 23, 1981. The best available copy of this document is illegible in spots; several parts have also been excised.

35. Jack R. Binns, daily diary.

36. Ibid.

37. U.S. Embassy Tegucigalpa cable 5623 (EXDIS), "Reported Arrest and Expulsion of CARE Employee for Aiding Salvadoran Guerrilla," July 31, 1981. Also see U.S. Embassy Tegucigalpa cable 5544, "UNHCR in Honduras," July 28, 1981.

38. U.S. Embassy Tegucigalpa cable 5666 (EXDIS), "Reported Expulsion of CARE Employee," July 31, 1981.

39. U.S. Embassy Managua cable 3230, title unknown, late July 1981; and U.S. Embassy San Salvador cable 5569, title unknown, late July 1981. Release of these cables was not requested.

40. U.S. Embassy Tegucigalpa cable 5637 (NODIS), "Concerns about Regional Policies and Objectives," July 31, 1981. The complete text of this cable, with minor excisions, is in appendix 3.

41. U.S. Embassy Tegucigalpa cable 5469, "*Halcon Vista,*" July 27, 1981.

42. Department of State cable 203317, "Regional Interdiction of Clandestine Infiltration," July 31, 1981.

43. USCINCSO cable 061435Z Aug 81, title not known, August 6, 1981. This cable is not available.

44. *New York Times,* "Green Berets Step up Honduras Role," August 9, 1981.

45. U.S. Embassy Tegucigalpa cable 5890, "Proposed USCINCSO/MOD Meeting," August 10, 1981.

46. The arms interdiction effort was definitely secondary if not just cover for the covert war against the Sandinistas. The visit of the CIA's regional operations chief, Duane "Dewey" Clarridge, later in August was billed as being related to arms interdiction. Actually he was laying the groundwork for the Contra campaign, as will be described.

47. U.S. Embassy Tegucigalpa cable 5902 (NOFORN), "Regional Interdiction of Clandestine Infiltration," August 10, 1981.

48. U.S. Embassy Tegucigalpa cable 6122, "Exercise Plans and First Planning Meeting," August 18, 1981.

49. U.S. Embassy Tegucigalpa cable 6539, "Leftist Allegations of Honduran Participation in Perquin Operation," September 2, 1981; National Security Archive, "El Salvador," p. 42.

50. U.S. Embassy Tegucigalpa cable 5940, "*New York Times* Story on Green Berets," August 12, 1981.

51. U.S. Department of State cable 212321, "Press Guidance 8/10," August 11, 1981.

52. Gutman, *Banana Diplomacy,* pp. 66–73. Gutman draws on Nicaraguan transcripts of these meetings and recollections of Ambassador Pezzullo and other participants in this episode and its aftermath. See also National Security Archive, "Nicaragua," p. 59, and the archive's other holdings on this subject.

53. Ibid., pp. 73–78.

54. Shultz, George P., *Turmoil and Triumph: My Years as Secretary of State,* Charles Scribner's Sons, New York, 1993, pp. 304–9 and 414–19, especially.

55. U.S. Embassy Tegucigalpa cable 6055 (EXDIS), "Visits of Presidents Fuel Rumor Mills," August 14, 1981.

56. National Security Archive, "Nicaragua," p. 59.

57. I am uncertain about the precise dates of Clarridge's visits. According to Gutman, Clarridge visited Honduras twice during August. I can find nothing in my daily diary, and my clearance of his visit was transmitted in CIA channels, so I have no record of it. Gutman placed the first trip in early August. For most of that period I was on vacation in Tela, so I could not have met him then. I believe he actually came during the second week of August. I recall meeting with Clarridge and discussing the arms interdiction program with him. In his book (*A Spy for All Seasons,* Scribner's, New York, 1997, pp. 207–10) Clarridge claims that both trips occurred in November 1981, conveniently after the Presidential Finding authorizing the Contra operation had by that time been signed. I believe he is mistaken. If he had come in November, I would not have been there to meet him. Whatever the dates, Clarridge visited Honduras in this general time frame, and the CIA engaged in a deliberate effort to deceive me as to its plans and activities.

58. Gutman, *Banana Diplomacy,* pp. 55–57.

59. Ibid. Enders and NSC director Richard Allen later disputed Clarridge's reported assertion that President Reagan had authorized his visit or had agreed that the USG would back the Contras.

60. Ibid.

61. Ibid.

62. U.S. Embassy Tegucigalpa cable 5996, "GOH and IMF," August 13, 1981.

63. U.S. Embassy Tegucigalpa cable 6055 (EXDIS), "Visits of Presidents Fuel Rumor Mills," op. cit.

64. U.S. Embassy Tegucigalpa cable 6092, "More on Paz/Duarte Meeting," August 17, 1981.

65. U.S. Embassy Tegucigalpa cable 6091, "Possibility of New Mining Investment Diminishes," August 17, 1981.

66. U.S. Embassy Tegucigalpa cables 6056, "Text of Draft Declaration of Tegucigalpa"; 6057, "CAP FonMins Meeting: Guatemala Participates; Declaration Analyzed"; and 6060, "CAP Foreign Ministers Meeting: Invitation to Nassau Group; Dust Up with Guatemala"; August 15 and 16, 1981.

67. Department of State cable 217262, "Orientation Travel of Mr. Nestor Sanchez (DOD/ISA)," August 15, 1981.

68. U.S. Embassy Tegucigalpa cable 6095, "Sanchez Meetings with Paz and Alvarez," August 17, 1981.

69. Valladares Lanza, *Honduras,* pp. 22–35. The specific cases that appear to relate to this insurgent supply network are 20 through 30; and 32 through 41. There is no doubt that the Hondurans uncovered an insurgent supply apparat, but it is less clear that those who were arrested and vanished were actually involved. It is also clear that these actions were contrary to Honduran law and represented major human rights violations.

70. U.S. Embassy Tegucigalpa cable 6167, "Further Fallout on Capt. Sheehan Case," August 19, 1981.

71. Antonia Stolper, memorandum "Investigation Report—Captain Sheehan and His MTT in La Virtud," August 19, 1981.

72. U.S. Embassy Tegucigalpa cable 6387, "Capt. Sheehan Case," August 27, 1981.

73. National Security Archive, "Nicaragua," p. 59.

74. U.S. Embassy Tegucigalpa cable 6539 (see note 48 above).

75. Jack R. Binns, to the Honorable Gerry E. Studds, September 29, 1981; also to Victoria Rideout (Studds aide), same date.

76. U.S. Embassy Tegucigalpa cable 6199, "Suazo Cordova on National Security Law," August 20, 1981.

77. National Security Archive, "El Salvador," p. 43.

78. Ibid.

79. U.S. Embassy Tegucigalpa cable 6221 (EXDIS), "Priests in Honduras Involved in Guerrilla Support Network," August 21, 1981.

80. U.S. Embassy Tegucigalpa cable 6248, "Additional Information on Visiting Church Group," August 21, 1981.

81. U.S. Embassy Tegucigalpa cable 6220 (EXDIS), "Suazo Declines Invitation to Visit Caracas," August 21, 1981.

82. U.S. Embassy Tegucigalpa cable 6244 (EXDIS), "Reported Decision to Delay Elections: Analysis and Strategy Recommendations," August 21, 1981.

83. Ibid.

84. U.S. Embassy Tegucigalpa cable 6258 (EXDIS), "Christian Democrats on Delay of Elections," August 21, 1981.

85. U.S. Embassy Tegucigalpa cable 6371 (LIMDIS), "Liberals on Possible Delay of Elections," August 27, 1981.

Chapter 9

1. U.S. Embassy Tegucigalpa cable 5637 (NODIS), "Concerns about Regional Policies and Objectives" (see chapter 8, note 39 above).

2. U.S. Department of State cable 227408 (EXDIS), "Concerns about Regional Policies and Objectives," August 25, 1981.

3. U.S. Embassy Tegucigalpa cable 6351 (EXDIS), "Concerns about Regional Policies and Objectives," August 26, 1981.

4. National Security Archive, "El Salvador," p. 43.

5. Ibid.

6. *La Prensa,* "American Congressman: World Interest Directed at CA"; *La Tribuna,* "U.S. Congressman Impressed by High Voter Turnout in '80 Elections"; *Tiempo,* "American Congressman in Honduras"; all September 1, 1981.

7. U.S. Embassy cable 6540, "CODEL Petri," September 2, 1981.

8. National Security Archive, "Nicaragua," p. 59.

9. U.S. Embassy Tegucigalpa cable 6504 (EXDIS), "Paz on Elections Issue, Summit Meetings and Travels," September 1, 1981.

10. U.S. Embassy Tegucigalpa cable 6519, "*Halcon Vista:* Suggested Press Guidance," September 2, 1981.

11. USDAO San Salvador cable 021625Z SEP 81, title unknown. This document is not available.

12. U.S. Embassy Tegucigalpa cable 6539, (see chapter 8, note 48 above).

13. Department of State cable 235800 (EXDIS), "Concerns about Elections," September 3, 1981. The document is not available.

14. U.S. Embassy Tegucigalpa cable 6565 (EXDIS), "Concerns about Elections," September 3, 1981.

15. U.S. Embassy Tegucigalpa cable 6587 (LIMDIS), "Military Plan to Delay Elections Has No Support," September 4, 1981. This document, which identified a number of embassy sources, is very heavily excised.

16. National Security Archive, "Nicaragua," p. 60.

17. U.S. Embassy Tegucigalpa cable 6646 (EXDIS), "GOH Request for Crowd (Riot) Control Training," September 9, 1981.

18. U.S. Embassy Tegucigalpa cable 6675 (EXDIS), "Meeting with President Paz and Senior Army Colonels," September 9, 1981.

19. U.S. Embassy Tegucigalpa cable 6723 (EXDIS), "Col. Alvarez on Elections," September 10, 1981.

20. U.S. Embassy Tegucigalpa cable 6698 (EXDIS), "GOH Request for Crowd (Riot) Control Training," September 10, 1981.

21. National Security Archive, "El Salvador," p. 43.

22. This cable, sent in military channels, is not available.

23. National Security Archive, "Nicaragua," p. 60.

24. U.S. Embassy Managua cable 4158, "Sandinistas Speak Out against *Halcon Vista,*" September 23, 1981.

25. National Security Archive, "El Salvador," p. 43.

26. U.S. Embassy Tegucigalpa cable 7037 (LIMDIS), "Honduran Military, Elections and Security Assistance," September 22, 1981. The State Department withheld this cable.

27. *La Tribuna,* "Silent Visit to Honduras of U.S. Ambassador to the OAS," September 23, 1981. Also see *La Prensa,* "Visit by U.S. Ambassador to the OAS," same date.

28. National Security Archive, "El Salvador," p. 43.

29. Jack R. Binns, daily diary. This account is based primarily on my recall of the incident. William Walker added several points that I had forgotten.

30. National Security Archive, "El Salvador," p. 43.

31. Jack R. Binns, text of speech to San Pedro Sula Rotary, September 23, 1981.

32. *New York Times,* September 25, 1981, 9:4.

33. National Security Archive, "El Salvador," p. 43.

34. At the time, the United States maintained bases in the former Panama Canal Zone, which had been American territory prior to the 1978 treaty with Panama providing for the zone's reversion to Panama (and the ultimate closure of our bases); in

Cuba, where our base rights at Guantanamo dated from 1902 and 1931 agreements with that country; and the Bahamas, where rights derived from a preindependence agreement with the United Kingdom. During WWII, the United States had also established a chain of bases along the Caribbean and Atlantic littoral and on several Caribbean islands; at the conclusion of the war those facilities reverted to the host countries.

35. U.S. Embassy Tegucigalpa cable 7214 (LIMDIS), "Joint Use Military Base in Honduras," September 25, 1981. The State Department withheld this cable.

36. Department of State cable 257250 (EXDIS), "Joint Use Military Base in Honduras," September 25, 1981.

37. *United States Treaties and Other International Agreements,* Vol. 34, Part 4, 1981–82, "Honduras: Defense Assistance," agreement entering into effect May 7, 1982.

38. U.S. Embassy Tegucigalpa cable 7231 (EXDIS), "Paz Still Pushing for Elections Delay: Liberal Problems," September 25, 1981.

39. *La Prensa,* "Democracy Cannot Exist Excluding Private Enterprise and Trade Unions"; *Tiempo,* "Administrative Corruption Undermines the Legitimacy of Government"; both September 25, 1981. Also, *La Prensa* editorial "U.S. and Our Development," September 26, 1981, and "A Complicated Inheritance," September 28, 1981.

40. See, for example: *Tiempo,* "Attack Will Not Change U.S. Plans"; *El Heraldo,* "Attack of U.S. Military Is Isolated Incident"; *La Prensa,* "Domestic Left Is Not a Danger to Honduras"; *La Tribuna,* "U.S. Is Not Converting Honduras into Policeman of CA"; and *El Heraldo,* "U.S. Doesn't Intend to Make Honduras Policeman of CA"; all September 25, 1981.

41. U.S. Embassy Tegucigalpa cable 7253, "DAS Briggs Travel to Honduras," September 26, 1981.

42. U.S. Embassy Tegucigalpa cable 7273, "Security Enhancement, or Promises, Promises," September 28, 1981.

43. U.S. Embassy Tegucigalpa cable 7283 (EXDIS), "Suazo on Negotiations with ALIPO," September 28, 1981.

44. U.S. Embassy Tegucigalpa cable 7288 (NODIS), "Political Leaders on Replacement of Ambassador," September 28, 1981.

45. USAFSO Howard AFB cable 291915Z Sep 81, "Joint Use Military Base in Honduras." This document is not available.

46. U.S. Embassy Tegucigalpa cable 7294, "Joint Use of Military Base in Honduras," September 29, 1981.

47. See *Tiempo,* "Change in U.S. Embassy in Honduras"; *La Tribuna,* "Negroponte Will Replace Binns as Ambassador"; *La Prensa,* "Reagan Replaces Binns"; *El Heraldo,* "U.S. Senate Will Soon Approve Appointment of Ambassador to Honduras"; all September 30, 1981. Also, *El Cronista,* "New Ambassador," October 2, 1981.

48. U.S. Embassy Tegucigalpa cable 7646 (NODIS), "Likelihood of Elections Delay Increases," October 9, 1981.

49. *La Prensa,* "Assistant Secretary of State for Hemisphere Visits Foreign Minister," October 2, 1981.

Chapter 10

1. National Security Archive, "El Salvador," p. 43.

2. U.S. Embassy San Salvador cable 7444, "FMLN/FDR Position on Negotiations with the Government of El Salvador," October 4, 1981. Part of the National Security Archive collection.

3. The Diplomat in Residence program afforded senior Foreign Service officers an opportunity to be assigned to universities as visiting scholars for a year, providing the receiving institutions with a foreign policy resource otherwise unavailable to them. In return, the host institutions were required to provide office space, secretarial and other support services. The visitors were then available as lecturers and in some cases actually taught classes.

4. Jack R. Binns to Enders, letter describing *Halcon Vista* and its impact from my vantage point, October 12, 1981.

5. Ibid.

6. Jack R. Binns, text of October 6 speech to Tegucigalpa Rotary.

7. *La Prensa*, "Government Intervention Has Become a Negative Factor in Development," October 9, 1981.

8. Jack R. Binns to Enders, October 12, 1981 (see note 4 above).

9. U.S. Embassy Tegucigalpa "Briefing Book for ambassador John D. Negroponte," October 9, 1981. A search of the embassy's retired files from this period failed to turn up a copy of this document. This description is based on the table of contents, which I retained in my personal files, and my recall supplemented by comments of Walker and others who were involved in its preparation.

10. U.S. Embassy Tegucigalpa cable 7646 (NODIS), "Likelihood of Elections Delay Increases."

11. This group apparently did not include all members of the Superior Council. Rather, it seemed to have been limited to only those senior officers holding major unit commands, thus excluding senior staff officers and others not actually commanding troops.

12. U.S. Embassy Tegucigalpa cable 7696 (NODIS), "Weekend Coup Narrowly Averted," October 13, 1981. An abbreviated account of these events appears in *Inside a U.S. Embassy*, "Nurturing a Fragile Democracy (Honduras)," The American Foreign Service Association, Washington, D.C., 1996.

13. U.S. Embassy Tegucigalpa cable 7674, "Armed Forces Pronouncement on Political Process," October 13, 1981.

14. U.S. Embassy Tegucigalpa cable 7696 (see note 12 above).

15. U.S. Embassy Tegucigalpa cable 7753 (NODIS), "Further Assessment of Aborted Coup Attempt: Problematical Elections Outlook Unchanged," October 14, 1981.

16. U.S. Embassy Tegucigalpa cable 7776 (NODIS), "Coup Maneuverings of Last Week: Junior Officers Input," October 15, 1981.

17. U.S. Embassy Tegucigalpa cable 7696 (see note 12 above).

18. U.S. Embassy Tegucigalpa cable 7833 (EXDIS), "Conditions Imposed on Political Leaders By Honduran Military," October 19, 1981.

19. U.S. Embassy Tegucigalpa cable 7834 (EXDIS), "Military Document Advocates Delay of Elections," October 19, 1981.

20. U.S. Embassy Tegucigalpa cable 7696 (see note 12 above).

21. U.S. Embassy Tegucigalpa cable 7723 (EXDIS), "Venezuelan Concern Over Threats to Electoral Process," October 14, 1981.

22. *Los Angeles Times*, "Wrong Signal to Central America," October 14, 1981.

23. National Security Archive, "El Salvador," p. 43.

24. U.S. Embassy Tegucigalpa cable 7815, "Ambassador's Endorsement of Elections Well Received," October 16, 1981.

25. *Tiempo*, "USA Is Not Going to Change Its Policy Toward Honduras"; *El Heraldo*, "Elections Will Go Forward, According to Binns"; *La Prensa*, "Jack Binns: The Possibility of a Coup Can Never be Discounted"; *La Tribuna*, "U.S. Does Not Discount a Coup"; all October 16, 1981.

26. *La Prensa,* "Change of Ambassadors: Why So Much Noise?" October 17, 1981.

27. U.S. Embassy Tegucigalpa cable 7833 (EXDIS), "Conditions Imposed on Political Leaders by Honduran Military," October 19, 1981.

28. U.S. Embassy Tegucigalpa cable 7857 (NODIS), "Political Outlook: Situation Fluid, Elections Problematical," October 19, 1981.

29. National Security Archive, "Nicaragua," p. 60.

30. Ibid.

31. Ibid.

32. Department of State cable 283212, "Senator Helms' Questions at Negroponte Hearings," October 23, 1981. This document is not available.

33. U.S. Embassy Tegucigalpa cable 7894, "Potential Foreign Policy Differences of Major Parties," October 22, 1981.

34. U.S. Embassy Tegucigalpa cable 7969, "Senator Helms' Questions At Negroponte Hearing," October 24, 1981.

35. U.S. Embassy Tegucigalpa cable 8040, "1981 and 1982 Balance of Payments and Fiscal Outlook Grim," October 26, 1981.

36. U.S. Embassy Tegucigalpa cable 7933 (EXDIS), "Military Involvement in Land Scandal," October 23, 1981.

37. U.S. Embassy Tegucigalpa cable 7945 (NODIS), "Honduran Elections: Outlook Brightens," October 23, 1981.

38. I do not have a record of the exact date of this phone call but believe it was about a week before my scheduled departure. Its precise timing, in any event, is not important.

39. U.S. Embassy Tegucigalpa cables: 7990 (EXDIS/STADIS), "U.S. Air Base in Honduras"; and 7991 (EXDIS), "U.S. Air Base in Honduras"; both October 26, 1981. The State Department has refused to release these cables; appeal of that decision was unsuccessful.

40. U.S. Embassy Tegucigalpa cable 8138 (STADIS/EXDIS), "Proposed U.S. Air Base in Honduras," late October 1981. Release of this cable too was denied, and appeal was unsuccessful.

Chapter 11

1. National Security Archive, "Nicaragua," p. 61.

2. *New York Times,* "Rightist Party Takes Big Lead in Vote," November 30, 1981, p. 5.

3. National Security Archive, "Nicaragua," p. 61.

4. *New York Times,* "U.S. Seeking Right to Use Air Bases in Caribbean," March 4, 1982, p. 1.

5. *United States Treaties and Other International Agreements,* Vol. 34, Part 4, "Honduras: Defense Assistance," signed May 6 and 7, 1982.

6. Jacqueline Sharkey, "The Tug of War...," *Common Cause Magazine,* September/October 1984, pp. 20–30.

7. Gutman, *Banana Diplomacy,* pp. 104–7. This account, based largely on interviews with some of those involved, appears generally accurate, although it does contain some minor factual errors (e.g., placing the onset of Argentine involvement in Honduras in mid–1981, vice 1980).

8. *New York Times,* "Hondurans Said to Hold Salvadoran Claimed Land," July 4, 1982, p. 10; "Honduran Commander Confirms Border Move," July 11, 1982, p. 3.

9. Ibid., "Honduran Officer Denounces His Chief," September 1, 1982, p. 3.

10. Ibid., "25 Honduran Rebels Said to Seize 200 at Meeting," September 18, 1982, p. 2.

11. Bob Woodward, *Veil: The Secret Wars of the CIA*, Simon and Schuster, 1987 p. 508.

12. Gutman, *Banana Diplomacy*, pp. 160–62; 276–80; 327–31; also see McNeil, *War and Peace in Central America*.

13. *New York Times*, "G.I.'s Join Honduran Soldiers in Maneuvers on Nicaraguan Border," February 2, 1983, p. 4.

14. George P. Shultz, *Turmoil and Triumph*, Scribners, New York, 1993, pp. 302–6

15. *New York Times*, "U.S. Plans to Train Salvadoran Soldiers at Honduran Base," May 27, 1983, p. 1.

16. Ibid.," Projected U.S. Maneuvers to Center on Honduras," July 21, 1983, p. 4.

17. Ibid., "Hondurans Divided on U.S. Maneuvers," August 28, 1983, p. 3.

18. Ibid., "U.S. Pilot Killed by 'Hostile Fire' on Honduras Trip," January 12, 1984, p. 1.

19. Ibid., "Human Rights Is Also an Issue in Honduras," January 22, 1984, Sec. 4, p. 3.

20. Valledares Lanza, *Honduras*, pp. 67–116.

21. Woodward, *Veil*, pp. 319–27.

22. New York Times, "Large Exercise with Honduras to Start April 1," March 24, 1984, p. 1.

23. Ibid., "Honduras Ousts Its Top General, an Ally of U.S.," April 1, 1984, p. 1.

24. Ibid., "Honduras Names New Military Commander," April 5, 1984, p. 6.

25. Ibid., "Honduras Seeking Changes in Military Training by U.S.," May 27, 1984, p. 12.

26. Ibid., "Honduras Bars Training of Salvadorans at Base," September 29, 1984, p. 4.

27. Sharkey, "Tug of War," pp. 20–30.

28. Gutman, *Banana Diplomacy*, pp. 232–33; McNeil, *War and Peace*, pp. 266–67.

29. *New York Times*, "FBI Charges 8 with Plotting Honduran Coup," November 2, 1984, p. 1.

30. Ibid., "Hondurans Ask the U.S. for a Fleet of Jet Fighters and Big Increase in Aid," November 20, 1984, p. 9.

31. Ibid., "The Mystery Over a Killing in Honduras," September 29, 1985, p. 7.

32. Ibid., "Honduran General Arrested in U.S. in Assassination Plot," November 22, 1985, p. 15.

33. McNeil, *War and Peace*, pp. 227–32; Valledares Lanza, *Honduras*, pp. 260–71. McNeil's account is based on evidence developed by the Intelligence and Senate Select Committees in the Iran-Contra hearings; Valledares Lanza cites the court records of *United States v. Oliver North*.

34. Woodward, *Veil*, p. 508.

35. *New York Times*, "General's Resignation Accepted by Hondurans," February 2, 1986, p. 3.

36. Ibid., "CIA Accused of Tolerating Killings in Honduras," February 14, 1986, p. 3.

37. Ibid.," Honduran Buildup: A Variety of Means," July 14, 1986, p. 3.

38. Ibid., "U.S. Set to Offer Newer Jet Fighters to the Hondurans," October 31, 1986, p. 1.

39. Ibid., "3,000 U.S. Troops Begin an Exercise in South Honduras," December 31, 1986, p. 1.

40. Ibid., "Senate to Set Up Iran Inquiry Panel," January 7, 1987, p. 8.

41. McNeil, *War and Peace,* p. 10.

42. *New York Times,* "Honduran Army Linked to Death of 200 Civilians," May 2, 1987, p. 1.

43. Valledares Lanza, *Honduras,* pp. 160–86.

44. McNeil, *War and Peace,* p. 11.

45. *New York Times,* "A Bomb Wounds 12 Near Honduran Base," August 10, 1987, p. 7.

46. Ibid., "Honduran Bombing Suspect Is Given Asylum by Mexico," October 4, 1987, p. 20.

47. Ibid., "In Human Rights Court, Honduras Is First to Face Death Squad Trial," January 19, 1988, p. 1.

48. Ibid., "Hondurans Riot at U.S. Offices; Four Said to Die"; "Honduran Leader Acts to Put Down Anti-U.S. Protests"; "Honduran Anger at U.S. Is Product of Washington Policy, Officials Say"; April 8, 9 and 13, 1988, pp. 1, 1 and 10, respectively.

49. Ibid., "OAS Tribunal Finds Honduras Responsible for Political Killing," July 30, 1988, p. 1.

50. *Baltimore Sun,* "Unearthed: Fatal Secrets," June 11, 1995, part 1 of a four-part series on Honduran human rights abuses.

51. *New York Times,* "Latin Presidents Announce Accord on Contra Bases," February 15, 1989, p. 1.

52. Ibid., "3 U.S. Soldiers Slightly Hurt in Bomb Attack in Honduras," February 19, 1989, p. 14.

53. Ibid., "Bush and Congress Sign Policy Accord on Aid to Contras," March 25, 1989, p. 1.

54. Ibid., "North Honduras Blast Wounds 7 Americans," July 14, 1989, p. 3.

55. Ibid., "Nicaragua Calm in Heavy Turnout for Critical Vote," February 26, 1990, p. 6; "Nicaraguan Opposition Routs Sandinistas; U.S. Pledges Aid, Tied to Orderly Turn Over," February 27, 1990, p. 1.

56. Ibid., "Snipers in Honduras Wound 6 U.S. Troops," April 1, 1990, p. 3.

57. Ibid., "Strikes Strangling Nicaragua and New Leaders Cry Foul," April 24, 1990, p. 8.

58. Ibid., "Chamorro Takes Helm; Hails New Era," April 26, 1990, p. 1.

59. Ibid., "Salvadoran Chief and Rebels Reach Broad Accord," September 25, 1991, p. 1.

60. Ibid., "U.S. To Forgive Honduran Debt," September 27, 1991, p. 2.

61. Ibid., "Salvadoran Rebels Halt Attacks; Government Sees an End to War," November 15, 1991, p. 1.

62. Department of State fact sheet, "El Salvador," 1995.

63. Valledares Lanza, *Honduras,* p. 6.

64. *New York Times,* "Salvadorans, Ending War, Are Cautioned On Peace," December 16, 1992, p. 1.

65. *Baltimore Sun,* "Hondurans Charge Soldiers," July 26, 1995.

66. Ibid., "Military Can Be Tried in Honduran Civil Courts," January 20, 1996, p. 1.

Chapter 12

1. Robert Timberg, *The Nightingale's Song,* p. 424.

2. CIA Inspector General's report on Honduras, August 27, 1997.

3. National Security Archive, "Nicaragua," p. 57.

Appendix I: Instructions for New Ambassador

This document (Department of State cable 270099 of October 9, 1980) is a statement of U.S. policy toward Honduras and strategies for the dealing with the interim government. It was coordinated with other foreign affairs agencies and represents official instructions for the new Ambassador. It was transmitted by the State Department as an EXDIS cable in early October 1980 and remained in effect, with minor changes in operational strategies, through October 1981. It represented the Country Team's official marching orders and was binding on all U.S. agencies.

Department of State

UNCLASSIFIED

AN: D800483-0638

~~CONFIDENTIAL~~

PAGE 01   STATE   270,099
ORIGIN SS-30

INFO   OCT-00   ADS-00   SSO-00   /030 R

DRAFTED BY ARA/CEN: KANDERSON
APPROVED BY ARA- WGBOWDLER
HA -DSHAFFER
S/P -SPURCELL
S/S-O- DSANDBERG
ARA- JCHEEK
ARA/CEN - JOBLACKEN
ARA/CEN - RCBROWN
------------------116475 I-001462 /61
P 091956Z OCT 80
FM SECSTATE WASHDC
TO AMEMBASSY TEGUCIGALPA PRIORITY

~~C O N F I D E N T I A L~~ STATE 270099

EXDIS   **DECAPTIONED**

E.O. 12065: GDS 1019/86 (BOWDLER, W.G.)

TAGS: PGOV, PINT, HO, US

SUBJECT: UPDATED STRATEGY FOR PERIOD OF INTERIM GOVERNMENT

REF: TEGUCIGALPA 2058

1. ✓ ENTIRE TEXT

2. HONDURAN PROGRESS INTO THE TRANSITIONAL PERIOD BETWEEN
MILITARY AND CONSTITUTIONAL, DEMOCRATIC RULE HAS NECES-
SITATED A REVIEW AND UPDATE OF THE STRATEGY OUTLINED
IN REFTEL.   RECENT DEVELOPMENTS SUGGEST THAT IT IS NOW
TIMELY AND APPROPRIATE TO ENSURE THAT ALL SECTORS INVOLVED
IN THE TRANSITION FULLY UNDERSTAND: THE US STRONGLY
CONFIDENTIAL
CONFIDENTIAL

PAGE 02   STATE   270099

SUPPORTS THE PROCESS ITSELF; THE GOALS WE HOPE TO SEE

UNCLASSIFIED

Sidebar (rotated text, right margin):
DEPARTMENT OF STATE
IS/FPC/CDR   MR Cases Only: EO Citations
Date: 6/17/86
TS authority to.
CLASSIFY as ( ) S or
DOWNGRADE TS to ( ) S or
RELEASE   (X) DECLASSIFY
EXCISE   ( ) DECLASSIFY IN PART
DENY
DELETE Non-Responsive Info
( ) Exemptions
( ) Exemptions

UNCLASSIFIED

ACHIEVED; AND HOW THE ANTICIPATED ACHIEVEMENTS RELATE
TO OUR REGIONAL POLICY.

3. WE BELIEVE THE BEST ANSWER TO THE EXTREMIST CHALLENGE
POSED THROUGHOUT THE CA REGION IS TO FOSTER AND SUPPORT
THE EMERGENCE, THROUGH DEMOCRATIC PROCESSES, OF MODERATE,
REFORMIST GOVERNMENTS. WE SHARE, WITH THE OVERWHELMING
MAJORITY OF HONDURANS, THE BELIEF THAT THE CHALLENGE IN
HONDURAS CAN BEST BE MET BY THE POPULAR ELECTION OF A
CONSTITUENT ASSEMBLY WHICH, WITHIN 12 TO 18 MONTHS,

WILL DRAFT A NEW CONSTITUTION AND PREPARE FOR DIRECT
ELECTIONS, RETURNING THE COUNTRY TO DEMOCRATIC, CONSTI-
TUTIONAL RULE. THE 80 PERCENT OF THE ELECTORATE THAT
PARTICIPATED IN THE APRIL 20 ELECTION GAVE A SOLID MANDATE
TO THE RETURN TO CONSTITUTIONAL RULE. INDEED, THAT
ELECTION REPRESENTS A MANDATE WHICH CANNOT BE IGNORED.

4. IN SUPPORT THEREOF, THE US HAS MADE SUBSTANTIAL
POLITICAL (THROUGH PRESIDENTIAL MEETINGS AND COMMUNICA-
TIONS), DEVELOPMENTAL (THROUGH INCREASED AID ASSISTANCE)
AND SECURITY (THROUGH INCREASED FMS AND IMET PROGRAMS)
COMMITMENTS. HONDURAS CAN COUNT ON CONTINUED US SUPPORT
AS THE TRANSITION PROCESS CONTINUES TOMOVE FORWARD.
WHILE WE RECOGNIZE THAT THERE WILL BE INSTANCES IN WHICH
THE POLITICAL PARTIES AND OTHER INSTITUTIONS WILL NOT
AGREE ON THE SHAPE OF REFORM PROGRAMS AND/OR HOW THEY
SHOULD BE IMPLEMENTED, WE BELIEVE THE PROCESS MUST GO
FORWARD AND THE POPULAR WILL BE RESPECTED. OBSTRUCTION
OF THE TRANSITION PROCESS WOULD BE CONTRARY TO THE EX-
PRESSED POPULAR WILL AND, OVER THE LONGER TERM, INCREASE
THE SECURITY THREAT IN HONDURAS.
CONFIDENTIAL
CONFIDENTIAL

PAGE 03   STATE   270099

5. IN THE COMING WEEKS YOU SHOULD THEREFORE ENSURE
THAT INTERIM PRESIDENT PAZ, THE MILITARY, THE POLITICAL
PARTIES, THE PRIVATE SECTOR, THE LABOR MOVEMENT, THE
CHURCH AND THE MEDIA UNDERSTAND BOTH OUR GOALS AND OUR
EXPECTATIONS. REVISED GOALS, TOGETHER WITH SUGGESTED
TALKING POINTS AND A DISCUSSION OF MEANS FOR THEIR
DELIVERY TO THE VARIOUS SECTORS FOLLOW.

6. GOALS:

 UNCLASSIFIED

UNCLASSIFIED

--CONTINUATION,' DURING THE TRANSITION PERIOD, OF ON-GOING
REFORM PROGRAMS.

--RESOLUTION OF THE BORDER DISPUTE WITH EL SALVADOR,
WHICH CONSTITUTES A MAJOR OBSTACLE TO THE REVITALIZATION
OF THE CACM.

--THE DEVELOPMENT AND ARTICULATION, BY THE MAJOR POLITICAL
PARTIES, OF "PROGRAMS OF GOVERNMENT'S," EMPHASIZING THEIR
COMMON GROUND IN SUPPORT OF REFORMS.

--THE RATIFICATION OF A NEW CONSTITUTION GUARANTEEING
AN OPEN, DEMOCRATIC FORM OF GOVERNMENT.

--THE LEGAL REGISTRATION OF ALL DEMOCRATIC POLITICAL
PARTIES HAVING A REASONABLE CLAIM TO SIGNIFICANT POPULAR

SUPPORT AND WISHING TO PARTICIPATE IN THE ELECTIONS.

--THE POPULAR ELECTION OF A NEW, CONSTITUTIONAL PRESIDENT
WITHIN THE NEXT 12 TO 18 MONTHS.

--THE ACCELERATION, BY THE ELECTED GOVERNMENT, OF MODERATE
REFORM PROGRAMS, INCLUDING: EXTENSIVE ADMINISTRATIVE
REFORMS; THE REVITALIZATION OF THE AGRARIAN REFORM PRO-
CONFIDENTIAL
CONFIDENTIAL

PAGE 04   STATE 270099

GRAM; INCREASED EMPHASIS ON THE POOR; AND CONTINUED
ECONOMIC GROWTH, ESPECIALLY IN THE INDUSTRIAL AND AGRI-
CULTURAL SECTORS.

--THE DENIAL OF THE USE OF HONDURAN TERRITORY TO FORCES
HOSTILE TO NEIGHBORING GOVERNMENTS.

--THE CONTINUED EFFECTIVE CONTAINMENT OF EXTERNALLY
SUPPORTED SUBVERSION, WITH DUE CONSIDERATION TO HUMAN
RIGHTS.

7. TALKING POINTS: THE FOLLOWING TALKING POINTS MAY
BE USEFUL IN COMMUNICATING OUR POLICY GOALS AND EXPECTA-
TIONS TO THE RELEVANT GROUPS AND MAY BE USED AS THE
OCCASION WARRANTS:

--HONDURAN PROGRESS TOWARD RESTORATION OF DEMOCRATIC

UNCLASSIFIED

UNCLASSIFIED

GOVERNMENT HAS ENABLED US TO STRENGTHEN OUR CLOSE
POLITICAL RELATIONSHIP AND STEP UP ECONOMIC AND SECURITY
ASSISTANCE PROGRAMS.

--SIMILARLY, THE GOH'S CONSTRUCTIVE APPROACH TO THE
LONG-STANDING BORDER PROBLEM WITH EL SALVADOR HAS BEEN
A POSITIVE DEVELOPMENT. SETTLEMENT OF THIS ISSUE, WE
BELIEVE, WILL ULTIMATELY ENHANCE HONDURAN SECURITY AND
THAT OF THE REGION AS A WHOLE.

--TRANSITION TO DEMOCRATIC GOVERNMENT MUST NOT BE ALLOWED
TO FAIL, SINCE FAILURE WOULD FRUSTRATE THE POPULAR WILL.
IF THE POPULAR MANDATE IS NOT HONORED, BOTH THE
SECURITY OF HONDURAS AND THE CURRENTLY STRON
RELATIONSHIP WITH THE US WOULD BE JEOPARDIZED.

CONFIDENTIAL
CONFIDENTIAL

PAGE 05   STATE 270099

--AS WE SEE IT THERE ARE SEVERAL KEY ELEMENTS IN THE
TRANSITION PROCESS:

A. FIRST, THE TRANSITION PERIOD MUST BE KEPT RELATIVELY
SHORT; SAY RATIFICATION OF THE CONSTITUTION AND DIRECT
ELECTION OF THE NEW PRESIDENT WITHIN 12 TO 08 MONTHS;
B. SECOND - ON-GOING DEVELOPMENTAL AND REFORM PROGRAMS
MUST NOT BE ALLOWED TO LANGUISH UNDER THE INTERIM GOVERN-
MENT; AND

C. THIRD, THE PARTIES AND OTHER INSTITUTIONS MUST ENGAGE
IN A CONTINUING DIALOGUE. AS TO THE DIRECTIONS THE NEW
GOVERNMENT WILL TAKE AND, ESPECIALLY, THE MEANS FOR
ACHIEVING ADMINISTRATIVE REFORM.

--THROUGH THIS DIALOGUE THE POLITICAL PARTIES SHOULD
DEVELOP THEIR RESPECTIVE PROGRAMS OF GOVERNMENT WHICH
WOULD PROVIDE BASIC POLICY DIRECTION FOR THE NEW ADMINIS-
TRATION AND BENCHMARKS AGAINST WHICH FUTURE PERFORMANCE
COULD BE MEASURED.

--WE WOULD HOPE THAT THE PARTY PROGRAMS INCLUDE FIRM
COMMITMENTS TO: CARRY OUT ADMINISTRATIVE REFORMS; RE-
VITALIZE THE AGRARIAN REFORM PROGRAM; INCREASE ATTENTION
GIVEN TO THE PROBLEMS OF THE POOR; ADOPT ECONOMIC POLICIES
WHICH ENCOURAGE CONTINUED SOUND GROWTH, ESPECIALLY IN

UNCLASSIFIED

THE AGRICULTURAL AND INDUSTRIAL SECTORS.

--WE ALSO BELIEVE THAT OTHER SECTORS OF THE SOCIETY

--BUSINESS, AGRICULTURE, LABOR, THE CHURCH, THE MEDIA

--MUST BECOME OPENLY ENGAGED IN THE POLITICAL PROCESS
THROUGH REGULAR DIALOGUE WITH THE ELECTED GOVERNMENT
AND OPPOSITION PARTIES. THESE SECTORS HAVE A PARTICULAR
LY CRITICAL PART TO PLAY IN ENCOURAGING ADMINISTRATION
CONFIDENTIAL
CONFIDENTIAL

PAGE 06   STATE   270099

REFORM.

--WE TRUST THE MILITARY WILL CONTINUE TO SUPPORT THE
RETURN TO CONSTITUTIONAL GOVERNMENT, WHILE AT THE SAME
TIME DEVOTING THEIR PROFESSIONAL ATTENTION TO CONTROLLING
THE COUNTRY'S FRONTIERS AND CONTAINING INTERNAL SUBVER-
SION.

--HONDURAS CAN COUNT ON OUR SUPPORT IN ALL OF THESE
TASKS, PROVIDED -- AS WE EXPECT WILL BE THE CASE --
THE GOH CONTINUES TO OPERATE WITHIN THE ACCEPTED CONSTI-
TUTIONAL AND LEGAL FRAMEWORK. THE HONDURAN HUMAN RIGHTS
RECORD IS VERY GOOD, AND ITS MAINTENANCE WILL ASSURE
THE CONTINUATION OF OUR CLOSE COLLABORATION.

8. MODALITIES:

OUR GOALS AND EXPECTATIONS SHOULD BE COMMUNICATED TO
ALL SECTORS IN A DISCREET MANNER THAT WILL MAXIMIZE

THEIR IMPACT, ENSURE NO MISAPPREHENSION AND REINFORCE
EXISTING TRENDS., IN THIS REGARD, OUR CONTINUED WILLING-
NESS TO PROVIDE DEVELOPMENTAL AND SECURITY ASSISTANCE,
AND THE NEED FOR THE GOH TO SAFEGUARD HUMAN RIGHTS BY
AVOIDING REPRESSIVE ACTIONS, MAY BE STRESSED WITH APPRO-
PRIATE GROUPS. IT SHOULD BE EMPHASIZED THAT THE DECISON
TO RETURN TO DEMOCRATIC FORMS WAS TAKEN BY THE GOVERNMENT
STRONGLY ENDORSED BY OTHER INSTITUTIONS AND, ULTIMATELY,
APPROVED OVERWHELMINGLY BY THE HONDURAN PEOPLE. CARE
SHOULD BE EXERCISED TO ENSURE WE DO NOT APPEAR TO BE
DICTATING TO THE HONDURANS; RATHER, WE ARE SEEKING TO
REINFORCE THEIR OWN INITIATIVES. THE FOLLOWING IS A

UNCLASSIFIED
CONFIDENTIAL

SUGGESTED PLAN FOR APPROACHING EACH PLAYER OR SECTOR.
CONFIDENTIAL
CONFIDENTIAL

PAGE 07   STATE 270099

UNLESS SPECIFICALLY INDICATED OTHERWISE, THESE DISCUSSIONS
SHOULD BE PRIVATE.

A. PRESIDENT PAZ: AT THIS POINT WE SEE NO NEED FOR A
SPECIAL COMMUNICATION FROM PRESIDENT CARTER, THOUGH
WE WOULD BE WILLING TO CONSIDER SUCH A STEP SHOULD THE
SITUATION BEGIN TO DETERIORATE. THE AMBASSADOR, HOWEVER,
SHOULD COMMUNICATE TO PRESIDENT PAZ OUR GOALS AND EXPEC-
TATIONS AT THE EARLIEST OPPORTUNITY, ENSURING THAT HE
UNDERSTANDS THAT WE ALSO PLAN TO COMMUNICATE THESE POINTS
TO OTHER SECTORIAL LEADERS.

B. THE MILITARY: THE AMBASSADOR AND OTHER CIVILIAN
AND MILITARY MEMBERS OF THE CT SHOULD TAKE EVERY OPPOR-
TUNITY TO CONVEY THIS MESSAGE TO THE ARMED FORCES SUPERIOR
COUNCIL AND OTHER OFFICERS OF THE ARMED FORCES. WE DO
NOT AT THIS STAGE PERCEIVE A NEED TO REQUEST COMPLEMENT-
ARY APPROACHES FROM HIGH-RANKING US MILITARY FIGURES, BUT
WOULD BE WILLING TO CONSIDER SUCH ACTION SHOULD IT
APPEAR TIMELY AND USEFUL.

C. THE POLITICAL PARTIES: THE AMBASSADOR AND MISSION
OFFICERS SHOULD MAKE A CONCERTED EFFORT TO ENSURE THE
LEADERS OF THE TWO MAJOR AND ALL OTHER LEGALLY INSCRIBED
PARTIES COMPREHEND OUR GOALS AND EXPECTATIONS. MOREOVER,
IN THE FINAL ANALYSIS, THE SUCCESS OF BOTH THE TRANSITION
AND SUCCESSOR GOVERNMENTS DEPENDS ON THE MATURITY OF
HONDURAN POLITICAL LEADERSHIP.

D. PRIVATE SECTOR: THE AMBASSADOR AND MISSION OFFICERS
MUST ALSO COMMUNICATE OUR POLICY TO KEY MEMBERS OF THE
PRIVATE SECTOR, STRESSING THAT THEY TOO HAVE AN IMPORTANT
ROLE TO PLAY IN THE TRANSITION PROCESS AND REFORM PRO-
GRAMS. THE BEST GUARANTEE FOR THE FREE ENTERPRISE SYSTEM
IN HONDURAS IS THE EMERGENCE OF A STABLE, MODERATE RE-
FORMIST GOVERNMENT WHICH CAN EFFECTIVELY MEET THE
CONFIDENTIAL
CONFIDENTIAL

PAGE 08   STATE 270099

UNCLASSIFIED
CONFIDENTIAL

UNCLASSIFIED

MARXIST CHALLENGE. SELF-INTEREST, IF NOTHING ELSE, REQUIRES THAT THE PRIVATE SECTOR USE ITS INFLUENCE TO THIS END, SINCE THE SURVIVAL OF THE FREE ENTERPRISE SYSTEM MAY BE AT STAKE. THE PRIVATE SECTOR ALSO BEARS A SPECIAL RESPONSIBILITY TO SUPPORT MUCH NEEDED ADMINIS-TRATIVE REFORM -- GOVERNMENT CORRUPTION INVOLVES THE INTERACTION OF TWO PLAYERS -- AND IT'S THE PRIVATE SECTOR AS A WHOLE WHICH CAN BENEFIT DIRECTLY FROM THIS REFORM. THE DEPARTMENT WILL SEEK TO GET THE COUNCIL OF THE AMERI-CAS TO COOPERATE IN REINFORCING THIS MESSAGE, IF THE EMBASSY BELIEVES IT WOULD BE USEFUL.

E. THE LABOR MOVEMENT: WHILE CONSIDERABLE DISCRETION WILL BE REQUIRED IN DEALING WITH THE LABOR AND CAMPESIMO MOVEMENTS, THE AMBASSADOR AND MISSION OFFICERS SHOULD ENSURE RESPONSIBLE LEADERS UNDERSTAND OUR EXPECTATIONS AND THAT THEY HAVE AN OBLIGATION TO PLAY AN ESSENTIAL PART IN THE ENTIRE PROCESS, AND SHOULD WORK TO ESTABLISH AN EFFECTIVE DIALOGUE WITH BOTH MAJOR PARTIES AND WITH THE MILITARY. WE ALSO BELEIVE IT IS IMPORTANT FOR MOVE-MENT TO STRONGLY SUPPORT ADMINSTRATIVE REFORM, SINCE THE WORKERS TOO STAND TO BENEFIT DIRECTLY FROM THE ELIMI-NATION OF GOVERNMENTAL CORRUPTION.

F. THE CHURCH: THE AMBASSADOR AND OTHER MISSION OFFICERS SHOULD ESTABLISH A DIALOGUE WITH THE HIERARCHY CONCERNING OUR OBJECTIVES AND RELATING THEM TO THE CHURCH'S PASTORAL LETTER OF JANUARY. IN THIS REGARD, THE CHURCH IS A VITAL MORAL FORCE IN THE SOCIETY AND WOULD APPEAR TO BE IN AN ESPECIALLY STRONG POSITION TO ENCOURAGE HONESTY IN GOVERNMENT. WE ARE WILLING TO SEEK THE ASSISTANCE OF THE VATICAN OFFICE IN REINFORCING THIS EFFORT, IF
CONFIDENTIAL
CONFIDENTIAL

PAGE 09 STATE 270099

THE MISSION BELIEVES THIS WOULD BE USEFUL.

G. THE MEDIA: THE AMBASSADOR AND USICA SHOULD CONTINUE ITS OFF-THE-RECORD DIALOGUE WITH SELECTED MEDIA LEADERS, WHILE EXERCISING APPROPRIATE DISCRETION. THIS SECTOR HAS A UNIQUE RESPONSIBILITY TO INFORM AND INTERPRET EVENTS FOR THE HONDURAN PUBLIC AND CAN THEREFORE PLAY AN INFULENTIAL PART IN ENSURING THE TRANSITION MOVES FORWARD AND IN ENCOURAGING NEEDED REFORMS. MUSKIE

UNCLASSIFIED
CONFIDENTIAL

Appendix II: Honduran Armed Forces, Strength and Structure, 1980–1981

The Honduran Armed Forces (HAF) consisted of four service arms: Army, Air Force, Navy and Public Security (FUSEP). The provisional president, General Policarpo Paz Garcia, was commander in chief of the armed forces (CINCHAF). The CINCHAF position was always occupied by a military officer chosen by the Superior Council, a collegial body made up of the senior officers, which effectively ruled Honduras from 1975 until 1982, when the democratically elected government of Roberto Suazo Cordova took office. Even after that time, the Superior Council, not the government, continued to direct the HAF.

Overall strength of the HAF was about 17,000. CINCHAF exercised direct command over all service and unit commanders; some unit commanders also had additional duties as commanders of one of Honduras's ten military districts. This second post greatly enhanced the influence and independence of the officers so serving. The HAF General Staff functioned principally as an administrative support body for all services.

Services and Commanders

Army: Commander, General Policarpo Paz Garcia

STRENGTH AND STRUCTURE—Total force approximately 12,000 (900 officers and 11,000 plus enlisted, mostly conscripted). Principal operating units: eleven infantry battalions; three artillery (mortar) battalions; one engineering battalion; one armored reconnaissance battalion; and several support units (e.g., military schools, logistic support center, counterguerrilla unit). Units were dispersed throughout the country, with largest concentrations in the Tegucigalpa and San Pedro Sula military districts.

MAJOR EQUIPMENT—Eleven light-armored recon vehicles (British Scorpion); mortars (160mm and 120mm); light infantry weapons.

Air Force: Commander— Col. Walter Lopez Reyes

STRENGTH AND STRUCTURE—Total force about 1,000 (65 pilots, 50 other officers and 900 enlisted). Service was organized into headquarters unit, transportation section, aviation school (located in Tegucigalpa) and tactical sections (located in San Pedro Sula district).

MAJOR EQUIPMENT—Twenty-eight jet fighters (U.S., French and Israeli); 19 transport aircraft; 19 training aircraft; 16 helicopters; 19 light utility aircraft; and 1 bomber. Although its jet aircraft were obsolete and often out of service for lack of spares, this force was the strongest of its kind in Central America.

Navy: Commander— Col. Ruben Montoya

STRENGTH AND STRUCTURE—The smallest of the services, it consisted of about 400 men (40 officers, 350 enlisted). Headquartered in Tegucigalpa, the Navy had two operating bases: Puerto Cortez, on the Caribbean (north) coast, and Amapala, on the Gulf of Gonseca (south).

MAJOR EQUIPMENT—Six swift boats (ex-U.S.) at Puerto Cortez; six 75-foot support boats at Amapala.

Public Security: Commander— Col. Gustavo Alvarez Martinez

STRENGTH AND STRUCTURE—Approximately 3,500 men, directed and controlled by Army officers detailed to FUSEP. This force was responsible for all civil police operations throughout the country, including treasury and customs operations. It maintained operational units in all significant cities and towns. Also responsible for the National Investigations Directorate (DIN), which was responsible for countering subversion and terrorism. DIN was the CIA's principal liaison.

MAJOR EQUIPMENT—Police vehicles, riot-control gear and small arms, including light automatic weapons.

Appendix III: Concerns About Regional Policies and Objectives

This official Embassy cable (American Embassy cable 5637 of July 31, 1981) was sent to the Department of State in the NODIS channel for Assistant Secretary Thomas O. Enders. It describes Ambassador Binns' concerns about actual and potential conflicts in U.S. policy in Honduras and the Central American region. He also urged a coordinated, interagency examination of these conflicts and establishment of clear policy priorities so that increasingly chaotic operations could be conducted coherently. Neither the Department nor Enders ever responded meaningfully to this cable or its recommendations.

This cable has been retyped as portions of the original would not reproduce clearly. The text has been carefully checked against the original for accuracy. To enhance legibility, the text is rendered in standard upper-and-lowercase style, although the original cable was entirely in uppercase letters. Top-of-page markers repeating the cable number and the classification have been eliminated.

DEPARTMENT OF STATE

SECRET

SECRET
PAGE 1   TEGUCI   05637   01
OF 03   3117482Z
ACTION SS-20

INFO   OCT-01   ADS-OO   (illegible)
-----------------------052335   311755Z
0   311636Z   JUL 81
FM AMEMBASSY TEGUCIGALPA
TO SECSTATE WASHDC IMMEDIATE 4091

SECRET SECTION 1 OF 3 TEGUCIGALPA 5637

NODIS

ARA FOR ASSISTANT SECRETARY ENDERS ONLY

SECRET—WINTEL—NOFORN—NOCONTRACT—ORCON

EO 12065: OEAD RDS-2 7/31/01 (BINNS, J.R.) OR-M
TAGS: PEPR MILI ESEN HO NU ES
SUBJ: CONCERNS ABOUT REGIONAL POLICIES AND OBJEC-
TIVES

REFS: (A) MANAGUA 3238 (B) SAN SALVADOR 5569 (C) STATE
196527

1. SECRET—ENTIRE TEXT

2. It is truism that the pursuit of some policy objectives often jeopardizes
the realization of other, perhaps equally important goals. I believe this is
clearly the case regarding our policies toward El Salvador, Honduras and
Nicaragua, as has most recently been illustrated by cables from Ambassadors Hinton and Pezzullo. At least from where I sit, we do not appear
to have either defined our regional policy priorities or analysed the possible implications of various courses of action sufficiently to make the best
choices between conflicting objectives, actual and potential. I recognize,
of course, that my perception of the situation may only reflect inadequate
information.

3. As I see it, our overall objectives in these three countries might be summarized as follows: Nicaragua—prevent consolidation of the Sandinista regime by supporting pluralistic forces, and contain FSLN capacity to export subversion/revolution; El Salvador—prevent ascendancy of a radical regime and/or collapse of country by supporting JRG and its programs, and by assisting it to defeat the insurgency; and Honduras—help to ensure continued stability by encouraging the political transition proccontinued development and economic growth, and Honduras support for our objectives in Nicaragua and El Salvador especially. We also have a global objective of trying to increase international support for our policies in the region.

4. The above objectives (assuming the summaries are not too far off the mark) are to some extent complementary and in no way inherently contradictory. But sub-goals and specific courses of action pursued in each of the three countries may be inconsistent or in conflict.

5. As regards El Salvador. I am concerned that some of the courses of action being considered to deal with immediate problems in the frontier area may be counter-productive in terms of our larger goals for Honduras. It is clear that supplies, including arms and ammunition, move overland from Nicaragua through Honduras and across the border into El Salvador. While it is not clear that this is the most important supply route, we are moving to close it off through our joint [deleted] arms interdiction program. As I see it, this program is not inherently inconsistent with any of our objectives, but it could stimulate Nicaraguan or Salvadoran counter action (e.g., increased border incidents, stepped up subversion, joint operations by Salvadoran and Honduran subversives that would undermine Honduran stability). U.S. involvement in arms interdiction could also be used against us in international media as evidence of the "cat's paw" theory. But as our Honduran efforts to control this traffic are important, consistent with international law and practice and supported by most Hondurans, the risk is worth taking.

6. The presence of a large, uncontrolled refugee population near the border facilitates clandestine supply operations and provides relatively easy, if limited, safehaven for unarmed guerrillas. Indeed in early January we urged (Tegucigalpa 0077) that USG make concerted effort with GOH and UNHCR to get these people into camps situated some distance away from border. This process has now started, but will take time (and money) to complete. Ultimately these changes will permit better control of the

refugee population and relief supplies, and greatly inhibit clandestine traffic, as well as serve legitimate humanitarian purposes (e.g.,improved delivery of relief services and improved sanitary conditions). While this action also risks Nicaraguan or insurgent retribution and media exploitation, the risks are minimal and far outweighted by beneficial effects.

7. Anti-insurgent cooperation between Salvadoran and Honduran militaries is a different story. As you are aware, the Hondurans are reluctant to do too much (or, perhaps from Salvadoran viewpoint, enough) because of historical animosities and suspicion, the fragility of current political transition process and the likelihood that overt cooperation will trigger a negative popular reaction and extremist retribution. I believe their assessment on two latter points is correct and, in any case, they are in best position to assess the potential risks. They also believe overt cooperation would damage their international reputation. This does not mean we should not continue to urge greater cooperation, but that we should be sensitive to the constraints they perceive. As I see it, the Hondurans are amenable to cooperative actions that are low profile (e.g., coordination by local troop commanders), covert (e.g., intelligence exchange), or plausibly deniable (e.g., recent Salvadoran incursion near bolsones or Salvadoran "hot pursuit" incidents). They will act forcefully to prevent incursions into Honduran territory by armed salvadoran insurgents and will occasionally send patrols into the bolsones, but will not aggressively seek out the guerrilas in those areas, or engage in joint operations except, possibly, in small scale blocking operations where they remain entirely in Honduran territory). They believe that if they take the more aggressive actions they could trigger significant Salvadoran insurgent and possibly stepped up Nicaraguan counter actions in Honduras. Such a development would threaten several U.S. interests: the political transition process; private sector confidence; and GOH ability to maintain the pace of social/economic development programs. In short, it could be a classic example of desirable actions defeating higher priority objectives. The last thing we should want in Honduras, it seems to me, is increased terrorist/insurgent activity, an even weaker economy, deceleration in the development effort and/or greater social unrest. We don't need another active insurgency or economic basket case in the region. Accordingly, I have not yet carried out the instructions contained in state 196527.

8. My differences with Ambassador Hinton and others in this regard may be based on differing perceptions. I do not believe the outcome in El Salvador hangs generally on the situation in the border area or specifically

on whether the two armies conduct joint operations. Surely the border is an important problem, but its importance lies in the topography of the area and presence of refugees, both of which facilitate arms traffic, resupply operations and offer limited safehaven. We are making progress, albeit slowly, to diminish these problems, and joint military operations are not directly germane thereto. Nor is there any hard evidence I am aware of to suggest the guerrillas have major operational bases on the Honduran side of the frontier. And in any event I believe we can count on the GOH to move to prevent any efforts to develop such bases. Our current programs also enhance their capability to [*sic*] this regard.

9. In addition to the psychological, political and military contraints, there is an important financial constraint that inhibits the GOH of which I believe we must be contantly mindful. The central government budget is very tight: despite considerable resistance, taxes have just been increased and government expenditures cut to reduce the deficit and meet IMF conditions for the EFF. As a result, spending on social and development programs has slowed. Coupled with a stagnating economy and soaring birthrate, this means that living standards have declined after nearly a decade of steady improvement, thus increasing the potential for popular unrest.

10. Our efforts to get the Honduran military to do more usually imply new or increased costs for the defense budget, leaving them the choice of ignoring our suggestions, leaving some other defense activity or project unfunded, or diverting for military ends funds allocated for other desirable purposes (e.g., GOH operations or development investment). It is hard to get a precise fix on this problem, because: much of the defense budget is hidden under non-defense accounts; the full cost implications of actions we propose are rarely clear and their management of financial resources in the defense field is not always rational (see Tegucigalpa 5167). And we can do nothing to help offset operational costs.

11. In this context I am concerned about the proposed 200 percent increase in FY 81 FMS financing. While we cannot be certain how these funds will ultimately be used, the GOH list of "priority" requirements suggests that it will not be in the most rational manner. They are planning and spending for an "inevitable" war with Nicaragua. A good part of any eventual expenditure will no doubt be entirely wasted (e.g., massive quantities of anti-tank ammo which requires special storage facilities not now available and is being purchased "as is"), but even rational expenditures (e.g., new vehicles) will place increased demands on the operational budget,

as well as add to the long-term debt. But most significantly, an increase of this magnitude at this time, at least in my judgement, will send precisely the wrong signals. The Hondurans will read from our responsiveness that we: share their perception of inevitable war with Nicaragua; support their buildup for that purpose; and are prepared to underwrite irrational arms acquisitions. As for the GRN, we will provide substance for their paranoia and alleged fears of the Honduran buildup. Accordingly, I do not believe we should go forward with an increase of the magnitude currently under consideration, for all of the reasons described above. While these dangers are to some extent inherent in any additional funding, the size of the increase is important and, of course, a debatable factor. At this point, however, I am inclined to think an increase of more than five million dollars would be a mistake.

12. If we want to be most helpful in the security assistance field (and I realize the accounts are not fungible) we would provide $10 million (or more) in ESF rather than FMS. Such funds could be used immediately to help reduce the critical shortage of credit to the private sector, help maintain (or even increase) employment, add to FX reserves, ultimately produce tax revenue for the state, and avoid the negative economic consequences of increased FMS. Such action would also signal, in a very substantive way, our support for the private sector at a time when confidence is flagging. It would not assuage Honduran military fears of Nicaragua (there is a low cost way to do that, such as assurances pursuant to the Rio treaty), but it would not pander to these fears and would help strengthen the economy, which underpins the entire edifice.

13. The Nicaraguan issue has other facets as well. On the one hand, Ambassador Pezzullo urges that we bend our efforts to encourage the Hondurans to "build bridges" with the Nicaraguans in order to have a positive influence on their behavior. That is a purpose for which I have much sympathy, but it may no longer be feasible or germane. The GRN has made a policy decision to resume its material support for the Salvadoran insurgents. While one can reasonably argue (indeed, I believe) that many of the Nicaragua/Honduras frontier incidents are the result of or in response to provocations from anti–Sandinistas operating out of Honduras, such is clearly not the case with regard to GRN policy toward El Salvador. And while GRN paranoia about a U.S. attack on their "revolution" may provide a rationale for their arms buildup, the consequences of that buildup are real and must be dealt with. In sum, while I believe we should continue to counsel the GOH against rash or provocative actions

and avoid feeding their paranoia, it is probably too late to expect them to be interested in "building bridges."

14. But if we accept a strategy of counseling patience and restraint, how can we ignore the activities of the anti–Sandinistas in Honduras and the GOH's continued support of them? I have no idea how much of the GRN-originated frontier activity, support for Honduran subversives and bilateral tension is the product of anti–Sandinista provocations, but there certainly appears to be a linkage. By trying to face both ways on this issue we again risk serving some of our goals by defeating others. Where do our priorities lie?

15. I have other specific concerns about some of our actions in the region, but I have run on too long already. To begin the process of establishing a hierarchy of policy objectives that would guide subsequent action decisions, I urge that you call a meeting of the three ambassadors most directly involved (you might, however, wish to include ambassadors McNeil and Chapin) and your key advisors. The venue is less important than getting the process underway quickly. I would, however, be happy to offer Tegucigalpa as the site if you would prefer to meet in the area rather than Washington.

16. I have no objection to your sharing all or parts of this message with Ambassadors Hinton and Pezzullo.

Binns

Bibliography

Books

Clarridge, Duane R., with Digby Diehl. *A Spy for All Seasons: My Life in the CIA.* Charles Scribner's Sons, New York, 1997.

Department of State. *United States Treaties and Other International Agreements.* Vol. 34, Part 2, 1981–82. Department of State, Washington, D.C.

Gutman, Roy. *Banana Diplomacy.* Simon & Schuster, New York, 1988.

LeoGrande, William L. *Our Own Backyard: The United States in Central America, 1977–1992.* University of North Carolina, Chapel Hill, 1998.

McNeil, Frank. *War and Peace in Central American: Reality and Illusion.* Macmillan, New York, 1988.

National Security Archive. *El Salvador: The Making of U.S. Policy, 1971–1984.* Alexandria, Virginia, 1988.

_____. *Nicaragua: The Making of U.S. Policy, 1978–1990.* Alexandria, Virginia, 1991.

Shultz, George P. *Turmoil and Triumph: My Years as Secretary of State.* Charles Scribner's Sons, New York, 1993.

Timberg, Robert. *The Nightingale's Song.* Simon & Schuster, New York, 1995.

Valledares Lanza, Leo. *Honduras: The Facts Speak for Themselves.* Human Rights Watch/Honduras and the Center for Justice and International Law, Washington, D.C.

Walsh, Lawrence E., *Iran-Contra: The Final Report.* Time Books, New York, 1994.

Woodward, Bob. *Veil: The Secret Wars of the CIA, 1981–1987.* Simon & Schuster, 1987.

Magazines

Common Cause. Sharkey, Jacqueline. "The Tug of War," September/October 1984.
_____. "The Contra-Drug Tradeoff," September/October 1988.

Newspapers

HONDURAN

(Note: All headlines are translations from Spanish text)

El Cronista, Tegucigalpa
"North American Ambassador Denies Charges," January 29, 1981.

"There Was No Meeting of the PDCH with Binns," March 21, 1981.
"U.S. Supports Pacific Solution with Nicaragua," May 9, 1981.
"Ambassador Jack Binns Writes to University Rector," June 23, 1981.
"U.S. Does Not Criticize CEDEN or CARITAS," June 26, 1981.
"New Ambassador," October 2, 1981.

El Heraldo, Tegucigalpa
"Honduran Democracy Will Spring from Assembly," October 15, 1980.
Letter to editor, "The Ambassador Jack Binns Ought to Shut Up," October 14, 1980.
"Cuba Prepares Armed Invasion of Central America," January 10, 1981.
"The Problem Between Texaco and Government Is Purely Commercial," February 2, 1981.
"Binns Will Be Fired for His Intervention in Honduran Politics," March 20, 1981.
"Allegations of Binns' Intervention Follow Zuniga Thesis," March 21, 1981.
"USA Will Support Democratic Process," May 9, 1981.
"U.S. State Department Envoy Met with Paz," May 14, 1981.
"North American Military Assistance Remains at Announced Levels," May 20, 1981.
"Assistance Plan for Central America and Caribbean Does Not Include Military Aid," July 22, 1981.
"Attack on U.S. Military Is Isolated Incident," September 25, 1981.
"U.S. Doesn't Intend to Make Honduras Policeman of CA," September 25, 1981.
"U.S. Senate Will Soon Approve Appointment of Ambassador to Honduras," September 30, 1981.
"Election Will Go Forward, According to Binns," October 16, 1981.

La Prensa, San Pedro Sula
Editorial, "The Campaign Against Binns," March 23, 1980.
"Opinion" column, "Jack Binns: An Anguished Equilibrium," February 7, 1980.
"Cuba Trains Central American Guerrillas," January 10, 1981.
Editorial, "Cuba and Central American Subversion," January 13, 1981.
"Salvadoran Marxists Wanted to Win Diplomatic Battle in Tegucigalpa," January 22, 1981.
"U.S. Does Not Plan Armed Intervention in El Salvador or Other Country in Area," January 29, 1981.
"Nationalization of Refinery Gets Serious," February 4, 1981.
"U.S. Will Recognize Whatever Government Honduras Elects Democratically," March 14, 1981.
Editorial, "The Campaign Against Binns," March 23, 1981.
"USA Doesn't Want War," May 9, 1981.
"Washington Post Has Lied: Binns," May 9, 1981.
"Reagan Special Envoy Unreachable for Journalists," May 14, 1981.
"20 Million Lempira Increase in U.S. Military Assistance for Honduras," May 16, 1981.
"About U.S. Military Assistance for Latin America," May 20, 1981.
"He Won't Retract, Almendares Says to Binns," June 26, 1981.
Editorial, "New Campaign Against American Embassy," June 24, 1981.

"Will of Honduran People Will End 18 Years of Unconstitutional Rule," June 29, 1981.

"American Congressman Arrived Yesterday," July 2, 1981.

"U.S. Support for Elections a Serious and Consistent Policy," July 4, 1981.

"American Congressman: World Interest Directed at Central America," September 1, 1981.

"Visit by U.S. Ambassador to the OAS," September 23, 1981.

"Democracy Cannot Exist Excluding Private Enterprise and Trade Unions," September 26, 1981.

Editorial: "U.S. and Our Development," September 26, 1981.

"Domestic Left Is Not a Danger to Honduras," September 26, 1981

Editorial: "A Complicated Inheritance," September 28, 1981.

"Reagan Replaces Binns," September 30, 1981.

"Assistant Secretary of State of Hemisphere Visits Foreign Minister," October 2, 1981.

"Government Intervention Has Become a Negative Factor in Development," October 9, 1981.

"Jack Binns: The Possibility of a Coup Can Never Be Discounted," October 16, 1981.

Editorial, "Change of Ambassadors: Why So Much Noise," October 17, 1981.

La Tribuna, Tegucigalpa

"Honduran Road to Democracy a Wise Decision," October 15, 1980.

"University Bathes Car of Ambassador Binns in Paint," November 11, 1980.

"Cuba Incites and Trains People to Destabilize Central America," January 10, 1981.

"Cuba Sent Arms Decommissioned in Comayagua," January 29, 1981.

"Honduras Not Being Converted into Gendarme of Central America," March 14, 1981.

"Honduras: A Development Model for the Region," March 21, 1981.

"They Try to Discredit My Country and Me: Binns," March 21, 1981.

"Honduras Occupies Third Place in U.S. Military Assistance," April 10, 1981.

"USA Ratifies Support for Honduran Political Process," May 9, 1981.

"Aid for Refugees Goes to FMLN," June 22, 1981.

"U.S. Continues Supporting Return to Constitutional Government," June 23, 1981.

"CARITAS Attends to the Needy without Distinction of Color or Creed," June 23, 1981.

"Impossible to Control All Help for the Refugees," June 25, 1981.

"Won't Retract and Invites Ambassador to Listen to Tapes," June 25, 1981.

"I Have Nothing to Retract: Almendares to Binns," June 25, 1981.

Editorial, "The U.S. and Our Electoral Process," July 17, 1981.

"U.S. Congressman Impressed by High Voter Turn Out in '80 Elections," September 1, 1981.

"Silent Visit to Honduras of U.S. Ambassador to the OAS," September 23, 1981.

" U.S. Is Not Converting Honduras to Policeman of CA," September 25, 1981.

"Negroponte Will Replace Binns as Ambassador," September 30, 1981.

"U.S. Does Not Discount a Coup," October 16, 1981.

Tiempo, Tegucigalpa
  "University Repudiates Jack Binns," November 11, 1980.
  "Hidden Arms Were for Salvadoran Guerrillas," January 29, 1981.
  "Binns Doesn't Wish to Comment on Texaco Blackmail," February 2, 1981.
  "U.S. Ambassador Tried to Silence Salvadoran Army Atrocities," February 6, 1981.
  "Ambassador Binns Has Not Conversed with Salvadoran Marxist Leaders," February 21, 1981.
  "Director of AID in Honduras," March 6, 1981.
  "Honduran Political Situation Best in Central America," March 21, 1981.
  "What *El Heraldo* Says is Slanderous and False," March 21, 1981.
  "Binns Confident of Pacific Solution with Nicaragua," May 9, 1981.
  "Ex of CIA Spoke with Paz Yesterday," May 14, 1981.
  "Reagan Will Fill 'Oasis' with 20 Million in Arms," May 16, 1981.
  "U.S. Has Not Increased Military Assistance to Honduras," May 20, 1981.
  "American Congressman Visits on Mission of Peace," July 2, 1981.
  "American Congressman in Honduras," September 1, 1981.
  "Administrative Corruption Undermines the Legitimacy of Government," September 25, 1981.
  "Attack Will Not Change U.S. Plans," September 25, 1981.
  "Change in U.S. Embassy in Honduras," September 30, 1981.
  "USA Is Not Going to Change Its Policy Toward Honduras," October 17, 1981.

U. R. P., Tegucigalpa (Organ of the "Peoples' Revolutionary Union," published irregularly)
  "Jack Binns: Interference and Repression," March 21, 1981.

UNITED STATES

Baltimore Sun
  Binns, Jack R., "Departing Honduras to Where?" October 29, 1995.
  Cohn, Gary and Ginger Thompson, "Unearthed: Fatal Secrets," an award-winning series examining Honduran human rights abuses, 1980–88, June 11–18, 1995.
  "Honduras Charges Soldiers," July 26, 1995.
  "Military Can Be Tried in Honduran Civil Courts," January 20, 1996.

Diario las Americas
  "Cuba Trains Central American Guerrillas," January 13, 1981.

Los Angeles Times
  "Wrong Signal to Central America," October 14, 1981.

Miami Herald
  "2 Salvadoran Coalition Leaders: We Were Near Talks with U.S.," January 29, 1981.
  "Binns' Meetings: Same Set of Facts, Two Interpretations," January 31, 1981.

New York Times
  "Somoza Assassinated," September 15, 1980.
  "For Costa Rica, 2 Bombs Bring a Taste of Fear," March 22, 1981.
  "Three Injured in Honduras as Assembly Bombed," March 27, 1981.

"Rightist Exiles Plan Invasion of Nicaragua," April 2, 1981.
"Salvadorans Deny Killings," April 10, 1981.
"Ally of Honduran Army Expects U.S. Right Face," April 15, 1981.
"Green Berets Step Up Honduras Role," August 9, 1981.
"Demonstration in Honduras," September 25, 1981.
"Rightist Party Takes Big Lead in Vote," November 30, 1981.
"U.S. Seeking Right to Use Air Bases in Caribbean," March 4, 1982.
"Honduras Said to Hold Salvadoran Claimed Land," July 4, 1982.
"Honduran Commander Confirms Border Move," July 11, 1982.
"Honduran Officer Denounces Chief," September 1, 1982.
"25 Honduran Rebels Said to Seize 200 at Meeting," September 18, 1982.
"G.I.s Join Honduran Soldiers in Maneuvers on Nicaraguan Border," February 2, 1983.
"U.S. Plans to Train Salvadoran Soldiers at Honduran Base," May 27, 1983.
"Projected U.S. Maneuvers to Center on Honduras," July 12, 1983.
"Hondurans Divided on Maneuvers," August 28, 1983.
"U.S. Pilot Killed by 'Hostile Fire' in Honduras Trip," January 13, 1984.
"Human Rights Is Also an Issue in Honduras," January 22, 1984.
"Large Exercise with Honduras to Start April 1," March 24, 1984.
"Honduras Ousts Its Top General, An Ally of U.S.," April 1, 1984.
"Honduras Names New Military Commander," April 5, 1984.
"Hondurans Seeking Changes in Military Training by U.S.," May 27, 1984.
"Honduras Bars Training Salvadorans at Base," September 29, 1984 .
"FBI Charges 8 with Plotting Honduran Coup," November 2, 1984.
"Hondurans Ask the U.S. For a Fleet of Jet Fighters and Big Increase in Aid," November 20, 1984.
"Mystery Over a Killing in Honduras," September 29, 1985.
"Honduran General Arrested in U.S. in Assassination Plot," November 22, 1985.
"General's Resignation Accepted by Hondurans," February 2, 1986.
"CIA Accused of Tolerating Killings in Honduras," February 14, 1986.
"Honduran Buildup: A Variety of Means," July 14, 1986.
"U.S. Set to Offer Newer Jet Fighters to the Hondurans," October 31, 1986.
"3,000 U.S. Troops Begin an Exercise in South Honduras," December 31, 1986.
"Honduran Army Linked to Death of 200 Civilians," May 2, 1987.
"White House to Push Sale of Jets to Honduras," May 12, 1987.
"A Bomb Wounds 12 Near Honduran Base," August 10, 1987.
"Honduran Bombing Suspect Given Asylum by Mexico," October 4, 1987.
"In Human Rights Court, Honduras Is First to Face Death Squad Trial," January 19, 1988.
"Hondurans Riot at U.S. Offices; Four Said to Die," April 8, 1988.
"Honduran Leader Acts to Put Down Anti-U.S. Protests," April 9, 1988.
"Honduran Anger at U.S. Is Product of Washington Policy, Officials Say," April 13, 1988.
"OAS Tribunal Finds Honduras Responsible for Political Killing," July 30, 1988.
"Latin Presidents Announce Accord on Contra Bases," February 15, 1989.
"3 U.S. Soldiers Slightly Hurt in Bomb Attack in Honduras," February 19, 1989.

"Bush and Congress Sign Policy Accord on Aid to Contras," March 25, 1989.
"North Honduras Blast Wounds 7 Americans," July 14, 1989.
"Nicaragua Calm in Heavy Turnout for Critical Vote," February 26, 1990.
"Nicaraguan Opposition Routs Sandinistas; U.S. Pledges Aid, Tied to Orderly
    Turn Over," February 27, 1990.
"Snipers in Honduras Wound 6 U.S. Troops," April 1, 1990.
"Strikes Strangling Nicaragua and New Leaders Cry Foul," April 24, 1990.
"Chamorro Takes the Helm; Hails New Era," April 26, 1990.
"Salvadoran Chief and Rebels Reach Broad Accord," September 25, 1991.
"U.S. to Forgive Honduran Debt," September 27, 1991.
"Salvadoran Rebels Halt Attacks; Government Sees End to War," November
    15, 1991.
"Salvadorans, Ending War, Are Cautioned on Peace," December 16, 1992.

Washington Post
"Honduran Military Girds for War with Nicaragua," May 5, 1981.
Anderson, Jack (column), "Poland's Plight Prompts Two to Try to Flee," Sep-
    tember 4, 1981.

OTHER

El Mercurio, Santiago, Chile
"U.S. Will Honor Rio Treaty, Says Ambassador," November 13, 1980.

Unknown newspaper, Bogotá, Colombia
"Position of U.S. on Central America," November 12 or 13, 1980.

Official U.S. Government Documents

CABLES

(*indicates documents that are not available, either not requested or withheld)

Central Intelligence Agency, San Salvador Station
1980
    271810Z, concerning Cuban pressure on Salvadoran insurgents, September 27.
    011823Z, concerning slaying of opposition leaders, October 1.
    041941Z, concerning slaying of opposition leaders, October 4.

Defense Attache Office, San Salvador
1981
    021625Z, title unknown, concerning Perquin operation, September.

Defense Attache Office, Tegucigalpa
1981
    cable concerning activities on Salvadoran frontier, February 15 (NSA hold-
        ings).

Department of State
1980
    213030, "Salvadoran Elections," August 12, 1980

270099, "Updated Strategy for Period of Interim Government," October 9, 1980.

274568, *"Halcon Vista* Exercise," October 14.

339182 (NODIS), "Meeting with FDR Leader Hector Oqueli," December 24.

1981

03027, "Helicopters for OAS Observer Group," January 8.

09168, "Salvadoran Refugees in Honduras," January 15.*

11455, "Honduran Views on Events in El Salvador," January 16.

20713, "Press Guidance January 26," January 27.

30214, "Memorandum of Secretary Haig's Conversation with Honduran Foreign Minister," February 2.

56460 (EXDIS), "Honduran and Guatemalan Military Assistance to El Salvador," March 6.

77984 (EXDIS), "The Almost Visit of General Paz," March 27.

82952 (EXDIS), "Arms Infiltration and Military Assistance," April 2.

93666 (EXDIS), "Message for President Paz," April 11.

113419 (EXDIS), "Cols. Alvarez and Lopez Grijalva," May 2.

160064, title unknown, concerning disappearance of Concepcion Navarro, mid-June.*

170597 (EXDIS), "Assessment of Salvadoran Situation," June 27.

189539, "Nassau Conference on Caribbean Basin," mid-July.*

203317, "Regional Interdiction of Clandestine Infiltration," July 31.

212321, "Press Guidance 8/10," August 11.

217262, "Orientation Travel of Mr. Nestor Sanchez (DOD/ISA)," August 15.

227408 (EXDIS), "Concerns About Regional Policies and Objectives," August 25.

235800 (EXDIS), "Concerns About Elections," September 3.

257250 (EXDIS), "Joint Use Military Base in Honduras," September 25.

283212, "Senator Helms' Questions at Negroponte Hearing," October 23.*

Foreign Information Broadcast Service, Chiva Chiva, Panama

1981

120320Z, concerning alleged troop movements on frontier, February 12.*

U.S. Embassy, Managua, Nicaragua

1980

6100 (NODIS), "Meeting with FDR Leader Hector Oqueli," December 23.

1981

1448, "Hijacking of SAHSA 414: Chronology," March 28.

1452, "Hijacking of SAHSA 414," March 29.

2178 (EXDIS), "Regional Approach to Central American Security," May 21.*

3230 (NODIS), title unknown, concerning policy/action recommendations, late July.*

4158, "Sandinistas Speak Out Against Halcon Vista," September 23.

U.S. Embassy, San Jose, Costa Rica

1980

2242 (EXDIS), "Presidential Mission on Agriculture," April 23, 1980;* however, text of this cable was surreptitiously released to York mission and is in the "Garst File."

2535, "Visit to Costa Rica of Presidential Mission on Agriculture and Agro-Industrial Development," May 6, 1980;* text also contained in "Garst File."
1981
1117, "OAS Consultations on El Salvador," late February.*

U.S. Embassy, San Salvador
1980
8332, title unknown, concerning slaying of opposition leaders, November 30.*
1981
1368, "OAS Consultations on El Salvador," late February.*
4743 (EXDIS), title unknown, concerning Ambassador Hinton's assessment of the overall situation and policy recommendations.*
5569 (NODIS), title unknown, concerning policy/action recommendations, late July.*
7444, "FMLN /FDR Position on Negotiations with the Government of El Salvador," October 4.

U.S. Embassy Tegucigalpa
1980
6295, "Planned US-Honduran Exercise: *Halcon Vista*," October 9.
6296 (NODIS), "Reported Coup Plans," October 9.
6313 (EXDIS), "FonMin on Border Dispute and Other CA Topics," October 10.
6415 (EXDIS), "Liberal Party May Oppose Treaty with El Salvador," October 15.
6444, "Visit of Liberal Party Leader to U.S.," October 16.
6445 (EXDIS), "Peace Treaty with El Salvador: Tactical Considerations and Recommendations," October 16.
6489, "Arms Smuggling and Somocista Activity in Southern Honduras," October 17.
6490 (EXDIS), "Meeting with President Paz," October 17.
6522, "*Halcon Vista*," October 21.
6532, "*Halcon Vista* Exercise," October 22.
6544 (EXDIS), "Reported Coup Plans," October 22.
6766 (EXDIS), "Updated Strategy for Period of Interim Government," October 30.
6767, "Embassy Annex Hit by Gunfire," October 30.
6803, "Additional Terrorist Incidents in Tegucigalpa," October 31.
6853, "Translation of Pamphlet Sent by Group Claiming Credit for Attack on Embassy Annex," November 3.
6905 (STADIS), "Issue of Leased Helicopters," November 5.
6958, "Physical Security Enhancement," November 11.
6992, "Nicaraguan Helicopter Seized in Honduras," November 11.
7314, "ARDEN: Nicaraguan Exile Group," November 19.
7468 (EXDIS), "Assessment of Continuing Coup Rumors and U.S. Policy," November 26.
7549, "Visit of Senate Staffer Richard McCormack," December 2.
7550 (NODIS), "Coup Plotting," December 2.
7572, "Honduran Ratification of Peace Treaty with El Salvador," December 2.

7685, "Security Threat Analysis: Further Update," December 8.
7699 (EXDIS), "National Party Leader on Political/Economic Situation," December 8.
7816, "Tegucigalpa: Capital of the Americas," December 12.
7848 (EXDIS), "Situation of Honduran Side of Frontier," December 15.
7850, "Press Comment on Private Visit of SFRC Staffer McCormack," December 16.
7942, "Request for Assistance on Local Security Situation," December 19.
7979 (NODIS), "Vinelli Kidnapping: Carried Out by Salvadoran FPL," December.*
8007, "Another Look at the Honduran Security Situation," December.*
8025 (EXDIS), "Reina on Negotiated Solution to Salvadoran Situation," December 24.
8080 (NODIS), "Reina on Salvadoran Dialogue," December 30.
8094 (EXDIS), "Update on Vinelli Kidnapping," December 30.
8118, "Support for El Salvador/Honduras Border Observers," December 31.
1981
0077 (LIMDIS), "Salvadoran Refugees in Honduras: Need for Refugee Camps and Strategies to Achieve Them," January 6.
0138, "Most Recent Estimate of Salvadoran Refugees," January 8.
0178, "Helicopter Support for OAS Observers," January 9.
0184, "Letter of Resignation," January 10.
0201 (NODIS), "Reina Meets with FDR/DRU," January 12.
0248, "Proposed Meeting with Ungo," January 13.
0329 (EXDIS), "Paz on Border Situation: What Does the US Want Me to Do?" January 16.
0335 (NODIS), "Press Query Re FDR/DRU Approach," January 16.
0336 (LIMDIS), "Enhancement of Honduran Armed Forces, Especially on Salvadoran Border," January 16.
0337, "IMF and IBRD Programs in Honduras," January 16.
0343 (LIMDIS), "Honduran Views on Situation in El Salvador," January 16.
0345, "FonMin Elvir on Salvadoran Situation," January 16.
0346, "Salvadoran Refugees in Honduras," January 16.
0348, "Codel Studds: Message for President Carter and President-elect Reagan from Codel," January 17.
0362, "Text of Codel Studds 'Outline of Major Findings,'" January 19.
0389, "Codel Studds," January 19.
0390, "GOH Seizure of Arms Shipment," January 19.
0439, "Codel Studds/Edgar/Mikulski in Honduras," January 21.
0443, "Reported Honduran Military Operations on Border," January 21.
0457, "Honduran Request for Police Training," January 21.
0502 (EXDIS), "Possible Exchange of Arms Smuggler for Kidnapped Banker," February 23.
0615 (EXDIS), "Request for Guidance on Dealing with Nicaraguan Exiles," January 28.
0622, "GOH Refugee Committee Recommendations," January 28.*
0641, "Texaco/GOH Negotiations Continue Deadlocked," January 28.
0697 (STADIS), "Proposed Visit of Gen. Nutting," January 28.
0724, "IMF Position on Honduras," February 2.

0883 (EXDIS), "Costa Rican Role in Honduran Arms Seizure," February 6.

0991 (EXDIS), "Impressions of Col. Gustavo Alvarez," February 11

1069, "Alleged Honduran Troop Build-up on Salvadoran Border," February 12.

1133, "Honduras and the IMF," February 17

1144, "Elections, Ambassadors and National Party Leader Zuniga," February 17.

1146, "President Paz on Economic Situation and IMF," February 18.

1212, "Pro-Guerrilla Priest Arrested," February 19.

1310, "Proposed OAS Consultations on El Salvador," February 24.

1333 (EXDIS), "Possible Release of Arms Traffickers," February 24.

1335 (NODIS), "Possible Assignment of U.S. Military Personnel in Honduras," February 24.

1355 (EXDIS), "Socialist International Meeting in Panama," February 26.*

1448, "The Honduran Church: An Overview," March 2.

1584, "Private Sector Leader on Possible Coup," March 5.

1644, "A Cancer in the Vitals: Government Corruption in Honduras," March 7.

1673 (EXDIS), "Honduran Military Assistance to El Salvador," March 9.

1679, "Arms Infiltration Problem," March 11.*

1758, "Government and Private Sector Reach Accord on Tax Package," March 12.*

1795 (EXDIS), "Arms Infiltration and Military Assistance," March 13.

1800 (EXDIS), "Arms Infiltration and Military Assistance," March 13.

1802 (LIMDIS), "Reported Diversion of Refugee Relief Supplies to Guatemala [sic]," March 13 (title should read "El Salvador" vice "Guatemala").

1804, "Liberal Party Leader on Financial Problem/Tax Package," March.*

1842 (EXDIS), "Honduran Military Disquiet Over U.S. Assistance Levels," March 17.

1872 (EXDIS), "Honduran Military Disquiet Over U.S. Assistance Levels," March 18.

1959, "Local Newspaper Attacks U.S. Ambassador," March 20.*

1962, "Codel Long Visit to Tegucigalpa," March 20.

1991, "Further Reverberations from Attack on Ambassador," March 23.*

1998, "La Prensa (March 23) Editorial 'Campaign Against Binns'," March 23.

2142, "Demands of SAHSA Hijackers," March 28.

2144, "SAHSA Hijacking: GOH Position and Strategy," March 28.

2151, "SAHSA Hijacking," March 29.

2164, "SAHSA Hijacking," March 30.

2182 (LIMDIS), " SAHSA Hijacking," March.30

2248 (EXDIS), "Arms Infiltration and Proposed Interdiction," April 1.

2300 (EXDIS), "Arms Infiltration and Military Assistance," April 2.

2309 (LIMDIS), Honduran Military Desire for Additional Assistance," April 2.

2325 (EXDIS), "Aborted Paz Visit, Its Implications and Strategy Recommendations," April 2.

2342 (EXDIS), "Apparent Misuse of AID Funds," April 3.

2443, "SAHSA Hijacking," April 8.

2448 (EXDIS), "Arms Infiltration and Military Assistance," April 8.

2506 (EXDIS), "Arms Infiltration and Military Assistance," April 11.

2543 (LIMDIS), "Honduran Military Leaders to Visit Washington," April 13.

2558, "Ricardo Zuniga, a Rascal for All Seasons," April 13.*

2632 (LIMDIS), "Honduran Military Leaders to Visit Washington," April 20.

2795 (EXDIS), "General Walters Visit," April 24.

2835 (NODIS), "Honduran Scheme to Attack Nicaragua," April 27.

2936 (EXDIS), "Possible Honduran Attack on Nicaragua," April 30.

2968 (EXDIS), "General Walters Visit to Honduras," April 30.

2971, "Proposed Halcon Vista Exercise," April 30.

2987, "SAHSA Hijacking: Démarche to GOH," May 1.

2988, "Further Information on Border Situation," May 1.

3015, "Press Guidance for SOUTHCOM Survey Team," May 4.

3064 (EXDIS), "Paz on Nicaraguan Situation," May 5.

3074 (EXDIS), "Reported Misuse of AID Resources," May 5.

3086 "Reported Nicaraguan Attack on Honduras," May 6.

3089, "Constituent Assembly Passes Emergency Economic Plan," May 6.

3205, "Request for Consultations," May 11.

3223, "SAHSA Hijacking: Approach to Col. Torres Arias," May 8.

3225 (LIMDIS), "Honduras/Nicaragua Problems," May 11.

3253, "1981 World Refugee Report to Congress," May 11.

3254 (EXDIS), "General Walters Program for Honduras," May 11.

3291 (LIMDIS), "National Party Leader on Elections," May 12.

3333 (EXDIS), "Reported Misuse of AID Resources," May 13.

3336 (EXDIS), "Meetings with President Paz, FonMin and Military Leaders," May 14.

3368 (EXDIS), "Meeting with President Paz," May 14.

3427, "Survey Team Recommendations on Arms Infiltration," May 18.

3456 (EXDIS), "Assessment of Gen. Walters' Visit," May 18.

3572 (EXDIS), "Central American Chiefs of State Meeting," May 22.

3574 "Visit to Salvadoran Refugee Sites," May 22.

3610 (EXDIS), "Honduran/Nicaraguan Conflict: Regional Considerations," May 22.

3674, "Arms Interdiction Training Proposals," May 27.

3910, "Conversation with Chairman of National Electoral Tribunal," June 4.

4036, "Additional Thoughts on Proposed *Halcon Vista* Exercise," June 8.

4057, "State of National Party and Military in Politics," June 9.

4127 (NODIS), "Potential Problems with GOH and Exile Groups," June 11.

4289 (EXDIS), "Views of Junta President Duarte," June 16.

4300 (EXDIS), "Possible Appearance of Death Squad Type Justice," June 17.

4314 (NODIS), "Reports of GOH Repression and Approach to Problem," June 17.

4368 (EXDIS), "Possible Deterioration in Honduran/Nicaraguan Relations," June 18.

4395 (NODIS), "Allegations of Abduction by Honduran Security Forces," June 19.

4409, "Disappearance of Revolutionary Leaders," June 19.

4496 (EXDIS), "President Paz on Nicaragua and Tax Problem," June 23.

4545, "*La Prensa* Editorial Entitled 'New Campaign Against American Embassy,'" June 24.

4601, "Speculation About Delay or Frustration of Elections," June 25.

4625, "Paz Reports GRN to Return Alleged Honduran Spies," June 26.

4637, "AmCit Kidnapped by Alleged Political Terrorists," June 27.

4653, "Proposed Visit by Assembly President," June 29.

4696, "GOH Decides," June 29.

4710, "Second Kidnapper Arrested by Police," June 30.

4815, "Visit of Vice Presidential Candidate," July 1.

4822, "Another McBroom Kidnapper Killed by Police," July 3.

4823, "Chief of Staff on OAS Observers," July 3.

5056 (STADIS), "Texaco/Honduras Negotiations," July 13.

5167 (LIMDIS), untitled (concerning Honduran arms acquisitions), July 14.

5168 (EXDIS), "Soviet Tanks in Nicaragua," July 14.

5179 (EXDIS), "Soviet Tanks in Nicaragua," July 17.

5199, "Suggested Talking Points Honduran Liberal Party Visit," July 17.

5325 (LIMDIS), "Honduran Foreign Minister on Border Situation," July 22.

5332 (EXDIS), "FonMin on Nicaragua and Outlook in Honduras," July 22.

5373 (LIMDIS), "GOH Request for Increased FMS Credit for FY 81," July 23.

5420, "Nassau Conference on Caribbean Basin," July 23.

5469, "*Halcon Vista*," July 27.

5544, "UNHCR in Honduras," July 28.

5617, "Alleged Salvadoran Incursion into Honduras," July 31.

5623 (EXDIS), "Reported Arrest and Expulsion of CARE Employee for Aiding Salvadoran Guerrillas," July 31.

5637 (NODIS), "Concerns about Regional Policies and Objectives," July 31.

5666 (EXDIS), "Reported Expulsion of CARE Employee," July 31.

5890, "Proposed USCINCSO/MOD Meeting," August 10.

5902 (NOFORN), "Regional Interdiction of Clandestine Infiltration," August 10.

5940, "New York Times Story on Green Berets," August 12.

5996, "GOH and IMF," August 13.

6055, "Visits of Presidents Fuel Rumor Mills," August 14.

6056, "Text of Draft Declaration of Tegucigalpa," August 15.

6057, "CAP Foreign Ministers Meeting: Guatemala Participates; Declaration Analyzed," August 15.

6060, "CAP Foreign Ministers Meeting: Invitation to Nassau Group; Dust Up with Guatemala," August 16.

6091, "Possibility of New Mining Investment Diminishes," August 17.

6092, "More on Paz/Duarte Meeting," August 17.

6095, "Sanchez Meetings with Paz and Alvarez," August 17.

6122, "Exercise Plans and First Planning Meeting," August 18.

6167, "Further Fall Out [*sic*] on Capt. Sheehan Case," August 19.

6199, "Suazo Cordova on National Security Law," August 20.

6220 (EXDIS), "Suazo Declines Invitation to Visit Caracas," August 21.

6221 (EXDIS), "Priests in Honduras Involved in Guerrilla Support Network," August 21.

6244 (EXDIS), "Reported Decision to Delay Elections: Analysis and Strategy Recommendations," August 21.

6248, "Additional Information on Visiting Church Group," August 21.

6258 (EXDIS), "Christian Democrats on Delay of Elections," August 21.

6351 (EXDIS), "Concerns about Regional Policies and Objectives," August 26.

6367 (LIMDIS), "Liberals on Possible Delay of Elections," August 27.

6387, "Capt. Sheehan Case," August 27.

6504 (EXDIS), "Paz on Elections Issue, Summit Meetings and Travels," September 1.

6519, "*Halcon Vista*: Suggested Press Guidance," September 2.

6539, "Leftist Allegations of Honduran Participation in Perquin Operation," September 2

6540, "Codel Petri," September 2

6565 (EXDIS), "Concerns about Elections," September 3

6587 (LIMDIS), "Military Plan to Delay Elections Has No Support," September 4.

6646 (EXDIS), "GOH Request for Crowd (Riot) Control Training," September 9.

6675 (EXDIS), "Meeting with President Paz and Senior Army Colonels," September 9.

6698 (EXDIS), "GOH Request for Crowd (Riot) Control Training," September 10.

6723 (EXDIS), "Col. Alvarez on Elections," September 10.

7037 (LIMDIS), "Honduran Military, Elections and Security Assistance," September 22.*

7214 (LIMDIS), "Joint Use Military Bases in Honduras," September 25.*

7231 (EXDIS), "Paz Still Pushing for Elections Delay: Liberal Problems," September 25.

7253, "DAS Briggs Travel to Honduras," September 26.

7273, "Security Enhancement, or Promises, Promises," September 28.

7283 (EXDIS), "Suazo on Negotiations with ALIPO," September 28.

7288 (NODIS), "Political Leaders on Replacement of Ambassador," September 28.

7294, "Joint Use of Military Base in Honduras," September 29.

7646 (NODIS), "Likelihood of Elections Delay Increases," October 9.

7674, "Armed Forces Pronouncement on Political Process," October 13.

7696 (NODIS), "Weekend Coup Narrowly Averted," October 13.

7723 (EXDIS), "Venezuelan Concerns Over Threats to Electoral Process," October 14.

7753 (NODIS), "Further Assessment of Aborted Coup Attempt," October 14.

7776 (NODIS), "Coup Maneuvering of Last Week: Junior Officer Input," October 15.

7815, "Ambassador's Endorsement of Elections Well Received," October 16.

7833 (EXDIS), "Conditions Imposed on Political Leaders by Honduran Military," October 19.

7834 (EXDIS), "Military Document Advocates Delay of Elections," October 19.

7857 (NODIS), "Political Outlook: Situation Fluid, Elections Problematical," October 19.

7894, "Potential Foreign Policy Differences of Major Parties," October 22.

7933 (EXDIS), "Military Involvement in Land Scandal," October 23.

7945 (NODIS), "Honduran Elections: Outlook Brightens," October 23.

7969, "Senator Helms' Questions at Negroponte Hearing," October 24.

7990 (EXDIS/STADIS), "U.S. Air Base in Honduras," October 26.*
7991 (EXDIS), "U.S. Air Base in Honduras," October 26.*
8040, "1981 and 1982 Balance of Payments and Fiscal Outlook Grim," October 26.
8138 (EXDIS/STADIS), "Proposed U.S. Air Base in Honduras," late October.*

U.S. Air Force South, Howard AF Base, Panama
1981
291915Z, "Joint Use Military Base in Honduras," September 29.*

U.S. Southern Command, Panama
1980
081507Z, concerning *Halcon Vista*, title unknown, October 8.*
1981
061435Z, concerning region Defense Ministers meeting, title unknown, August 6.*

Other Official Documents

Central Intelligence Agency
"Central American Arms Trafficking: The Comayaguela Case," February 20, 1981.
Inspector General Report, "Selected Issues Relating to CIA Activities in Honduras in the 1980s," August 27, 1997 (released with extensive excisions, October 22, 1998).

Department of State
Memorandum, "DAS Cheek Meeting with FSLN Political Committee," Sept. 27, 1980.
Office of Central American Affairs memorandum, "Ambassador Binn's [*sic*] Appointments," undated.
Fact Sheet, "El Salvador," 1995.

General Accounting Office
Report, "Applicability of Certain Laws That Pertain to U.S. Military Involvement in El Salvador," July 27, 1982.

Inter-Agency Intelligence
Memorandum, "Growth and Prospects of Leftist Extremism in El Salvador," January 1980.

National Foreign Assessment Center
Memorandum dealing with El Salvador, February 19, 1980.
Memorandum dealing with Cuban supply routes into El Salvador, June 20, 1980.

Reagan Transition Team
Memorandum from Pedro Sanjuan to Robert Neumann, "Interim Report of the Bureau of Inter-American Affairs and Related Bureau and Policy Areas, Department of State," November 1980.

U.S. Embassy, Tegucigalpa
  Press Release, "U.S. Military Assistance to Honduras," March 9, 1981.
  USIS transcript of General Vernon Walters's press conference, May 15, 1981.
  Memorandum from Antonia Stolper, "Investigation Report—Capt. Sheehan and His MTT in La Virtud," August 19, 1981.
  Issues Paper: "What Role, If Any, Should USG Play in the GOH/Texaco Dispute?" October 9, 1981.
  "Briefing Book for Ambassador John D. Negroponte," October 9, 1981.*

Miscellaneous Documents

BINNS, JACK R.

  Daily diaries, 1980–81.
  Letter to Ambassador Mari-Luci Jaramillo regarding Garst letter to President Carter, September 8, 1980.
  Notes from first Country Team meeting, October 6, 1980.
  Text of "Speech for American Association Luncheon," November 11, 1980.
  Memorandum, "The Frontier Problem," December 29, 1980.
  Statement for January 28 press conference and anticipated questions (undated).
  Letter to Thomas M. Tracy, Assistant Secretary for Administration, March 5, 1981.
  Letter to *La Prensa* and *La Tribuna,* March 15, 1981.
  Letter to Francisco Morales Calix, editor, *El Heraldo,* March 30, 1981.
  Letter of notification of possible reprimand to unnamed Milgroup technician, March 30, 1981.
  Letter of reprimand to unnamed Milgroup technician, April 6, 1981
  Letter to editors of all major newspapers concerning military assistance levels, May 18, 1981.
  Draft text of "Ambassador's Comment," concerning Honduran plan to attack Nicaragua, undated.
  Letter to Rector Juan Almendares, with copies to major newspapers, June 19, 1981.
  Letter to Assistant Secretary Thomas O. Enders, July 17, 1981.
  Letter to CEDEN executive director, Naomi de Espinoza, concerning refugee relief supplies, with copies of media and other refugee relief organizations, June 24, 1981.
  Memorandum to Assistant Secretary Enders, "Improved Honduran/Salvador Cooperation," July 9, 1981.
  Letter to Hon. Gerry Studds concerning actions of his staff aide, September 29, 1981.
  Letter to Victoria Rideout (Studds's aide) on same topic, September 29, 1981.
  Text of speech to San Pedro Sula Rotary Club, September 23, 1981.
  Letter to Assistant Secretary Enders concerning *Halcon Vista,* October 12, 1981.
  Text of speech to Tegucigalpa Rotary Club, October 6, 1981.

BLACKEN, JOHN D.

  Letter to Jack R. Binns concerning aborted Paz visit to U.S., March 27, 1981.

BOWDLER, WILLIAM G.

Letter to Jack R. Binns, November 14, 1995.

BROWN, RICHARD C.

Letter to Jack R. Binns concerning aborted Paz visit to U.S., March 27, 1981.

CARITAS (CATHOLIC RELIEF AGENCY)

Letter to editors of major papers, with copy to Jack R. Binns, concerning controls on supplies provided for Salvadoran refugees, June 23, 1981.

COMMITTEE OF SANTA FE

"A New Inter-American Policy for the Eighties," May 1980.

GARST, DAVID

File of correspondence, memoranda and other documents concerning the views of Garst and others opposing President Carter's human rights and land reform policies and my nomination as ambassador to Honduras; consists of 35 documents, 94 pages.

MCCORMACK, RICHARD

Memorandum to State Department Counselor Bud McFarlane, "Visit of President Paz," March 24, 1981.

NATIONAL EVANGELICAL COMMITTEE FOR
DEVELOPMENT AND EMERGENCY (CEDEN)

Letter to Jack R. Binns concerning control of refugee supplies, June 27, 1981.

PREWITT, VIRGINIA

"Hemisphere Hotline—A Private New World Intelligence Service," January 30, 1981, p. 3.

SCHWEITZER, GEN. ROBERT A.

Memorandum of conversation "Honduran Military Delegation Visit with NSC Staff Members, June 19, 1981," June 26, 1981.

UNNAMED MILGROUP TECHNICIAN

Memorandum to Col. Goodwin concerning meeting with Superior Council of the Armed Forces, March 24, 1981.

Index

Abrams, Elliott 305
Agency for International
Development, Honduras
(AID) 68, 86, 144, 181,
183; appropriate technol-
ogy 130; attack on 44;
Codel Long 130; Eco-
nomic Support Fund
(ESF) 120, 147, 187, 246,
296; misuse of AID
funds 148–149, 171–172;
part of Mission 15, 18;
performance 119; pro-
gram 12, 120–121; public
awareness of 103–104,
120–121, 125–126;
regional office reports
economic crisis 295–296;
support for Nicaraguan
refugees 229–231
Agency for International
Development, Washing-
ton (AID/W) 227; dis-
aster relief office 75;
meeting with 187; on
misuse of AID funds 149
Air attaché *see* Defense
Attaché
Algeria 225
Allen, Richard 90–91, 124,
315
Almendares, Juan 49–50;
alleges U.S. responsible
for repression 201–202,
205, 207–208
Alvarez, Colonel Gustavo
39, 51, 65, 93, 107–108,
167, 226, 242, 253,
309–310; American kid-
napped 210; on

Argentina 104–105;
assassinated 307; atti-
tudes 104–106, 316, 317;
as commander of armed
forces 302; conflicting
interests 258–259; efforts
to constrain 284; election
assurances 264, 272;
impressions of 105; on
insurgent support net-
work 247; land scandal
277; meets with Sanchez
246–247; meets with
Walters 263; on needed
reforms 104–105; ousted
and exiled by junior
officers 304; ousts Torres
Arias and Bodden 302;
plan for Contras and to
attack Nicaragua
157–160, 163–164; plan to
attack Salvadoran insur-
gents 198–199; relations
with junior officers 192,
304; secret trip to U.S.
202–203, 207; on South-
ern Command joint use
bases 297–298; view of
Zuniga 191; visits to U.S.
152–153, 159–160,
163–164, 167
Alvarez Cordova, Enrique
59
American Institute for Free
Labor Development
(AIFLD) 74, 261
Anderson, Jack: plug for
ambassador 214
Anti-Sandinistas *see* Contras

Arce, Bayardo 261
Arcos, Cresencio 29,
46–48, 49, 50, 82, 93, 94,
95, 110–111, 125–126, 127,
130–133, 149, 151, 154,
168, 172, 177–178, 180,
208, 256, 259, 267, 276,
289–290, 298; *La Prensa*
interview 209–210; on
National Party and
Zuniga 191–192; perfor-
mance award 298–299;
press briefings/confer-
ences 93–94, 98–99,
126–127, 269–270,
290–292; press release
111; public affairs officer
18–19; relations with
media 273; on repression
allegations 202; San
Pedro Sula trips 42–44,
268, 269–270; support
for AID 103–104
Argentina 104–105, 164,
166, 295; alleged support
for Honduran plan to
attack Nicaragua 159,
203; as CIA front 14,
188, 243, 302; Col.
Mario Davico 243; with
Contras 33, 71, 103, 203,
204, 242; invades Falk-
land Islands 188, 302;
presence in Honduras
13–14, 33, 51; visas for
military intelligence
officers 215–216, 220–221
Arias, Oscar: Central
American peace plan
306, 307

383